THE EMERGENT ORGANIZATION

Communication as Its Site and Surface

LEA's COMMUNICATION SERIES
Jennings Bryant/Dolf Zillmann, General Editors

This title is included in the Organizational Communication subseries (Linda Putnam, series advisor):

Berger • *Planning Strategic Interaction: Attaining Goals Through Communicative Action*

Dennis/Wartella • *American Communication Research: The Remembered History*

Ellis • *Crafting Society: Ethnicity, Class, and Communication Theory*

Greene • *Message Production: Advances in Communication Theory*

Heath/Bryant • *Human Communication Theory and Research: The Remembered History*

Riffe/Lacy/Fico • *Analyzing Media Messages: Using Quantitative Content Analysis in Research*

Salwen/Stacks • *An Integrated Approach to Communication Theory and Research*

For a complete list of other titles in LEA's Communication Series, please contact Lawrence Erlbaum Associates, Publishers.

THE EMERGENT ORGANIZATION

Communication as Its
Site and Surface

James R. Taylor
Emeritus Professor, University of Montreal

Elizabeth J. Van Every

2000

LAWRENCE ERLBAUM ASSOCIATES, PUBLISHERS
Mahwah, New Jersey   London

Lawrence Erlbaum Associates, Inc., Publishers
10 Industrial Avenue
Mahwah, New Jersey 07430

Cover design by Kathryn Houghtaling Lacey

Library of Congress Cataloging-in-Publication Data

Taylor, James R., 1928-
    The emergent organization : communication as its site and surface
/ James R. Taylor, Elizabeth J. Van Every.
        p.   cm.
    Includes bibliographical references and index.
    ISBN 0-8058-2193-7 (cloth) : alk. paper). -- ISBN 0-8058-2194-5
(pbk. : alk. paper)
    1. Communication in organizations. I. Van Every, Elizabeth J.
II. Title.
HD30.3.T388   1999
658.4'5--dc21
                                                    99-39626
                                                       CIP

Books published by Lawrence Erlbaum Associates are printed on acid-free paper,
and their bindings are chosen for strength and durability.

Printed in the United States of America
10   9   8   7   6   5   4   3   2

Contents

Preface

This book is the culmination of a long quest: to explain organization in the language of an authentically communicational theory. The quest began with what is on the surface an innocuous enough question: *What is an organization?* But the closer one looks at the literature on organization the less evident the answer to the question becomes. The problem is that, although it is correlated with many material manifestations, organization has in and of itself no materiality. We can only know organization by forming an image of it. Yet as Morgan (1986) has astutely observed, the image we have of an organization is based in metaphor and metaphor hides as much as it reveals. Is organization a machine, an organism, a brain, a culture, a political system, a psychic prison? The answer is always going to be "yes" and "no"; none of these metaphors is so all-encompassing that it provides a definitive answer to our question.

Despite the great diversity of writings on organization there are, we believe, two principal classes of established answers to the puzzle we have posed ourselves, or perhaps a better term would be two attitudes. For the sake of convenience, let us call the two attitudes essentialist and anti-essentialist. The essentialist attitude takes the existence of organization as a given and then goes on to address the issue of how to investigate it scientifically: what theories are appropriate, what methodologies are the most effective in investigating organizational structures and processes. The objective is to arrive at a theory or model of organization that is sufficiently robust to deal with the variety of forms of organization with which we are confronted in daily life. Its ultimate goal is effective management. Movements such as Total Quality or Business Process Reengineering illustrate this attitude. Essentialism forms the basis of traditional management science and some branches of the sociology of organization.

The anti-essentialist view has a different starting point. It assumes organization to be a secondary phenomenon: a kind of battleground where powerful forces contend in a struggle to have their ideology prevail in an ongoing redistribution of the world's resources. Some end up winners, and some losers. From this perspective the essentialist preoccupations of the scientific community are part of a smoke screen that hides the reality of the struggle for power from our view. In this perspective, ideologies, historically grounded in divisions of class, race, gender, among other factors, inform the actions of practitioners, consciously or unconsciously, with the result that they are led to institute systems of power and privilege that underlie the functional hierarchy of the organization and give it its real meaning. Analysis and research, in this view, should aim to reveal the hidden dynamics and structure of the system. Organization becomes not so much phenomenon as epiphenomenon. Anti-essentialism is sometimes known as critical theory. It has sociological roots.

The book that follows is neither essentialist nor anti-essentialist. We neither question the reality of organization nor the role of ideology in it. But what strikes us about both attitudes is that, although each makes assumptions about the enabling role of communication, neither foregrounds communication, or treats *it* as "essential." In this book we reverse this implicit figure/ground relationship and promote communication to become the center of our concern. We make the simplifying assumption that there is no organization nor any ideology other than that which emerges in communication. If organization is emergent in communication, as we believe, then it is not a *being,* but a *becoming.* What we ought to be studying is not organization or ideology, because neither has any ontological status independent of communication, but the processes of communication by which we continue to construct both to become the world we live in.

We propose, in other words, to look at the translations that communication effects in order to turn a lived experience of organization into a theory of it, on the one hand, and an idea of organization into a realization of it, on the other hand. We will argue for a communicational view of organization that is simultaneously conceptual and pragmatic. Organization is pragmatic in the sense that, whatever conception lay behind it (managerial or other) that which is realized in the day-to-day depends on the construction of relationships of work: people and their objects and technologies, on the one hand, and people with people, on the other. No matter how elegant the designer's plan or subtle the ideology the crucible of the quotidian is the ultimately determining factor in what the organization will be like. It is this that we mean by communication as the site of organization.

Our approach is conceptual in the sense that how people relate to each other in a working group explains the kind of intelligence they produce: how they recognize the organization they live in and its environment. It is this that we mean by saying that communication furnishes the surface on which organization can be read—made sense of, in Weick's (1995) terms.

A principal consequence of taking communication rather than organization as a starting point is to force the role and dynamics of language and discourse to the forefront of our consciousness. We devote the entire first half of the book to looking at language and discourse, and how they operate to become a site and a surface of organization. If organizations are realized in the discourse of their members then there is no privileged observation point to study organization—no way to ever arrive at a definitive theory of organization. The theories of its members (everyone is a theoretician of organization) are realized in their talk and their texts, so that any description of organization is a construction of text whose object is a complex configuration of many conversations and texts. But to choose one text in particular, let us say that of the manager or the scientific analyst, is to have selected out of the set of possibilities a single one, and, in so doing, to have negated the nature of organization as a continuing reinterpretation of itself, with no stopping point. All that is scientifically feasible, we argue, is to describe, not the organization, but the process by means of which it realizes itself. To put our claim differently, the study of organization is in fact the study of communication. The existence of organization is by this fact inherently problematical; it must emerge in communication to exist as an organization (as opposed to several incompatible ones coexisting uncomfortably in a single speech community). There is no finality; it is a continuous process.

The second half of the book uses our inquiry into language and discourse to begin thinking about organization in a new way, as an emergent reality. Our theory supposes that communication occurs in different modalities, as transmission using the symbols of language, and as interactive medium by means of which conversation, and the basis of sociability, are established. Cognition, then, we argue, is both an individual and a collective achievement. The second half of the book is an exploration of the seldom explored translations from one kind of cognition to the other and their implication for organizational dynamics.

A book's history does not always start at the moment that it was first thought of as "a book": Often, it begins much earlier as an irritant that, *because* it irritates, doesn't go away—cannot easily be extruded—becomes the core around which one's own speculations and reading of other people's writings on similar themes collect and are gradually transformed into something different, the germ of an idea. Only when the idea-formation process has matured does it even become worth looking at as perhaps publishable. The source of this book can be traced back to just such an irritant: an experience that left behind a niggling trace of mental irritation that would become, bit by bit, this kind of collector. For us, that irritant was a single question: What is an organization? In this book, we offer our answer.

ACKNOWLEDGMENTS

Our book has emerged in the course of many acts of support from friends and colleagues over the past four years. Special thanks are due to Linda Putnam, who initially encouraged us to submit a manuscript for publication, to François Cooren, Gail Fairhurst, Bruno Latour, and Stuart Sigman, all of whom read and critiqued an earlier version of the book, to Yrjö Engeström, who used a draft manuscript as a text in a course he was teaching at the University of California at San Diego, to Jyri Engeström, who helped us with graphics, to Nicole Giroux, Hélène Giroux,

Carole Groleau, Lorna Heaton, Jo Katambwe and Daniel Robichaud for their continuing helpful critiques of parts of the book in an ongoing seminar at the Université de Montréal. A special vote of thanks goes to Luc Giroux and André Lafrance who, as Chairs of the Department of Communication, Université de Montréal, made it possible for us to take the time we needed to finish the manuscript, and to Arthur Bochner and Eric Eisenberg at the University of South Florida for welcoming us as guest scholars while we were preparing and revising it. Very special thanks go to Linda Bathgate, our editor, and Sondra Guideman, our production editor, both of Lawrence Erlbaum Associates, for providing the invaluable and always highly professional editorial and production guidance that smoothed the path throughout. Finally, a word of thanks to Matthew and Gavin, who cheered us up when the road seemed especially long.

James R. Taylor
Elizabeth J. Van Every

Part I

THEORY OF COMMUNICATION

Organizational Communication: A New Look

This book develops a thesis, that communication is the essential "modality," to use Giddens' (1984) term, for the constitution of organization and, more generally, of society. By modality, Giddens means that which explains how those properties of a society that give it continuity over expanses of time and across many geographically dispersed situations come to be manifested in day-to-day human interaction. It is how social structures inform social systems (to again use his terminology) and, vice versa, how organization can be both local (systemic) and global (structured), bounded by constraints of space and time and yet also transcending them.

This modality has, however, two distinct manifestations, that we term *symbolic* and *subsymbolic*. In its role as symbol system, communication serves as a medium by means of which people's thoughts, transcribed into either spoken or written form (as what are often called *messages*, and we call *texts*), may be conveyed by some persons to some other persons for them to interpret and fit into their frame of reference. This is a concept of communication that is sometimes known as transmission theory. But, communication has another role to play in the organization of people's social interchange. That role is not so much to transmit one person's knowledge to others as to permit both together to construct interactively a basis of knowledge, which becomes their joint property and thus cannot be said to belong to either of them individually. Although they participate in its construction, they do not separately own it.

This is a theory of communication—and knowledge—of much more recent vintage than the transmission view and has become known as the theory of "distributed cognition" (Hutchins, 1995) or "group mind" (Weick

& Roberts, 1993). It borrows from a radical departure in artificial intelligence and computing known variously as neural net theory, connectionism, or parallel distributed processing (McClelland, Rumelhart, & the PDP Research Group, 1988; Rumelhart, McClelland, & the PDP Research Group, 1986). These researchers view cognition not as it is conventionally conceptualized as symbol manipulation but as the product of the interaction of the parts of a network, each of which, separately considered, is a local information processor but which, collectively considered, form a patterned representation of their environment that none of them singly can be said to hold. The intelligence is thus lodged in the configuring of the network as well as in the information processing activities of its component parts. It is for this reason that these researchers think of knowledge as subsymbolic rather than symbolic. The knowledge is a function not of the symbol processing as such, but of the way it is interconnected subsymbolically to generate a collectively synthesized image of the world that transcends the set of individual images that generated it.

On the basis of this work, the team of Weick and Roberts, and Hutchins generalize the connectionist principle to hypothesize that cognition is not contained within the skull of the brain but is a continuous phenomenon linking what goes on in the mind and what occurs in the human conversation of people engaged in practical work. However complex the operations of the brain, it is still the case that conscious thought uses language as its medium and so does conversation. Because of this, the flows of knowledge rehearsal and development that make up the sum of what a society collectively knows are not strictly boundaried by the individual cognitive system but flow out into the conversation, which is thus doing its own kind of thinking.

It is the implications of this radical new hypothesis that this book explores. A bimodal theory of information as both transmission and generation of knowledge throws an entirely new light on the genesis of organization and its relation to communication. Such a theory transcends the unimodal assumption of transmission theory that holds that communication occurs in or within organization (R. C. Smith, 1993) and reveals instead that it is equally true to say that organization emerges in communication (and nowhere else). It emerges, furthermore, in two distinct ways: as described, and thus an object about which people talk and have attitudes, and as realized, in its continued enactment in the interaction patterns of its members' exchanges. It is both locution (representation) and illocution (action, with practical consequences). Language becomes not only a way to record experience, but also a way to furnish a script for it. This theory, in other words, is both interpretivist and constructivist in its orientation. It constitutes an introduction to the study of organizational communication in a new way, and it is this novelty that inspired the preparation of the book.

PRECEDENTS

As with most new ideas, what follows is not really, in another sense, new at all. On the contrary, the symbolic/subsymbolic division has been in the literature on communicative discourse all along, but has not been identified as such, or at least has not used those terms. Instead, the two distinct perspectives are revealed by the kinds of emphases that writers adopt in their analyses of communication-mediated-by-language. The intensive study of discourse in the social sciences and the founding of disciplinary traditions dedicated to naturalistic analyses of communication can really be said to date only from the 1960s. Prior to that decade the social sciences, with the partial exception of anthropology, were largely dominated by a positivist philosophy of research, which pursued laws of behavior measured quantitatively and supported by statistical analysis. In this interpretation of how to do science, language in its naturalistic contexts of use figured almost not at all. When in the 1960s positivism began to lose its hold on research method and the framing of research questions, investigators also started to venture out to consider language-in-use. When they did so, two quite different approaches became apparent. For some, in order to see what role language was playing, studying language use meant mixing in normal contexts with people who were interacting with each other in the usual way. For others, studying language use meant the analysis of the texts people produce and read, independent of interactional context, and more concern with a rather different kind of context, that is, the universe of other texts that either tied them to historical evolutionary trends in texting or to the different genres of texts that coexist within a given time and society.

A bimodal theory of communication makes no attempt to refute either of these ways of seeing, but instead perceives them as dimensions of a complete theory of communication in language.

It is this spontaneous branching of the literature on discourse (a catchall term if ever there was one) that we consider in this first chapter. This chapter situates our whole discussion in a historical framework. But, it also takes us to a more focused consideration of where these two orientations in the literature lead when their attention is directed to the theme that most directly preoccupies us, namely, how organization emerges in communication. In this respect, we consider two contrasting perspectives: one, ethnomethodological and the other, critical.

Ethnomethodology focuses first and foremost on interaction-mediated-by-talk: conversation in its multitudinous manifestations. From this perspective, language is an instrumentality, a necessary support for the negotiated developing through interaction of an account of how the world is and how the interactants are with respect to it. It looks into the interactive mechanics of the process of making joint sense—of getting on with things and of dealing with events to produce an intelligible universe of meaning. Organization, in this view, is a constructed entity generated by people in their talk.

Critical theory, by contrast, focuses on the texts of communication or what has been called, following Foucault (1972), its "discursive formations." Its metaphoric basis is not so much language as instrumentality, but rather, as we see in this chapter, language as colonizer. It is less preoccupied with dynamic processes of interaction and the negotiation of meaning than it is with how language subtly frames the interaction, determines its orientation, and calls into being the identities of organizational members, independent of their own willing. It sees the performance of organizational members as already shaped by language, even before it takes place.

Now let us consider in turn each of these orientations to the study of discourse.

THE REDISCOVERY OF THE NATURAL WORLD OF COMMUNICATION—ITS "CONVERSATION"

Arguably the two most influential influences on discourse analysis dating from the 1960s were Erving Goffman (1959) and Herbert Garfinkel (1967). Between them they initiated the study of conversation as a serious discipline.

Goffman made the telling point that social organization is situated. It always involves specific people in particular circumstances, and it always has a history (you and me or us and them, in a here-and-now or a there-and-then). He captured the tenuous nature of everyday life by expressing the logic of people's interaction with each other as a "presentation of self." Daily life is like a drama, he argued, where people realize that if their own identities are to be accomplished successfully and social situations sustained, they must improvise in playing out the plot together. There has to be an interactive order established for communication to be even minimally successful. For this reason, Goffman's image of organization is of a collectively produced interaction, of a fragile equilibrium, vulnerable to accidents. One false step and the whole drama runs the risk of falling apart: loss of face, confusion, and embarrassment all around.

Garfinkel originated a school of thought known as "ethnomethodology." Given its importance as an element on which our own work builds we shall devote a longer discussion to it. Its roots are in a turn-of-the-century philosophy called "phenomenology" whose spokesperson was Edmund Husserl.

Phenomenological Reduction: Edmund Husserl

Husserl (1964, 1976) built on the philosopher Kant's perception that there are features of experience, such as our perception of time, space, and causality, that must already be present, a priori, in categories of the mind.

Otherwise, the familiar shapes of the world around us would not appear to us to be shape-like (but merely a meaningless array of uninterpreted information). A chair is a chair because it looks like a chair, no matter what angle we see it from or in what light. It is our seeing it as a chair that makes it a chair, not just its intrinsic natural properties, as they are recorded on the retina. The subjective structures of meaning do not just come into play, passively, at the moment of perception, as a filter, but rather actively participate in the constitution of the perceived world (something that Karl Weick, much later, would call "enactment"). We are, in this view, not a neutral material on which signals from the world out there are physically sensed and cognitively recorded; we are actively engaged with a world of objects that we know about, have feelings about, and manipulate—objects that are of our own making. The result is to change the focus of attention from the world (positivism) to our knowing of the world (phenomenology).

Husserl thus emphasized the primacy of the constitutive role of consciousness: not to study how psychological factors intrude into perception and bias it, as did his contemporary Freud, but how perception is normally accomplished. To this end, he distinguished between what he termed *the natural attitude*, which is to take the phenomenal world as it comes, as "just there," as most people do and as positivism does, and what he called a *phenomenological reduction* in which the researcher sets aside—temporarily brackets out—the question of whether what is perceived as natural is truly a representation of the world in order to focus on the process by which perception of it is accomplished. When such a change of focus has been accomplished, there will be two things to consider: the experiencing process itself (which Husserl called *noesis*) and the content of what is experienced (which he called *noema*). It was the first of these, the constructing of an experienced world, that would become the object of study of ethnomethodology. But to be interpreted as relevant to communication theory, there had to be an intermediate step of translation, and that step was taken by one of his students, Alfred Schutz (1962, 1964, 1967, 1970).

The Intersubjectivity Riddle: Schutz

Suppose that we accept Husserl's idea that the ability of ordinary people to function effectively in normal circumstances depends on their adopting a natural attitude. Ordinarily, the objects and events that surround us do not seem to be filtered by complex procedures of deliberate consciousness on our part. The world is simply there. The problem, Schutz realized, arises elsewhere—when someone wants to communicate their experience to others. We can never have immediate access to what someone else is experiencing. The instrument of communication we have is language, and

language is made up of a network of *typifications* that we inherit along with
our learning of language in the circumstances of daily life: commonsense
constructs of typical actions, events, motives, identities, and contexts that
arise not out of personal experience but are inherited from the community
where we learned to speak. Such typical constructions inevitably fall short
of an understanding of *this* particular action, *this* event, *this* context. Because the categories of language are typifying, rather than specific to any
single individual or experience, they always underspecify the individual's
experience. No matter how clear you try to make yourself, there is always
a residual ambiguity.

Yet, Schutz said to himself, people do communicate easily, naturally,
without any sense of artificiality. How can this be? How can something as
problematical as communication be pulled off so effortlessly, on a routine
everyday continuing basis?

Part of the answer, he thought, is that the commonsense categories and
constructs that we unthinkingly employ to experience our personal world
were already social to begin with and that they are part of what we learn
when we begin to speak. It is not just that we can only communicate the
unique character of our experience through a code that turns it into
generalities, that is, typifies it; it is that even the original experience had
to have already been mediated by that code. So one thing that makes the
mundane intelligibility of social life possible is that our experience was
framed in a shared language from the start.

But this still does not solve the problem of the categorial underspecifi-
cation of individual experience.

The key to the puzzle, he reasoned, is that people treat understanding
each other not as a technical or a scientific or a philosophical problem,
but as a practical problem to be solved in a practical way. They, unlike a
philosophical movement of the 1930s known as logical positivism, do not
try to invent a new language to eliminate ambiguity. Instead, they assume
that, for all practical purposes, their world is intersubjectively shared with
others, that the standpoint of the person they are talking to is reasonably
interchangeable with their own (if you were in our position you would be
feeling pretty much what we do), and that the world other people talk
about is one that we do, or at least could, share. Now when someone
speaks to you and you do not quite grasp what they are saying, you still
are convinced that you could get the drift, and perhaps will later, as the
conversation unfolds, or that you already have enough background information to fill in most of the unstated but intended meanings. You can live
with the ambiguity in the interest of getting on with the conversation.
Although a risk is involved, you assume you understand enough, until
shown otherwise. Communication is thus inevitably elastic. As the conversation analyst and sociologist Heritage puts it:

[T]he type constructs with which the actors navigate the natural and social worlds and with which they communicate through natural language are inherently approximate, open-ended and revisable. They may undergo change, elaboration or qualification at any moment subject to local contingencies. Their development and use is shaped by the practical experiences and relevancies which arise in the course of the actors' engagement with the world around them.[1] (1984, p. 53)

Communication, then, is not just messaging; it is instead a continuous process of adjustment in which each participant's speech provides the material for the interpretive skills of the hearer to fill in the gaps, to guess at the speaker's meanings and motives, to verify assumptions, and to correct misapprehensions. To speak is to open oneself up to inferences, to make one's own capacity to express oneself contingent on others' understandings and sanctions. Intersubjectivity is something to be achieved: Its maintenance is a practical problem, routinely solved in social interaction through an ongoing process of mutual adjustment of perspectives. There is no external guarantee of success. But there is a payoff: "[A] world of shared experience—extruded, as it were, through language—is brought into being" (Heritage, 1984, p. 60).

Garfinkel and Accountability

This is the platform on which the ethnomethodologist Harold Garfinkel (1967) built. Garfinkel was a doctoral student of Talcott Parsons, a reigning authority in sociology of the time. Parsons, a complex figure who had tried to marry a voluntaristic view of human action with a general theory of social systems and structures, felt obliged by his preoccupation with the systemic to postulate that people internalize social norms. Only in this way could he explain the sociality of human action that was necessary to make it functional for the achievement of collective social action. Garfinkel reacted against this way of reasoning because he considered that it reduced people to "judgmental dopes," or mere tools of society in the realization

---

[1]Cf. Goffman (1981, pp. 10–11): "Commonly a speaker cannot explicate with precision what he meant to get across, and on these occasions if hearers think they know precisely, they will likely be at least a little off. . . . Indeed, one routinely presumes on a mutual understanding that doesn't quite exist. What one obtains is a working agreement, an agreement 'for all practical purposes.' But that, I think, is quite enough. The edging into ambiguity is only significant, I think, when interpretive uncertainties and discrepancies exceed certain limits or are intentionally induced and sustained (or thought to be by hearers), or are exploited after the fact to deny a legitimate accusation concerning what the speaker indeed by and large had meant. A serious request for a rerun on grounds of faulty reception is to be understood, then, not as a request for complete understanding—God save anyone from that—but for understanding that is on a par with what is ordinarily accepted as sufficient: understanding subject to, but not appreciably impaired by, 'normatively residual' ambiguity."

of its objectives. There must be a better way, he argued, to explain the stability of social life than by this essentially patronizing mainstream social science view. To support his position he turned for inspiration to Schutz, who by this time had immigrated to the United States. Through his famous breaching experiments, Garfinkel was able to display, convincingly, the taken-as-given basis of human intersubjectivity that Schutz had hypothesized: how much of how we make communication work depends on unspoken assumptions of normality and shared typifications. There was no need to postulate the rule of norms other than those we use to successfully interact in society and establish ourselves as persons.[2]

Garfinkel developed the idea of intersubjectivity in an important new way: He showed the centrality of "accounting." People in interaction, he suggested, are engaged in making what is occurring around them accountable to each other, in the sense of furnishing comprehensible descriptions and explanations of what is going on (they are in effect generating a jointly accessible text through their shared speech). The accounts people develop, he maintained, never constitute self-contained semantically complete descriptions; they are always occasion-framed or *indexical.* To understand what someone is saying, you have to have a sense of what he or she is doing, you have to supply context (such as who is speaking, what the circumstances are, and what went on before to which the current utterance might be related). The meaning of what people say is never self-contained, never strictly textual, communicationally speaking. Hermeneutics[3] is an everyday scientific method (which is what led him to describe his branch of sociology as *ethnomethodology*, i.e., the study of how ordinary people proceed methodologically to make sense of their world).

But Garfinkel went further. If accounts, to be comprehensible, require a situation, the obverse is also true. The situation is not merely given; it is constituted by the accounts that occur in it. Consider a court of law. What is it?—other, that is, than witnesses accounting for their behaviors; counsel making accounts of the witnesses' accounts or of what the legal texts say; juries giving an account of their verdict; judges passing judgments on the events unfolding before them; and reporters reporting on the

---

[2]Garfinkel's breaching experiments exploited a simple device: Question the normally taken-for-granted. He might, for example, have a student return home at night and to his or her partner's formula question "So how was your day?" reply with a response such as "What do you mean 'how was it'? Do you mean what was the weather like, or how many hours did I work, or what?" The usual response was flat-out exasperation: "What got into you? Are you crazy?" Or he might have a student ask someone on a subway train to give up their seat (the students found this very hard to do). In every case, the object was to point up the existence of tacit understandings in the conduct of interaction.

[3]Hermeneutics is the science of interpretation, especially associated with the branch of theology dealing with the principles of exegesis, or interpretation of the Scriptures. As Hawes (1977) puts it, it is interpretation of that which manifests itself in and through language.

reporting of witnesses, lawyers, jury spokespersons, judges (and sometimes other reporters), and of the public who has been present. Take away the accounts, and, as with the core of a peeled onion, there is nothing left. But similarly for all organizational occasions: The accounts are not just in and about the situation; they are it.

This is a radical new view of organization: a self-organizing system.

Conversation Analysis: Sacks, Schegloff, and Jefferson

Schutz' and Garfinkel's work was evocative, but not particularly systematic. For ethnomethodology to become fully empirical, a further step was required, and it was Harvey Sacks and his colleagues, notably Emmanuel Schegloff and Gail Jefferson, who took it. The field that has come to be known as conversation analysis (CA) dates from an article they published in 1974 entitled "A Simplest Systematics for the Organization of Turn Taking for Conversation."[4] The authors observed that, in spite of the remarkable diversity of conversational situations, certain regularities are observable. Mostly, only one person talks at a time, and, when more than one does, the overlap is brief; changeovers from one speaker to another occur constantly and do so with little or no gap; and, in a conversation with multiple participants, the allocating of turns of talk is accomplished regularly and, when troubles arise, they are dealt with, that is, repaired. None of this smoothness could be managed, they argued, if there were not an underlying mechanism at work in the form of unspoken rules that people follow in the course of their otherwise unprogrammed interaction. Using their own analyses of recorded conversations as a basis, they outlined what they thought might be such a set of implicit rules (the "systematics"): how to self-select oneself as the next speaker, how one speaker selects another, when it is acceptable to go on speaking. It was these kind of elementary rules, they speculated, that make conversation a possibility, whatever the context.

The seeming triviality of this explanation is deceptive. Sacks and others are drawing implications that, in line with Garfinkel's insight, represent a break with previous thinking on organization. They make points such as these:

1. Participants in a conversation do not have the luxury of coasting— they have to be alert to the cues that indicate they now either must, or can, enter the conversation.

---

[4]Sacks died tragically young, yet he left a brilliant legacy of original thinking, on a variety of topics (see Sacks' lectures, edited by Jefferson, 1989, for a collection of his lectures and occasional writing). Conversation analysis has been carried on by Schegloff, Jefferson, Hopper, Heritage and others, to become a well-established field.

2. Many conversational exchanges consist of paired utterances ("adjacency pairs"), where the selected speaker is under a constraint to
   answer.
3. Understanding of other people's interventions is not only taken for
   granted, but also must be actively displayed in the responses and, if
   it turns out to be faulty, this constitutes a "trouble."
4. The whole process is actively monitored by participants, and if there
   are troubles, they have to be repaired.

The authors conclude that conversation is thus a locally managed organizational system: "party administered." The administration is not predetermined, but interactively constituted. It is not the speaker who unilaterally
decides on the boundaries of his or her turn, for example; the turn, as a
unit, is interactionally determined. They think of these properties of local
turn-by-turn management, self-administration, and interactional control as
an instance of the general principle of *recipient design*, by which they mean
"an orientation and sensitivity to the particular other(s) who are the co-
participants" (Sacks, Schegloff, & Jefferson, 1974, p. 43). The principle
covers an impressive range of the features of a normal conversation, including word selection, topic selection, how sequences are ordered, how
the conversation is initiated and terminated, and so on.

Why is this so important to a student of organizational communication?
Functionalists in an earlier Parsonian tradition (Parsons was Garfinkel's
thesis advisor) had assumed that social continuity depended on the internalization of values and norms by the individual. The Human Relations
school of management theory assumed that managerial stability depended
on taking account of individual needs and motivation. But the CA researchers are saying something different: that continuity is a product of
the dynamics of interaction as such, independent of individual values and
norms. The conversation has its own internal governing mechanisms. Accounting, the very basis of a shared understanding on which stable organization depends, is not accomplished by sender-to-receiver messaging but
is a locally managed, interactively controlled, jointly monitored phenomenon that is not under any single person's control. The conversation has
its own self-organizing dynamic. But, does this principle apply in contexts
larger than that of face-to-face interaction?

Scaling Up?: Boden

Because of its spartan methodological commitments, many of the published
accounts of CA research have tended to seem irrelevant to organizational
inquiry—too micro to be informative about anything as transsituational as

contemporary organization. It is evident that CA researchers have themselves begun to feel uncomfortable about the restricted range of their
analysis (they are sociologists, after all). This changing focus is evident in
the appearance of published works that directly address organizational
questions (Bargiela-Chiappini & Harris, 1997; Boden, 1994; Boden & Zimmerman, 1991; Drew & Heritage, 1992). Of these publications, Boden's
book is easily the most relevant to an organizational communication researcher, because it integrates not only principles of ethnomethodology
informed by a grounding in conversation analysis, but also is sensitive to
both sociological theories (the structuration theory of Giddens, in particular) and several well-known management theories of organizations (Weick,
Stinchcombe, Pfeffer, and March among others). Methodologically, she
adopts an intermediate position: not quite as austere as pure CA, more
open to interpretation, but respecting throughout CA's emphasis on self-
organization. (We return to consider Boden's ideas again, in a different
context, in chap. 7.) The summary that follows serves to introduce her
general approach.

Boden observes that the participants in an interactively constructed
exchange are doing more than merely keeping the turns straight; they are also,
as Garfinkel had insisted, interactively working through an account, and they
do so in the same self-managed and mutually monitored way that we have been
describing in our discussion of conversation analysis. As Sacks was among
the first to point out, it is in this context that membership categories—the
whole hierarchy of an organization—are affirmed and recognized. Boden
argues that, to the extent that there is an organizational life at all, it must pass
through the wringer of a locally managed conversational exchange. In her
words (1994, p. 74) "[T]he structuring properties of turn-taking provide the
fine, flexible interactional system out of which institutional relations and
institutions themselves are conjured, turn by turn."

Among Boden's imaginative contributions (based on a suggestion of
Goffman, 1974) is the concept of the *lamination* of conversations, by which
she means the interlacing of many locally realized interaction episodes
into a pattern that knits together the organization as a whole. Conversations
may be linked by their common preoccupation with shared objects and
roles. Through the focus on a common object, a complex tissue of discourse
is built up, involving multiple actors in a variety of conversational sites.
Out of this emerges an account that has pan-organizational implications:
a common text for all the conversations.

Boden sees organizational discourse as having an episodic character.
She thinks that it is by "segmenting [it] into meaningful units" that organizational actors make sense to each other locally and, in this way,
develop "the practical structures of action" that constitute the organization
(we come back to the issue of segmenting in chap. 2). To describe the

episodes of interaction, she takes as her mapping device the principle of adjacency pairs developed within conversation analysis. Queries, for example, "carry their own interactional and organizational force"[5] (1994, p. 126). Organization is an arena not only of interpretation but also of action: "The turn-*taking* system is also a turn-*making* opportunity for asking questions, soliciting advice, clarifying issues, expounding opinions, developing projects, negotiating agreements, resolving conflicts (and even creating them) and, in the broadest sense, achieving the *essential*, ongoing understandings that make social life work" (1994, p. 73, emphasis in original).

From this it is an easy step to argue that, if all social life is episodic, it is also local (Boden, 1994, p. 4: "organizations run in the 'informal mode' *all* the time"), and therefore (p. 5) "the world is of a piece, single and whole . . . there is no such thing as 'micro' and 'macro'" (a position that, as we find in chap. 5, allies her with the structurational view of Anthony Giddens). As she puts it: "The tiniest local moment of human intercourse contains *within* and *through* it the essence of society, and vice versa" (p. 5, emphasis in original). Global issues are necessarily "grounded in local conditions of concrete action" (p. 10). Yet as we read her (frequently quite detailed) analyses of the organizational episodes of discourse she studied, one is struck by how intensely situated they are and how specific the concerns are to the individuals involved. How is it possible to be at the same time local and global, situated and transsituated?

The first clue she gives us is in the objects being transacted. The transaction may be local, but what is transacted can be as global as we like and, in many of her analyzed instances, is: university and state budgets, for example. So conversations, although local, become linked by the commonality of their objects. The second clue is agency. Although the people who participate in the conversations are necessarily place-and-time-constrained human actors the agencies—the roles—they instantiate in the transacting of verbal exchanges are not. Human agency comprises the involvement in action of social actors who are always, without exception, confronted with specific conditions and choices. Boden is insistent on the central importance of agency, as are we; she too sees human beings as knowledgeable agents in the production (and reproduction) of their lives and their history. People's actions are made relevant through their treatment of each other as agents, who are accountable for their actions, *"morally accountable"* in fact (1994, p. 14, emphasis in original). On the other hand, agency, although realized in the local circumstances of an exchange, is not locally limited in its scope: "[H]uman actors both produce and expect agency in immediate and distant others who, *through their actions*, constitute the organizations and institutions of their society" (p. 14, emphasis in original).

---

[5]The distinction between questions and queries is Goffman's (1981).

It is that telltale phrase "and distant others" that we call attention to here. The organizational actors in question are not just John or Jane Does. They are types of actor, organized by "membership categorization devices" (a concept borrowed from Sacks), or "highly selective and interactionally variable mechanisms for 'doing' *social* relations" (Boden, 1994, p. 57, emphasis in original). Some of those "devices" have a universal scope (categories such as gender, age, race) but some may be organization-specific (university deans, TV station managers), and, when they are, they constitute the means by which agency is able to spread from one conversation to another. This is how, as she puts it, conversations become laminated, one on another. This is how the macro is regenerated by the micro.

None of this would work at all in the absence of a shared body of frame knowledge (a theme we pick up in chap. 3). How else would you read the meaning of the objects and agents you encountered if you did not already have them typified in language? As a result, Boden reports, organizational members spend an inordinate amount of their time making accounts of their activities and decisions, accounts that are, as she puts it, "not some flawed version of an otherwise objective 'reality,' or rationalizations of 'irrational' or unreasonable strategies and decisions that are being given a gloss of 'retrospective rationality'; they *are* the organization in action" (1994, p. 14, emphasis in original). Accounting is not a personal achievement; it too is accomplished interactionally ("Cognition," she says flatly, "is not an 'individual' matter," p. 20, a view that we return to develop in chaps. 6 and 7). Its effect is to "fit current actions (and inactions) to some immediate problem in ways that retrospectively mesh with earlier actions and prospectively will be seen to adequately accommodate projects organizationally shared agendas" (p. 21). As she says elsewhere, organizational actors look back, and forward, because they need to frame their actions to *look* consistent; their attention to the past and the future is selective, in the interest of constructing an account that "will look credible" (p. 57).

Finally, Boden describes the informational preoccupations of organizational members as an ongoing scanning of the horizon for relevant signs and a continuous updating of the store of knowledge needed to construct and maintain a plausible account of one's own and others' actions: "[O]rganizational members continuously position their current activities and emerging agendas in terms of the larger stream . . . In the process, that recursiveness of action lays down the steps of the organizational dance that others must, with their own variations, follow" (1994, p. 188). The beat, you might say, goes on: a "*blur* that needs constantly to be clarified, refocussed, and occasionally completely realigned through talk" (p. 152).

Boden has, with great skill and a truly remarkable facility of language, drawn a communicational portrait of an intersubjective universe, always locally grounded, yet nevertheless globalizing. Its procedures of accounting are both situationally reconstructed, yet simultaneously translocal in their scope. Essential to this universe's continued vitality is the body of frame knowledge that is used for interpreting the objects and roles of organization, continually regenerated interactively to produce a shared cognitive surface of understanding and assiduously sought and exchanged in networks of links that both discriminate between and bridge the multiple conversations of organization. Part of what makes that frame knowledge work is how it "categorizes and segments" actions, actors, and their objects, and how it "filters, screens, selects, and organizes" (Boden, 1994, p. 57). She makes good sense of the sensemaking process, to our way of thinking. But hers is less than a complete account. It is, in fact, only one way to look at the unfolding of organizational communication. We are now going to consider an alternative set of explanations, and oddly enough, although they take their jumping-off place in the same theory as ethnography, namely, phenomenology, they arrive at radically different interpretations. Again, the turning point was the 1960s.

CRITICAL THEORY AND ORGANIZATIONAL PROCESS

Semiology in the 1960s

All of the developments we have been discussing were part of an Anglo-American tradition. Paris, during this same time, was witnessing its own rebirth of interest in the discursive dimension of communication but, typically, it developed in a radically different direction from the trans-Atlantic world. In good part, this was because the progenitors of European discourse analysis were markedly different in training and outlook from their transoceanic counterparts who were, in North America, associated with the empirical social sciences and cognate fields such as psychotherapy, and, in France, were among scholars versed in philosophy, literature, and European linguistics (more speculative and less data driven than in the United States).

In 1961, a new journal, named *Communications*, appeared, which was published by the *Centre d'Étude des Communications de Masse* (Center for the Study of Mass Communications), located in the prestigious *École Pratique des Hautes Études* in Paris. The authors who published there constituted a select group that included Claude Bremond, Violette and Edgar Morin, Tzvetan Todorov, Julia Kristeva, Roland Barthes, Christian Metz, Umberto Eco, and Algirdas Greimas—names that resonate in French thought and are almost unknown in the United States (with the exception of Barthes and Eco). Two issues, Number 4 (1964) and Number 8 (1966), explicated the principles of the new science of semiology (Barthes' "Éléments de sémiologie" appeared in the 1964 issue, for example, and the 1966 issue was devoted to a discussion of the theoretical underpinnings of a scientific narratology).

The new movement, which was to define communication studies in the French-speaking world for a decade and more, drew for its inspiration on currents of linguistic analysis inspired by the Danish specialist Hjelmslev (the definitive interpreter of the pioneering studies of de Saussure, whose ideas are briefly considered in chap. 4), and also on structuralist analysis in anthropology as represented by the British ethnologist Radcliffe-Brown and by Lévi-Strauss. In striking contrast to North American tendencies of the time, the study of communication in Paris was seen through the lens of a detailed analysis of text. It is this work that began to explore systems of semantics, not limited to language, since Barthes and later, Baudrillard, would go on to document the multiple ways in which meaning is incorporated into every object of our everyday existence.

Barthes and Baudrillard wrote with more flair and for a wider audience, but the true systematizer of the new movement was Greimas (1987; to whom we acknowledge our own profound debt). It was Greimas who developed a body of theory, and it was around him that a group of researchers—still active—clustered to form a school. In essence, Greimas argued that the analyst needs to recognize three logically distinct levels of discourse. There is first the surface, or figurative, level. This is the level of ordinary talk, and it is immediately interpretable because it is composed of all the words we normally use to identify people, their objects, and the events in which they are caught up—everything that is figurative because it names (what we later call "frame knowledge").

Skipping the second level for a moment, the third, or "deep" level, is that of basic semantics. For Greimas, the deep level is an austere world of elementary contrasts, whose binary oppositions allow us to see, precisely because they distinguish one thing from another (a very well-known principle in the psychology of perception where contrast is recognized as the basis of all vision).[6] There are, he thought, two kinds of contrast characteristic of basic semantics: contraries and contradictions. *Contraries* are bipolar oppositions such as black–white, male–female, rich–poor, young–old. These are concepts that are literally mutually defining. Why, for example, would you carve up the world into male and female if everyone in the population were hermaphrodite? Why worry about rich and poor if everyone were rich? Wealth would cease to matter: It would not even need to

---

[6]Some of Greimas' successors, including our colleague Pierre Boudon, reject the Greimasian assumption of binarity in favor of a trinary logic, which they trace back to the system of logic of Charles Saunders Peirce, who has enjoyed a recent revival in France (although not, we think, in his native United States).

exist. Contraries are how any society cuts up the world, or classifies it, to make it comprehensible. *Contradictions* are produced by simply adding the qualifier "not": To be *not young* is not necessarily to be *old*, but it does imply aging.

Greimas' second level is that which comes between the surface and the base. It explains how a domain of abstract, quasimathematic, binary distinctions—the deep semantic—might come to be translated into the figurative speech of ordinary discourse, and thus inform it with meanings that we are sensitive to, but often without knowing why (think of how many irrational prejudices cluster around terms such as *black–white, male–female, rich–poor, young–old,* and so on). This intermediate level of analysis is, for Greimas, that of narrative.

It is in narrative that the binary oppositions of the base are turned into the unfolding events of a narrative interpretation of the world. To effect this translation, Greimas makes some simplifying assumptions:

1. Every story is a chaining together of states of affairs and their transformation, in the form of events.

2. A state is defined as the linking of a subject and an object or quality (the verbs of state are *to be* and *to have*). Because we have already seen that he thinks of qualities as having a binary basis, the association of quality (in an object) with a human subject thus serves to, as he puts it, "anthropomorphize" the semantic primitive: to give abstract qualities a human face, in other words.

3. An event constitutes either the gain or the loss of some object or quality by some human subject, essentially a gain or loss of some valued property, and thus attitudinally motivating, and the starting point of a story. Obviously, what is gain for one subject is loss for another, and vice versa, and it is to this feature that we can trace what he calls the "polemical" character of stories: why there are bad guys as well as good guys.

4. Events have causes, and for this reason, it is necessary to postulate a second kind of subject: an actor or agent, human or otherwise (the relevant verb here is *to do*, either expressed directly or as part of some other verb such as *to open* or *to make*).

5. To act ("perform") one must be able to act, and be motivated to act, one must be "competent" and "qualified."

6. Competence and qualification are something that may be conveyed from one agent to another: You may give someone the information they need to act, or motivate them to do so, or authorize them to do so, or qualify them as professionally competent.

This, Greimas says, is the communicational dimension and from it all the identities that qualify as organizational flow: who does what for whom and why. (We come back to these ideas in greater depth in chaps. 2 and 3).

Side by side with the semiological movement, and to a degree in competition with it, there were other developments of equal or greater importance in the intellectual ferment of the 1960s Paris. We said earlier that some of the interest in discourse arose there among philosophers. In the French school system of the time philosophy occupied a much more prominent position than it did in North America. Philosophy was very much alive as it struggled to integrate the ideas of such thinkers as Husserl, Merleau-Ponty, Wittgenstein, Austin, and Heidegger, perhaps the most radical of all.

Michel Foucault

Heidegger's revolutionary proposal was that "it is in words and language that things first come into being and are" (Heidegger, 1959, cited in Hawes, 1977, and again discussed in chap. 2). Michel Foucault (1972) demonstrated what such a claim might mean to a sociologist and a historian. To do this, he draws a line between what he is doing, and what we might be tempted, in the ordinary course of events, to think someone is doing when they take discourse as their object of study. His focus, he insists, is not on discourse as a carrier of ideas, nor on the history of thought, as a historian's might be, nor is it on the structural properties of discourse, as a linguist's or semiotician's might be. Instead, he will look at the bodies of discourse he is analyzing from the cold-eyed view of an archaeologist (later, he would change the metaphor to a geneologist). He will study language as object, setting aside its intersubjective functions. He will look not through but at language. "[W]hat we are concerned with here," he says, is "the regular formation of objects that emerge only in discourse. To define these *objects* without reference to the *ground*, the *foundation of things*, but by relating them to the body of rules that enable them to form as objects of a discourse and thus constitute the conditions of their historical appearance" (Foucault, 1972, p. 48, emphasis in original).

Notice that phrase: "objects that emerge only in discourse." His task, he says, "consists of not—no longer—treating discourses as groups of signs (signifying elements referring to contents or representations) but as practices that *systematically form the objects of which they speak* [our emphasis]" (p. 49). The objects he is concerned with, in other words, are those not of the world but of the map of the world that the subject brings to the encounter, and that are given in language and, furthermore, a language that is institutionally grounded and legitimated, within a historical context.

It is not, he is saying, that there is first a world to be represented to ourselves by framing it in language. That would "neutralize" language. It is rather, he is arguing, that the things we deal with in our lives are "objects that emerge only in discourse," formed by practices, generated by a body of rules that "constitute the conditions of their historical appearance." Language, he is insisting, is consequential: It is in discourse that organization actually comes to exist.

Some of the Foucault flavor can be found in a book by Jacques (1996) who has studied the history of industrial work relationships from the Federalist era to the present. He observes that

> [T]oday, the division *manager/employee* is habitually used to distinguish the primary boundary between organization members. This would have been a meaningless division within Federalist reality. One would have referred to *owner/worker*, which is not analagous. Neither can one move directly from the Federalist to the industrial pairings. Between them lies an unbridgeable gulf created during a time when a society fell apart and was recreated, not from scratch, but along radically different lines. The pairing more representative of that period is *capital/labor*.[7] (p. 44)

Words matter. The almost magical power of words is in their capacity to engage us, without our even meaning to be caught up. How do they do it? One answer is a property of statements called their presuppositions (Levinson, 1983). A sentence can be seen as having two components, that which it explicitly asserts (its *focus*) and that which it takes for granted, or treats as something already given or established (its *presuppositions*). Suppose someone says "U.S. management has failed to meet the challenge of the postindustrial economy." Your normal reaction is to take up the cudgels, to argue pro or con ("I disagree. I think U.S. management has shown real adaptability" or "I agree. Management is caught in a time warp" or something of the sort). What is impossible to do without stepping out of frame is to question the presupposition that *management* or *postindustrial economy* are meaningful concepts. Yet why should we consider *management* or *postindustrial economy* just a given part of reality? Is not each possibly just a reification—a word without any real referent? Yet to step out of frame is to brand yourself as odd. There is a powerful constraint at work here: Presuppositions are not easily challenged.

---

[7]As Bennett (1990, p. 53) observes: "As late as the Civil War, the word 'employee' wasn't even in the lexicon of an ambitious young person." Both Jacques and Bennett speculate that, fueled by the downsizing campaigns of recent years, we are in turn evolving out of the managerial era, as downsizing practices of business have made employeeness less secure and attractive. (But note that the concept of *downsizing* is itself a discursively constructed object.) It is plausible that, as we enter the 21st century, we will evolve in the direction of other, but still discursively grounded, social objects.

What Foucault is proposing, then, is no longer to focus on (or at least to bracket out) what people say, but instead to concentrate on their presuppositions. Do not get involved in an argument with the prevailing ideology; stand back and ask when and how the presuppositions came to be presuppositional. What was the discursive surface on which the taken-for-granted object appeared? Management, for example: Was it something first taught in the business schools that began to spring up late in the 19th century? Did newspapers, magazines, and films provide a surface for it to emerge? Were congressional hearings, or court actions, involved? Was it part of labor's turn-of-the-century rhetoric? On whose authority did the idea rest? How did the concept come to be differentiated (staff vs. line, for example)? And so on. What we take to be the natural order of things is in fact the outcome of institutionally rooted historical contingencies: It could have been otherwise, and if it had that too would have seemed inevitable.

Out of this emerges a view of discourse (and communication) as no longer a transparent window on reality: "not the majestically unfolding manifestation of a thinking, knowing, speaking subject, but, on the contrary, a totality, in which the dispersion of the subject and his discontinuity with himself may be determined. It is a space of exteriority in which a network of distinct sites is deployed" (Foucault, 1972, p. 55). It is that "space of exteriority"—that "network of deployed distinct sites"—that is the organization in its textual constitution: a world that has been fitted to the word.

Foucault resurrected the role of language in the context of an institutionally grounded discursive formation; it remained for Jacques Derrida to draw a line in the sand separating a discourse-based (emphasizing the role of text) from a naturalistic version of communication (emphasizing conversation).

Jacques Derrida

There has been historically, according to Derrida (1988), a persistent prejudice to see verbal, face-to-face nonmediated communication as primary and writing (text) as derived and secondary. The rationale for this assumption is that with writing something has been added or substituted (a "supplement"): marks, or traces, that, unlike the ephemerality of conversations, survive beyond the moment of their actual production. A typical way of conceiving of writing, in this spirit, is to see it as an extension of presence: a widening of the radius of coverage of speech, through mediation, to reach a greater audience. But what strikes Derrida as crucial is not the enhancement of presence, but the marvel of absence. A piece of writing—a text—does not lose its viability because it is detached from its author and its recipients; liberated from its interactional circumstances of enunciation, it goes on leading an autonomous existence in their absence (and its absence from them).

This old notion of the text as a supplement—the extra that results from writing down what was first spoken—is, says Derrida, to put things wrong way up. The issue is not physical, but semiotic independence. Texts do not depend for their existence on their insertion in any specific context. The plays of Shakespeare and Aeschylus are not less plays because every point of reference in their societies was different from ours. Texts may have required a context to exist at all to begin with, but they continue to operate as conveyors of meaning even after all their initial reference points have vanished. That is what makes them *texts*.

Now consider again the so-called "unmediated" conversational utterance. The only way communication could occur is if the utterance had an existence autonomously of its speech context: "Our plane got to Denver at 1:30 p.m. Sunday" is meaningful only if such a formula of language can function in multiple contexts, that is, to be repeated ("iterated," is Derrida's term) across specific situations, and thus serve as a vehicle of communication for many people in many contexts (assuming we substitute some other location for Denver). In the absence of such semiotic autonomy of language, we would all be reduced, like the lower species, to pointing and grunting. So, says Derrida, even the utterances of ordinary conversation are themselves a form of writing, or text (*écriture*).[8]

Now Derrida will say that even our experience of the present (*la présence*) is a representation. Experience is re-presented in the sense that it is in the writing of it that we know it (remember that for him writing really means language). Experience, by the fact of its re-presentation, is already past and so is distanced from us.[9] In its re-presentation in language it has become a trace, a vestige, of something that is already absent: a remainder (*une restance*). "This," says Seung (1982, p. 144), "is his way of saying that perceptual objects are encountered never in their naked presence, but always through their representation or conceptual mediation." In the context of our discussion, this would mean that the subjective experience of organizational life is only possible through its representation in language. Organization must have been a discursive text before it could be given life in the intersubjectivity of a conversation.

---

[8]Where others might employ the word *sign* he uses *writing*; rather than call the science of signs (writing) *semiology* he names it *grammatology*.

[9]Much the same point is made by Weick (1995a) in his discussion of the retrospectivity of sensemaking (in a more accessible language than that of Derrida): As he puts it "people can know what they are doing only after they have done it" (p. 24). He expands on the idea this way (p. 25): "[P]ure duration is a 'coming-to-be and passing-away that has no contours, no boundaries, and no differentiation' (Schutz, 1967, p. 47). Readers may object that their experience seldom has this quality of continual flow. Instead, experience as we know it exists in the form of distinct events. But the only way we get this impression is by stepping outside the stream of experience and directing attention to it. And it is only possible to direct attention to what exists, that is, what has already passed."

The implications of this for organizational research have been outlined
by Cooper (1989). If human experience is existentially equivocal (as Weick,
as well as Derrida, believes), then it is in language that organization is to
be found. It is language that constructs the structure of organization (its
categories, its hierarchies, its logical processes and "good reasons").[10] But
what someone as deeply versed in language as Derrida (and here he echoes
Greimas) knows is that language achieves its power to structure organization (both of meaning and, by extension, of what is meant) by a combination of affirmation and denial, of positivity and negativity. Such binary
oppositions are, inevitably, marked in the sense that one pole dominates
the other, or seems more primary than the other (it is the latter that is
then marked by its being different). To say that a society is underdeveloped
is to have marked it as deviating from the primary state of being developed.
It is this that leads Cooper (p. 480) to interpret Derrida as saying that
"organization always harbors within itself that which transgresses it, namely,
disorganization." To the extent that language reveals the organizational
world to us, "it is a process that reflexively includes its own antithesis" (p.
480). When such underlying differences are stretched out in time, or
"deferred," then Derrida treats them no longer as differ-ence, but as de-
fer-ence, and they are the motor of the organizational dynamic, which in
affirming itself has simultaneously created the possibility of its own eventual
disaffirmation.[11] In the at-one-time almost total masculine hegemony of
management, there was already the seed of the feminist movement. Much
the same can be said for the current exclusion of minorities. The rationality
of any model of management is thus accomplished only at the expense of
a simultaneously created irrationality.

When an ethnomethodologist such as Boden analyzes a recorded managerial conversation in a meeting (of Provost and Dean, or Dean and Comp-
troller, or TV Station Manager and Producer) she emphasizes the synthetic
character of the exchange: how, in the sequentiality of the talk, identities
and agendas take shape and eventually, to use her term, become laminated
to form an organization. For Foucault, such an encounter would be one
more instance of the power of an underlying discursive formation to structure organizational objects. And Derrida might well see in the particular
circumstances of any one organization a demonstration of the iterability
of language and its capacity to create the illusion of immediate presence.
And both Foucault and Derrida might find not only the language iterable,

---

[10]In Cooper's words (p. 484): "Writing is the process by which human agents inscribe
organization and order on their environments."

[11]The French verb *différer* means both *to differ* and *to put off* or *defer*. Derrida invented a
neologism *différance* (the usual noun is *différence*) to emphasize that every presence of
something is made possible by an absence (of the latent opposed term), and thus meaning
unfolds only over time.

but also the roles that are expressed in and through it: A company president is, after all, also an iterable function!

All these ideas were soon to begin to filter into the organizational communication literature to become the basis of what is known as *critical theory* (Deetz & Kersten, 1983; Putnam, 1983). Stanley Deetz's (1992) *Democracy in an Age of Corporate Colonization* offers an interpretation of critical theory that is directly relevant to the study of organizational life.

Stanley Deetz

Deetz, as do Schutz (1964, 1967, 1970), Garfinkel (1967), and Heritage (1984), starts with Husserl, and yet, as we have said, the implications he draws are almost startlingly at variance with theirs. As Deetz interprets Husserl: "There is no route to the world or other persons except through *the experience of them*" (1992, p. 116, emphasis added). This may sound like a banal statement of the obvious, but it is not. It was the beginning of a radical new way of thinking that is only obvious in retrospect. The dominant philosophical tradition of the modern Euro-American world (beginning in the 17th century) has typically fostered a dualistic conception of (a) an objective world "out there" and (b) a subjective world "in here." The goal of empirical science, based on this dualism, has always been to perfect our knowledge (the "in here") to the point where it accurately matches the facts (the "out there"), by repeated verificatory acts aimed at testing the reliability and validity of subjective images through experimentation, thereby arriving at a consensus interpretation of the truth (establishment of a "scientific fact"). The problem that this nice dichotomization poses, which Husserl was among the first to point out, is that the "out there" is actually a construction of our own knowing processes, so that what we are observing as fact is already a projection of what would now be called our *cognition*. We can see only that which we are predisposed to see: We are caught in an epistemic loop. What we are predisposed to see reflects our particular purposes and involvements. There is no value-free knowledge.

This may have seemed like a radical idea at the turn of the century, but it is now a cliché of the psychology of perception. Gregory (1966, p. 11), for example, puts it this way: "Perception is not determined simply by the stimulus patterns; . . . [T]he senses do not give us a picture of the world directly; rather they provide evidence for checking hypotheses about what lies before us." The hypotheses come, of course, from us, not the world outside, and they inevitably reflect, as Gregory points out (pp. 160–163) culture-bound predilections (visual illusions that fool Europeans and U.S. observers do not work for Zulus, for example, or at least those who still live in a village world of round houses). Indeed, biologists such as Varela (1979) now believe there is no possible way to see the world other than by constructing it mentally: Perception is a closed system (J. R. Taylor, 1995).

The implication of the shift of perspective that critical theory highlights is that, if different people start with different premises, they will end up with different interpretations of the world, each in its own way as authentic as any other. Why does this make the historical dualistic foundation of modern science problematical? Not because subjectivity was eliminated by the methodologies of science but because, in Deetz's words, "a particular shared subjectivity became privileged" (1992, p. 117). (By "shared subjectivity," he means the intersubjective world of scientists and other such experts who regularly communicate with each other in a specialized language that they have themselves invented.) Science, in other words, has been muscling other interpretations of the world to the sidelines, on the grounds that its descriptions have a special status not shared by any other. Everybody else is limited by the subjectivity of their perceptual singularity, or by stale tradition, but not science, because it has transcended (it claims) the normal bounds of perception by substituting a more reliable access to the real world, namely, via instrumentation and measurement. It is the implications of this unequal contest pitting the socially sanctioned voice of science against all comers in the conversations of society that Foucault and Habermas called to our attention, and the logical extensions of the contest which Deetz has rephrased in his discussion of large organizations.

The mechanism by which science overshadows every other discipline is its monopolization of language. Recall from our earlier discussion of Schutz that language is a system of typifications that are treated by people in conversation not as tokens to which it happens that we assign an arbitrary meaning (*tree* in English vs. *arbre* in French, for example), but as a transparent window on the world.[12] It is this suspension of disbelief, this treating what is said not as a text but as a text-world, that Schutz identified as the vital clue as to why conversation works the way it does and why communication is possible. But the implication the critical theorist draws is this: If you can get other people to accept as normal your typifications, then you have established the platform on which people are now going to interact with each other. The way to do this is to persuade them that the typification is not arbitrary, nor a reflection of someone's subjectivity, but natural—just a fact. You rarely find phrases such as "I believe" or "I think" or "This is how I see it" in scientific reports, even though such articles invariably are reporting someone's current belief. This is even less tolerable in the social (where it springs from a tradition that Durkheim gave a name to, that is, the study of *social facts*) than in the physical sciences, because it is not even clear how society could be measured. Yet as Deetz remarks:

---

[12]One of our friends was overheard telling an acquaintance in a supermarket that her husband, David, "still loves little schoolboys!" It helps to know that "Little Schoolboys" is a brand of cookie; otherwise the casual passerby might have got a somewhat wrong impression!

"[M]ost social science in the United States today is practiced *as if* such naturalist assumptions were true" (1992, p. 119).

It is easy to see why people are tempted to naturalize. To set the terms on which other people engage in interactive languaging is a very special kind of power (to see why think about "TQM" or the "learning organization" or "re-engineering" or "self-organizing systems" and then reflect on how many organizational communities have been turned upside down, with real human fallouts, as a consequence of management's giving credit to such terms). Language determines, as Deetz puts it, a "mode of living" or a "style of being in the world" (1992, p. 129). And the effect is cumulative: The oftener a typification is used in conversation, the more natural it begins to seem—a phenomenon that Deetz, following the lead of Berger and Luckmann (1966), calls *sedimentation.*

Let us now follow Deetz further by delving deeper into the logical implications of such sedimentation. One of the typifications that language supplies (remember, such typifications are treated as a property of the world, not of language) is the subjectivity of individual intentionality. When we think of "being a subject" we usually tend to think of individual motive, attitude, and intention, but for those in the critical tradition, such as Deetz, this is yet another illusion: The "intending act" is "thoroughly social and historical." As he puts it:

> In phenomenology the "subject" or intending act is not a "real" person or psychological state, but rather a structuring possibility which precedes the individual who takes it on as his/her own. Only on the basis of the structuring possibility can an individual have the experience at all. The structuring possibility is shared and thoroughly social before the individual actualizes it in a particular experience. (1992, p. 125)

Again, the medium by means of which the "structuring possibility" is "shared" is language, which appears as "discourse" and is thus "an ideological practice [that] mediates between individuals and the conditions of their existence" (1992, p. 125).

According to Louis Althusser (1969; a French philosopher and sociologist writing in the 1960s) the individual "becomes a subject" by a process he called (in French) *interpellation.* The word interpellation has usually been translated into English as *hailing* but this gives an entirely false sense of what he was getting at. A much better translation would be *calling upon* (as when someone is called upon to speak up in a meeting) or perhaps *summoning.* When someone addresses you as *Doctor* (in the appropriate circumstances, to be sure) you are, in effect, being called upon to act like a doctor, with all that implies in both duty and authority. You have been what Deetz, playing with words, calls "subject-ed." The subject, says Deetz, "is always an image or constructed self rather than an individual in the full set of relations to the world" (1992, p. 135).

So far, we have concentrated on the cognitive consequences of the typifying property of language—what we refer to (beginning with chap. 2) as the constituting of a text-world. But this is to ignore a second dimension of languaging. The discourse-world (people in talk, such as Boden describes) is itself a world, not just a description of one. The doctor who is called up into a socially recognized subject status is not merely a figure in someone's texted representation; he or she is someone who realizes doctorness in the context of an ongoing world of talk, with colleagues, with patients, with nurses, with administrators, with students, with politicians, with reporters, with journal editors, with people who run conferences, and so on and on. He or she is enveloped in discourse. It is a discourse-world that, as Deetz insists, is justified by the texting, but after the justification is admitted, it is perpetuated in "routines and standard practices" that develop, in their quotidian ordinariness and their "accomplishment of everyday life," their own built-in justification. They become what Deetz thinks of as institutionalized, and their plausibility is all the greater because they are clothed in buildings and technologies, and other material signs of substantiality, that go hand in hand with recognizable social arrangements. "Every building, every sidewalk," says Deetz, "institutionalizes a point of view" (1992, p. 128).

It is this whole interconnected nexus of text-world/discourse-world that is the focus of attention of the critical theorist. It is here that he or she perceives we must look if we are to understand why it is that social structures, such as complex organizations, seem to replicate certain patterns of association, over and over, to produce the culture of a given society, or what Deetz calls "a way of being and experiencing in the world." It is a universe of being that is constituted by language, in that language carries both the knowledge in the institution and of the institution, both what it knows and what it is. It is language that is the mother of all the institutions, the universal support system of every domain of activity. "Language," in Deetz's words, "does not represent things that already exist. In fact, language is a part of the production of the thing that we treat as being self-evident and natural within the society" (1992, p. 128). It holds, he says, "the possible ways we will engage in the world and produces objects with particular characteristics"(1992, pp. 129–130). It is how we distinguish one thing from another.

From this, it is an easy step to defining what an organization is:

> The corporation is a special type of fiction held in place by a set of discourses including legal statutes, contracts, and linguistic production of roles, authority and meaning. It usually resides at a site and has members, but both the physical site and members can change without it being lost. Its material character rests on a discursive production and reproduction institutionalized

as routines, expectations, payments, deliveries, and so forth. Its constancy has
to be produced as a sequence of texts drawing together events and things having
a particular meaning regarding the corporation. (Deetz, 1992, p. 307)

In one sense, we could think of it as the same universe described by
Boden, a lamination of conversations, but the terminology, with its emphasis on distinctions and the power relations they presage, tells us the
angle of view is quite different.

There are two ways that we can look at the distinctions that language
makes. One is to look at language qua language. This is what the early
20th century linguist Ferdinand de Saussure (1966) did: He observed that
words are related to the objects and concepts they stand for by arbitrary
convention (the fact that we say *apple* in English and *pomme* in French is
a historical fact, because the words have no intrinsic appleness to them).
Instead, what makes language the flexible instrument it is are all the distinctions internal to it (apple vs. peach, plum, or pear; fruit vs. vegetable;
vegetables vs. meat or dairy products, and so on). It is how we cut up the
world into perceptible chunks. Part of that world is the one that we live
and communicate in, and part is the identities that language furnishes us
to live it. Language, in other words, defines the people who speak it as
well as what they speak about.

In a second sense, however, it is when these distinctions, inherent in
language, cease to be seen as characteristics of language to become, because
language is normally treated as transparent, characteristics of the world
described by language—the text-world/discourse-world of everyday life—
that they begin to institute the power relations that are the primary concern
of the critical theorist. It is the legitimizing, justifying property of language,
realized in discourse, that makes it such a potent instrument of control
over people's actions—a control that depends as much on self-monitoring
as it does on external discipline. Distinctions result in asymmetries, so that
the unequal distribution of privilege and power typical of every society,
our own included, is an inevitable consequence of discourse. Power, like
discourse, is not a property of the person, but of the relationship ("Power
relations are not external to other relationships but immanent in them,"
in Deetz's words, 1992, p. 307), and relations, as de Saussure discovered,
are what make language *language*. Power exists in the "reciprocal relations
of the haves and the have nots" (p. 307).

The gulf in perception separating the ethnomethodologist Boden and
the critical theorist Deetz is nowhere better illustrated than in their treatment of meetings. Like Boden, Deetz views meetings as a "reoccurring
feature" of corporate life. Like her, also, he sees the legitimacy of decisions
taken there as dependent on proper membership, resulting in the inclusion
and exclusion of certain people. He, too, notes that the relative status of
people is determined by this pattern of inclusion/exclusion. He, as she

does, emphasizes how much time is spent in meetings, how they serve as a place to make contacts with people outside one's immediate circle, often senior people, and how important they are in sharing perceptions and information and in cementing commitments to decisions. He, also, agrees with Boden that meetings may be hazardous because one risks being embarrassed or pressured or surprised in them, with the curious result that, although their ostensive function is to take decisions, critical decisions are rarely risked in that context. They are not just an activity, meant to further the interests of the organization; they are the organization—or, at least, a sign, a signifier, or an index of it. They are its ritualistic reenactment. All this is close to Boden's image, and yet in one respect their two accounts differ: Deetz never actually describes the occurrence of a meeting.

Why not?

The key is that concept of distinction. To describe a meeting in a positive way is to concentrate on what is present there. But Deetz argues for a different way of looking: one which equally takes account of what is absent. Consider a meeting of managers. What we observed (if we were observing) would be the managers talking among themselves. We would think of them as present. This is what Boden does. But are managers "managers" when they are not managing? Obviously not, no more than a farmer who does not farm is a farmer. So, what enables them to go on being "managers" in their meeting of managers is what is absent (or perhaps virtually present?): the managed. It is this submerged manager/managed relationship that Deetz wants us to see even when it is experientially absent (not in our field of immediate view).

For Deetz, as for Derrida, the meaning of this is that we should not think of speech and writing as how one person conveys an intentional meaning to another, but rather the converse: how what Derrida calls the *iterability* of text (the fact that it can be used over and over in many different contexts, can be stored, reproduced, and distributed) is what gives meaning to people's acts. Think, we could interpret both of them as saying, not of how those managers in the meeting are transacting their world, but how words such as *manager* (with all its connotations) lend their transactions meaning and make them and their preoccupations present for us. Their inclusion in the meeting, in other words, only works if there is simultaneously an exclusion. That is a function not of pragmatics but of semantics, dictated by the logic of language. In the absence of such an exclusion, the meeting ceases to have any organizational significance at all. It would be meaningless jabber. It is language that makes the occasion managerial and not just an encounter of more verbal and more fully clothed, if less hairy, primates (a comparison to which we return in chap. 5).

Thus, Deetz cannot give an empirical description of an actual meeting because to do so would make him an accomplice of the very system of inclusions and (unspoken but crucial) exclusions to which he is trying to call attention by his use of words such as "ideology." For him to concentrate on the voices that speak would imply his complicity in the silencing of the voices that are not speaking (or at least are not there). It is this that he means by expressions such as "language and the politics of experience," "disciplinary power," "discursive formations at work," "the imaginary world of work" (all taken from chapter headings in his book).

The shift of perspective from Boden to Deetz is like the alteration of perspective that occurs when the camera is moved from close-up to long shot: The close-up ignores the context (in Boden's case, context of power relations) whereas the long shot obliterates detail (in Deetz's case, the actual dynamics of interaction).

When we think of conflict we usually have in mind a contest of human actors. From the critical perspective, there is a much more profound conflict underway: one that pits one "discursive formation" (a term borrowed from Foucault) against another. It would be a mistake to picture a discursive formation in the short term. The structures of language are remarkably durable. It may take centuries for a discursive formation to develop (as Foucault argued in his history of how Europeans have historically conceived of madness and how our conceptions about it changed in an era of science). The point about such a formation is in how it links together a whole body of words, sentences, ideas, and practices. Meaning is not present in the single sentence or statement (message) but in how it ties together with other elements in the discursive formation of which it is a component. In Deetz's words: " 'Managerial discourse' for example does not denote who the speaker is external to the discourse nor a set of intentions, but a particular construction of the speaker and a specific social/historical set of distinctions, interpretive practices, and integrative unities." It is "a set of [. . .] structural principles which arise in a social/historical/economic/geographic area" (1992, p. 262).

WHY STUDY ORGANIZATIONAL COMMUNICATION IN A NEW WAY?

It is evident, from even such a cursory review of the literature as we have offered, that there are alternative conceptualizations of how organization emerges in communication, even when you have committed yourself to believing it does. One of them, which takes the conversation as its point of departure (Boden being a perfect example), emphasizes the intersubjective dynamics of a negotiated cognitive and social order. The other begins from text (and here Deetz is the exemplar), and emphasizes how, as the semantic screen of meanings that inevitably separates us from direct experience, our own discourse imposes a pattern that both organizes the conversation and yet transcends it, historically and geographically (Foucault's "discursive formation"). We have described these elsewhere (J. R. Taylor, 1993) as *worldviews*. Our aim in this book is not to choose between them nor to refute them, but to build on them.

One of the seminal ideas of the theory of self-organizing systems is that life occupies the space created by two boundary conditions that have been described (somewhat poetically) as "the crystal and the smoke" (Atlan, 1979). *Crystal* is a perfectly structured material, in its repeated symmetry of pattern, but because its structure is perfect, it never evolves: It is fixed for eternity. It is not life. But it is order. *Smoke* is just randomness, a chaos of interacting molecules that dissolves as fast as it is produced. It is not life either. But it is dynamic. Life appears when some order emerges in the dynamic of chaos and finds a way to perpetuate itself, so that the orderliness begins to grow, although never to the point of fixity (because that would mean the loss of the essential elasticity that is the ultimate characteristic of life). Chaos theory shows that there are, even in the most turbulent of processes, strange attractors around which patterns emerge and then, if they reproduce themselves, generate structure and order.

We perceive the emergence of organization to be similarly boundaried by two contrasting conditions. One of them is the relatively permanent structuring of text (the domain of the symbolic); it is this materialization of language to give it permanency that permits organization to transcend the strictly local conditions of its own production and, through its agency, to organize many conversations, in many places, and at many times. The other is the relatively chaotic (or at least unpredictable) processes of conversation (the domain of the subsymbolic), in the absence of which text, as the clay tablets of Sumeria, would describe organization, but would not be it. This book is an exploration of this one basic idea and its implications. It is an attempt to demonstrate how the texts of language portray, in immanence, an eventual organization, as well as how the conversational discourse makes the actualization of such a structure feasible but always problematical. It is the essential tension between two perspectives on discourse, one conversation-based, one text-based, that we perceive to be the fertile ground for the emergence of organization in communication.

Our analysis, however, expands the usual interpretations of those words *conversation* and *text* to recognize conversation as an essential sociality and text as a structuring principle with more than one manifestation: as immanent code of organization (that which is not said but on the basis of which all saying is made possible), as verbal and written expression in the context of a conversation, and as the physically transcribed traces that are what are left to us of previous conversational episodes.

The structure of the book is dictated by the centrality of this theme. In the three chapters that follow, we consider the structuring properties of discourse in its manifestation as text. Chapter 2 sets out a general theory of organizational communication in which the intersection between conversation and text is seen to be the ground for the emergence of organization. Chapter 3 delves into those properties of language-as-text that qualify it to be a surface for the emergence of organization, by that we mean those features that correspond to the actors, objects, and events of organizational life. Chapter 4 pursues this same analysis further to explore the deep semantic structures of language and how they condition our perception of the world we live in. Together, these first four chapters constitute Part 1, which we call "Theory of Communication."

The remaining chapters form the matter of Part 2, "Theory of Organization." Chapter 5 turns to an exploration of the concept of self-organization, presented as a reanalysis of reflections on the subject of three theorists of human organization: Weick, Giddens, and Latour. Chapters 6 through 8 focus on the organizing role of the conversation and include a reconsideration of Boden's analysis but in the new perspective we are proposing. Chapter 9 takes up the organizing role of text in the emergence of organization as a kind of interactively constructed map.

From the analysis of chapters 6, 7, and 8, a thesis emerges, and it is this thesis that constitutes the originality of the book. There are, we claim, two ways in which communication is related to knowledge. In one, it serves as a medium for the transmission of information. Our manner of conceptualizing this is to see knowledge as transcribed in language and passed on to others through speech. This is the matter that is transacted in human conversational exchanges. However, conversation serves a different role as well: not in the transmission of knowledge, but in its collective development to produce an understanding that is properly that of the community of conversationalists rather than of any single one of them. This is distributed intelligence. It is in the translation of this shared (or distributed) knowledge through its voicing by some socially legitimated agent or spokesperson that creates the structuring of the community of work into what we usually think of as "the organization."

Chapter 6 explores the basis of this idea by borrowing from a contemporary theory of computation, which demonstrates the deep relationship between understanding and the configuration of networks. Chapter 7 reexamines the literature on conversation analysis to show how the human conversation can be understood as a generator of collective knowledge. Chapter 8 examines the implications of this theory for the analysis of organizational processes and shows how organizational structure and communicational process are intertwined. Chapter 9 investigates, through the medium of a fictional case study, how authority structures emerge through the collectively negotiated mapping of actors and their objects.

Chapter 2

Communication as Coorientation

There are, we saw in chapter 1, two basic approaches to the study of the organization–communication link, assuming the latter to be mediated by discourse. One is a conversation-based, ethnomethodological view that perceives organization to arise out of communication through the laminated sensemaking activities of members, endlessly renegotiated. The second is a text-based, critical view that sees organization as already inscribed in the forms of language we inherit as part of a larger "discursive formation" and reproduced spontaneously (even unconsciously) in communication to instantiate a structuring of society that privileges some voices and silences others. You could think of these as alternative conceptualizations, mutually exclusive. In this chapter, we argue for a different interpretation. We conceive of the approaches as complementary perspectives within the framework of a more encompassing theory of communication and organization. We treat them as corresponding to dimensions of communication that lend themselves to alternative readings of the organizational phenomenon but that are not inherently contradictory. We see communication as fundamentally bidimensional. We try to show that the difference of perspective of the two approaches is just that—a difference of perspective, one that is the result of a decision of what to treat as figure (conversation or text) and what as ground (the other): a choice of "worldview" (J. R. Taylor, 1993).

The chapter unfolds as follows: Section 1 outlines a two-dimensional model of communication. It sees communication as a dynamic ongoing process, bringing into play two kinds of resources and being framed by two kinds of elementary constraints, which we conceive of as dimensions of conversation and text. Communication takes the form of a talking out in which there are two outcomes: (a) a situation is talked into being through the interactive exchanges of organizational members, to produce a view of circumstances including the people, their objects, their institutions and history, and their siting in a finite time and a place; and (b) a body of discourse is generated through the talk, such embodied discourse accounting for the ongoing reproduction, historically speaking, of the kind of enveloping discursive formations Foucault's work sensitized us to. These are the two perspectives we have considered, both being generated by the talking out of organizational members to produce two versions of what an organization is: (a) a lived world of practically focused collective attention to a universe of objects, presenting problems and necessitating responses to them; and (b) an interpreted world of collectively held and negotiated understandings that link the community to its past and future and to other conversational universes of action by its shared inheritance of a common language. Werth (1993) calls these, respectively, a discourse-world (that of the conversation) and a text-world (that of the discourse it produces). We see these two dimensions as corresponding to the *site* and the *surface* of the emergence of organization in communication: site, because as Boden observed, organization depends entirely on the existence of conversations for its continuance; surface because for organization to be recognized by its members it must be made present to them in a medium that allows them to read it, and this we understand to be the role of discourse—texting.

The model we present in this chapter conceptualizes two kinds of resource, and two kinds of constraint. The resources available to people who enter into communication include (a) the circumstantial advantages and disadvantages inherited from one's previous history of communication, including who one is, how one stands with respect to others, what kind of material resources one has control over, and what kind of patterns of behavior one has learned; and (b) language, the unique human ability to verbalize. The constraints are similarly of two kinds: (a) the rules of interaction one is obliged to respect to continue to be part of the community as a participating member; and (b) the rules of correct use of language (where *correct* is always to be taken with respect to the discourse community one is part of, never an absolute standard).

Section 2 of the chapter begins an exploration of the concept of language as surface—an exploration that will be continued in the following two chapters as well. Here we concentrate on one of the dimensions of communication, language, in order to better understand it as both resource and constraint. We introduce as our basic position the hypothesis that organization is made real to people in communication and tangible—an object they can relate to—primarily by its narrativization. Narrative furnishes a framework of understanding of action and its objects, of agents and their relationship, of community and its ethical codes, which makes it possible for organizational members to comprehend and to deal practically with their own and others' actions and situations. It provides the *modality* they need to signify, to legitimate, and to control both the material and the social world and to be controlled by either or both (Giddens, 1984). Its functions are mirrored in the elementary sentences of language. Narrative thinking does not just represent a world; it instantiates it. When we have understood how people narrativize experience, we understand how they can enact it.

Section 3 addresses the issue of how the parameters of conversation and text enter into the structuring of the dynamic processes of communication on a moment-by-moment basis, that is, how the ongoing events of communication begin to take on self-organizing properties and to thus explain the continuities that we associate with organizational life. We describe this as a *translation* of one dimension into another (essentially of circumstances into language and language into action), which has the effect of talking a situation into being to generate a universe of discourse that describes it, and thus becomes, because of the time-insensitive character of text, the means by which one situation influences another to produce a coherence that transcends the strictly local and makes the discourse produced by one conversation a resource to be used in others.

In Section 4 we offer some general reflections on the conduct of research, in particular with its relevance to the study of organizational processes, the topic of chapter 3.

TOWARD A BIDIMENSIONAL TEXT/CONVERSATION MODEL OF COMMUNICATION

Some Terminological Clarifications

We use some terms differently from ordinary usage, in particular, conversation and text. We employ both words in a special way. *Conversation*, as it is usually thought of, is what occurs in occasions of casual talk, when people group themselves together in verbal interaction without a formal agenda, not governed by the kind of institutionally sanctioned procedures that might be found in a courtroom, parliament, or television interview. Similarly, when people speak of *text*, they usually have in mind something written down, stored, displayed, or sent through the mails. Because our preoccupation is with organizational communication, the way we use these terms is considerably more inclusive.

Conversation

We take the organizational *conversation* to be the total universe of shared interaction-through-languaging of the people who together identify with a given organization. This obviously includes all the informal occasions of talk they take part in, whether over a drink or supper, in the washroom or on a golf course, in a casual encounter in the corridor or on the way to the airport. But it also includes the more arranged and circumscribed encounters of meetings, interviews, appraisals, briefings, union–management negotiations and so on, that collectively carry forward the interactively constructed themes of organizational life and situate the people who accomplish such an accounting process with respect to each other to create a recognizable system of relationships linking them to what they do and who they do it with.[1] There is no reason, on theoretical grounds, to exclude mediated as well as unmediated interchanges, including such phenomena as memos, reports, and communication software (although there are obviously practical reasons to take account of the medium of interaction and its effects, which we as practicing researchers are interested in).

This broader comprehension of the term *conversation* is close to Boden's (1994), who prefers to think of the discourse that goes to make up an organization, as we have already noted, as a lamination of conversations.

Broadening the definition of conversation in this way is not an arbitrary decision on our part; it is motivated, as we discuss further in chapter 7, by what we perceive to be tendencies in the principal scientific discipline concerned with the study of conversation, conversation analysis (CA). This body of research has convincingly demonstrated that even the most casual interaction through talk has a procedural basis. Over time, CA, although it was initially principally concerned with informal occasions of talk, has gradually enlarged its field of view to consider more structured situations, such as television interviews, medical consultations, court proceedings, and so on, and has concluded that, although context is of great importance in understanding the way the exchange unfolds, basic conversational rules of procedure always apply. Their results suggest what is more a spectrum of conversational occasions than a conversation/nonconversation dichotomy. There are, it can then be argued, genres of conversation, ranging all the way from unprogrammed to programmed, from relaxed to rhetorical and/or argumentative, from (to use a classic distinction) informal to for-

---

[1]Cf. Goffman (1981, pp. 70–72): "What, then, is talk viewed interactionally? It is an example of that arrangement by which individuals come together and sustain matters having a ratified, joint, current, and running claim upon attention, a claim which lodges them together in some sort of intersubjective, mental world. Games provide another example, for here the consciously intended move made by one participant must be attended to by the other participants and has much the same meaning for all of them. . . . Yet, of course, conversation constitutes an encounter of a special kind. It is not positional moves of tokens on a board that figure as the prime concern; it is utterances, very often ones designed to elicit other utterances or designed to be verbal responses to these elicitations. . . . And what conversation becomes then is a sustained strip or tract of referencings, each referencing tending to bear, but often deviously, some retrospectively perceivable connection to the immediately preceding one."

mal. We need to take account of all these possibilities if we are to grasp how the business of organization (Boden's "business of talk") is transacted.

Text

We use the word *text* to capture the quite ordinary idea that speech is built of words and phrases, strung together in more or less systematic ways to produce a coherent, understandable piece of language. In a conversation, this happens to be mostly spoken (or, among people with a hearing disability, signed), but it could have been written, and when it has been recorded and transcribed, as often happens, it is. Once again, there are of course practical reasons why language may exhibit different features when it is first spoken (and then perhaps recorded or transcribed) than when it is first written, but the basic material basis of spoken and written exchange—that which makes communication possible—is, theoretically speaking, the same: strings of language.

Again, our use of the term *text* to cover both possibilities is not entirely idiosyncratic. The functional-systemic school of linguistics associated with M. A. K. Halliday (which we discuss in chap. 4) has consistently favored this approach, for many of the same motives as we have just described (Benson & Greaves, 1985; Halliday, 1985; Halliday & Fawcett, 1987; Halliday & Hasan, 1985/1989; Hasan, Cloran, & Butt, 1996; Hasan & Fries, 1995).

Our choice of perspective leads us to conceive the basis of organization to be in the generation and regeneration, within conversational contexts, of texts: multiplexed (in the sense of composed of many layers that correspond to the simultaneously ongoing occasions of communication that collectively realize organization), to be sure, but nevertheless, conceptually, texts (or what could be called a layered, multiply interconnectable hypertext). Conversation is the site of organizational emergence, text, its surface. We assume, in other words, that the structure of organization is a property of communication.

Modeling Communication

What do we mean by *site* and *surface*? Consider Fig. 2.1.

This is our image of how the elementary communication event is framed: its parameters. We conceive of the actual communication as unfolding in the following way. First, people enter communication possessing a repertoire of stored material, a language resource base, out of which they can construct a spoken (or written) intervention. The repertoire includes what linguists would call a *lexicon*, which is to say the vast storehouse of words that everyone learns in an established language community. Second, verbalized exchange with other communicators is invariably framed by explicit

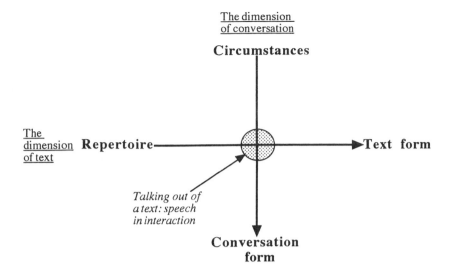

FIG. 2.1. Communication as the intersection of two dimensions, text and conversation.

circumstances (of time, place, participants, and occasion). The circumstances constitute a framework of identities and habits, not just of the participating members, but also their physical and symbolic context—a carryover from both their personal and inherited previous experience of interaction. Third, in the interaction itself there is always one person filling (holding the floor) with the other(s) backing (paying attention or in other ways exhibiting that they are an encouraging audience, what is called in CA the "back channel"). The resulting complementarity of roles produces a discursive structuring that is referred to in CA as "adjacency pairs"—the back-and-forth of ongoing talk. The filling/backing complementarity is explained as a formal constraint on conversation, called in Fig. 2.1 conversation form, in that it is only by the alternating of turns of speech that an interactive order is sustained and comprehension made possible. Finally, speakers must also know how to put words and elements of the repertoire together to make phrases, enunciate sentences, tell stories, formulate excuses and arguments, and do everything else that can be done using language in an interactive context. This is what we mean by text form: It is the syntactic/semantic constraint imposed by the necessity to produce a sentence or sentences that others will understand because they possess the same linguistic code.

Speakers enter communication, in other words, with resources that are both real (circumstantial) and symbolic (linguistic), but they must obey constraints of form that are respectively explained as the need to generate orderly interaction, one person at a time, and to enunciate strings of spoken language that conform to the normal rules of syntax and semantics of their community. Through their communication, they arrive at a situation in which both subjects and their objects are constituted and thus turned into a site of organization. As they construct their situation, they also give it discursive form and a kind of cognitive as well as lived reality, in that they now can talk about what they are living. We see the role of language in this realization as providing the surface on which organization can be read.

Figure 2.1 illustrates the framework within which communication occurs: its resources and constraints. The circle we have drawn at the intersection of the dimensions of text and conversation is meant to represent the space within which communication takes place. Figure 2.1 is thus a static representation of the framing constancies of communication; it makes no attempt to show its dynamic. Later in the chapter, we return to consider how the parameters become operationalized in the flow of talk.

We need by no means be restricted to spoken language; we admit as part of the repertoire nonverbal gestures and paralinguistic expressions for conveying ideas and adding emphasis, and all the technical skills needed to use microphones, blackboards, and overheads, or whatever goes into stringing together a communicative performance. The result of talking out is what we mean by *text* in the most basic sense. It is the text of the conversation—its support base. In the dynamic sense, each intervention follows from what was said before, impelled by the imperative of interaction, so that as each new addition to the text is produced it has, as its context, those texts which preceded it. The process is cumulative. The additions have become part of the circumstances of some future interaction. Text in this sense is the necessary input to and inevitable output from communication: both raw material and product.

Conversation Form

We touch only briefly on conversation form in this chapter, reserving consideration of that topic until chapter 7. We confine ourselves here to the following observations.

• People engaged in conversation must, to begin with, phrase their interventions phonologically, in the rhythms that are recognizably those of a given community. They have to sound right when they talk. Furthermore, their gestures and body behavior in space have to look right. In linguistics, sounding right would be seen as respecting the constraint of phonological form, or PF (Chomsky, 1995); in the domain of nonverbal research, the constraint in question would be conceived to be determined by kinesthetic rules (Birdwhistell, 1952, 1970), or spacing rules (E. Hall, 1959, 1966, 1976; Scheflen, 1965, 1973; Scheflen & Ashcraft, 1976).

• People must also behave in a conversational manner, and this supposes knowledge of correct conversational form (or CF). Briefly explained, the concept of *conversational form* is derived from a bedrock finding of conversational analysis that there is a *systematics* (Sacks, Schegloff, & Jefferson, 1974) at work in conversation—a kind of conversational grammar, if you like—which makes it possible for people to take turns talking in an orderly way and generally to keep the conversation on its rails in other relevant fashions (such as making one's contributions thematically relevant to what is being talked about or being cooperatively reactive to what others are saying). This grammar had to have been learned and operates as a fundamental constraint on communication. Conversation analysts find that individual contributions typically fit together structurally as interactive complements (called adjacency pairs), thus connecting the elements of the conversation together in a way that makes them locally coherent. In addition, there are generalized conventions in play (to open and close a conversation, for example) to provide a degree of global coherence. It is because of these coherences that we see communication (and the organization it realizes) as inherently conversational, even when it takes the form of such non-face-to-face exchanges as memos or interaction through the medium of competing press releases (as occurs in labor–management negotiation, for example). There is always a tacit protocol underpinning the discourse-world of interactive talk and mediated exchanges.

It is the conversational constraint on communication that makes it ineluctably contextual, situated, occasional, grounded, iterative, and cumulative. We, along with the authors discussed in chapter 7, recognize that situatedness. From the perspective of conversation, text (the intersecting dimension) is merely its support system, one that constitutes what might be called the bridge over which all the commerce of organization must ultimately pass (and in the absence of which the traffic of conversation would come to a halt). Conversation is the site of emergence of organization—where organization is enabled to disclose itself, to appear.

Text Form

If the finality of conversation is to sustain interaction, the finality of text is to produce a collectively negotiated interpretation of the world: to turn circumstances into a situation that is comprehensible and that serves as a springboard for action. What is important is how the texts of language, produced in interaction, effectively represent both the world around the conversation and the conversation itself—how they furnish a surface. It is the question of how language creates a surface of apprehension that now preoccupies our attention, for the remainder of this chapter. To answer it, we introduce an additional component of our theory, that of narrativity. We draw on the work of two individuals, the psychologist Jerome Bruner and the semiotician Algirdas Greimas.

THE THEORY OF NARRATIVE

The Narrative Mode of Reasoning

There is a tendency to think of narrativity as limited to explicit storytelling, especially because there is a well-developed research literature on the functions of stories in organization (Boje, 1991; Bormann, 1983; Czarniawska, 1997). Stories, of course, are one of several ways of using language to make a rhetorical point. This is not, however, what Bruner (1991) or the semiotician Greimas (whose work is described in the following section) mean by narrativity. Both Bruner and Greimas, although coming from very different disciplinary backgrounds, attribute a much more basic role to narrative than mere storytelling. They both see the narrative form as a basic trait of all forms of cognitive processing of social information: "how we go about constructing and representing the rich and messy domain of human interaction" (Bruner, 1991, p. 4).

As Bruner points out, there has been a dominant preoccupation in Western science with those processes of thought that come into play in understanding the natural or physical world; much less is known about how the social world is, or should be, understood (Bruner, 1991, p. 4). Typically, mental constructions appropriate to physical or natural phenomena are recycled as tools to represent the processes of social knowledge construction. Bruner's hypothesis is that, unlike the logico-mathematical basis of thought that someone such as Piaget assumed in his studies of cognitive development in children, "we organize our experience and our memory of human happenings mainly in the form of narrative—stories, excuses, myths, reasons for doing and not doing, etc." (Bruner, 1991, p. 4).

This is a considerably broader conception of narrative than just storytelling.

The Narrative View in Greater Detail

What is a "narrative mode of thought"? What are "forms of narrative discourse"? (Bruner sees the two terms *thought* and *discourse* as practically indistinguishable, although one is mental, the other language-based; 1991, p. 5). We see these properties as essential:

1. Narrativity is not a property that can be reduced to single, isolated sentences or propositions, nor to "semantic networks" of interconnected lexical items, such as are often studied in cognitive science; narrativity emerges only in longer strings of language than the sentence. It is this property that leads to the idea of an hermeneutic circle. A story is told sentence by sentence but its meaning is not conveyed by any particular sentence. It was the pioneering narratologist Vladimir Propp (1958) who conceptualized the contribution of the sentence to the narrative as its "function," that is, a component of a larger structure. As a consequence, the meaning of a sentence is determined not by what it itself says in so many words, but in what it adds to the meaning of the whole. On the other hand, the meaning of the whole is no more than a composition of its parts—its sentences. This is the *hermeneutic circle*: The meaning of the parts depends on the meaning of the whole, but the meaning of the whole depends on the meaning of the parts. You have to try to read both levels simultaneously, if either is to be made transparently meaningful. It is one of the reasons stories can be so absorbing: They excite the imagination because they take interpretive work.

2. Narrativity deals with the unfolding of action over time, a property called *diachronicity*; a narrative is an account of events that, as he says, is "irreducibly durative" (Bruner, 1991, p. 6). It is episodic.

3. A subtler point: Narrative, in all its manifestations, is a relating of specific events involving specific actors in specific circumstances, and yet the essence of narrativity is that the sequence of events is an instance of generic form. In Bruner's words, the ostensively referred to particular happenings are a "vehicle," not a "destination" because the particulars of a story are "tokens of broader types": "Particularity achieves its emblematic status by its embeddedness in a story that is in some sense generic" (Bruner, 1991, pp. 6–7). It is this specific/generic distinction that Greimas (1987) sees as a contrast of figurative and structural levels. Not just any old sequence of related events constitutes a story, narratively speaking (that would be specific but not generic). A story becomes a story because it is recognizable, generically, as a story, so much so that the listener can fill in the blanks if the speaker leaves something out. On the other hand, stories, as the generative basis of narration, are made accessible only by translating the generic into the specific, by cloaking the spare structural in the dressy figurative. Narrative, thus, has a grammatical basis (and it is the relationship of story to sentence grammar that Greimas, as we shall see, was at pains to elucidate).

4. Attributions of agency are an intrinsic part of narrative: people acting with an intention, making choices. Later (in chaps. 3 & 4) we explore the grammatical property of modality as the logical link joining speaker to spoken; modality is part of the logical form of a sentence—its inherent

circumstantiality—that is conveyed in the sentence through devices such as mood. The root of modality is not in the sentence, however (although it is mirrored there, syntactically), but in the narrative structure that enfolds the sentence. The branch of sentence semantics that treats of modality is in fact derivative on narrative semantics: It is here that agency is explained (more on this later). As Bruner points out, narrative accounts do not provide causal explanations (because an intention can be realized in action in a multitude of alternative and, thus, unpredictable ways), but a basis for interpreting why a character acted as he or she did. "Interpretation is concerned with 'reasons' for things happening, rather than strictly their 'causes' " (Bruner, 1991, p. 7).

5. Combining the assumptions of 2 and 3, it follows that narrative actors lead a double life. They are at one and the same time specific psychological actors, in a specific sociological situation, and yet also generic actors in an abstract narrative situation where intentionality is no longer to be thought of as that of a psychological subject but rather an obligatory function in a genre of narrative origin—a necessary motive force in a predetermined pattern of events (we come back to this in chap. 4). It is for this reason that Greimas reserves the word *actor* for the figurative or purely circumstantial level of narrative and invents a neologism, *actant*, for the generic or structural. The same bivalence applies to the objects of a story, that on which attention is focused. They, too, are both specific to a time and place, and generic—conceptual, not circumstantial. At the generic or structural level, subject and object are mutually defining, in the sense that their meaning is not reducible to circumstances, either psychic or physical, because they are components in a logical structure of relationships that not only has no expression other than in the form of narrative but also is what gives meaning to happenings in a purely circumstantial world (a crucial part of what we later describe in this chapter as translation).

6. Narrative starts with the breach of some social order. As Bruner puts it:

> [N]ot every sequence of events recounted constitutes a narrative . . . Some happenings do not warrant telling about and accounts of them are said to be "pointless" rather than storylike . . . For [it] to be worth telling, a tale must be about how an implicit canonical script has been breached, violated, or deviated from in a manner to do violence to what Hayden White terms the "legitimacy" of the canonical script. This usually involves what Labov calls a "precipitating event." (Bruner, 1991, p. 11)

Bruner uses a favorite of artificial intelligence, Schank and Abelson's (1977) "script" that describes how to order a meal in a restaurant, as an instance of a canonical script but the concept has much wider relevance. Getting the restaurant script wrong might work as a precipitating event in a *Seinfeld* episode, but it is hardly the stuff of high drama; there the precipitating event is more likely to resemble what Greimas (1993, p. 22) calls the "destruction of the social order"—a breach of a different dimension—the total destruction of a town by a volcano, for example, or a plot to kidnap (or humiliate) the President. Precipitating events can thus be very small or very dramatic.

So important is the concept of *breach* that Greimas thinks of it as the motivation for what he calls the "economic organization" of narrative, with two parts, the breach and the reparation of the breach (or the return to the order specified by the canonical script). The implication of Bruner's principle, of course, is that a society—any society—rests on the basis of a canonical script or scripts. The principal activity of organization is repair: correcting deviations from the script.

7. Stories are for telling. Narrative is social. Because of the hermeneutic circle and specific/generic codependency, the meaning of a narration is often negotiable (as researchers in CA attest). In narration, skill is involved both in composing (selecting the specifics in such a way as to exemplify the generic and thus tell a good story or give a plausible explanation) and in interpreting (navigating the hermeneutic circle): "For narratives do not exist, as it were, in some real world, waiting there patiently and eternally to be veridically mirrored in a text. The act of constructing a narrative, moreover, is considerably more than 'selecting' events either from real life, from memory, or from fantasy and then placing them in an appropriate order. The events themselves need to be *constituted* in the light of the overall narrative" (Bruner, 1991, p. 8). Narration thus has an argumentative dimension. The listener has to, in turn, not only listen but also interpret— reconstitute—the events for him- or herself, and, if necessary, contribute to the telling. As Bruner puts it, "It is not textual or referential ambiguity that compels interpretive activity in narrative comprehension, but narrative itself" (1991, p. 9). The success of a narrative depends not on its verifiable adherence to the truth, but on its verisimilitude—its plausibility as an interpretation of events, its acceptability. The social world is never "verifiable" (Gilbert & Mulkay, 1984). The facts of the social world are attributions of reasons, not determinations of causes. Narrative and rhetoric thus have much in common.

8. Finally, there is the principle of narrative accrual. Bruner's concept of accrual is grounded in a cognitive theory of the understanding of understanding, of the making sense of sensemaking. Mental capacity is not, he says, a set of cognitive skills or programs to be applied independent of context. Contemporary learning psychology sees cognitive abilities as specific to a domain: "a set of principles and procedures, rather like a prosthetic device, that permits intelligence to be used in certain ways, but not

in others" (Bruner, 1991, p. 2). The transfer of cognitive skill from one domain to another remains problematical. Intelligence is not universal—a mythical context-free IQ. Acquired habits of thought can be thought of as "a culture's treasury of tool kits" (p. 2), or as we have been calling it, a "surface of emergence." Applied to narrative, the same principle holds: People's knowledge of the social and organizational world is procedural, manifested in their explanations and stories, a "culture" or a "tradition" that is "never point-of-viewless" (p. 3), never "solo," and never understandable without taking into account "the network of friends, colleagues, or mentors on whom one leans for help and advice" (p. 2). Story comprehension, it follows, supposes frame knowledge, or what Werth (1993) called a common ground of established understandings shared by conversants.

"Once shared culturally—distributed in the sense discussed earlier— narrative accruals achieve, like Émile Durkheim's collective representations, 'exteriority' and the power of constraint" (Bruner, 1991, p. 19). Through its translation into a narrative text, the organization is both naturalized and socialized: it is made an object like any other and legitimated socially, as Deetz proposes.

Bruner's version of narrativity is grounded in cognitive theory, whereas that of the theorist we now turn to consider, Algirdas Greimas, is grounded in logic and linguistics.

Greimas and the Reinterpretation of Propp

Vladimir Propp was a folklorist in the Russian formalist tradition who published his findings in the 1920s, although they were not translated into English or French until much later. Propp's research consisted of collecting a corpus of some 150 Russian fairy tales in which magic plays a major role. His analysis led him to conclude that, in spite of the wonderfully rich figurative variety of the tales, they all, without exception, could be explained as variants of one and only one story. This generic construction had, according to his theoretical reconstruction of it, 31 components that he called "functions" (actions, really), which, without exception, were sequenced in the same order, although not all were always present in any given variation. (Much the same conclusion, but more contemporaneous, is found in Wright's 1975 analysis of Hollywood Westerns and Taylor's 1976 analysis of television detective series.)

In his initial analysis of narrative, Greimas, working out of a continental tradition of linguistics, set out to show that Propp's system of 31 functions could be simplified to a much more elementary logical structure. Greimas' subsequent elaboration of his theory is daunting in its formalistic complexity and opacity of expression, even for one who is French-speaking by birth, and many of the popularizations of his thinking are hardly less obscure. The presentation that follows is intended to be more accessible. It is inspired directly by Greimas, but his ideas are freely interpreted to adapt to the context of a book on organizational communication. (For a more conventional presentation of his thought see Greimas, 1987.)

The Building Block of Narrativity: Exchange

Whether in the context of narrative or of ordinary life people confront the issue of coorienting to others. One of Greimas' important contributions is to have identified two classes of coorientation, one structured around the exchange of an object of value, the other around attributions of agency. What Greimas thinks of as the *narrative economy* of a story is an articulation of these two levels of coorientation. The same may safely be asserted for human organization, as we argue in chapter 3.

Consider first the structure of an exchange relationship as illustrated by such mundane activities as a trip to the supermarket or getting the car fixed. There is an object, X, on which attention is focused. It could be groceries, a problem with the car, or any other of the myriad concerns that occupy our attention every day, whether we are home or at work. The circumstances for an exchange relationship are created when the attention of more than one actor, at minimum an A and a B, is focused on the same object, X. The concept of exchange implies that the object in question undergoes a change of state (it gets exchanged). As it does, the coorienting actors are affected by either giving up or acquiring a possession or a quality. At the supermarket that which is acquired by the buyer (and no longer possessed by the seller once the transaction is complete) is a cartful of groceries; at the garage what is acquired by the owner (and what is delivered into his or her hands by the garage) is a car that works as opposed to one that did not when it was taken in for repairs. Groceries count as possessions; cars that run (as opposed to those that do not) as a quality. The effect of the exchange is thus to create a triadic relationship, A-B-X, in which A and B are seen to occupy complementary roles that are explained by their respective orientations to a joint object, X. The purchase of groceries instantiates a checkout counter clerk/customer relationship, the repaired car a garage mechanic/car-owner relationship.

There is, Greimas observes, a simple way to capture the notion of an A-X or a B-X orientation. The idea of possession of an object by a subject is conveyed by the verb "to have"; the verb "to be" describes a relation of the actor to a quality. The buyer *has* groceries; the owner's car *is* working. What the exchange accomplishes, for both the A and the B, is to change a *not have* into a *have* (or vice versa) or a *not be* into a *be* (or vice versa). It is the value of the object that motivates the exchange; but the exchange is what gives rise to the value of the object. There is a chicken-and-egg logic at work here: Customers are customers because of the objects they buy but the objects become saleable products because there are customers to buy them.

A central property of narrativity, as we saw earlier, is that it is generic. The simple stringing together of a sequence of events to produce a chronicle is not enough to qualify it as a narrative. The chronicle of events must exhibit evidence of generic form. To be generic, however, means to be stripped of everything that is specific to a particular situation. In the generics of narrativity there are no Marys and Toms, no supermarket customers and counter clerks, no car owners and mechanics. In the austere world of narrative form objects are defined only by the subjects with which they associate, and vice versa. As and Bs are subjects through their being related to an object X and, reciprocally, an object X becomes an object by its association with a subject A and/or a subject B. The A-B-X unit is like an algebraic expression, entirely relational. But this logical primitivism nevertheless captures a feature of ordinary language-in-use. One becomes a customer because there are things such as supermarkets and yet supermarkets exist because of their customers. One is a driver because one has a car, but a car is something to be driven. The logic is circular, self-enclosing. To mark the distinction, Greimas introduces a neologism, *actant*, to refer to actors whose only coordinates are relational, reserving the usual term, *actor*, for real-life, breathing people.

It is this very property of abstraction from the concrete circumstances of any particular context that gives narrative form its applicability to an infinite variety of situations. Storytelling is enabled by the wedding of the generic and the specific. The story is full of detail; its narrative form is generic.

We are here close to the heart of the structuralist project, to which Greimas was a notable contributor. It is not a question of denying that there are real-life people along with the things they relate to and the activities they engage in. It is that when they reconstruct these activities in their talk they do so through the technology of language. Language offers a wealth of ways to refer to people, their objects and their activities and in this respect it may seem like a neutral instrument of simple description. But language is not quite so innocent in another way, in that it is constructed around a repertoire of generic forms. Greimas' goal is to explore the properties of these forms, and to understand how they mold our construction of experience, even as we report it.

There are, for example, some interesting things we can say about an A-B-X exchange without entering into the specifics of any particular situation. First, exchange can be either one-way or two-way. If it is one-way then there is a gain involved for one party but it is associated with an uncompensated-for loss for the other. If you walk out of the store without paying for the items you have put in your bag this is called shoplifting and it is against the law. Similarly if you fail to pay the garage for the car they repaired you are delinquent and may be hauled into small claims court. If you give your fortune to charity you are a benefactor. If you turn the other cheek when others transgress against you then you may be on your way to sainthood.

Stories exhibit many instances of one-way exchanges. What narratologists such as Labov and Bruner call a *precipitating event* and Greimas calls a *breach* occurs when one actor, identifiable as a villain, takes something without giving anything in return. At the opposite end of the scale, when the hero becomes qualified in some special way that provides the means to rectify the transgression the villain has committed it is frequently in the form of a gift offered by someone, such as a weapon or a vital piece of information. And, of course, everyday life offers many instances of people who feel they have had less than a fair shake or of extraordinary acts of kindness, sacrifice, and renunciation. Each of these words, *kindness*, *sacrifice*, and *renunciation*, is a way we have to refer to generic properties of one-way exchanges. It is because one-way exchanges are characterized by gains and losses, where A's advantage is correlated with B's disadvantage, or vice versa, that Greimas sees all human interaction as potentially polemical, that is, vulnerable to displays of opposition.

Two-way exchanges have the character of a transaction. Much of economics is taken up with the study of two-way exchanges and their dynamics. Stories, too, commonly have a two-way exchange relationship as their framework. The sacrifices made by the hero in carrying out a mission for someone else must be rewarded at the end for the story to feel right. Ordinary organizational dynamics are marked everywhere by two-way exchanges: payment for work done, offering a service to an internal client or customer or, more informally, one good turn deserves another. In fact it could be said that two-way exchanges are the norm of all human interaction. That is evident enough for positive transactions, but even transgression followed by retribution can be thought of as a two-way exchange whose character is polemical. On the other hand, all two-way exchanges are susceptible to degenerating into a one-way exchange, whenever one of the partners is perceived as having taken advantage of the other. Exchange transactions, one-way and two-way, are the stuff of narrative (as they are, of course, of organization as well).

Notice how much we have been able to say about the transactional dynamics of both narrative and everyday life based solely on analysis of the abstraction A-B-X. And yet it is quite easy to illustrate these abstract properties of exchange by examples drawn from ordinary circumstances. This again suggests the power of language in molding the construction we make of our experience. It is a theme to which we return again and again in this book.

Greimas' Model of Exchange

We have one last observation to make on the subject of the exchange relationship. Figure 2.2 illustrates the components in Greimas' model of exchange. One actor, let us say A, is identified as a source, S. For there to be an exchange the object O must have initially been possessed by one person (S) and not by the other (R). A second actor, let us say B, becomes the recipient of the exchanged object (R). The exchange results in a transfer T which expresses the idea of change of possession (from the perspective of S and R) or of location (from the perspective of O). In addition Greimas observes that transfers take place only when they are caused (C) by some agent (Ag), who might be either of the two actors concerned in the exchange. It matters which, of course, since in a one-way transaction an object transferred voluntarily by S to R is a gift; an object taken by R without the consent of S is a theft. Consenting two-way transactions suppose two exchanges, where one object Y is returned in compensation for the other X. Here the agent of each contributing exchange is the source. In polemical two-way transactions the agent is the receiver (i.e., the taker).

We will have a good deal more to say about the structure represented in Fig. 2.2 in this and succeeding chapters. Among other findings we will discover that it is, as Greimas claimed, a component of all narrative, but also of the grammar of ordinary sentences. The significance of this latter correspondence is one to which we return later in this chapter and again in chapters 3 and 4.

Coorientation Involving Agency

Greimas identifies a second kind of coorientational exchange. In this kind of exchange intentionality becomes central.

The concept of intentionality was a preoccupation of the literature on phenomenology that we alluded to in chapter 1. Without engaging in a prolonged discussion the idea is this. People are always involved in a world

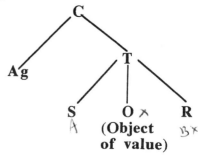

FIG. 2.2. The structure of a one-way exchange.

and the intelligence they develop in dealing with that world will inevitably by marked by an attitude. Knowledge is never completely neutral; it is always situated, and reflects the boundaries of experience of the people who develop it. What we can know is always tied to our experience, and our experience is that of people who do things, have commitments, and take positions. In the context of our presentation of Greimas, coorientation can be taken to mean two actors who are attitudinally related to some object in the same way. According to Newcomb (1953), from whom the notion of an A-B-X system is taken, when attitudes are lined up in this way a stable social unit exists. Greimas would agree.

What Greimas adds to Newcomb's more static formalization is the idea of a transaction whose outcome is the formation of an A-B-X unit. Where Newcomb thinks of B as *having* the same attitude as A, Greimas focuses on how B *comes to have* the same attitude. To accomplish this goal, Greimas adapts the general model of an exchange (Fig. 2.2) by reinterpreting one of its components. The object is now thought of, no longer as an object of value, but as an attitude. To transfer an attitude means that the intentionality of one actor, A, is communicated to become that of a second actor, B (Greimas, in fact, calls this transfer the "axis of communication"). In Greimas' language, the A becomes a *sender*, the B a *receiver*, and the transferred object (that we call "attitude") a *modal object* (we return shortly to consider why Greimas chose modality to be his key term). When the transfer is complete a relationship of agency is established in that B is now a vehicle for the subsequent transmission of A's intentionality. B has become A's agent, both acting and acting *for*.

We have many words in English to convey this idea of attitudinal dependence of one person on another. Depending on the context we use words such as envoy, instrument, executor, representative, employee, deputy, associate, delegate, missionary, spokesperson, emissary, proxy, ambassador, dupe, puppet, and so on. Agency is a central property of narrative (as indeed it is of organization). As in all transactions agency implies complementary roles. Unlike exchanges that center only on the symmetric exchange of an object of value, the agency relationship also implies hierarchy, since one person's intentionality takes precedence over the other's. And, as in the case of exchanges involving objects of value, coorientational exchanges that instantiate agency also imply a reciprocal exchange: pay for work, for example (in organizational contexts) or the hand of the princess in marriage (in fairy tales whose hero is a handsome prince).

Modality

The basic idea of modality is actually very simple (we consider its more complex organizational implications in chapters 3 and 4). A modal expression is one that communicates attitude. For example, suppose a student you know says in frustration, "I wish they'd send me my marks!" The *I wish* part is a modal expression. It tells you about what the student feels rather than what he or she has those feelings about. The object of the verbal expression *I wish* is, grammatically speaking, *they'd send me my marks. They would send me my marks* is already a sentence that describes an exchange. In fact, modal expressions typically take as their object a sentence that describes some state of affairs, or (as in this example) some action. The fitting of one kind of sentence (a descriptive) into another (a modal) is termed *embedding*. It is a standard feature of all language, spoken or written.

Note that since, as Greimas observes, coorientational exchanges resulting in agency are modal constructions whose structure of exchange is identical with nonmodal constructions (Fig. 2.2 is applicable to both) the difference between the two kinds of exchange is not formal, but an effect of embedding. In the study of language, whether natural or artificial, this kind of embedding of one component in another which has an identical structure is called *recursivity*. Because of recursivity language may also be reflexive (in that it can refer to itself). The classic instance is the liar paradox. If someone says "I am lying" they are in effect asserting "It is true that what I am telling you is a lie." The contradiction becomes self-evident once we understand "what I am telling you is a lie" as a descriptive expression embedded within a modal expression "it is true that." The embedded descriptive sentence nullifies its modal qualifier and in doing so undermines its own basis of credibility.

There are two kinds of modality, depending on what is being qualified (i.e., what the focus of the embedded descriptive sentence is). When the modal expression takes as its object a report on a certain state of affairs then the qualifying modal is called *epistemic*. Epistemic verbs and expressions are "I believe that," "I think that," "probably" (as an adverbial qualifier), "it is true that," and so on—any kind of formulation, in fact, that conveys knowledge of the speaker's probable beliefs. When the object of a modal expression reports on an event or an action, however, the modality is *deontic*. Deontic expressions are such expressions as "I wish you would (do something)," "Please" (in the context of a request), "I promise," and so on. (Chapter 3 offers a more detailed consideration of epistemic and deontic expressions and their organizational significance.)

It happens that in the French language the principal modal verbs form a neat paradigmatic set: *savoir, devoir, vouloir,* and *pouvoir* (roughly translated, to preserve the paradigmatic feel, as *know, should, would,* and *could*). Now of course there are in ordinary language many, many more ways to convey modality than these four verbs (a topic of chapter 4). Nevertheless, Greimas is making a valid point. If the issue is how to form a coorientational system in which one actor, B, becomes the agent of another actor, A, then the question is how to transfer attitude from one actor to another. Greimas' four modal verbs are a classification device intended to get at the dynamics of attitude transmission. One way to get people to act is to persuade them of the reality of a certain situation (this is *savoir*). Another is to remind them of their duty (this is *devoir*). Another is to appeal to their desires (this is *vouloir*). And finally sometimes all it needs to get them to act is to give them the means to do so (this is *pouvoir*). So the point Greimas is making is that much of narrative is about motivating people to act and mobilizing the resources to make their action possible (we return to consider the question of mobilization of resources in our discussion of Giddens in chapter 5). But of course organization is also about motivating and mobilizing.

Because modality is a qualifier it is not always explicitly marked in speech, since it may be perfectly self-evident to the hearer from context what the modal intention is. Consider the sentence *John just bought a new Buick!* The mood of the verb in this sentence is indicative (a typical expression of modality in sentence grammar), which is the unmarked or default form of the modal: a factual. There is no direct surface evidence that John's buying of the car (a description of a transaction) is embedded in a modal construction other than the indicative. His doing so is stated as a simple fact. But suppose we were to ask, "Did John need a car?" Chances are your reply would be something like, "Well, yeah, sure; probably. People don't put up that kind of money unless they need something." So, without saying it in so many words, we took John's need for granted (Greimas' *devoir*). Suppose we now asked, "Did John want a car?" Again, you would tend to answer, "Well, of course, why would he buy it if he didn't want to?" So we have taken will or desire as a given (Greimas' *vouloir*). Then, we ask, "Does John know how to buy a car?" and you might now begin to be, reasonably enough, a bit irritated: "For Heaven's sake, if he didn't know how, he couldn't have done it, could he?" (Greimas' *savoir*). But we persist: "Did he have the means, could he, buy a car?" And the answer seems even more obvious to you, because if he could not have he would not have (Greimas' *pouvoir*). So buried beneath the surface of a simple declarative utterance is a whole set of modal preconditions, corresponding to those postulated by Greimas, that we have, without giving it conscious thought, fed into the interpretation of what is, on the surface, a quite uncomplicated sentence: *John just bought a new Buick!*

What an explicit narrative does is uncover those tacit modal understandings that go into comprehending the meaning of an utterance, so that the bald performance of buying a car (or doing anything else) is contextualized by the reasons for it. There is a multitude—an infinity, in fact—of ways we could turn *John just bought a new Buick!* from an isolated sentence into one component of a narrative sequence. Suppose we began by *John didn't even know he needed a new car until one day. . . .* : What story is this part of? (the reader is invited to fill in the blank from his or her imagination), or *John didn't really want a car but last Friday* . . . (again up it is to you to imagine the sequel), or *John didn't have a clue about dealing with car salespeople but fortunately* . . . (same as before, think of a story), or *John would never have been able to afford a new Buick if it had not been for* . . . (you have the idea).

What we have done in each case is to have problematized the modal conditions of an act or performance by calling attention to—highlighting—conditions of action: necessity, willingness, know-how, and means. Every sentence carries traces of its modalizing context, but they often remain implicit and outside of awareness because we have called upon our general knowledge of default conditions that apply to standard situations (as in our example) or because of a particular set of knowledges specific to a lived situation (where, if the hearer already knew who John was and a lot more about him, saying "John just bought a new Buick!" might carry a considerable freight of additional meaning and lead to a reaction such as "Oh really! Oh my! So he actually did it! Who talked him into it in the end?").

It is those residual traces of narrativity expressed through the mood of the single utterance that signal the link from sentence to the story (generically speaking) in which it is embedded. But notice a truly significant shift of perspective that has quietly taken place. As long as we stayed within the grammar of sentences, the subjective intentionality that is expressed in the grammatical category of modality was conceptualized as a property of the individual. In a grammar of texts—a narratively based grammar—intentionality is conceptualized differently, as an object of communication—a modal object—involving more than one subject. This is what we believe Bruner was getting at when he criticized the dominant focus in Western society on the natural or physical world. Its chronic neglect of narrative reasoning arises from a failure to address the communicative basis of society (and of individual identity). It is the shift of perspective to center our attention on communication that makes Greimas' exposition of narrativity the most fully elaborated and subtle of any we have encountered.

Communication is never just information, nor is it ever something as neutral as a message.[2]

---

[2]In introducing his book on *Discourse as structure and process* the editor Teun Van Dijk (1997) writes this: "One characterization of discourse that embodies some of these *functional* aspects is that of a *communicative event.* That is, people use language in order to communicate ideas or beliefs (or to express emotion)" (p. 2, emphasis in the original). This is an instance of a conventional sentence-based, or message-based, approach to the analysis of discourse. It assumes that the communication event is initiated by an intrapsychic state that then is expressed discursively. The effect of this is to decontextualize the intentional states of the communicator by bracketing out their source in previous interactive exchanges and their context of an ongoing activity. What we are proposing respects Bruner's principle of the hermeneutic circle, in that we assume that the intentional states of the individual and their social (communicative) context are *co*-created. We are thus in fundamental disagreement with Van Dijk on his characterization of a communicative event.

Articulating the Levels

We have now isolated two kinds of exchange, one centered on an object
of value and the other on an attitude, and we found that, although their
formal structure as exchange is identical, they differ from each other in
that one is embedded within the other, as its object.[3] At the level of the
embedded exchange we are in the domain of action: things going on such
as buying groceries and getting the car fixed. At the level of the embedding
exchange we are in the domain of intentionality, understanding, and attitude. On the basis of the action/intentionality distinction Greimas identifies two dimensions, that he calls cognitive and pragmatic. The *cognitive*
dimension is that of intentionality. Here action figures only as a virtual
possibility. The issue is double: (a) establishing the facts of a situation,
and (b) preparing the ground to do something about it. The themes at
this level are motivation (of an eventual actor), and establishing the actor's
qualification or competence to act. The *pragmatic* dimension is where the
action occurs: the domain of performance. It is the instantiation of an
agent, through the transfer of intentionality, that effects the articulation
of levels by means of which the narrative action is motivated. The "sender"
to which Greimas refers in his characterization of the transfer of a modal
object exists at the level of cognition. The sender knows and yet is unable
to act in the absence of an instrumentality. The "receiver" can act but his
or her acting must be reoriented for it to carry out the intention of a
principal. The receiver at the level of cognition is transformed into an
agent at the level of pragmatics. It is this interlinking or articulation of
levels of cognition and pragmatics that confers its economic character on
narrative: economic because the engagement of the agent is explained as
a contract (which may be implicit) whose fulfillment supplies the energy
to drive the story forward toward its dénouement.

A story is characterized by what Greimas calls a "narrative program." By
this he means (as Propp before him had concluded) that there is a logical
sequencing of events from a beginning to an end. Stories begin, typically,
by an event which in some way is recognizable as a breach of the normal
social order of things. It could be something as trivial as a missing file, or
as momentous as ethnic cleansing in the Balkans. It is this event that
establishes a theme of communication, expressed cognitively as knowledge
and motivation. The passage from cognitive to pragmatic supposes the
recruitment, motivation and qualification of an agent who possesses the
competence to act. In a film such as *Star Wars*, for example, the sequences
that unfold leading to the eventual mobilization of Luke Skywalker exem-

---

[3]It is because of attitude that the object has value: an effect of embedding a descriptive
statement within a modal. Attitude is always toward something.

plify the critical articulation of the cognitive (knowing what must be done) and the pragmatic (doing it). The core of the story is the doing—the performance. Finally the story is brought to an end when the outcome of the performance is recognized, both in the sense that there is a dénouement and that the hero's performance is given its appropriate reward (the contract has been fulfilled).

The implications of Greimas' investigation of the articulatory dynamics of linking the cognitive and the pragmatic dimensions of narrativity go far beyond the field of literary analysis of formal or informal storytelling (the application of the narrative model most actively explored in the literature). The utility of perceiving action as a program in which the intentionality of one participant (cognitive dimension) figures as the motivator of another (pragmatic domain) has caught the attention of at least one school of computer system design, committed to what it calls a language/action perspective (or L/AP). It has, for example, developed what is called a DEMO (Dynamic Essential Modeling of Organization) model (Dietz, 1990, 1994; van der Rijst, 1997). In the DEMO model communication is conceived of as a two-actor transaction, such as booking a room in a hotel. This is "the basic pattern of organizational behavior," according to one of its developers (van der Rijst, 1997, p. 4). A transaction (e.g., booking a hotel room) is conceptualized as evolving in three phases: negotiating the conditions of the transaction, executing the agreed-upon service, and evaluating, and if necessary negotiating, the result. The negotiation that precedes the performance is called an "actagenic conversation" (since it generates an order to do something), and the postperformance evaluation of the "essential action" is known as a "factagenic conversation" (Fig. 2.3). The performance is sandwiched between the two conversations.

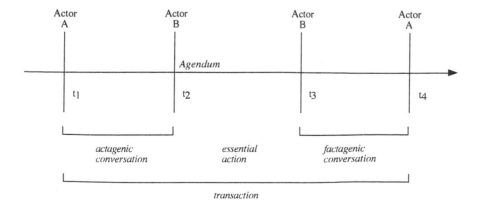

FIG. 2.3. The DEMO transactional pattern (after Steuten, 1998; see also Dietz, 1994).

	Necessity	Capability	Achievement	Evaluation
Sender role (knowing)	Manipulation	Qualification		Sanction
Receiver role (doing)		Competence	Performance	

FIG. 2.4. The stages of a narrative program.

These system developers have evolved their model independently of the theory of narrativity. The parallel is nevertheless striking. Greimas' narrative program has four phases: manipulation, qualification/competence, performance, and sanction (Fig. 2.4). By manipulation he means all those strategies by which a sender is able to motivate a receiver (the eventual agent of the performance) to act: through persuasion, or the inculcation of a sense of duty, or premise control, or intimidation, for example, or simply making available the means to act. As with the L/AP analysts Greimas perceives such manipulation as a form of entering into a contractual arrangement, in which the performer of the act—the agent—will henceforth act as the instrumentality of the principal. This is essentially the actagenic conversation of the DEMO model. Greimas thinks of this as a modalization of action (*modalisation du faire*). In the DEMO model the agent's qualifications, or competence, is taken for granted. In narrative theory it has a central place because much of stories concerns the acquiring of the means to act by the central protagonist, or eventual hero. Greimas' performance is DEMO's essential action. And finally Greimas' sanction becomes DEMO's factagenic conversation, which Greimas conceives of as a modalization of state (*modalisation de l'être*).

Thus the organizational system modelers are thinking narratively, even when they are not consciously doing so.

Concluding Observations on Greimas

There is of course a great deal more that could be written about a theory as dense and elaborate as that of Greimas and his school. Much of it, however, is not relevant to our concerns in this book since it relates to the discourse analysis of texts, not our preoccupation. There are, however, two further observations that are pertinent to our topic.

First, Greimas' theory strongly emphasizes the interconnectedness of knowledge and action, and the inevitable situatedness of knowledge. It makes no sense, if we follow his reasoning, to think about communication outside of the context of activity in which it is embedded, and which it influences. This reminder of the grounding of communication in the material world of everyday performances seems to us a salutary corrective to the occasional tendency to think of communication as "just messaging."

In this respect, although their backgrounds and styles of discourse are so totally different there is nevertheless a similarity of perspective in Greimas' thought and that of an author whose work we consider in greater depth in chapters 5 and 8, Karl Weick. Weick, like Greimas, is fascinated by the interdependency of cognition and practice. Both authors perceive the world to be enacted, and not simply discovered. Greimas, however, adds a further nuance that forms the topic of chapter 8. Because he thinks of the cognitive and the pragmatic as complementary dimensions that are linked contractually he perceives all action to have a moral basis. If agents are motivated to serve the interest of a principal it is because such an interest is legitimate, and justifies obedience to its dictates. But this poses a great problem, which is the basis of legitimacy in organizational affairs. We introduce the topic in chapter 5 in our discussion of Giddens, and return to it in chapter 8 to offer what we believe is a plausible answer.

Although it is not a major theme of this book, a second feature of Greimas' work that we see as important, and relevant, is his idea that for every subject there must be an antisubject, for every protagonist an antagonist. Stories, of course, are normally about contests, about failing and succeeding in the face of opposition, about guilty secrets and their unveiling. Again what is true for narrative has resonance for other realms of experience. Companies have competitors, countries have enemies, political parties have rivals for power, and so on. But Greimas' analysis goes far deeper than this trivial observation and has deeply disturbing implications. His theory of narrative sits on top of a second theory, which is a theory of semantics. At the core of his idea of semantics is what he calls a semiotic square (Fig. 2.5).

For every positive term, let us say for the sake of illustration, "honest," there are two negative terms. One is called a *contrary*. For example, the contrary of honest is *dishonest*. A contrary is negative in the sense that it is the opposite of the positive. The other negative is a *contradictory*. The status of contradictory is more ambiguous, in that it is not the opposite of the positive quality, but its absence. The contradictory of honest, for

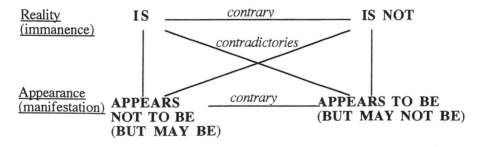

FIG. 2.5. The semiotic square.

example, might be *unreliable*: not necessarily dishonest, but not reliably honest either. Stories are contests pitting a positive against a negative, but the dynamics of the story are worked out on a battlefield peopled by the contradictories: characters who waver, or are seduced, or repent, or turn out not to be what we thought they were. The troublesome implication of this analysis to which we have alluded is that in narrative theory no positive identity can be assumed by any human actor other than by the denial of some other person's identity. To exist as a positive there must be an immanent negative. This is an insight (if it is indeed an insight) that is characteristic of the thought of several of Greimas' contemporaries, including two we mentioned in chapter 1, Foucault and Derrida. It leads to a less than optimistic view of social life. In a world still riven by interethnic prejudice and conflict, and marked by varieties of chauvinism, we, as do members of the critical school we described in chapter 1, find this idea troubling. It is not, however, a major theme of this book.

Let us now consider what is a major theme of the book: how narrative theory can be employed to enrich a theory of organizational communication. Narrative theory has, as we have observed, been mainly used in textual analysis. What we now consider is how it can be employed in a very different context, to resolve issues in our own field.

COMMUNICATION AS COORIENTATION

What is the dynamic of communication? How do its parameters of conversation and text (Fig. 2.1) become instantiated in the activity of communication to produce organization?

We see communication as an ongoing process of making sense of the circumstances in which people collectively find ourselves and of the events that affect them. The sensemaking, to the extent that it involves communication, takes place in interactive talk and draws on the resources of language in order to formulate and exchange through talk (or in other media such as graphics) symbolically encoded representations of these circumstances. As this occurs, a situation is talked into existence and the basis is laid for action to deal with it. Communication thus concerns both descriptions of existing states (the epistemic function of speech) and what to do about them (the deontic function of speech, with the focus on virtual or as yet unrealized states). Communication is how situations are resolved interactively at the level of the cognitive.

In the perspective of conversation, people interact to deal with their world. Sensemaking, however, involves translating experience into language through the production of texts, spoken or written. Here it becomes important to take account of the means that language affords to structure the expression of experience. This is the domain of semantics.

Linguists such as Goldberg (1995) distinguish between two domains of semantics: frame knowledge and construction knowledge (more on Goldberg's analysis in chapter 3). *Frame knowledge,* Goldberg specifies (p. 25), is that which relates to some background frame or scene. *Construction knowledge* corresponds to sentence types that "encode as their central senses types that are basic to human experience" (p. 39, the meaning of the distinction will become clearer in chapter 3). What we showed in Fig. 2.1 as "circumstances" become frame knowledge (that we referred to there as repertoire) by their being translated into language. (Basically this amounts to giving a name to things, people, and events.) What we showed in Fig. 2.1 as "conversation form" (the mechanics of keeping an interaction going) becomes construction knowledge through the medium of talking out to produce text. (The back-and-forth conversational patterns of interaction take on the meaning of an episode in which coorientational relationships are made manifest.) Figure 2.6 shows this correspondence of circumstance and frame knowledge, and conversation and construction knowledge.

Communication accomplishes the mapping of (a) circumstances to frame knowledge in order to produce an epistemic interpretation of the state of affairs that characterizes the situation the participants are in, and of (b) conversation exchanges to construction knowledge in order to produce a deontic interpretation of what is to be done and who is to do it. Getting people to think and do things has been called the function of speech as act (Austin, 1962; Searle, 1969).[4] In the process, through the exchange of modal objects (to use the Greimasian terminology), the interagent relationships typical of all human organization are both generated and regenerated. Figure 2.7 visualizes how this mapping occurs.

Of course the mapping of the conversation to construction knowledge, and in the process generating a resolution of the situation the conversants are in as well as a reconstitution of themselves as a group engaged in talk, itself constitutes a change of circumstance. Similarly the unfolding of the conversation depends on an understanding of the nature of the occasion of talk, which in turn depends on frame knowledge (interviews have a different conversation form than meetings, for example, or debates, or conferences). The conversation thus cycles back on itself (Fig. 2.8).

The cyclic mapping of one dimension to the other is a continuous phenomenon. Its effect is to produce resolution of the situations people find themselves in, mediated by communication. And since circumstances are affected by and form a linkpoint to other ongoing conversations, involving other people (and often the same people in a different role), the

---

[4]Speech act theory, like narrative theory, is concerned with the expression and communication of actor intentionality. For a comprehensive discussion of the correspondences between speech act and Greimas' narrative theory see Cooren (in press).

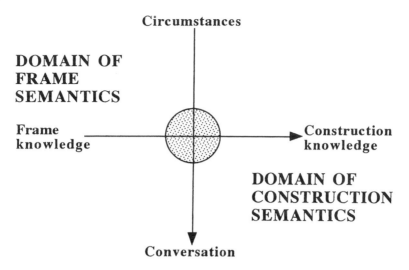

FIG. 2.6.   The domains of frame and construction knowledge.

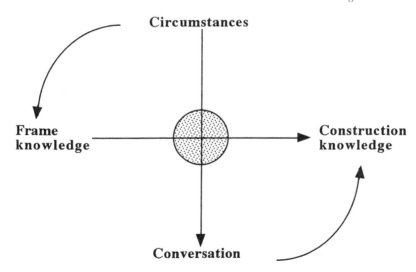

FIG. 2.7.   Mapping circumstance to frame knowledge and conversation to construction knowledge.

conversation as a unit of talk has self-organizing properties (J. R. Taylor, 1995) but is also open to influences from without. Because of the immediacy of feedback and the continuity of participation of its members the organizational conversation forms a unit of ongoing talk that is typically tightly coupled (Weick, 1979a). It remains connected to other organizational units of conversation in a more loosely coupled association. In chap-

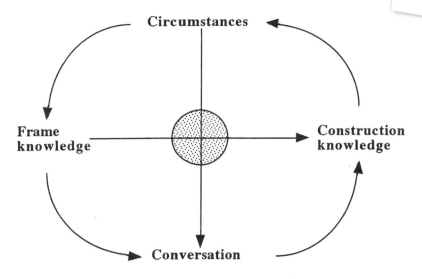

FIG. 2.8. The conversation–text cycle.

ter 5 we pick up this thread of analysis for closely attention in our consideration of Weick's approach.

The Relevance of Narrative Theory

The relevance of narrative theory becomes evident against the background of a model of organizational communication which sees communication as a cyclic (and simultaneous) translation of conversation into text and text into conversation. Conversations have many manifestations. Often they are merely desultory exchanges of talk with little specific focus other than the maintenance of a sense of sociability and neighborliness. Organizational conversations, however, tend to be more focused and problem-oriented. It is here that we can put narrative theory to good use.

We employ the notion of *text* in two distinct ways. In one sense the text of a conversation is what it produces as a conscious (or even unintended) product. It could be the minutes of a meeting, or a press release, or even just a recording of the session. It could be the stories that people tell to make sense of the conversations they have been in. This is an interpretation of text that obviously lends itself to narrative analysis (and indeed most narrative analysis has continued to take this kind of text to be its subject matter). There is now a growing literature that analyzes organizational stories and documents and it furnishes many important insights into organization.

A second way to think of the organizational text, is as the script (or generic form) that people follow in order to produce the conversation.

This view emphasizes the coorientational dynamics of talk, as the site where problems are not only addressed but agency relations are established. Such an interpretation draws directly on the Greimasian notion of the centrality of modality as the transactive basis for the formation of an organizational hierarchy in which a collective intentionality takes form to produce a group capable of acting as a single unit (a theme we take up in chapter 5 in our discussion of the work of Latour and again in much greater depth in chapters 7 and 8). In conversation the "X" of the A-B-X unit that we discussed earlier remains a virtual focus of attention, or theme of talk. Conversation is not the performing of an action with the exchange of an object of value as its effect. It is instead about developing an attitude to such exchanges: an attitude that is sufficiently shared to constitute a basis for organization to exist. In conversation the articulation linking the cognitive to the pragmatic must be accomplished for the organization to begin to emerge. This is thinking narratively: always seeing the sequence of communicative events as they unfold before us as occurring within a larger (if unstated) scene of action. In their exchange of modal objects conversants establish themselves as a social unit. To think narratively means always seeing the sequence of communication as it occurs in the larger context of situated action. In chapter 3 we turn to consider what those modalities are and how they become the basis of organizing.

CONCLUSION

To conclude this chapter, and before we continue our discussion of the conversation/text model in chapter 3, let us first explore the general question of what it is that a communication theorist should be trying to explain about organization and how to go about it.

In a perceptive article published in 1977, Hawes drew a distinction between two contrasting traditions of research in communication.[5] His analysis delineates a crucial aspect of what we take to be the inescapable challenge we, as students of organizational communication, collectively face: how to plausibly be at one and the same time both communicational and organizational. The coupling of these two terms in the phrase "organizational communication" is an instance of bridging what has been called the macro–micro gulf (Alexander, Giesen, Munch, & Smelser, 1987; Cicourel & Knorr-Cetina, 1981; Layder, 1994; Weick, 1983) and that others (Crozier & Friedberg, 1977, for example) see as pitting actor against system. Two levels of reality are in play simultaneously. Communication is invariably

---

[5]Hawes was a prolific contributor to the debates on the bases of a communication science during the 1970s, a critical period in its development. He is now professor of communication at the University of Utah.

situated in a single time and place; organization, in the sense of large organization, is not—it transcends the local and is never only here and now. It has sometimes not been clear how to be consistently both organizational and communicational without somehow forgetting that organization would cease to exist in the absence of communication, or that communication is always at least organizing, if not organizational (Cooren & Taylor, 1997; Haley, 1976; J. R. Taylor & Cooren, 1997).

Hawes' article develops what we take to be an avenue to a reconciliation of the two perspectives. As he analyzes the practices (and presuppositions) of the social sciences, there are two ways of going about the task of research. One of them, which he thinks of as "positivistic," is epistemological in its principal emphasis; the other, to which he gives the (daunting!) title of "hermeneutic phenomenology," is, by contrast, more preoccupied with ontology.

What is Hawes getting at here? The crucial element that distinguishes one approach from the other, as he describes it, is in the order of question that a positivistically, as opposed to a phenomenologically, bent scientist would begin with. The positivists start, he claims, by predicating the existence of the object they are studying—taking it for granted—and then go on to questions of its "how" and "why": to explain through the elaboration and experimental testing of hypotheses or through the use of nonexperimental empirical methods (surveys or directed interviews) the properties and underlying causal dynamics of the assumed object. This is why the emphasis is epistemological: The issue is not *what* exists, but *how to know it*, and *what are its underlying causal dynamics*, using the established methodologies of scientific investigation. The ontological issue is finessed by assuming that things are what they are commonly said to be: If people in research freely talk about "socialization of new members," or "supervisor-subordinate relations," or "organizational climate," let us say, then there must be such things, and it is reasonable to study them.[6]

Organization, in a positivist way of thinking, is one such thing.

We call this an expression of the *symbolic* perspective on human discourse: language as instrumentality for the recording and storing of an already interpreted experience.

---

[6]Hawes would, along with Gregory Bateson, "declare war on nouns" (p. 36). "Nouns," he says, "work to objectify or hypostasize social worlds." The result is that "[p]ositivist scientists, and the people they study, take everyday social worlds for granted. Rather than asking what communicative work members do to accomplish perpetually their being and how they do it, a social world is presupposed and *why* questions are asked about it" (19XX, p. XX). For a more extended exposition of nominalization and its pragmatic uses, see Hodge and Kress (1993). The latter point out how common constructions of language such as nominalizations both mask information about process and turn actively engaged-in events, with purposive actors and their intentions, into reified, inert objects and, in doing so, create an impression of social substance that obscures the fluidity of the event itself. We discuss their ideas further in chapter 5.

Phenomenologists, Hawes thinks, have a different and less intuitively natural point of departure: They are preoccupied with the question of what. To be a student of the *what* of things (as opposed to their *how* or *why*) is to begin by questioning the categories we normally take for granted and then to attempt to open oneself to a confrontation with experience, as a stranger who is living it for the first time. One tries to grasp how people (including the research community itself) are using the words they use, but not as one for whom understanding of what is occurring is already clear enough, on the basis of everyday, established meanings.[7]

This approach is to recognize the subsymbolic as distinct from the symbolic. It assumes that discourse is itself an experience and that the use of language in interaction is part of what has to be understood, because meaning cannot be self-evident on the quite simple grounds that this would confound the interpret-er (the texts of language) with the interpret-ed (the use of language to encode experience). It is the same point that Foucault made, as we described in chapter 1. Looking at language-in-use is not the same thing as looking through language-in-use to what it represents.

He claims the divergence of approach between positivist and phenomenologist can be traced to a single factor: how we understand the role of language in communication. One way of viewing language—the positivistic—is to take it as a window on reality. At the heart of this way of thinking is the belief that the real to be studied is not language, but that which language names: social and psychological phenomena that exist independently of their being talked about. Even if we were to admit that from time to time the naming process is biased, incomplete, or a bit artificial,

---

[7]Husserl's influence on Hawes is evident. Hawes (1977) writes, for example: "If one's ontological interest is in this practical world and how it is communicatively constituted, one ought to work from a perspective which enables one to make problematic for study that which everyone else presupposes. . . . To foundationally explicate communication, it is necessary to put its superficial features out-of-play; that is, to consider common-sense assumptions completely out of the network of relations which render them common-sensical. . . . By putting out of play one's everyday assumptions of practical reality, one has made the first move in thematizing communication. One has rendered the familiar unfamiliar, the mundane bizarre, the routine foreign, and the taken-for-granted problematic. One has transformed a 'here and now' practical world into a 'there and then' unfamiliar world; a 'there and then' requiring interpretation to be *foundationally* understandable, not *practically* understandable as it was prior to the putting out of play of the non-essentials" (p. 33). Elsewhere, in addressing implications of this approach for his own field research he interprets this as ". . . constantly attempt[ing] to make strange what I was seeing, hearing, and reading" (p. 39). This is what Husserl thought of as a phenomenological reduction. For a subtle application of the "naive anthropologist" approach to doing research in a contemporary setting, see Latour and Woolgar (1979/1986). They take a scientific research laboratory as their object of study and show how treating it as an exotic site visited by curious outsiders makes science, as an activity, reveal itself in terms quite different from the authoritative exterior image we are accustomed to accord it.

nothing disturbs the basic faith that, at its best, language provides a transparent window on the outside world—just a way of talking about it, comprehensibly, so that other people can grasp our meaning and benefit from our perceptions. This has been taken in the positively oriented philosophy of science to be an issue of establishing, by whatever means that maintain objectivity, the truth or falsity of a proposition (or set of propositions) framed as a statement (or set of statements, such as a theory).

The phenomenological perspective on language is different from this. Hawes cites Heidegger this way: "[W]ords and language are not wrapping in which things are packed for the commerce of those who write and speak. *It is in words and language that things first come into being and are*" (Hawes, 1977, p. 31, citing Heidegger, 1959, emphasis added). Language, as speech, is not, therefore, merely the outward expression of an inward perception. "It is a situation coming to explicitness in words" (Hawes, 1977, p. 31). Communication is not about a social world; it is, literally, the constituting of a social world. The reality lies not behind communication, or through it, but in it.[8] "Socialization of new members," "supervisor–subordinate relations," "organizational climate," or "organization" come into existence at precisely the moment we name them and begin to treat them as things in our world to be talked about. How we choose to construct the map of our world by naming it is the first preoccupation of phenomenology.

To a phenomenologist, language is not a window through which to observe social reality but a canvas on which it gets painted. The positivist uses language as a tool, an instrument by means of which to better know reality. The phenomenologist enjoys no such luxury. For him or her, the language of communication is not just medium or means or instrument (although it

---

[8]Stewart and Philipsen (1984, p. 184; see also Stewart, 1986) also discuss Heidegger's rejection of language as mere tool. "[L]anguage," they say, in their interpretation of Heidegger, "does not function to 'represent' objects and qualities; instead it functions to *disclose* them." For Heidegger, they say, it is in words and language that things first come into being and continue to exist: "[T]here is being only when there is appearing, entering into unconcealment, when unconcealment occurs, when there is disclosure" (Heidegger, 1959, p. 139), and disclosure occurs through language. Heidegger's European phenomenology is not unique in emphasizing the link between language and the appearance of reality. The U.S. pragmatic school of thought (Peirce, James, Dewey, Cooley, Mead, Burke, etc.) offers an alternative conceptualization. Cheney and Tompkins (1988), for example, cite Burke (1966, p. 466) as urging us to realize "just how overwhelmingly much of what we mean by 'reality' has been built up for us through nothing but our symbol systems." As they say, "our symbol systems construct what we call the reality of a given situation, and words are the most taken-for-granted facts of these constructions." This means, of course, that communication becomes both what we study, and how we report our findings on it; this doubling of logical levels in a single symbolic event is the property of reflexivity (Handel, 1982; Leiter, 1980) and it establishes a limit to what it is possible to accomplish through social science (Ashmore, 1989), because research, in its turn, is also not only a report on reality but also a constitution of it (Tompkins, 1993).

is that too) but theme, because it is in language that reality comes into being, and it is there that the study of communication must be focused.

The distinctions Hawes draws have a special cogency when we apply them to the study of organization. Consider the following simple fact. There is no object that we can directly apprehend by the senses that corresponds to what we are in the habit of terming an "organization." It cannot be seen, heard, touched, or smelled. The point is made by the philosopher Ryle (1973, cited in Button, Coulter, Lee, & Sharrock, 1995, p. 63), who tells a story about showing a visiting fireman around his university (Oxford). After being taken to several of its colleges, the visitor then asked: "Very impressive; now could I see the University?" How was Ryle to tell the visitor he had been seeing the university all along (because Oxford is a university composed of colleges, each with its own buildings)? How would you have explained the nuance to him?

There is involved here what Ryle thinks of as a "category mistake" but that is exactly the point: The University is a category—a category of language. It is not that there is nothing beyond language that corresponds to a university. Obviously there is, and it is something we are all perfectly familiar with in our own lives. It is that the university does not exist independently of our constituting of it in language: We would not even have an experience of university if we had not first instantiated it in our collective discourse. If the organization is a territory and our representation of it in language is its map, then, unlike the usual order of mapping, the map preceded the territory (we come back to this idea in chap. 9). It is a general principle: There would not have been an organization unless we had said there was. Words make things exist for us by naming them: The name comes before (or at least simultaneously with) the thing.[9]

---

[9]And with the name comes the naming, and that supposes an institutional instance responsible for it. Button et al. (1995, pp. 217–8, emphasis in original) cite Winch to argue that "the very identification of much of human conduct by anyone presupposes social institutions: saluting presupposes armies and their rules of comportment, buying and selling presupposes markets, and voting for someone presupposes representative political institutions, and so on. These 'institutions' are not 'simply invented by people to *explain* what happens' (Winch, 1958, p. 127), but enter into their lives in a *variety* of ways. The spectatorist view of our 'psychological' concepts commits a similar error. It is as if we first observed other people engaged in a host of activities, and *then* required some terms with which to describe and explain the regularities in what they do. Against this (impoverished) view, we would note that we use (such) language not just to talk *about* other people, but to talk to them as they talk to, and with us, to enter into *variegated* lines of conduct with them." It is notable that Searle (1995), now seems to argue in much the same terms: not that the action and its description are autonomous domains (language as descriptor), but that institutional realities enter integrally into the meaning of a term and its effects (J. R. Taylor & Cooren, 1997). In the absence of an institutionally determined meaning of the names of things, there would be no such "things." But then where did the institution come from; are we not into a chicken-and-egg riddle? Part of what this chapter is about is clarifying that question.

If organization emerges and is constituted as a social object in the language of communication, then the macro–micro issue is not so much resolved as dissolved. Communication would be not a report on organization nor a support to it, but a revelation (or in Heidegger's terms, "disclosure" or "uncovering") of it. Whatever there is about organization that transcends our knowing, it will remain in the domain of the subsymbolic—latent, perhaps, but not yet manifest.[10]

An A Priori System of Forms?

We are, however, confronted with a puzzle. If you believe that organization emerges only in communication, then how would you recognize it? When could we, like Archimedes in his bath, call out triumphantly: "Aha, there it is; I see it!" ("Eureka!"), "There it comes, in at least visible outline, the emerging, self-disclosing organization—*there!*"?

Hawes' argument goes to the heart of this central issue (which is very much the theme of the present book). He cites Kockelmans (1967), a student of Husserl and a translator of Heidegger, who asks why it is that, even though psychological science has borrowed from the exact natural sciences the whole spectrum of their methodological and operational apparatus for conducting a scientific investigation, it has nevertheless failed to achieve anything like the latter's exactness. Kockelmans' answer emphasizes the ontology/epistemology distinction once again. It is not, as we might be tempted to think, methods that produce exactness but what he calls an "a priori system of forms."[11] By *a priori forms*, Kockelmans has in mind such structures of thought as make up the basis of pure geometry or mechanics—typically, although not always, mathematical in origin. Without such a framework of criterial bases of comparison, the natural sciences, he thinks, would have stayed "vague, inductive, empirical." It is through the interpretation of data as signs or indices of the a priori forms that scientific analysis attains the status of exactness. Science is above all a conceptual investigation (with rhetorical overtones)—a voyage in the realm of theory, a struggle to have one's interpretation of the world admitted to the canon (J. R. Taylor & Gurd, 1996).

---

[10]The original German was written in Heidegger's highly idiosyncratic style, even for a native German speaker; its translation into English tends to sound even odder, but the oddness is deliberate and reflects Heidegger's determination to compel us to question our comfortable (and unreflective) habits of language use and to see familiar things in a new light.

[11]Parenthetically, although Kockelmans (1984) translated Heidegger, it is by no means evident that the concept of *a priori forms* is derived from the latter, or that Heidegger would have even approved of it; on the contrary, the idea appears to owe more to Heidegger's mentor, and eventual rival, Husserl, than it does to Heidegger. For criticism of Kockelmans' interpretation of Heidegger, see Dreyfus (1991).

If organization emerges in communication through the mapping of experience to language, then the challenge we face is to discover an a priori system of forms of language that both constitutes the backbone of communication and explains the emergence of the reality of organization in it. Our task is rendered even more delicate by the qualification that we are speaking not of language in the usual sense that it is treated in a technical field such as linguistics, content analysis, semiotics, or cognitive science, but of communicative language. For almost the entire span of scientific interest in human language, language has been treated as an object in its own right, abstracted from its practical contexts of use. This has led to the development of some extraordinary insights, but it has stubbornly obscured from view what Boden (1994) calls the "business" of talk: the contribution it makes to the construction and reconstruction of organization. It has encouraged many to see language as a psychological, rather than a communal, phenomenon—and certainly not the locus of organization (J. R. Taylor & Cooren, 1997).

The task of the phenomenologically bent communication theorist and researcher, as we see it, is to explicate an a priori system of forms that is communicative in essence and that may then become an underpinning for the conduct of empirical research. Unless the epistemology of communication research is supported by an adequate ontology, there can be no exactness, precision, or rigor. "Certainly epistemological and ontological questions can be divorced only at the expense of brute oversimplification" (Hawes, 1977).

In chapter 3, we consider what such a priori forms might look like. Our hypothesis is simply this: The forms of narrative, realized as the fundamental semantics in the ordinary language of people in interaction, serve to structure experience and provide the surface of emergence of organization. This chapter has outlined how narrative theory supplies us with a priori forms; the next takes up the question of why they are appropriate to the study of the emergence of organization in communication.

Chapter 3

How the A Priori Forms of
Text Reveal the Organization

Social reality is not merely described by language but emerges in it. To cite the great early 20th century U.S. logician and pragmatist, John Dewey (1916/1944), "Society not only continues to exist *by* transmission, *by* communication, but it may fairly be said to exist *in* transmission, *in* communication. There is more than a verbal tie between the words common, community, and communication. Men live in a community in virtue of the things they have in common; and communication is the way in which they come to possess things in common" (p. 4, emphasis in original).

It is a property—and power—of spoken and written language that it instantiates the meanings that give form and substance to our collective experience of the world.[1] As Hawes points out, this is an assumption that runs against the grain of much conventional thinking, which tends to hold that facts are one thing but the words that announce them are another. One of the firmly held premises of the social sciences, dating back at least to the sociologist Durkheim (1933, 1938), has been that it is legitimate to draw a line of demarcation between what he called "social facts" (*des faits sociaux*) and the linguistic descriptions of them employed by scientists.

---

[1]One of the core meanings of the word *instance* (not the only one, because it is also used as a synonym of *example*) is a decisional or judgmental procedure or process (as in a court of law), but, as often happens in ordinary language, it can also be used to refer, metonymically, to the body responsible for the taking of the decision or the making of the judgment. So when we say that the elements of the organization are instantiated by discourse, we mean that both the basic processes of a social institution and the actors associated with them are brought into being and become part of what Searle (1995), the philosopher, calls "social reality."

Social facts for him were things like religion and a propensity to commit suicide; the terms *religious affiliation* and *probability of committing suicide* would then merely describe facts, such facts being taken to exist independently of our speaking of them.[2] This belief was in turn encouraged by an early 20th century philosophical movement known as logical positivism, whose avowed goal was to lay the basis for a purified scientific language, uncorrupted by the messy connotations of vulgar speech (Carnap, 1959; Hempel, 1959; Rappaport, 1953; Reichenbach, 1947, 1949).[3]

Positivism, in its several guises, inspired attempts on the part of empirical researchers to discriminate "operational" from "literary" (or even—horrors!—"artistic") kinds of definition, on the grounds that what is measured, with instrumentation, can be taken to be an objective, authentic reflection of the real world, whereas that which is merely described in language is in danger of being biased by the subjective prejudices of the researcher. Listen to how Underwood (1957), a widely respected authority on the methodology of psychological research during the 1970s, saw it: "[W]e must guard against thinking that our literary statements about a phenomenon which we believe exists, and which we wish to measure, are inevitably identified with the phenomenon we finally measure" (Underwood, 1957,

---

[2]The classic reference is Durkheim's (1951) book, *Suicide.* Durkheim claimed to have measured a link from religious affiliation to the suicide rate of adherents (see also his *Rules of Sociological Method,* 1938). The methodological problem this has consistently raised since is that there are no objective measures of suicide, because the recording of a suicide is judgmental and reflects cultural practices of policing, insurance, and family values. Nor is religion a cut-and-dried matter: Not every Protestant resembles every other, nor every Catholic. There is no escaping the problem of linguistic contamination until the focus shifts from the objective facts that language records to the recording process itself and what it tells us about human organization.

[3]The word *positivist* is now mostly used as a blanket term to refer to schools of research that adhere to one form of quantitative operationism or another. It came into the language with Auguste Comte, an early 19th century French sociologist who advocated the appropriation of a style of inquiry borrowed from the exact natural sciences. Logical positivism was a 20th century branch of philosophy associated with what became known as the Vienna School. It was very influential in the 1930s and 1940s, and the exact date of the waning of its influence is controversial. Campbell (1986, p. 131), for example, claims that it was in 1959 that "Fiske and I struck one of the first public blows in psychology against logical positivism as epitomized in the 'operational definition' of theoretical terms." "We were," he goes on, "promptly scolded by logical positivists for this heresy." Meehl's (1986) take is somewhat different (p. 315): "It was agreed that logical positivism and strict operationism won't wash. Logical positivism, in anything like the sense of Vienna in the late twenties, turned out not to be logically defensible, or even rigorously formulatable, by its adherents. . . . The last remaining defender of anything like logical positivism was Gustav Bergmann, who ceased to do so by the late 1940s." The term *positivist* continues to be used but there is no longer any school of thought that would describe itself as such; it makes, as we saw in chapter 1, a convenient point of reference for interpretivists who are less than committed to the strictly quantitative strictures imposed on the conduct of research by the dominant practitioners of a previous generation.

p. 55). Underwood's preferred "statements" would limit themselves to recorded measurements. The "measurements" to which he was referring in this particular passage, however, were respondents' reactions to experimenter-scaled statements (intended to index ethnocentrism). The latter obviously had been framed in language by the researcher (on the basis of his own intuitions and experience) that Underwood is citing, and thus still reflected (and incorporated) that researcher's literary concept of ethnocentrism through, as Underwood puts it, a "translation" that "usually remains private." The researcher would not have made those particular measurements if he had not first had a conception of them that could be enunciated in language—and was.

The dilemma to which Underwood was reluctantly referring has no solution in communication studies (J. R. Taylor & Gurd, 1996). There are no uncontaminated-by-language social facts to be objectively measured by social scientists (with instruments, that is), for the very good reason that, as the management theorist Karl Weick (1995a) points out, knowledge, or the making of sense (including the activities of social scientists) is inevitably retrospective and mediated by the typifications introduced by the categories of language. If there are real social facts, we have no unmediated access to them. Time exists, Weick argues, in two distinct forms: as pure duration and as discrete segments. As *pure duration*, life is a continuous stream of experience—"a coming-to-be and passing-away that has no contours, no boundaries, and no differentiation" (Schutz, 1967, p. 47, cited by Weick). For it to take on a factive meaning, it must be experienced differently, as made up of episodes or distinct (and distinguishable) events.[4] But to perceive the episodic character of experience means, as Weick says (Weick, 1995a, p. 25), "stepping outside the stream of experience and directing attention to it. And it is only possible to direct attention to what exists, that is, what has already passed." Being preoccupied, retrospectively, with something is how we "can impose a figure–ground relationship on elapsed experience" (p. 28)—the here and now of experience is knowable only by transforming it into a there and then.

The medium we possess to "step outside the stream of experience and direct attention to it" is language: "Sense is generated by words that are combined into the sentences of conversation to convey something about our ongoing experience" (Weick, 1995a, p. 106). People, he says again

---

[4]We chose to use the word *factive* rather than *factual* to emphasize a point. The term *factive* is used by Lyons (1977), in a discussion of the modal functions of language, to mean "straightforward statements of fact" (Palmer, 1986). But as Palmer points out (p. 17), "dictionary definitions relate it to the notion of 'making' rather than that of 'fact,' and the more natural term, or even correct, is 'factual,' together with 'factuality,' etc." We see Weick to be saying precisely this: that facts are indeed made, and they are never just straightforward: factual = factive.

and again, will "know what they think only when they see what they say." Words matter (Weick, 1995a, p. 106): "Words constrain the saying that is produced, the categories imposed to see the saying, and the labels with which the conclusions of this process are retained." Underwood's researcher who measured ethnocentrism by scaling responses to a questionnaire he had devised and administered was not tapping the stream of experience of ethnocentrism but the experience of filling out a questionnaire. These were questions dictated by the researcher's own literary construction and interpreted by the respondents, in the circumstances of a survey, as an episode in their lives. And the researcher's subsequent analysis was his stepping out of the stream of experience of the survey to interpret its results using the categories of ethnocentrism he began with. The process is perfectly circular. The researcher did not measure ethnocentrism; it was instantiated as a social scientific concept that could now be presumed to have been measured. It was the measurement that gave it its existence. There is no simple unmediated fact of ethnocentrism; what we know of it is our reconstruction of it.[5]

IN SEARCH OF THE A PRIORI FORMS

By *a priori forms*, we understand properties of text through which social organization is made present and recognizable to us: organization not as a given or presumed, but found. To discover organization means to look at, not through, the discourse of communication, that is, to take discourse as a site and a surface of emergence, which are uniquely capable of revealing or disclosing it. It is in the constraints that are built into the act of communicating that we expect to find the a priori forms of organization. We thus make an assumption that communication is not incidentally, but fundamentally, organizational, in that people engaged in communication do so, always, as both the makers and the made of their own organizational environment. As its *makers*, people in interaction must and do construct the sequences of talk in which they engage in such a way that organization results: Work gets done, and hierarchies are produced. As the *made* of organization, people's identities, and the objects they value (positively or negatively), are circumscribed by and inscribed in the forms of language they employ. Language furnishes both the constructive instrumentality and the conceptual frame to make and understand organization.

---

[5]It is this reconstructive basis of meaning that Weick (1979a) attempted to capture in his concept of *enactment*. Weick's raw environment is equivocal, lending itself to multiple readings, depending on the reader. It is never directly knowable; it presents itself as "an environment of puns" (Weick, 1985). It is the enacting of it (such as the measuring of ethnocentrism) that creates the illusion of univocality, of certitude.

So if we are seeking an a priori system of forms, the locus of our investigation must be the discursive formations that mediate the text–conversation cycle. The challenge we described at the end of chapter 2 is to see organization emerging, or being produced, in communication. That seeing raises three questions that we address in this chapter: What to look for?, Where to look for it?, and How to look?

What to Look For?

There is no consensus among management theorists or sociologists as to what to take into consideration in characterizing an organization. It is an elusive concept that a century of intensive reflection has left, if anything, more problematical than ever. We do not try to resolve all the issues of ecological dependency, institutionalization, reengineering, and deconstruction that form a good part of the current diet of organization theory. We limit ourselves to those perceptions that can be supported empirically by the analysis of organizational discourse. For us, therefore, an elementary, even simplistic, definition of *organization* suffices: that which serves to constrain interaction by structuring its occasions of talk and, by so doing, to generate a kind of common accord (not necessarily unanimous) as to the objects and agents of communication. Organization, as it emerges in communication, both empowers and constrains and, as it does, creates a universe of objects and agents.[6] How the objects and agents are constituted in the basic meaning structures of human language is the focus of our attention.

Where to Look?

If conversation is the indispensable stream of experience of collective existence and text is how that stream is mediated to us so that it is made meaningful, then communication must exist at the intersection of conversation and text. For it to have the intersubjective character of a commonly shared stream of experience, conversation must be realized in a talk-supported flow of copresence (mediated technologically or not). Yet, if that flow is not re-experienced as episodic, through its textualization, then the communicational character of the conversation, although present, remains unrecognizable. On the other hand, text is not itself the conversation but merely a record of it. So what we must look at is the (often simultaneous) translation of the conversation into the text and of the text into the conversation, that is, communication as the intermediation of two modes of

---

[6]The dictionary concept of *organization* connotes constraint as well as empowerment (Oxford): arranging, systematizing, giving orderly structure to.

experience, materialized by text, in the conversation. But, as Weick has pointed out, the only access we have to the naked stream of experience is through its being re-presented to us in meaningful form, that is, in language. This means, therefore, that we have to examine on the one hand, not text per se, but the conversation in the text, either as that which is prefigured in the text, pointing to a future conversation, or as that which is past, pointing to a conversation already over and done with (even if only a microsecond ago). And, on the other hand, we must examine the text in the conversation, or how the texting of the speakers in the discourse situation is constructed into a conversational event that can be recognized.

The first of these translations, conversation into text, raises questions of syntactics and semantics; the second, text into conversation, of pragmatics. So the places to look for the emergence of organization are two. One is in the analytical constructions of language that, by making of the conversational exchange an episode or event, thus allow us to make sense of it. And the other is in the synthetic patterning of the spoken exchanges of conversation itself: how a jointly constructed account is arrived at out of the ongoing interaction. These perspectives correspond to the two main sections of this chapter.

How to Look?

All the researcher can ever know of the conversation is its text—that which has been said—yet the meaning of an organization is in that which is done: Organizations have a utilitarian end. How to go from the said to the done, and the done to the said, is another way of thinking about the text–conversation dialectic. But the doing is always specific to a unique context whereas text perdures, to figure in many contexts. It is here that the methodological challenge of organizational communication research appears. As we noted in chapter 2, Hawes (1977), in his characterization of his own philosophy, described himself as committed not only to a phenomenological, but also equally to a hermeneutic, approach. Hermeneutics, broadly defined, is the science of interpretation of texts. Its traditional debates have turned on the role of context in the reconstruction of a text's meaning. Because text is both local (a symbol system whose tokens need to be interpreted indexically by speakers in order to convey meaning each to the other) and global (a symbol system shared by every member of the language community, however situated circumstantially, and thus conveying meanings that transcend the local), there is no self-evident answer to the hermeneutic conundrum (and in chap. 1 we illustrated two contrasting positions on it). Communication researchers who choose to pursue the path of discourse analysis are not immune to the same dilemma of what weight to give the text-as-such as against the text-as-situated-act, even though, unlike the hermeneutics of scriptural analysis, the texts being analyzed are contemporary. If interpretation figures inherently in the act of communicating, how can analysts be certain that their interpretations mirror that of the people they are studying? On the other hand, the typifications of language are precisely how standardization is accomplished across situations to produce the complex social organizations we are familiar with, and, therefore, the local is never more than a sample of the global. The researcher cannot escape a limitation of perspective, and all research necessarily manifests a choice of point of view.

Now, for the remainder of the chapter, let us consider in turn each of the three questions we have raised.

WHAT TO LOOK FOR: THE SEMANTICS OF ORGANIZATIONAL COMMUNICATION

Frames and Constructions of Language

A useful analytical distinction, to which we alluded in chapter 2, has been proposed by a group of linguists who have developed what they call a "construction grammar" (Brugman, 1988; Fillmore & Kay, 1993; Fillmore, Kay, & O'Connor, 1988; Goldberg, 1995; Lakoff, 1987; Lambrecht, 1994). A *construction grammar* is concerned with the link between structures of meaning (semantics) and the patterns of spoken discourse that give expression to them (syntactics).[7]

---

[7]The origins of this school can be found in earlier work, including Gruber's (1967) thematic analysis (Jackendoff, 1972), Fillmore's (1968) case grammar, Langendoen's (1969) analysis of basic sentence forms, and others. All of this work draws on the insights provided by Chomsky's (1965) magisterial analysis of syntax and in particular his distinction between categorial and functional meaning on which the distinction between frame and construction is based (J. R. Taylor, 1978). Construction grammars are in turn only one of several contemporary schools of thought that incorporate somewhat similar ideas (Dowty, 1991; Jackendoff, 1990; Wierzbicka, 1988; etc.). Related ideas are to be found in the systemic-functional school inspired by the work of M. A. K. Halliday in Australia (Hasan, Cloran, & Butt, 1996). It is interesting that the Extended Standard Theory associated with Chomsky and others has also evolved in the direction of a limited set of elementary structures, at least in part semantically inspired, that are viewed as composing the "universal grammar" on the basis of which all actual languages are erected: truly a priori forms. There are clear parallels here with the construction grammar view. Chomsky (1995, p. 31) speculates in 1995 that the subcategorization feature that was central to his 1965 book is "artifactual, its effects derived from semantic properties." In this view (Grimshaw, 1979; Pesetzky, 1990), the primitives of subcategorization would be traceable to those of a semantic theory based on thematic analysis (agent, patient, goal, etc.), in that they meet the condition of epistemological priority. However, Chomsky reserves judgment: "This is an attractive line of reasoning, but, given our current understanding of these issues, it is not conclusive" (p. 31).

The grammar builds on a hypothesis that meaning has two bases. The first of these is called *frame semantics*. Here the meaning of a word (a noun or a verb, for example) is defined relative to some particular background frame or scene (Goldberg, 1995, p. 25). Such meanings relate to a practice: *Caught stealing* means one thing to a baseball fan and something quite different to a policeman or a social worker. Meaning, in this sense, ". . . must include reference to a background frame rich with world and cultural knowledge" (Goldberg, 1995, p. 27). The kind of distinctions that Jacques (1996) writes about, management versus employees, for example, fall into this category. Frame semantics describes the structuring of the language resources that go to make up what we called in Fig. 2.1 the repertoire.

Meaning has a second base in construction semantics, and this is the principal preoccupation of a construction grammar: the underlying, se-mantically inspired, structural patterns of phrases and sentences. As lin-guists Lakoff, Langacker, Fillmore, Goldberg, and others see it, language draws on a finite set of possible event types, and ". . . constructions which correspond to basic sentence types encode as their central senses event types that are basic to human experience" (Goldberg, 1995, p. 39). Lan-guage, according to Langacker (1991), is constructed on the basis of con-ceptual archetypes, and it is these archetypes that structure our knowledge of the world (including, as we shall see, organization).

Such a limited repertoire of possible event types includes someone causing something, someone experiencing something, something moving, something being in a state, someone possessing something, something or someone causing a change of state or location, something undergoing a change of state or location, something having an effect on someone, and so on. We are now in the domain of the abstract: "someones" and "some-things" (context-free variables, not situationally grounded constants). These abstract constructions, this linguistic school argues, form the under-lying skeleton of every sentence and are particularized in actual speech or writing by substituting for the abstract variables ordinary nouns, verbs, pronouns, adverbs, and adjectives, which are drawn from a lexicon of words that incorporates frame knowledge. The frame/construction distinc-tion thus has a practical linguistic equivalent in the lexicon/grammar cou-plet studied by linguists. The grammar is the bedrock, constructive, abstract part that dictates how the sentence must be built out of words to be syntactically admissible (the order of its components). The lexicon, drawing on culture-specific frame semantics, supplies the components themselves which are more susceptible to evolutionary change over time than the construction-based sentence builder, which evolves very slowly and, in its most general aspects, is a universal basis for every language (or at least so many contemporary linguists believe).

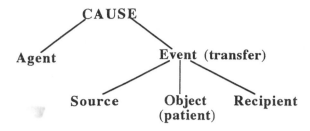

FIG. 3.1. The basic ditransitive construction.

All of our experience, however specific to a unique cultural matrix, must be poured into the mold of a universal constructive device in language, which conforms to ideas of deep-rooted elementary types of human experience. This is why we see semantics as the principal source of a priori form. *Hillary Clinton is a saint* is a (potentially controversial, from the perspective of frame semantics) statement about a particular person having a particular profession in a particular circumstance, but it is also an assertion that must conform to a structure of both thought and syntax that says that "someone is something": [*is <someone, something>*]. That structure is a construction.

The Ditransitive: The Backbone
of the Communication Event

Of these elementary filters, or constructions, one is of particular importance to our discussion because it involves the event of a transaction and explains how the enablements and constraints of organization arise in the flow of communication. Its technical name is a *ditransitive*. The basic event expressed by a ditransitive construction is that of an agent acting to cause transfer of an object from a source to a recipient (it is ditransitive because there is syntactically both a direct object, called the *patient*, and an indirect object, called the *recipient* or *goal*). It is the construction type, semantically speaking, where the communication exchange event takes place (Fig. 3.1).[8]

The reader will immediately recognize that what we are calling a ditransitive construction is formally identical with what we termed in chapter 2 an exchange. This is not an accident, but it deserves a brief explanation. Semantics has, throughout the years, remained a controversial domain of linguistics because, unlike syntactics, which studies the objectively observ-

---

[8]Note that the embedded phrase *source-object-recipient* has the same structure as *source-message-destination*, which is the classic Shannonian formulation. The difference is found in the additional presence of a matrix phrase that specifies an agentive cause for the transfer.

able ordering of the parts of a spoken sentence, semantics concerns how people assign meaning to those same components and thus has seemed to introduce into linguistics an unwanted psychological element, taken by some to be a threat to the scientificity of pure linguistics. The contribution of Greimas has been his perception that the meaning present in sentences derives from the fact that, as we cited Bruner earlier, sentences are fragments of larger entities, whose basis is narrative. If the meaning of a sentence is never reducible to the parts of which it is composed but may be traced back to its place in a larger structure of discourse regulated by rules of narration, as Bruner thinks, then the problem of meaning is not that it is psychological but that it is hermeneutic (and many grammarians have not wanted to open up this black box). The semantics of sentences, which is what Goldberg and her associates study, is thus perfectly compatible with the semantics of narrative, because it is derived from the latter. The advantage of focusing on sentence semantics, and the reason we do so in this chapter, is that it furnishes an instrument to analyze organizational discourse and a means to identify the a priori system of forms of organization, as the latter emerges in communication.

The ditransitive construction has an operator (syntactically, a verb) that incorporates, as part of its most basic meaning, a sense of "cause-(someone)-to-receive" and argument slots that specify an (a) agent or operator, and (b) a transfer (i.e., that which the agent causes to happen). The transfer thus effected is in turn an event constructed from an operator (a verb) whose argument slots include roles of (c) source, (d) patient, and (e) recipient. Formally, the construction is written as: [CAUSE-RECEIVE <**agt, rec, pat**>] where the agent (*agt*) is the causer, the recipient (*rec*) the receiver and the patient (*pat*) what is received: giver, givee, gift, in effect. This construction is read as having the sense of ". . . successful transfer of an object to a recipient, with the referent of the subject agentively causing this transfer" (Goldberg, 1995, p. 33). The agent causes the receiver to receive the object or patient.[9]

An additional precision is required, however, for the model to be applied organizationally. Figure 3.2 illustrates this special interpretation of the ditransitive construction.

In this second version of the ditransitive construction, two transfers and two objects are implicated, with one transfer figuring within (embedded in) the other. The "within" or lower level transfer (the embedded construction of Fig. 3.2) is directed to an *object of value*. (This is the usual

---

[9]This formulation makes an unstated assumption that the agent and source roles are played by the same person. It is, of course, possible for the agency role to be colocated with the recipient, so that the expression would then read 'cause (oneself)-to-receive' (or more colloquially, to take, as opposed to give). See our earlier discussion (Fig. 2.8).

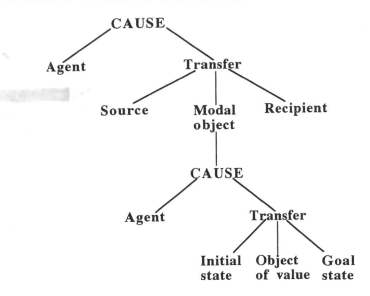

FIG. 3.2. The expanded ditransitive model of communication.

commonsense connotation of *object*: ordinary things that people work on and manipulate in the everyday world.) Here, the embedded construction may or may not be ditransitive. If it is, possession is involved. If it is not, the transfer in question results in a change of state or location of some object (but not necessarily a change of possession). It could be, for example, reorganizing a warehouse; here objects change location but not possession. If the embedded expression is a simple transitive, the term *recipient* is replaced by *goal state* and the resulting event need not involve a transfer, but simply a change of state. Industrial and commercial processes fall under this heading. Mining, manufacturing, processing, packaging, sales, accounting and so on, all take the form of either a change of state or of location, effected on some object, semantically thought of as the patient of the operation. All suppose the same logical components of active agency (not, however, necessarily human, or at least not overtly so), change (transfer or transformation), object (patient), and goal state (that involves a recipient, if a transfer is involved). The nature of the object of value and the kind of process in which it figures determines the character of the enterprise, private or public: insurance company versus car manufacturer versus State Department. It is by the objects of value it transacts that we know the mission of the organization.

The kind of transfer with which we are uniquely concerned in the remainder of this chapter, however, is represented as the embedding (or upper level) construction of Fig. 3.2. It must be a ditransitive. Its object, semantically speaking, is a description, in language, of the embedded transfer specified in the previous paragraph. Here, what is transferred is not an object in the usual sense of the term, but an idea, expressed as the propositional content of the utterance (we therefore term it a *theme*). The object of the embedded proposition is, as before, an object of value; the object of the embedding proposition is a *modal object*. The concept of *modality*, as we explained in chapter 2, is intended to capture the idea that the meaning of the embedding sentence is not so much to represent a state of affairs or an action in the world as to express an attitude of the speaker, or convey an intention with respect to it, to a recipient. The kinds of verbs that can figure in a modal construction are ones such as *think, feel, ask, like, wish, want, tell, hope, request,* and so forth: precisely those verbs that are followed by an expression such as "that such-and-such is or will be true or will or should occur."[10] They thus demarcate a different order of organizational process from those that are described as concerned with objects of value. They are the basis of management and administration. The specificity of an enterprise is indexed by the objects of value it transacts, not by its modal objects; modal objects are common to every organization, although the processes by which they are transferred may be specific to an organization. Communication transacts modal objects directly, objects of value indirectly.[11]

Consider an example drawn from a corpus of recorded conversation. The situation is a roundtable discussion involving a number of senior public administrators who had been meeting regularly for 3 years to consider the implications of globalization for the practices of government in a contemporary postindustrial society (Rosell, 1999). Each has agreed to develop and present a case study that exemplifies the impact of globalization in their sphere of executive responsibility. The excerpt is taken from the introduction of one of the participants to the person he has hired to conduct his departmental study. He concludes his introductory remarks this way: "Well that was my introduction, a bit longer that I had anticipated, but Jeff why don't you take them through the model and then I'm going to reflect on how much I should say in addition to what I've already said in the conclusions."

---

[10]It is a property of ordinary language that some verbs take as their object an embedded sentence. The verbs *think* or *feel*, for example, have as their object a statement as to what is thought or felt, and this embedded statement in turn can be described as a construction. Verbs that take sentences as their object are modal constructions. What the semantics of constructions adds to this syntactic analysis is the pragmatic perception that such embedded sentences refer to virtual states or actions—that which would or should or could be done or become.

[11]There is actually a second criterion, namely that the recipient be human, or at least possess the capacity of being able to grasp the sense of a spoken sentence. The source, if not human, must be interpretable as capable of expressing an intention. We return to develop this idea in greater depth later when we take up the question of where to look.

The ditransitive construction we have in mind is found in these words: *Jeff why don't you take them through the model.* We have an agent (the speaker) who, by his words, has transferred an object (the floor) to a recipient (Jeff), the agent having been the source (he had the floor and has now willingly ceded it to Jeff). In addition, his words refer to a second (embedded) transfer, in which the agent (causer) will be Jeff, the object will be the model and the recipient will be them (i.e., the other members of the roundtable). Again, a source is assumed: Jeff, who at the moment of speaking is still in possession of an object, the model, that has not yet been transferred. A transaction within a transaction is thus specified, by and in the speaker's words.[12]

Although the prototype expression corresponding to a ditransitive supposes a concrete object, the common extensions of the construction (the ones of most interest to people in communication science) are, as our example suggests, metaphorical: *Jeff why don't you take them through the model, Marcel gave me a new understanding of European politics, The prosecutor had unwittingly handed the defendant the perfect alibi,* and so on. Similarly, as the example shows, the concept of role (agent, recipient) includes not only individual actors but also collective entities (them, in this instance).[13]

If organization, as we believe, implies constraint exemplified in transactions, or the exchange of objects of value, concrete or other, from a source to a destination, such exchanges (transfers) must be brought about by responsible agents. The senior bureaucrat's act, in the example cited,

---

[12]This is what Werth (1993) calls a "text-world" within a "discourse-world." We return to Werth's ideas later in the chapter.

[13]An anonymous reviewer of one of our papers commented as follows: "The metaphor of *giving*, which is central to the revised view of the process of communication, is outdated, and for good reasons; it is wrong. It is an absurd idea to suppose, for example, that a speaker first possesses permission, which he then gives to the listener, who receives it, after which the speaker is no more in possession of this object." Not quite as "absurd" as the reviewer thinks. To begin with, ordinary language regularly includes mentions of "giving permission" and, in fact, such a giving may well figure as the hinge on which court cases turn (as in responsibility for a minor or a subordinate, for example). More fundamentally, the giving construction is precisely that: a *construction*, and furthermore a prototype for many derived secondary constructions, as, for example, buying and selling (Jackendoff, 1972). Fascinating work by Rosch (1973, 1978, 1981; Lakoff, 1987) indicates that some kinds of construction are more basic than others; we believe that giving and receiving (and the construction of transfer in which they occur) constitute such a prototype. Finally, our anonymous reviewer confounds two versions of possession, the psychological and the communicational. Within the communication frame, if something is given, it is given. It is no longer possessed by the giver within the framework of the communicational event. You cannot, logically, inform someone of the same thing twice (they have already been informed), and unless information is defined in other than communicational terms (which it often is, in spite of the fact that the root verb *inform* requires, grammatically, a recipient), a loss of possession is in fact occurring. After you give someone possession, he or she has it; you do not (unless you contrive a new transaction to recover it).

both instantiates an existing organization and gives shape to one in process of instantiation. If communication is where organization emerges, then conversation must be the arena for the realization of transactions. It is through such transactions that the modal objects and agentive roles of organization are produced and reproduced in communication. As they are, the organization begins to emerge.

The Principal Modal Objects of Communication

Having established the nature of a modal object, we now take the next step and begin to look at different classes of modal objects and, thus, different modalities of organizing. In previous work (J. R. Taylor, 1993, for example), we typically used speech act theory for this purpose. We now prefer to use a different framework of explanation of how interaction is mediated: one which is based on the transfer of modal objects. Speech act theory associates illocutionary point with what is enunciated and how it reflects states of the speaker such as his or her intentionality; modal transfer theory is communicational in its basic premise. It is based on the concept of a transfer requiring two agents for its accomplishment. In important respects, however, the effect is the same (Cooren & Taylor, 1997). In fact, later in the chapter, we return to the theme of speech acts to show its understanding of the interpretation of action through speech. There are three kinds of modal objects; and they point to three kinds of ditransitive communicative exchanges (transfer of a statement about the world), and, by implication, three kinds of organizing.

Transfers That Develop a Shared Image of the World. Through communication we construct an image of the factual basis of experience—the state of affairs that is assumed to hold in the world. Communications that aim to obtain agreement on the facts have been called *constatives* (Austin, 1962). The modality involved is known as *epistemic.* When the source of the constatively or epistemically oriented communication is also the agent, we commonly refer to this as *transmitting information.*[14] But other possibilities exist. Goldberg, for example, gives as an illustration the case where the speaker concedes a point to someone who is fabricating a structure of explanation, for example, *I'll let you have that much* (Goldberg, 1995, p. 150). Here it is the recipient who is making information, reflexively (he or she is both source and recipient). What is transferred is not the

---

[14]Cooren (1995a, 1995b) distinguishes assertives (as a class of speech act) from informatives. Our analysis would suggest that the difference between an assertive and an informative is that the former is merely a transitive (it establishes a relationship between an agent and a theme, i.e., that which is asserted) whereas the latter is ditransitive (the recipient or beneficiary of the assertion is explicitly indicated by the presence of a dative, as in *I told you so!*).

information but the sanctioning of it. What is important is that information is socially situated action involving transfers of more than one kind, bringing into play agency relationships, not just about facts, but also about the making of a shared basis of understanding of the situation, or what the philosopher Peirce (1940/1955) so felicitously called the "fixation of belief." Developing a shared image of the situation has always been recognized as a basic organizational function.

Transfers That Serve to Bring About New States of Affairs. Through communication we orient, direct, promise, and sanction the performance of activities, both our own and others'. Following Jakobson (1962), we term this class of communicational exchange the *conative* function of language. The modality involved is known as *deontic*. The simplest form of such a communication, from a management point of view, is presumably to give a command. The object in such a ditransitive construction is that which is commanded (people do in fact talk about "giving" commands, or orders, in everyday language). In speech act theory, this is called a *directive*. It is the giver of the command who functions as agent, the person to whom the request for action is directed being the recipient. Most of the time, the directive is softened (technically, mitigated), as in our example, where it is clear to everyone present in the roundtable discussion that this particular senior administrator is giving Jeff a directive (including Jeff, who obediently responds), even though he phrases it in the form of an invitation, "Jeff why don't you . . . ?"

Note, as before, the action-within-an-action character of the exchange. The actual communicative act is ditransitive; the directed action that constitutes the object of the communicative event is embedded, both syntactically and semantically—a description of some future or wished-for event, which may or may not in turn be communicational (in this case, it was).

Directives, however mitigated, are only one of a class of constructions whose embedded object is a transfer of a deontic modal object and thus a change of state of the implied organization. The complement of a directive, for example, is a *commissive*—the making of a promise. What distinguishes a commissive from a directive is the location of agency. In a commissive, it is the person designated to eventually perform the action (the source) who plays the argument role of agent in the ditransitive construction, whereas in a directive, the recipient in the ditransitive construction is the eventual performer of the action designated by the ditransitive object: *Do me a memo, please* versus *I'll do a memo*. Cooren (1995a) proposes a further category, which he terms an *accreditive*. An accreditive covers that class of verbs that refers to the giving of permission or the sanctioning of an act. It is related to the directive in the same way a double negative is related to a positive: not *You must* but *You may* (i.e., *I do not prohibit you doing*).

Again, we are reconfirming the obvious. It has always been known that organizations have hierarchies of command and authority. All we have done is to reframe the observation in discursive, that is, communicational, terms.[15]

Transfers That Actually Make a State of Affairs Happen. Through communication, we cause states of affairs to exist by the mere speaking of them. This is the most "magical" (Searle, 1989) of all communication events. It is characterized by the fact that, because someone declares a certain state of affairs to exist, then exactly that state of affairs ipso facto does now exist. This class of communicative events has been designated a *declarative* (and sometimes a *performative*). Modal logic makes no special provision for this kind of act. Here are examples: By a priest declaring a couple to be married, they are in fact married; by a judge declaring an accused guilty, that person is now found guilty; by a baseball umpire declaring a runner safe, that runner is in fact safe; by the President of the company announcing the layoff of 2,800 workers, effective immediately, the workers are in fact laid off; by the Governor of Georgia declaring the name of a boat to be the *Jimmy Carter,* then that is the name of that boat; by the Chair declaring the meeting open, the meeting is open; by willing and bequeathing your fortune to a niece, that niece is now the inheritor of your fortune; by shaking hands on a bet, the bet is on; and so on.

Searle (1989) points out a peculiarity of this construction. What he calls its "direction of fit" is simultaneously word-to-world and world-to-word. In a constative construction (an assertion of fact), the fit goes from word-to-world, that is, we try to make what the sentence says match up with what we perceive to hold objectively in some world. In a conative construction, the reverse holds: The purpose of a directive or a commissive is to program a change to occur in a future or possible world—the world should come to fit the word. In a declarative, the direction of fit is both world-to-word (it is the world that must accommodate itself to the word, i.e., the declarative has an executive effect in that the speech act is the effective cause of the new state of affairs) and word-to-world, because the state of affairs now created is also accurately described. It is the simultaneity of the direction of fit that is here at issue. It is not about what was or has become true (as a result of previous actions), nor about what will or should be true as a result of future actions, but what is now being made true as a result of the speaking. The declarative, as its title suggests, is self-referential—not just communicative about action or about states, but action and

---

[15]Fernando Flores (Winograd & Flores, 1986) even developed a software product called "The Coordinator," which would track people's commitments and obligations and call them to account regularly when they were tardy in carrying them out. Perhaps not too surprisingly, this software was not universally popular!

state combined: what it describes is what it does. The world in question (other than in the practice of magic) is obviously a social world. As Searle (1989, 1995) observes, worlds only come to conform themselves to words when there is an institutional understanding that this shall be so.

Again, we are restating the obvious in a different language. Part of what makes every organization work is the taking of executive decisions. Such executive acts constitute the strictly institutional basis of organization—its "magically" declared reality of subjects and objects (as Searle thinks), reconstituted on the basis of no more than a shared understanding that this is now the way the world will be. This is how organizations come into existence, how their officers are named, how they hire and fire, how they open and close plants, certify or decertify unions, merge and acquire, buy and sell, work.

The Concept of Role in a Construction Grammar

Goldberg (1995, p. 43) distinguishes between two concepts of role. A *participant role* is delimited by frame semantics. Categories and names such as *senior bureaucrat* and *Jeff* are participant roles. All you need to know to understand them is something about bureaucracy and how personal names work. *Argument roles*, by contrast, are associated with such abstract functions as agent, patient, source, recipient, or, in other words, the argument slots in a construction. In the making of an assertion, the semantics are fused in the syntactic components of the sentence. The senior bureaucrat (frame role) in effect steps into the role of agent (construction role), and Jeff (frame role) is designated as a recipient in the speech situation (construction role).[16]

The Interaction of Frame and Construction Semantics in Role-Playing

Consider an example. The verb *to recognize* has two distinct meanings. On the one hand, as any standard dictionary would show, it means to identify as already known (*I recognized my sunglasses in his glove compartment*). On the other hand, it means to acknowledge the validity of a claim or to admit a point. In this latter usage, it can mean to grant a person the right of speaking in a meeting (such as Jeff). Let us call the first sense *recognize₁* and the second *recognize₂*. The first is a simple transitive construction (*Martha recognized her cousin Fred*) whereas the second is, semantically, a ditransitive construction (as in *The Speaker of the House recognized the Member*

---

[16]The concept of agency occupies a special place in our theory. It is here that the micro–macro link so vital to understanding the organization/communication link is located. The discussion is expanded on in chapters 7 and 8.

from Vancouver South). *Recognize₂* is communicational in a way that *recognize₁* is not: The Speaker has transferred to the Member from Vancouver South a "right to speak"—a *recognition* (and in French the equivalent expression is *donner la parole*, i.e., literally to *give speech* or, less literally, *leave to speak*). Such recognition is the equivalent of the object of a ditransitive construction—a modal object or theme.

Using this example, we can get some idea of how frame semantics and construction semantics interact and how, as they do interact, the nature of the role/object relationship may be altered. Clearly, a noun phrase such as *The Speaker of the House* involves frame semantic meaning, including reference to ". . . a background frame rich with world and cultural knowledge" (Goldberg, 1995, p. 27). One has to know something about parliamentary roles, ritual, and procedure. It is this frame knowledge that encourages us to interpret *The Speaker of the House recognized the Member from Vancouver South* as a ditransitive construction. If we were to replace the subject of the sentence *The Speaker of the House* by *Martha*, however, so that it read *Martha recognized the Member from Vancouver South* the construction would no longer be so easily interpreted as a ditransitive; it would be simply a transitive. Our frame knowledge would tell us that individuals called *Martha* do not have the right to accord speaking rights to figures belonging to political parties in the context of official House business (not even if the Speaker's name happened to be Martha). So given frame knowledge we substitute one construction for another to arrive at a sensible interpretation (Martha might be someone in the Visitors' Gallery, for example, perhaps a constituent from Vancouver). A similar transposition would occur for *The Speaker of the House recognized her cousin Fred.* Once again, we would assume this was a case of *recognize₁*, not of *recognize₂* (now it is Fred who is in the Visitor's Gallery, being recognized, rather than—like Martha—recognizing).

It is not that we could not construct a situation where the sentence, *The Speaker of the House recognized the Member from Vancouver South,* would be construed as a simple transitive construction, as for example: *On her way back from the Cairo conference, in the airport, the Speaker of the House recognized the Member from Vancouver South seated at the bar, deep in conversation with an extraordinarily beautiful young woman, who, as it happened, the Speaker knew to be a member of the King's entourage. The Speaker passed discreetly on without calling attention to her own presence.* Here there would be no issue of *recognize₂*. No communication occurred or was meant to occur between Speaker and the Member from Vancouver South—no question of giving a right to speak.

Frame knowledge can be manipulated and as it is, our reading of the construction of the sentence is affected. The words in the lexicon of the language are constrained in their application by selectional considerations imposed by the construction grammar, but there is not necessarily a one-to-one fit. Frame and construction meanings are both in play, and they interact. As they do, they determine how the organization emerges in the discourse for us.

Agency as the Micro–Macro Link

It is the fusion of frame and construction semantics that explains how there can be corporate actors: agents that represent a collective intentionality, that of the organization itself.

Webster's New World Dictionary gives two principal readings of *agent*: either (a) "a person or thing that performs actions" or (b) "a person, firm, etc. empowered to act for another." The difference is between acting and acting for. What makes the Speaker (and not Martha) eligible to recognize the Member from Vancouver South is not Webster's first meaning, which is the capacity to perform the act (that is a necessary but insufficient condition of performance, something that Martha could master with a little training) but the second meaning, which is her being "empowered to act for another." The "other" in question is not, however, an individual, but is rather a collectivity: The House (and ultimately Parliament, or even the people of Canada). There is illustrated here a fundamental cornerstone of organizational communication. The exercise of authority (and the synonymous realization by an actor of agency in a ditransitive construction) is conditional on its being institutionally empowered to act for the collectivity. (This was Searle's point in his discussion of the role of the institution.) The collective (or macro) sense of agency is lodged in frame semantics (text as context) whereas the expression of it must occur in a ditransitively structured exchange (the micro sphere of conversational interaction, where text is the content).[17]

---

[17]This is an idea to be explored more fully in chapter 6. To our knowledge, the first statement of this idea is to be found in Durkheim's work (1915). Briefly, to anticipate the later discussion, he reasoned somewhat as follows (J. R. Taylor & Cooren, 1997): The collective takes precedence over the individual because the marshalling of collective energies creates an agency whose power supercedes the individual's; such an "agency," however, has no capacity to act on its own and can only find expression in the voice of some individual; when an individual is recognized by the community as giving legitimate expression to the collective agency, then that person's voice has a force that no single individual can aspire to—it is literally *power-ful*; this force is what makes command work because people recognize that it is the collectivity that speaks through the agent; the recognition of legitimacy depends, however, on the existence of a shared opinion, or view of the world (a "collective representation") that is generally understood to be the basis for action; it follows that the aspirant to authority must successfully vocalize the community's view if his or her voice is to be recognized as legitimate; the corollary, however, is that the community may withdraw recognition of legitimacy when authenticity is lacking. Reinterpreting Durkheim in the terms of Goldberg's theory, we would say that the former's "collective representations" coincide with the latter's frame, or scene, knowledge.

It is not just that, ditransitively speaking, the agent personifies frame semantical knowledge. He or she must also enunciate transfers that correspond to the parameters of frame semantical knowledge: appropriate objects and recipients. The relationship of representative (agent) and representation (embedded object of transfer) is reciprocal. Roles are defined by the activities they are authorized to perform and activities by the agentive contexts in which they do and may occur.

Frame semantics specify, among other things, participant roles (such as Speaker). Part of the definition of a participant role is to identify for whom the role occupant is authorized to speak or on whose behalf he or she is empowered to act—which *agency*, in other words. When the principal for whom the agent may speak is the community itself, then authority is already inscribed in the collective representation, and the playing out of agency in actual exchanges that conform to the grammar of constructions is part of the common expectation of where such participant roles will occur. It is why Jeff did what his principal asked, that is, explained the model.

Recognizing someone's right to speak by giving him or her the floor, as the Speaker does, or passing a turn to talk to Jeff, is accomplished communicatively: *Recognize$_2$* is a ditransitive construction. Who gets to play that role, and how the role is conceived, however, is part of frame, not construction, semantics. It is specific to a given society and culture. It is part of macrostructural knowledge: frame knowledge that certain participant roles fit with certain argument roles and not others. Generals give orders, privates do not. Similarly, scientists speak with authority on certain subjects that laypersons may not. Only judges judge (in a court of law).

The Organization in Semantic A Priori Forms

The significance of a construction grammar is this: An organization is also at one and the same time a frame and a construction—a structure with two dimensions. The participant roles (Speaker, Member, bureaucrat, Jeff) are part of the frame semantics of the organization, as is everything else that is circumstantial about organization, including places (such as the House) and times (being in session, for example). But the sum of all the participant roles and circumstances, because they are merely a frame, is not yet an organization, other than virtually. To be an organization in the full sense of the term, the participant roles must be realized, constructively, by fusing them with argument roles, which is to say becoming an agent in the transfer of some object of value from some source to some destination. The Speaker has to actually say "I (or The Speaker) recognize(s) the Member from Vancouver South." This is the organization realized in the communication—the actualization of participant roles through their translation into argument roles and, in particular, those of agent and recipient, that is, destinator and destinatee. To the extent that the communication succeeds, so does the organization, whose frame roles are thus once again reconfirmed.

Similarly for the objects of communication. Every organization (as every conversation) is ultimately oriented to objects in the real material world—objects of value—but the communication that makes concerted, cooperative action possible is not just about concrete objects. It is about getting the facts straight, directing action, asking for and giving commitments to act, creating institutional realities (roles such as Speaker or Member, and instances such as the House) through declaring them to exist—modal values, in a word. Again, as communication succeeds, so does organization. When communication fails, the organization is in (more or less serious) disarray.

The relationship between agent/source (giver) and agent/recipient (taker) is necessarily mediated by an object or theme to which they are mutually oriented, at least for the duration of the exchange. Organizationally speaking, such objects are, as we have seen, establishing the facticity of a situation, determining who is responsible for carrying out which tasks, and declaring, by executive intervention, states of affairs affecting the status of the actors to exist. If any of these objects become problematical, they index (a) uncertainty as to the actual state of affairs in a common environment, (b) more serious, a breach in the system of hierarchical command and, at the maximum, (c) failure of the underlying institutional basis of executive authority. When macroidentities are involved, such uncertainty means that the established order of the organization is, to greater or less degree, in question. Uncertainty will vary in intensity from discussion as to the facts (low uncertainty) to negotiation of the hierarchy (greater uncertainty) to questioning of the institutional bases of executive authority (very great uncertainty). At some point, the survival of the organization may even be in jeopardy.

WHERE TO LOOK: INTERACTIVE EXCHANGES

From Ditransitive to Diagentive

In chapter 2 we introduced what we called the polemical property of communication. A construction grammar takes no account of this property, because it is still a grammar of sentences. It is a useful tool for the analysis of kinds of organizational exchange, but it furnishes no more than a truncated view of communication. It may be true that people make sense of the interactions in which they are caught up by translating them semantically, but they almost certainly do not do so adjacency pair by adjacency pair. Instead, conversational dynamics have to be read hermeneutically in that a particular exchange is, as Bruner put it, a specific instance of a generic pattern. It follows from this that the act of communication is not only ditransitive, but also diagentive.

There are, we have said, three principal text-defined communication-describing (ditransitive) constructions, depending on the nature of their embedded object: (a) saying how the world is, or was, or predictively will be (direction of fit: word-to-world); (b) saying how the world must or should or could or is likely to be (direction of fit: world-to-word, with a connotation of desired future states); and (c) making the world be by declaring it to be so (direction of fit: world-to-word, instantaneously and, by that instantaneity, word-to-world as well). The objects of communication, in this linguistic, sentence-based, semantic interpretation of a priori forms of communication also turn out to be objects of organization: arriving at a shared understanding of the world, directing and controlling one's own and others' actions, making executive decisions, and constituting through instititutionally recognized acts the occasions and identities that go to make up the frames of organizational communication.

Managers have good reason to think in these terms. Large organizations must assume transactive stability because only then can the products and services (the ultimate objects of exchange that generate value) and the agentive relationships that frame them (both individual and institutional) be planned and concretized (installing production machinery, hiring permanent staff or contracting out, implementing systems, setting up sales divisions, etc.). The whole thrust of management is to reduce uncertainty and to control reactivity on the part of clients, workers, and regulators, to the extent possible. The ditransitive constructions of language fit into this pattern: They speak to the fixing of states, the orientation of objects (material and other), and the realization of established actantial roles.[18]

But this is not what is usually meant by *communication*—at least not as process. As we noted, we have been concentrating until now (in our discussion of a construction grammar) on the transaction in isolation from its enveloping context. But we have done so at the risk of underplaying

---

[18]The contrast of perspectives is apparent in the literature on the computerization of work. On the one hand, the exigencies of computer programming make the formalization of communication and organization inevitable; on the other, real work contexts remain, as Suchman (1987) put it, "situated." How far it is legitimate to go in the direction of formalizing organizational process is an issue in the systems design community (J. R. Taylor et al., in press; Van Every & Taylor, 1998). The debate is well illustrated by an exchange between Suchman and Winograd (Winograd, 1994) in which Suchman claims that the categorization of work that precedes and makes possible formalization is an exercise of power. Winograd defends the necessity of such abstraction where a system's complexity is such as to outstrip the usual practices of control that are typical of situated work.

the importance of the interactive, exchange-like properties of communication.

Communication, carried on as conversation, is inherently bipersonal, involving in its adjacent exchanges complementary agencies for its achievement. The ditransitive construction described by Goldberg specifies only one agent, uniquely responsible for the caused action of transfer. The recipient is merely a goal of the action, in Goldberg's characterization (Fig. 3.1). The constructions of text thus impose a point of view—that of a singular agency. That is not totally unrealistic. It is a point of view that manifests the presence of organization, from the perspective of a textual construal. It is because of the fixing of perspective that we accord a status of permanence to organization, in everyday life. It is how organization comes to be accorded a place in our universe, as one more object among others. But the conversational dynamics of communication are not characterized by a single point of view.

Let us be clear what we saying here, because the point is fundamental. We, as did the linguist Edmondson (1981), see conversation as also being, as the ditransitive representation of the communicational act portrays it, concerned with exchange (transfer). However, an exchange, Edmondson says, ". . . consists of the passing of a good from A to B, *and a reciprocal passing of a good from B to A*" (p. 83, emphasis added). Even the "passing of a good" from A to B ". . . may be said itself to consist of two acts, which we informally term 'offer' and 'acceptance'" (p. 83). His view of exchange, we note, starts ditransitively, but a further dimension is involved that is not to be found in the ditransitive construction: reciprocity of agentness. There are two, not one, agents involved: one to offer, one to accept. So communicational behavior is not only about *transferring* (as in a ditransitive construction), but also about *uptaking, replying,* and *reciprocating* (B to A, as well as A to B)—all parts of an ongoing exchange process involving agentive complementarity. Browning and Henderson (1989) distinguish between one-way and two-way (or bilateral) exchanges. The ditransitive construction describes one-way exchange. Edmondson is talking about a two-way exchange. If we are to retain the concept of a ditransitive construction, we must amend it to specify that not only must the source but also the recipient have properties of agency. Both figure in the CAUSE of the transfer (Fig. 2.7).

This change of perspective has important consequences. As Beach points out, conversational exchanges are not preordained, but interpretable, on the basis of fluid perceptions of situation and role:

> The next turn-at-talk may be the foundational building block of human understanding. It is here that next speakers contribute to an already un-folding interactional environment, producing a wide variety of actions (e.g., agreeing/affiliating, disagreeing/disaffiliating, attending/disattending, ac-

cepting, rejecting, closing, opening, reconciling, mitigating, canceling, de-
leting, avoiding) and a considerably more diverse set of possibilities (in both
kind and degree). Each possibility evidences little more nor less than how
participants display and detect one another's orientations to the occasion
at hand. Exactly what gets achieved is undeniably the upshot of how speakers
fashion, shape, and make available to one another their understandings of
the local environment of which they are an integral part. (1995, p. 125)

This strikes us as a fair statement of interpersonal communication in
practice, whether organizational or not, that is, centered on exchange but
interactive and problematical in its outcomes. It is precisely not what a
single-agent perspective on organization is about. Organization, in this
view, is about the reduction of interactive ambiguity and the fixing of
outcomes.[19]

Complementary agencies—not just one—are involved in interactive
communication. Conversation is a negotiated process—not merely ditransitive but diagentive. *Bill loaned Mary his copy of Putnam and Pacanowsky* may
well refer to the same conversational event as *Mary borrowed Bill's copy of
Putnam and Pacanowsky* but the attribution of agency, ditransitively speaking, is different. In communication, there are two actions in one.

An appearance of isomorphism between language structure (the ditransitive construction) and conversation (A-B exchange) arises because even
in conversation there is an initiator to whose opening act there is a response
(together constituting an adjacency pair). It is the opening act that proposes the text of the exchange (its theme or object), and, if the response
is favorable, there is closure. We might say that an organization had been
expressed in conversation through the realization of its object in the context of its transfer from agent to recipient. But if agency is problematical,
then the objects of communication are open to interpretation, something
to be constructed, not a given, and roles themselves are no longer strictly
determined by frame. If we admit that the transfer of an object (patient
or theme) to a recipient may be rejected as well as accepted then, because
the recipient is also an agent (a cause), the act of transfer is also problematical. It depends on the respective values they have placed on the
object and how they perceive the transaction to be going.

It is important that the communication researcher try to recognize closure when it occurs because it indexes an emergence of organization. The
analyst must explain not just the communication situation, but the com-

---

[19]The issue is at least as old as the Greeks. As Meyer (1993) points out, the tension arises
because of what he calls the "unavoidable ambiguity" (*l'incontournable problématicité*) of practical
knowledge as against the need to arrive at a firm interpretation. The tension is expressed,
in the classical literature, as a distinction between logic and rhetoric—between certainty about
a few things and probability about many, between a narrow but controlled world and a broad
but open-ended one.

munication situation as the realization (and/or reflection) of an organization. It is that point, in other words, at which the organization is taken as a given, in the sense of assumed or established. It is equivalent to the denarrativization of communication: its reduction from the kind of Greimasian narrative model that we described in chapter 2 to the simpler ditransitive structure that has been the topic of this chapter. The reduction derives from the suppression of the polemic dimension of narrativity: the transposition of a diagentive into a uniagentive view of interaction, by means of which the organization is endowed with an intentionality and a personality.

How is this reduction, so essential to organizational stability and continuity, accomplished?

The Problematic of Coorientation

Consider again the issue of agency, within the context of the A-B-X system logic that we introduced in chapter 2.

Newcomb's idea was that "just as the observable forms of certain solids are macroscopic outcomes of molecular structure, so certain observable group properties are predetermined by the conditions and consequences of communicative acts" (1953, p. 132). (Where he uses the word "group" we substitute that of "organization.") Systemic stability assumes congruence between A's and B's orientation to X. The question then comes down to how congruence is maintained to produce a system that is, as he puts it, "at rest" (p. 135). If it is not, the resulting disequilibrium constitutes a pressure to change. But there is, we have just been arguing, nothing in communication that seems to guarantee congruence. The source of systemic stability and organizational continuity, in the face of the apparently unpredictable outcomes of unconstrained communication, must lie elsewhere.

Narrative theory provides a route to an answer. This theory assumes that any particular A-B-X configuration may be embedded within a larger structure where it figures as an X in a higher level A-B-X unit. The structuring principle is "fractal": units within units within units, each structurally isomorphic to the others, but embedded to form complex configurations in which the levels are linked by means–end articulations.

In the original *Star Wars* movie, for example, the initial step that propelled the story was the recruitment of Luke Skywalker. But Luke was incompetent to act until he had in turn mobilized the agency of the Force. In the end his capacity to act was explained by his recruitment of the effective agent, the Force itself.

Or take a more everyday event, let us say booking a room in a motel. The communicative transaction that is in direct focus involves you and a front desk clerk. But notice what happens. The clerk immediately turns to his or her computer. Now there are two principal/agent relationships in play: one involving you and the clerk, the other the clerk and the computer. But this, of course, is the tip of an iceberg of A-B-X relationships. The motel is a matrix of means–end relationships, involving clerks, managers, accountants, maintenance, cleaning staff, owners, investors, auditors, suppliers, state regulatory agencies, and so on. And you may well be an agent too: for a spouse and family waiting in the car, perhaps, or the company you represent. Most of those buried relationships are backgrounded in the transaction that is currently in focus, namely, that transaction linking you and the clerk, but in the absence of those relationships nothing would work, and there would be no institutional reality of a motel.

Here is the answer to the puzzle of how organization stabilizes in spite of the seemingly problematical outcomes of a conversational exchange involving individuals. Everybody is caught up in a web of agency relationships.

We have described elsewhere (J. R. Taylor et al., in press) this complex embedding of A-B-X units as a form of *tiling*, or *imbrication*. Our rationale is this. Organization becomes a necessity at the point where one agent (let us say you booking a motel room) is only capable of accessing a crucial resource (the motel room) by mobilizing the intervention of another agent (the motel clerk). The resulting interaction is a tile, but like tiled structures everywhere (roofs, the scales on a fish, the leaves of a tree), it is in turn supported by another tile, which in turn rests on another, and then another, until some lower level of elementary performance is attained, namely, in our example, a materiality of rooms, beds, facilities and services. The ultimate result is a kind of construction, composed of multiple A-B-X units, each of which expresses an instrumentality where one agent B has enlisted the assistance of another agent A in the accomplishment of some object, X. Some of those agents are human, many are not. The important consideration is that in their totality they constitute an infrastructure of routinized performances whose effect is to realize a predictable X-ness. Each constrains all the others to which it is linked. Because the tiles are really standardized A-B-X exchanges they tend to become invisible: just part of a taken-for-granted practical world where things one wants to happen do happen. They stop being thematic: no longer a matter to be resolved in communication. Instead they become a framework of agencies out of consciousness and certainly out of discursive awareness. People no longer concentrate on organizing but instead are enabled to preoccupy themselves with the mundane business of ordering supplies, billing customers, submitting travel expenses, manufacturing widgets, selling insurance, or whatever.

It is not that communication generates organization so much as that communication was organizational to begin with. And we are all agents of organization. It is the cycling back of the conversation onto itself, through the medium of the discourse it generates and the rearrangement of the material world such discourse enables, that makes organization both a frame and a construction and limits our freedom of movement in it.

This very tendency to routinization presents the toughest challenge to a researcher in organizational communication because, to the degree that an organization has been successfully tiled, it is by its own routineness rendered invisible, just infrastructure. Communication, authors such as Labov, Bruner, and Greimas insist, is initiated by a precipitating event, a breach, a breakdown of some kind; otherwise there is no theme, no semio-narrative basis of talk. Such a consideration led Garfinkel (1967) to engage in his famous "breaching experiments." Only in this way could he render the tacit infrastructure of out-of-consciousness assumptions supporting the day-to-day world of talk transparent to the investigator.

Most organizational researchers do not have the luxury of provoking artificial breakdowns as part of their research strategy. There is, however, an alternative: the study of organizational conflict. No organization ever becomes completely tiled. This was one of Newcomb's points: that A-B-X structures are not always congruent, and, when they are not, they introduce what he called "strains" (1953, p. 135). The reason is clear. Every princi-pal/agent relationship supposes rights and obligations on the part of both of those engaged (we come back to this theme in chapter 9). A breach occurs when one member of the pair is perceived by the other to have failed to respect the terms of the contract, or what Greimas called the "fiduciary engagement" that presides over their transactions. Given the binding power of tiled systems with multiple embedded A-B-X linkages, no single breach is likely to be sufficient to provoke organizational change. The conditions of change are created when many people sharing some sense of common fate are persuaded of the reality of a breach.

It is in this circumstance that the organization becomes visible to the researcher. And this brings us to our final question, once revealed, how it may be studied.

HOW TO LOOK: DISCOURSE DIMENSIONS

So now as researcher you confront an organization struggling with some internal incongruence in its A-B-X system that has become a theme of communication and thus is accessible to you to study precisely because it has become thematized in the discourse of organizational members. You wish to be sensitive to two dimensions of discourse: how the participants in their talk constitute an image of their organization, and how they, in the very process of interacting, are constituting the organization—reenact-ing it, perhaps in a new way. How do you go about your task?

Discourse and Representation:
Text-Worlds and Discourse-Worlds

Werth (1993) conceives of the discourse generated by an ongoing conversation as not just a sequence of isolated statements, each self-contained in meaning (a conventional linguistic approach) but as a unit of speech that has to be understood in relation to its context. The context is partly, but not uniquely, verbal. Nor is it merely the accumulation of previous interventions: it includes both the extralinguistic situation (the circumstances) and the knowledge of those taking part (frame knowledge). The already acquired knowledge base of those engaged in an ongoing conversation consists of "given" information which, to the extent that it may be considered part of the collective experience of the people involved, can be backgrounded, that is, assumed to be present, and taken for granted, even when it is not explicitly highlighted. People come to take this backgrounded knowledge as a given in their subsequent talk. If they did not, the conversation could not proceed in the normal way; it would be what Barwise and Perry (1983) call "inefficient."

A discourse is built up progressively. Each new intervention both relies on an already existing basis of common knowledge for its comprehension and introduces "new" information that may, depending on the processes of interactive negotiation that compose the conversation, then in turn be incorporated into the body of knowledge shared by participants. Such a shared, taken-for-granted body of knowledge Werth (1993) calls the "common ground" (or CG) of the conversation. Werth's common ground is thus very similar to what we have been calling frame knowledge, with the difference that it is restricted to that part of frame knowledge that is actively forefronted in the context of an exchange.[20]

A CG may be conceptualized, as Werth sees it, as being constructed from a universe of propositions that refer to (but do not necessarily describe) situations. Propositions are of two kinds, those that are already incorporated into the CG, and those that are not (they are, in other words, either given—backgrounded—or new—foregrounded). If not yet in the CG, they are candidates for inclusion. However, because no proposition is comprehensible in isolation, for propositions to be introduced into the CG they must already have notional links with other propositions that are there. The comprehensibility of the proposition depends on such links.

---

[20]The term *ground* is significant. Werth is arguing that language functions similarly to other processes of perception, in that it requires both a figure (on which our attention is centered) and a ground (which provides the contrast necessary to make the figure both stand out and be comprehensible). The specific feature of language is that language continuously operates to create both a figure and a ground, the figure being the focus of a statement, the ground that which frames it.

The usual way to think of such cross-propositional links, in sentence-based approaches, has been to consider the supporting platform on which the explicit proposition rests as its presuppositions (see Levinson, 1983, for extensive discussion). *Presuppositions* convey assumptions about such factors as the existence of the objects and people being referred to as well as knowledge of prior states and events. Werth argues for a different interpretation of what makes notional links. Rather than the linguistic construct of a presupposition, he proposes that we see them as being the relevant parts of the CG, that is to say, those unexpressed but present understandings that are necessary to make sense of what is being currently said. To try to explain them from within sentence-based linguistics, he thinks, leads to artificial complexity and a host of unnecessary arbitrary conventions.

The idea can be made clearer by an example. Suppose someone says *There's been an accident on Côte-des-Neiges.* One formal presupposition of this sentence, linguistically speaking, is that Côte-des-Neiges exists. But this is not very helpful, especially to someone who does not connect to the reference, let us say, someone from San Antonio, Texas. If this sentence is addressed to a Montrealer, on the other hand, it can be taken for granted that it is part of his or her common fund of knowledge (CG) that Côte-des-Neiges is a main artery of the city and that car accidents are not infrequent on it (including one famous one involving the then Premier of the province of Québec). The effect of the statement is simultaneously, then, to both communicate information (There's been an accident) and to evoke a situation in the mind of the hearer. Part of what is called up is explicit (on Côte-des-Neiges), thus physically placing the event described in people's minds, but much of it is implicit: a car accident (nobody said it was an automobile, but we somehow know it would be), on a main street leading to downtown (it was not explicitly specified that it was a street, certainly not a main street, and nothing was said about downtown but that also we know), accidents are frequent there (everybody in our society knows about where accidents tend to occur), and so on. The only new proposition is the "accident on Côte-des-Neiges" part; all the rest was already available as part of the CG, or given information, not as presuppositions, but as notional links.

Having now called up an image of a situation in the hearer's mind, a next statement (that would otherwise be ambiguous) is in turn made meaningful: *Fortunately, no one was hurt.* The statement *no one was hurt* is informational, but its full meaning depends on the context created by what went before. Each statement thus alters the perception of the situation and frames the following statement; it both conveys information and builds a framework of perception in the absence of which meaning becomes equivocal. We will not be surprised if the next thing we hear is *The two drivers got into a furious argument, and the police came.*

What he calls a discourse (and we call a conversation) may thus be defined as a fusion of a text and its relevant context (or CG). (This is very close to what we argued for in chap. 2: the mapping of one dimension, the lived, to another, the interpreted.) The context is grounded in the practices of the people exchanging the information (Halliday & Hasan, 1985/1989; Werth, 1993). Each speaker arrives in a conversation with a given knowledge base about the world in which he or she lives, and it is this that allows for the making of notional links with the propositions expressed in the unfolding discourse of the conversation.

Such contexts are not constant. All of these notional links constitute, at the start of the discourse, areas of potential relevance to the propositions of the text, and, as the text proceeds, some of these areas are activated by the text—they become salient—while others are deactivated. The context, as the role of the speaker alternates with that of listener, is thus being jointly negotiated by the people involved in the verbal exchange. The text (spoken or not) of discourse is constructed progressively.

Werth thinks of this process as the construction of a text-world, such text-building processes in turn supporting, and being supported by, a discourse-world (that of the participants to the ongoing talk, or what we call the conversation) within which the text-world is embedded. The discourse produces the text, but it is the text, endlessly renewed, that supplies the matter and frame for the discourse: the output is also an input.

It is important to clarify a point here. The text is treated by the people involved in discourse production as being *transparent*. That is to say, they react not to the text as an opaque web of linguistic tokens but rather to what it stands for, semantically and/or pragmatically. People react to what is being asserted about their common world. This is why Werth speaks not about the text, but about the text-world.

The task of the researcher is first to record the unfolding text, and second, to begin to reconstruct on its basis the mosaic of common knowledge informants have of their organization.

The concept of situation is central in this characterization. The world, for us, is made up of situations (Barwise, 1989; Barwise & Perry, 1983; Devlin, 1991). The text itself is composed of propositions that indexically refer to (without defining) the situations that constitute its ground, so that it is the situations and not the propositions that point to them that we react to. Such situations are characterized by a set of deictic terms: time, place, nominated entities, relationships with the speakers, and knowledge relating to all of these categories (Werth, 1993, p. 51). It is this highlighted set of circumstantial parameters (where, when, who, etc.) that Werth thinks of as constituting a text-world—a figural universe or "conceptual space" that frames, cognitively, the actual verbal output of participants and allows it to take on meaning. To make a meaningful statement, there has to be a world about which what is stated could be saying something because, otherwise, the statement would be vacuous—it would have no reference.

In summary, text-worlds evoke situations, which are "complex units made up of entities in relationships" (Werth, 1993).[21] Propositions both serve to situate speakers and listeners with respect to situations (this is given information), and convey new information about them. To be acceptable, the informational content of a communication has to be seen as coherent with features of the situation to which it refers. When it is accepted, the new information is transformed into given or old, and the situations are updated. It is in this way that text-worlds are constantly being built and modified. The researcher is in the position of trying to read these text-worlds.

Speech as Act

If text-worlds describe discourse-worlds, as Werth claims, it follows that the a priori forms of text must have an equivalent in the patterns of spoken discourse. And in fact one has been proposed. It is called a *speech act.*

As it was introduced by its original exponent (Austin, 1962), a speech act was conceived of as a performance.[22] As Austin pointed out, there is an entire class of acts that can be accomplished only through speech: such things as getting married, making a will, baptizing an infant or a boat, committing to a bet. Clearly these are acts that have real consequences. Equally clearly, they are acts that are uniquely mediated by the instrumentality of speech. They form, in fact, an important class of speech. Everything we included earlier under the category of a declarative falls under this

---

[21]Cf. Devlin (1991, pp. 30–34): "In *situation* theory, ... an agent's world divides up into a collection, or succession, of situations: situations encountered, situations referred to, situations about which information is received, and so on. That is to say, our theory reflects the fact that agents discriminate (by their behavior) situations. ... The agent individuates a situation *as a situation,* that is to say, as a structured part of Reality that it (the agent) somehow manages to pick out. ... *Real* situations are the 'parts of the world,' picked out by some individuation scheme; *abstract* situations are mathematical constructs built out of the relations, individuals, and locations of our ontology."

[22]Notions of speech as action can be found in the literature previous to Austin (B. Smith, 1990). Bühler's Sprachtheorie (1934/1990) identified functions of language other than representative (expressive, appelative). Récanati (1991) identifies Gardiner's (1932/1989) *The Theory of Speech and Language* as the real start of speech act theory. Nevertheless, most of the contemporary literature on speech acts takes the 1955 lectures as its reference point. Obviously, the ideas expressed there had been in development for a considerable time, and much of the same material can be found in earlier lectures delivered at Oxford and elsewhere in the early 1950s (Austin, 1970b; Caton, 1963). Some of the central concepts are adumbrated, for example, in Austin's essay "Other Minds" (1946/1970a). The Harvard lectures have, however, become the standard source. Our own interpretation of Austin's ideas is developed in greater depth in Taylor and Cooren (1997).

heading, from passing a judgment of "guilty" in court to making a call of "safe" in baseball.

Austin (1962, pp. 14–15) saw such a speech-mediated performance as conforming to a number of conditions:

- an accepted conventional procedure, defined by him as "the uttering of certain words by certain persons in certain circumstances";
- the appropriateness of the procedure to the context of the performance, in that the persons and circumstances should be understood to be the right ones for that procedure to be effective in that context;
- the correct and full execution of the procedure by all participants;
- the sincerity of all those involved, in that their intentions should be authentic.

It is not hard to see in this characterization the properties of a ditransitive construction. The term "the uttering of certain words" connotes a construction of language (with a theme) and the "certain persons, in certain circumstances" points toward an interrelating of agency roles of the kind found in a ditransitive. Like the ditransitive the structure of a performative speech act is that of a speaker-agent, addressing a remark to a hearer-recipient, where the object is an embedded sentence.

Austin's original characterization of a speech act targeted a limited (if not insignificant) class of verbal constructions (performatives), but in his subsequent elaboration of the theory, he was to argue for a much more radical view that claimed that every utterance of speech can be seen as an act. Consider R's introduction of Jeff: "Jeff why don't you take them through the model?" He did not say, in so many words, "Jeff, I instruct (or tell, or order, or command) you to take them through the model" but everyone in the room knew perfectly well that, given these persons in these circumstances, this was in fact what he was doing (especially since Jeff, as the targeted participant, obediently and promptly did as he was told). Furthermore, the members of the roundtable equally understood that what was then presented to them as a statement of the facts of the study was in fact a *telling*, a performance which engaged both the teller (R, and his delegate Jeff) and the told (themselves, as engaged participants). They had to take it seriously not so much because the recounting was, or was not, true, but because it was R, directly, and via an agent, (and, behind them both, R's department) who was telling them. Even a mere telling is thus an act that, as Austin pointed out, presupposes a "procedure designed for use by persons having certain thoughts or feelings" (e.g., R's). In the context of the roundtable this implied, if Austin was right, that R and his spokesman Jeff "must in fact have [had] those thoughts or feelings," and it further implied "the inauguration of certain consequential conduct on the participants' [his and his audience's] part." Otherwise the act would have been improperly performed, and would have been not merely infelicitous or unhappy, but sanctionable. It was not that R (and Jeff) were simply telling the participants in the roundtable something, but that they truly believed what they were saying and that they could be held to account for what they had said, if it should prove wrong and to have tangible consequences. The assumption of sincerity is thus a consequence, not a precondition, of the success of the act (Cooren & Taylor, 1997).

Austin's assertion that for a speech act to work the participants must be sincere is questionable (it has been criticized). But he was surely right in claiming that the "thoughts and feelings" of participants are engaged in the act of speaking. Edmondson (1981) we cited as saying that communication is about exchange not only from A to B but also reciprocally from B to A. Even the A-to-B transfer supposes not one but two acts, an offer and an acceptance (such acceptance having been designated by Austin an *uptake*). Part of the frame knowledge that goes into interpreting the illocutionary force of, and intention behind, an act of speech is the understanding of both speaker and listener as to the nature of the underlying mutuality of continuing obligations that frame their ongoing relationship, and their understanding of their respective roles. R knew he had contracted with Jeff for a certain service, and Jeff knew he had been hired to perform a service. Every other participant understood the relationship between R and Jeff, Jeff and themselves, and R and themselves, and their accepting (taking up) of R/Jeff's joint act of speech (the reported case study) was conditioned by that knowledge (it was accepted, and subsequently it figured as part of the discourse of the roundtable). The explicit illocutionary force of the act (Austin, 1962) never had to be stated; it was part of the common ground of the participants—part of their frame knowledge, not only relating to this situation but also to others like it, those involving principals and their agents, or administrative outsourcing and its rules.

The act of speech is not itself the exchange (although it is a transfer) but merely a part of it, so that the meaning of the transfer cannot be grasped in isolation from the two-way exchange in which it figures. Its meaning derives from what it, as a part of the exchange, points to, metonymically, that is, the mutuality of obligations of the participants and how the act fits—or fails to fit—into such an underlying set of contractual arrangements.[23]

---

[23]Later, in chapter 4, in the context of a discussion of what is known as the "Sociology of Translation," we will look into an implication of this metonymic property, namely that the material, or textual expression of an act-in-speech may effectively create a tissue of obligations, even in the physical absence of the actor.

Toward an Interpretive Research Strategy

One of the truly insightful investigations into the role of speech acts in a naturalistic context is that of Labov and Fanshel (1977), in a book that is now a classic of the literature on discourse analysis. Drawing on their reading of speech act theory and their understanding of the empirical literature on discourse analysis, they distinguish between two planes of conversational behavior: what is said and what is done (p. 71). If you want to understand why conversational sequences unfold as they do, they argue, it is more productive to assume that people react not to what is said, but to what is being done in the saying. The "saying" furnishes the text of the conversation, but the meaning of the text, although constrained by the constructional form it takes, is not intrinsic to the text as such. Its meaning, rather, is in the bearing it has on the relational economy it makes a contribution to—the underlying exchange system of interpersonal trans-actions. The two planes must thus be connected by what Labov and Fanshel (p. 71) call "rules of interpretation and production." The "sequencing rules" of discourse, they claim, are not rooted in the syntactic connections visible in the surface linguistic forms people employ in formulating their spoken interventions, but in the illocutionary force these forms index: "It is not the linguistic form of interrogative which demands the linguistic form declarative, but rather requests for action which demand responses— to be complied with, put off, or refused" (p. 70).

Jeff understood that principle very well, as did everyone else at the roundtable. He (and they) knew R's "Jeff why don't you . . ." was not the open invitation it superficially resembled, but a definite request for action, and he immediately complied.

The rationale for a certain shift in communication studies of organization toward an interpretivist approach since 1985 is well enunciated by Labov and Fanshel (1977): The act of communication implies by its very essence an interpretation. The meaning of communication lies not on the textual surface, to be measured objectively, but is rooted in the structure of rights, duties, and obligations that bind people together into permanent patterns of association and frame a discourse-world. It is those "patterns" that anchor the organization and extend it beyond the localized conversation. They orient the sequence of communication, and they are negotiated and renegotiated in communication. As Labov and Fanshel put it (p. 30): "[C]onversation is not a chain of utterances, but rather a matrix of utterances and actions bound together by a web of understandings and reactions."

How does a communication researcher look at discourse? He or she looks at the invisible but vital surface created by the translation from the text of the utterance into its actional meaning, textually interpreted. He or she assumes the constraining power of text form on the talking out of conversation to produce the actual conversation-text. He or she looks to the text-world for clues for the underlying organization of the discourse-world. He or she takes the ditransitive construction that organizes the act of speech as his or her starting point but he or she sees in it a token of a relational arrangement linking agents into a pattern of organization, necessarily characterized by the power of one agentive intentionality to command another, at least within the context of that exchange. He or she sees in the communicational exchange evidence of an organization that is confirming itself by the instantiation of object and role, yet is simultaneously asking for its own confirmation in the interactive dynamics of two interlinked agents, one offering, the other accepting, rejecting, or putting off.

There are different kinds of organizational objects. Requests for action are one. Having an account of how the world is accepted is another. Taking executive decisions and making them stick is still another. The point is that in the transacting of such objects, however accomplished, roles and agencies come into play, and because the exchange process is not just ditransitive (sender–receiver, in effect) but diagentive (proposer–accepter, giver–taker, teller–told), the playing out of the roles necessarily supposes frame knowledge as to the agencies involved and their respective rights, duties, and responsibilities with respect to each other—a moral, not a market, economy (Silverstone, 1994).[24] But the link from utterance to its actional meaning involves a step of interpretation and thus lends itself, in a fundamental way, to argumentation. The organization is not only established but also (potentially, at least) negotiable: It depends on how "common" the "ground" is. Cooren (1995; Cooren & Taylor, 1997, 1998) makes a convincing case that, in some circumstances (a parliamentary inquiry, in his example), certain objects are treated as procedural, whereas others are recognized as essentially rhetorical. Thus what may legitimately be argued may, in stable contexts, be itself subject to rule.

A last word on the positioning of the communication researcher. What is available for analysis is the spoken text, but if Labov and Fanshel, and other like-minded discourse researchers, are right, the text we should be concerned with is only partly spoken. That which is unspoken are the underlying decisional premises, or what they call "propositions." These are, even if unspoken, part of the organizational text, because it is their existence that makes possible the linking of text and discourse, words and their meaning, or as we prefer to say, text and conversation.

---

[24]Silverstone's concept of a moral economy is developed in relationship to family viewing of television, but it could apply equally well to any form of organization. As he sees it, how the members of a family work out their use patterns of household objects such as the television set reflects as much the configuring of their roles—their "moral economy"—as it does the pragmatics of use of the facilities in question.

Labov and Fanshel's answer to our "how" question is: keep looking until the pattern appears. Textual form is a surface of emergence of organization, not a recipe for its discovery. In chapter 9, we consider how their counsel might work out in an actual research situation.

CONCLUSION

To summarize, we claim that organization does not precede communication, nor is it produced by it (otherwise, we would have to assume that it could exist in the absence of communication, which is absurd). It emerges in it. Communication is produced as a conversation (in the multiple modes that we admit in our definition of the latter). It is experienced by participants as an ongoing discourse-world, constrained by conversational and textual form, that generates a recursively framed conversation-text, or text-world, in which a common ground is brought to bear and endlessly renewed. The organization being generated in that discourse-world is only recognizable when it is itself translated into a text-world. We assume that "translation" to be already part of what gives a discourse-world its coherence, in that the reading of its textual form is what participants must do to make sense of their own role as agents in a transactively driven set of exchanges. That which makes discourse interpretable as organization is its action character. The act quality of a verbal performance is explained ditransitively as the agentive investment of utterances in the transfer of attitude and intention from one participant to another through the mediation of an exchange of texted references to the world (that we could, in conventional language, call "messages"). But acts are not autonomous units: Their meaning comes from their position within a larger unit, which is that of the exchange. Exchange in turn supposes understanding of rights and obligations. It follows that all communication has a hermeneutic character, in that we are obliged to read from others' performances how their present action fits with respect to the implicit understanding of mutuality of rights and obligations that continues to frame our own action and theirs.'

The researcher is placed in the position of an interpreter of interpretations. He or she looks for the structure of acts in the conversation—its a priori forms—and, from the visible dynamic of exchange, tries to understand how the participants make sense of their world and, in so doing, realize organization. It remains to be seen, however, how the macroworld of organization, itself a site of many conversations, is constituted.

Chapter 4

Language as Technology and Agent

In this chapter we explore some of the ways that language, even as it serves as the medium of communication, also independently structures the latter's outcomes. We look at language as a technology that, as with many other technologies, is the end product of a long history of cultural development, resulting in its having its own built-in agencies, traces of yesterday's experience and learning. It is these built-in agencies that make it capable of shaping our purposes, as we shape its. If conversation and the circumstances in which it occurs take on meaning by being mapped to text then we are here concerned with what might be called the value added of the mapping, that is how the text not only translates, but defines, reality for us and thus simultaneously enables *and* constrains our interaction.

The chapter has two parts. In the first, we review a current theory that treats language as technology: the science of language-as-object, modern linguistics. In the second part, we consider what kind of agencies language may be incorporating and how it might thus mediate action.

Some readers may find the material of this chapter difficult because it introduces figures borrowed from linguistics. For those readers we suggest they turn immediately to chapter 5 since the investigation we undertake here is not essential to understanding the ideas developed there or in later parts of the book. Our purpose in this chapter is to explore the conceptual bases of the theory of coorientation we introduced in chapter 2, and some of its implications.

LANGUAGE AS TECHNOLOGY

In no other era has language attracted the intense scrutiny it has in the 20th century. It has, for example, been a prime concern of philosophy.[1] The quintessential scientific discipline of language, however, is not philosophy but linguistics.

Modern linguistics found its first persuasive advocate in the person of an obscure Swiss academic whom we mentioned briefly in chapter 1, Ferdinand de Saussure (1966; for discussion, see Hodge & Kress, 1988, chap. 2). He made a fateful cut-of-the-pie when he drew a distinction (in French) between language as *langue* and as *parole*. This is a dichotomy that requires a bit of explanation because the translation to English is not as obvious as it might at first appear to be. It is true that the word *langue* can be literally translated as "language," and *parole* as "speech." The problem is that French has two words for "language" (*langue* and *langage*) where English has only one. The French word *langage* expresses the general concept of language and is not limited to verbal expressions alone. As in English, it is possible to talk about the languages of architecture, of jazz, of politics, or even of love! The term *langue* has a more limited range, more like a language. English, for example, is a language—*une langue*. Arguably, it may even be two: British and American English, each with its own vocabulary and dictionary. (It may even be more than two, as occasional debates over the identity of African-American English—Ebonics—and Latin American English—Spanglish—and, in the late 1990s, Montreal English—would suggest.)

It is this identifiability of a language (as opposed to language in the more diffuse sense) that led de Saussure to propose that it can be treated as a system—a code—amenable to the procedures of scientific analysis fully as much as any physical object that is constructed of analyzable parts and their relations. Language, in this sense, can be taken out of its historical context of ongoing evolution, and treated, specimen-like, as a kind of cadaver to be dissected into its component symbolic elements.

Modern linguistics, ever since de Saussure, has taken its cue from the *langue/parole* distinction. Language is typically studied outside of not only its historical but also its social context, as an object whose internal mechanisms can be reconstructed analytically and turned into scientific knowledge. Speech—*parole*—is set aside, excluded from serious consideration, because it is too messy, too circumstantial to lend itself to systematic study. On the other hand, the language part—*langue*—has become an object to be scientifically scrutinized, precisely because it has been abstracted from its communicational context.

---

[1]Fogelin (1996, p. 39) describes it as "a century in which philosophers have been obsessed with problems concerning the nature of language."

NOAM CHOMSKY AND HIS SCHOOL

Beyond a doubt, the best known contemporary linguist is Noam Chomsky. His slim volume, *Syntactic Structures*, published in 1957, set the field of linguistics on its ear—an intellectual shock treatment followed up and elaborated on by his more substantial *Aspects of the Theory of Syntax* in 1965. Even those who oppose his ideas on how language works—how what we call *text* is produced and what kind of an object it is—have to take account of them, if only to point up what they think are limitations in his conceptualization. (Chomsky's way of studying language is far from shared unanimously among linguists. It is even highly controversial. The systemic-functional school, for example, including Halliday, 1996, and Stubbs, 1996, argues we should always begin with the uses of language, before considering its structures; more on their point of view later in the chapter.)

If we were to take Chomsky literally, communication would essentially be wished out of existence. What makes communication work in the first place, the dialogic of conversation and text, is, with de Saussure, declared ultra vires, or evidence not admissible within the Supreme Court of Science—making communication a maverick of the human sciences. Chomsky has not merely maintained but accentuated that tendency. Of all de Saussure's successors, none has been more rigorous (some might say dogmatic) in his exclusion of any consideration of the communicational contexts of the use of language (Stubbs, 1996, documents Chomsky's aversion to data based on actually spoken, as opposed to made-up, sentences). It is hardly an exaggeration to characterize him as being on a single-minded mission to demonstrate, beyond reasonable doubt, that language is, at its root, a universal competence, physically wired into the human brain from birth as an essential part of our cognitive capacity, and that there is, under the apparent heterogeneity of the many tongues spoken by humankind, one basic universal language—one tune played with variations, or in his jargon, one set of "principles" modulated by "parameters."

In this picture, communication figures not at all. Chomsky is in search of the single unvarying original pattern of language, not its situated variability in the production of human society. He searches for its biological foundations, not its sociological employments (de Saussure thought of his new semiological discipline as a branch of psychology). In the age of cybernetics—Chomsky's age—the link is with cognitive psychology and artificial intelligence. They assume, as he does, that the structures of language mirror the structures of the brain. What people do with language is no part of the picture.

A restricted view of language is thus inherent in the linguistics project we are describing. Yet, as it turns out, the Chomskian version of linguistics is exactly the point of departure we are seeking, precisely because of its stubborn rejection of the intersubjective role of language. His eye is focused

on the objective properties of language, and that is what we have been
looking for: that which makes language, to cite Dawkins (1976/1989), a
"replicator" or carrier of social conventions and practices from one conversation to another.

The structuralist movement that de Saussure launched was conditioned
on the choice of object to be analyzed. It placed the emphasis of linguistics
on the sentence (a choice Chomsky has respected) as opposed to other
structures of speech. It is true that the sentence is a self-contained entity
that lends itself to study, similar, perhaps, to the way the cell does in
biology. Its internal complexity turns out, furthermore, to rival, if not
exceed, that of the cell. It easily justifies the formation of a scientific
discipline. Sentences, however, are not really self-contained entities at all
(any more than the cell). They typically are constituent elements in larger,
narratively based ideational structures, in which they contribute functionally to the attainment of a textual objective of getting an idea across (somewhat as, we hope, this sentence is doing). The classical study of language
dating from Aristotle had a wider scope, taking the form of a tripos that
included logic, rhetoric, and poetics. Rhetoric and poetics are concerned
with textual structures larger than the sentence; logic is more tightly tied
to the sentence.

Modern linguistics focused our attention on the logic of sentence construction and turned it away from the role of sentences in more extensive
textual constructions such as arguments, stories, and explanations. Linguistics thus gave a special and restricted meaning to the word *text*. Nevertheless, in spite of these reservations, there are important lessons to be
learned from Chomsky's version of language study, as we hope to show,
precisely because he treats it as object.

What marks Chomsky's approach as special, and why it was thought to
be revolutionary, is that it is computational. Computationism is of course
not unique to linguistics; by no means coincidentally, it was at almost
exactly the same time as Chomsky was proposing his new approach to his
colleagues in linguistics that the computational way of thinking was also
coming into favor in management sciences as a way to model human
organization (March & Simon's *Organizations*, which we look at in chap.
6, appeared the year after Chomsky's *Syntactic Structures*).

The theory of computation did not originate with Chomsky (although
he did make notable contributions to it in the 1950s). It got its contemporary formulation in the 1930s as a solution to a logical problem in
mathematics (Turing, 1936). It gained popular recognition with the construction in 1946 of the first all-purpose digital computer (which is, as its
name suggests, just a special kind of computing, or applied logic, machine).
Chomsky's triumph was in showing, by exploiting what is called in computer

sciences an *algorithm*, how to look at language in a new way, that is, as a system that could be computationally generated and transformed.[2]

Phase 1: The Generative-Transformational

Initially, Chomsky built on the standard practice of the descriptive linguistics that preceded him, whose tool of analysis was the parsing of a sentence (known as constituent analysis). To *parse* a sentence means to break it down, progressively, into the simpler units of which it is composed. Consider the sentence *Mary had a little lamb.* It combines two main parts, an actor ("Mary") and an action or condition ("had a little lamb").[3] So we could, using traditional terminology, call "Mary" the subject of the sentence and "had a little lamb" the predicate. We would thus have broken the sentence down into two parts that we can illustrate, using brackets, as [[*Mary*][*had a little lamb*]]. The predicate, however, now lends itself in turn to a finer analysis as composed of a verb ("had") and a direct object ("a little lamb"). Using even more brackets, we write [[*Mary*][[*had*][*a little lamb*]]]. In turn the phrase "a little lamb" consists of an article "a" (called a determiner in linguistics) and a noun phrase "little lamb." So the parsing continues: [[*Mary*][[*had*][[*a*][*little lamb*]]]]. Finally, "little lamb" can be broken down into its components, an adjective "little" and a noun "lamb," yielding as a final outcome of the parsing [[*Mary*][[*had*][[*a*][[*little*][*lamb*]]]]].

We can think of the result as a sort of embedding hierarchy of Russian dolls:

SENTENCE: (*Mary had a little lamb*)
  NOUN (Subject): (*Mary*)
  VERB PHRASE (Predicate): (*had a little lamb*)
    VERB: (*had*)
    NOUN PHRASE (Direct object): (*a little lamb*)
      DETERMINER: (*a*)
      NOUN PHRASE: (*little lamb*)
        ADJECTIVE: (*little*)
        NOUN: (*lamb*)

---

[2]An *algorithm* is an elementary procedure or routine that performs one well-defined operation. It can be called on repeatedly, in the context of a program, to perform a simple task, always in the same way but on different objects, and thus contribute to the progressive building of a more complex and ambitious computation. It is the ideal analytic device for turning complex problems into doable operations.

[3]Note the link with our earlier discussion of the ditransitive construction.

Chomsky's innovation was in picturing the parsing process in a new way. He saw it not as an analysis done by a professional linguist (or the ordinary grade school student in the days before teaching grammar was dropped from the curriculum), but as an operation susceptible to being programmed and even, eventually, run on a machine (which might be, some in artificial intelligence believe, the human brain, so that a principled explanation of parsing would then turn into a theory of the competence people possess that allows them to use language in the first place). To accomplish this goal, Chomsky reasoned, all you would have to do is write a separate procedure—an algorithm—for each of the individual steps we have just described. He did this by setting out what he called "rewrite rules," such as (glossing over the technicalities and the terminological novelties he introduced) "rewrite sentence as noun phrase (subject) followed by verb phrase (predicate)," "rewrite verb phrase (predicate) as verb followed by noun phrase (direct object)," or "rewrite noun phrase as determiner followed by a noun."(What we call "followed by" is an operation known in linguistics as *concatenation*.) The final step is to rewrite the abstract categories of noun, verb, determiner, and adjective by words drawn from a lexicon, such as *Mary, lamb, had, a,* and *little*. When the rewrite task has been completed, the result will be a "tree" such as illustrated in Fig. 4.1.

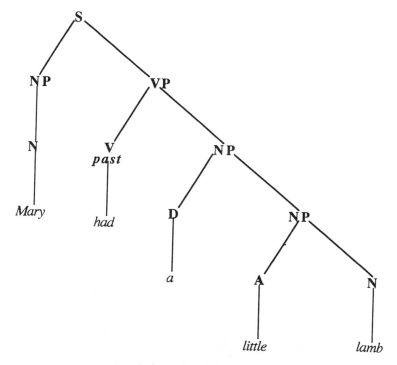

FIG. 4.1. A typical tree description of a simple sentence.

You can confirm yourself that each of the branches of the tree corresponds to one of the sets of brackets, or steps of hierarchical level, that we showed in our initial analysis. The advantage is that the tree makes it easier to visualize the underlying structure of the sentence. It displays in a new way the structural relation (Chomsky called it *syntactic*) linking *Mary* to *had* to *a little lamb*. (It also meant Chomsky could discard the conventional terminology of subject, predicate, direct object, and indirect object, because the relational patterns they were meant to make salient are instantly visible in the tree representation of the structure of the sentence.) A new insight into the nature of language had been gained.

The set of all such structures now becomes thought of as the base of a language. Chomsky astutely observed in 1957 that, using only a few rewrite rules, an infinite number of sentences can be produced. This explained a feature of the language facility and of how it might be learned that no one had previously been able to do, that is, its extraordinary productivity and the rapidity of its acquisition at a very young age in spite of its daunting technical complexity. Because such elementary structures or trees are very similar to the structures generated by modern formal logic (and remember that it was the formal logic of mathematics that gave rise to the idea of a computer in the first place), logicians, as well as linguists, began to enroll in the movement. (The pattern is one that is quite familiar to sociologists of scientific knowledge. Chomsky had become what Callon, 1986, and Latour, 1987, call an "obligatory passage point" for specialists in linguistic analysis—a view that might be contested, but not ignored.)

Chomsky now took a second step. His dissertation advisor, Zellig Harris (1963, 1965), had earlier written on the intuitively evident link between sentences such as *Marshall has taken out a life insurance policy* and *A life insurance policy has been taken out by Marshall*, or *You borrowed my copy of the Odyssey, didn't you?* and *Did you borrow my copy of the Odyssey?* in which one sentence seems to differ from the other by no more than what Harris called a *transformation.* Once again, Chomsky incorporated this intuition into his theory by restating it in terms of elementary operations such as deletion, substitution, inverting the order of components, and so on. From *Mary had a little lamb* we derive *Mary's little lamb, The little lamb that Mary had* (or a bit more subtle, *The little lamb that was owned by Mary*), *Whose little lamb was that, Mary's?*, and ditransitive "cousins" (like those in chap. 2 & 3) such as *Give Mary back her little lamb.*[4] Chomsky had been able to demonstrate how one sentence could be progressively (algorithmically) changed

---

[4]Of course, if you took the whole nursery rhyme into consideration ("Mary had a little lamb; His fleece was white as snow; And everywhere that Mary went; that lamb was sure to go"), even more transformational possibilities open up, such as "The lamb that followed Mary wherever she went" and so on.

into the other by the application of discrete rules, a bit like the visual trick you sometimes see in newspapers where an artist makes a well-known face (such as Bill Clinton's) seem to turn little by little into another (such as Teddy Roosevelt's) to make an editorial point.

This transformational apparatus became, for Chomsky, a component of his theory of language—or grammar—distinct from the generative mechanism we have described and allowed him to postulate two levels of language: the *base* (close to elementary logic, and thus where the meaning of the sentence could be read off), and the *surface* (composed of those structures that would be recognizable, when enunciated in speech, as the sentences of a living language).

Chomsky transformed more than the theory of language; he altered the discipline sociologically. From a profession dedicated in principle to collecting and analyzing the languages spoken in naturalistic contexts, on the model of botany, he turned it into a discipline of quasi-computer scientists, writing ingenious scripts, or proto-algorithms, to explain the possible dynamics of a theoretically justified transformational grammar: the kinds of transformations that could be shown to have empirical grounds and the order in which they should be applied. And in the process, he installed an ideology: language as computation.

Phase 2: The X-bar Hypothesis

The difficulty with an exercise of ingenuity on this scale soon became evident. The transformational rules necessary to explain a phenomenon as complex as language, with its unlimited ways of saying things, multiplied like rabbits in a pea patch. But it is not very plausible to believe that language can be as quickly and easily acquired as it is at an early age, even by people of otherwise limited intelligence, if they had to figure out and memorize a plethora of rules that nobody else in their growing-up environment could possibly have taught them (unless their parents were professional linguists—and even they had their doubts!). Disenchantment with the rules view grew. There must be a simpler explanation. After 1970, Chomsky and others began to explore what is called the "X-bar hypothesis."[5]

The intuition on which the X-bar hypothesis is based is this. Tree structures, such as that illustrated in Fig. 4.1, are not just randomly branching, as one idea after another is incorporated into the sentence (by adding

---

[5]The transition is marked by a paper Chomsky published in 1972 (but which had been circulating since 1967) defending what was called the "lexicalist hypothesis" (see Jackendoff, 1977, for discussion). Later in this chapter we offer a (very) abbreviated version of the lexicalist hypothesis.

qualifying clauses, for example, *Mary, the girl with the strawberry curl, had a little lamb, that had been given to her by her uncle*). They are compositions of varying complexity, "Lego-constructed," you might say, step by step, by the putting together of parts based on one elementary pattern, the planks out of which the whole scaffolding of the sentence is built up, to shift the metaphor. *The girl with the strawberry curl* and *had been given to her by her uncle* must be mirror images of *Mary had a little lamb* in the way they are, in turn, constructed internally, with one structure neatly fitting, or embedding, into the other. Otherwise, they will not be syntactically acceptable.

This basic building element of all sentences has the following hypothetical properties. There must be a single *head*. A head might be a noun, a verb, an adjective, a preposition, or a more abstract element such as an inflection that marks agreement, tense, or mood (we come back to that latter idea later in the chapter). Consider the simple sentence we have just been analyzing. "Lamb" is a head (a noun), "have" is a head (a verb), "Mary" is a head (a noun), and finally the past tense is a head (an inflection of the verb that changes it from *have* to *had*).

Heads, however, as the term connotes, must be heads of something. The head (let us say "lamb") becomes a head by having a complement adjoined to it ("little," in the example, is an adjective adjoined to the noun "lamb"). The result is a phrase, which may be, as here, a noun phrase (NP): "little lamb." If the head were a verb, the complement would be a verb phrase (VP): "had" [head] "a little lamb" [complement]. (The direction of the adjoining is irrelevant. In some languages, such as English, when the complement of a noun is an adjective, it comes before the noun; in others, such as French or Spanish, it generally, but not always, comes after. Similarly, in German, unlike in English, the past participle of the verb usually follows the direct object.)

A second adjunction has a different purpose: to specify which or who (otherwise the phrase "had . . . little lamb" would have no definite reference). In our example, "little lamb" is specified as *a* (but it could have been *the, that,* or *every*). The "little" in a "little lamb" is called a *complement,* the "a" a *specifier.* The result is a new noun phrase *a little lamb* that has within it, embedded, the noun phrase *little lamb,* that has in turn within it the head noun *lamb,* the whole being specified by the determiner *a* (Fig. 4.2).

According to the X-bar hypothesis, it is the resulting three-level phrase that constitutes the basic building block of a sentence grammar, not just for English, but for every language. The same structure that we have illustrated for verbs, prepositions, adjectives, or for inflections such as tense and agreement, works for the sentence as a whole! The "X" in X-bar covers all these possibilities. This is a principle that is invariant across languages; how such elementary patterns are put together to form a particular sen-

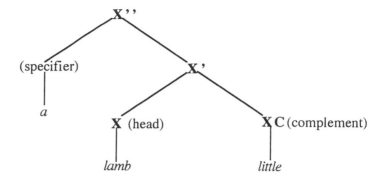

FIG. 4.2. An elementary X-bar configuration.

tence, in a particular language, is determined by the local rules of combination, or *parameters* (putting the adjective before the noun, as opposed to after, is just one instance of the operation of such a parameter).[6]

The three-level structure is still present, even when there is no surface evidence in the spoken sentence for it. Take "Mary" in our example. There is no visible complement (unless we were to add *the girl with the strawberry curl*) but there could be, so there is a slot for it, even if it is unfilled. Similarly, there is no specifier (such as *that* with "Mary") and no need for it in the case of a proper name, which already specifies the person in question, unless there is a cause for ambiguity (two Marys might have been mentioned in the preceding conversation, for example).

Sentences are built by fitting together, in a hierarchical (or tree) structure, several such elementary patterns in which what is head at one level is a component of the complement at the next higher. The verb *have* must take a complement and does so in our example (Fig. 4.3). The verb phrase formed by the adjoining of the noun phrase *a little lamb* to the verb *have* is now specified in its turn by tense—the past tense in our example (this is designated as **I**, for inflection). This adjunction triggers an intervening step (that in the interest of simplicity we glide over) that assures the agreement of the verb and thus changes *have* to *had*. Finally, the inflected verb phrase is in turn specified by the adjunction of *Mary* to produce the complete sentence. The highest node in the structure is **I**, and so this is equivalent to the sentence itself. (Just why inflection should be the topmost node is a question we return to shortly.)

---

[6]The term *X-bar* is used because the same principle applies for nouns, verbs, prepositions, etc. (therefore, "X" rather than "N" or "V" or "P"; the "bar" is used to designate level: X^0 is a head, X′ (i.e., X single-bar) its immediately superior noun phrase, and X″ (i.e., X double-bar) its eventual root, or "maximal projection."

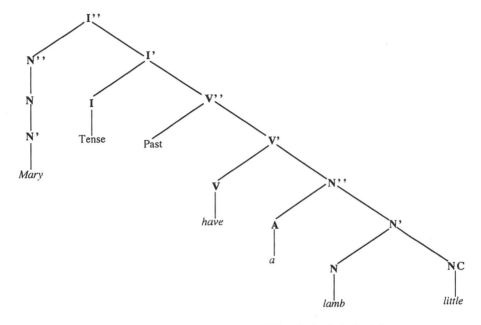

FIG. 4.3. The X-bar structure of "Mary had a little lamb."

It is this internal hierarchical complexity of even the simplest of sentences that has led Chomskian linguists to argue that, because in the speaking of a sentence one word follows another sequentially even though its syntactic structure is logically hierarchical, there must be a lot of (unconscious) internal processing going on in the brain in parallel with the enunciation of the sentence; otherwise, more spoken sentences would be ungrammatical than is actually the case. It is the necessity for that subconscious internal processing that leads members of this school to assume an inborn natural capacity for language.

The significant implication of all this is that the production of even the simplest of texts (sentences) is structuring our image of the world in nonaccidental and nonobvious ways. The heads in the simple three-level phrases we have been describing come out of a *lexicon*—the store of words we have at our disposal as the speakers of a language—with conditions attached as to what kind of constructions they can figure in. A *lamb* can have the adjective *little* adjoined to it but not the adjective *intrinsic*, to take but just one example. Similarly, if the sentence were to read *Mary ate a little lamb*, it would not be the same lamb: It would more likely be cooked and served with mint sauce than it would be gamboling about chasing after her. It would no longer be a "little" (i.e., small) lamb, but a "little bit of" lamb. So lamb is really two words. Coming out of the lexicon, each word projects to its eventual sentence environment certain conditions: A*live* lamb can be "had" (in the sense of "owned") but not eaten (unless by mosquitoes). Similarly, only someone like a "Mary" is allowed, grammatically, to "have a little lamb."[7]

Phase 3: The Minimalist Program

Chomsky (1993, 1995) in the 1990s is proposing what he calls a "minimalist program." Rather than analyze a sentence into its parts, his new approach constructs, synthetically, a whole out of parts by the successive adjunction of one element after another to form increasingly complex structures, through very simple operations that are called *merge* and *move*. The construction logic is no longer top down, as it was at the beginning, but bottom up.[8]

One effect of this change of perspective (that we do not attempt to present in detail) is to put even greater emphasis on what is called *projection*. As long as the analytic approach was top down, the sentence structure appeared to precede the selection of items from the lexicon. Suppose you had a partially completed sentence structure, *Mary had a little. . . .* The ". . ." indicates a slot to be filled, with certain restrictions imposed by the overarching structure of the already mostly completed sentence: Only a noun will do (and there are even conditions for which kind of noun, which we ignore in the interest of simplicity). So now when the procedure turns to the lexicon of available words—its building materials—it starts with a shopping list and is selective. This is (approximately) what Chomsky presented in 1965 as rules of selection and subcategorization.

When you go bottom up in your imaginary reconstruction of how language works, you have to proceed differently. If you have started with *have*, and if, to cite Abraham, Epstein, Thráinsson, and Zwart (1996, p. 28), "we want to integrate a head, say V, into a syntactic structure, we need to combine it with something, its complement, say DP [for DP read Noun Phrase], and the combination of V and DP yields a new syntactic object, V'," then, they are saying, the term *have* is already projecting outwards and upwards an environment for itself, that is, something that can be had (a complement), a *little lamb*, for example, and somebody who can have it (a

---

[7]We only have one word in English for *lamb* as farm animal, and *lamb* as meat, but we do have two for other animals: *sheep* versus *mutton, calf* versus *veal, pig* versus *pork,* or *cow* versus *beef,* for example (*sheep, calf, pig,* and *cow* are Anglo-Saxon in origin; *mutton, veal, pork,* and *beef* Latin, via Old French, which tells you something about the status system of post-Norman conquest England).

[8]There is a seeming parallel between this shift of tactic from top down to bottom up with the move in artificial intelligence (and cognitive science generally) to what is called parallel processing or distributed intelligence. In chapter 6, we delve into the reasons for this change and its implications for organizational theory.

specifier), that is, a *Mary* (these are called the internal and external environments of *have*, respectively).

The words in the lexicon now appear not so much like inert pieces in a Lego set but more as one of those do-it-yourself assembly toys—instructions included—that you have been unfortunate enough to think you could put together on a family holiday eve to be ready for your kid the next day. Chomsky and his colleagues, in other words, in their quest to simplify the syntactical operations of sentence-formation (merge, move) to the point where it is arguably an approximation to a culture-free grammar of universal language, have had to push more and more of what is specific to any one particular language into the lexicon. The result is that words are no longer just a bundle of synonyms, as the dictionary treats them; they come carrying, in immanence, the shadow of the set of sentence environments in which they will eventually be found.[9]

A Controversial Illustration of Head-ness

To see an implication of this innovation for our purposes, consider an analogy. Take the notion of *husband*. Let us write "husband," in the spirit of formalism, as H^0. Husband is now conceived as a head. To this initial head, let us adjoin a complement, *wife*, which we will call HP. (After all, husbands are not husbands in a vacuum; they become husbands at the same moment that wives become wives.) In everyday parlance, the new node, H', just formed, is a couple. The husband/wife couple is still, however, merely conceptual; to make any kind of definite statement about them we would have to specify which couple, so we add a specifier, to produce the familiar three-level logical construction postulated by X-bar theory (Fig. 4.4). This is now recognizable as a traditional nuclear family, that we show as H'' (i.e., H with two bars).

One of Chomsky's (1995) assumptions is that when one potential head (let us say *wife*) is "adjoined" to another (let us say *husband*) only the latter—the one to which something has been adjoined—"projects its features" (p. 243f, p. 256f). A different way of saying this is that there can only be one head in a nominal, verbal, prepositional, or adverbal phrase. To apply Chomsky's logic in this new context, in many traditional societies it is the husband's name that gets "projected," not the wife's, to take for purposes of illustration only one feature of people who enter into marriage.

---

[9]Although it is not part of our chronicle, we note the development in generative linguistics of studies into the link between syntax (structural patterning of sentences) and morphology (the underlying structures of word formation). These include Halle (1973), Kiparsky (1982), and Bresnan (1976). The concept of a Head-Driven Phrase Structure Grammar is defended in Pollard and Sag (1987).

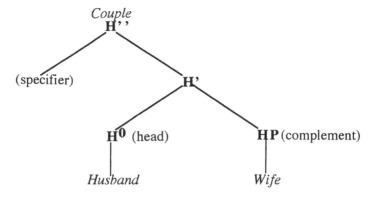

FIG. 4.4. The family conceived of as an X-bar configuration.

The force of the idea now begins to be evident. It is well known that patriarchal and matriarchal cultural systems differ from each other precisely in how such key features as family name get projected (inscribed in the form of the traditional marriage vows: "cherish" vs. "obey"). In a matriarchal society, it is the name of the wife that is projected to the combination consisting of the couple, and the husband is thus conceived to be adjoined to the wife and not the contrary. Western societies are patriarchal. Many others are matriarchal. In some societies, the feature being projected is the locality of the residence. If patrilocal, the couple locates in the vicinity of the husband, if matrilocal, that of the wife. Occidental patterns of localization seem to be less regular than naming: Sometimes the new couple locates close to one branch, sometimes the other.

It would be easy to elaborate on the illustration. Suppose the couple has a child. A further merge and move produces a new node—let us name it FP—that we would interpret, by the adjoining of the infant, as a family-with-children. The feature of name is projected to the new node, and the infant takes the head's name (as well as residence). As brothers and sisters are added and as children in their turn have children, what started as a simple merge in which one head was adjoined to another to create a root turns into a complex, many-branched structure—one that anthropologists have studied across the world's societies under the rubric of *kinship systems.* As they did, they discovered that such systems are quite regular within a society (although probably never totally homogeneous) and vary widely across societies. Some societies have arranged marriages; others (such as ours) do not. Some societies tolerate, and even encourage, polygamy; others (such as ours) forbid it. And so on. The force of Chomsky's view is striking. Family formation may be based on an elementary principle with a biological imperative lurking in the background, but the parameters are highly variable and the resulting patterns are a kaleidoscope in their mixtures of patterns.

A society-specific patterning is already inscribed in the meaning of words such as *husband* and *wife* for the people in a given society. A dictionary may give definitions of *husband* and *wife* such as "a man who is married" and "a married woman" (Webster's New World Dictionary), but the pragmatic and semantic projections of such words are also part of our collective common ground of frame knowledge. If it is true that words such as *husband* and *wife* come out of the lexicon with an assemble-it-yourself toolkit of instructions as to how they can be used in constructing a grammatically correct sentence, then the implications are not merely syntactical. In present-day North American society, talk about a wife being "adjoined" to a husband, and a husband "projecting his features to the couple" should be accompanied by a friendly smile, pardner. Those terms are loaded. They may be just words, but they translate into real social consequences. It is why some women decline to give up their names when they marry, so as not to abandon head status. At our university, women are automatically identified and registered under their original family name. Whether a same-sex couple is a "couple," is, as everyone knows, a matter of debate, especially when it comes down to whether they should have a right to be parents or to become eligible for each other's entitlements (such as a pension). Language is much more than a verbal support to interaction; it has built into it a whole ideology of what adjoins to what, and what projects to what, that can be felt as not just syntactical/semantic, but societal, structure. It is no wonder that the language of organization can be experienced as a psychic prison (Morgan, 1986).[10]

⟨ Words such as *manager* and *employee*, for example, are the visible tips of icebergs of meaning—a meaning that Chomsky's theory does a good deal to explain, because the meaning is not some static list of qualities associated with the word, but a potential for figuring in structures of interaction that

---

[10]The *New York Times Magazine* of February 2, 1997 (McPhee, 1997, p. 68), included a recollection by a woman of attending a dinner party in Florence, Italy, in the company of her husband, who was a native of that city. In the course of conversation, it came out that her recently born son's last name would be McPhee (*her* family name, not that of her husband). This announcement left the room speechless (but not for long). Her Italian relatives were scandalized, and said so bluntly; they made no attempt to hide their chagrin. She writes: "I have been asked the same question, in milder tones, many times since that evening, and I am still not sure how to answer it. What I do know is that every time I am asked why I gave my son my name, my gut response is deep embarrassment. . . . For a man, passing on his name is expected, traditional, unnoteworthy. For a woman to do so is a radical act, a gesture of defiance, an invitation to attack. It is also illegal for a woman to pass on her name without a court order in some countries, like Italy. Even here, as recently as 1996, a judge in Missouri ordered a divorced woman and her son to use the father's surname. Another judge justified a similar rule, saying, 'It's a philosophical matter.' "

Actually, less philosophical than philological! It probably seemed to them, whether they knew it or not, to go against a structural principle of language.

can only be built and rebuilt using the word as the building material—proteins of meaning, you could say. Managers go to meetings, have secretaries and executive washrooms; employees do not (yet managers are, in reality, employees too!). When Boden (as described in chap. 1) describes the common ground of management-in-interaction, she emphasizes its information seeking and staying up to date. It is keeping ahead of the blur. But the kind of common ground we have just been describing is well below the surface of everyday consciousness—part of how we structure the universe—and is not susceptible to much change in the short term.

Sentences, Chomsky thinks, are constructed on pretty much the same principle as kinship systems, and they are even more complicated! Or wait, maybe we have that backward. Are kinship systems perhaps constructed on the same principle as sentences?

Meaning in Generative Linguistics

The goal of Chomskian linguists is to construct the syntactic architecture of sentences—the structural framework of the spoken sentence. They recognize two constraints on the operation of the syntax. The products of such a syntax must be phonologically acceptable (they have to sound like real sentences when they are uttered) and they must be logically acceptable (they have to mean something). To be *logically acceptable* means having an interpretable argument structure such as we described in chapters 2 and 3.

To recall briefly what we said there, the verb is the linchpin in reading the meaning of a sentence. It is the verb that creates the links joining the several elements of a sentence. Verbs are distinguished from each other by the kinds of link they make. Suppose you say (in a game of bridge, for example) "I pass." There is only one link, from the action of passing to the person ("I") doing the passing. But now if, over supper, you say "Would you pass me the butter, please?" there are three links indicated: what is to be passed ("the butter"), to whom it is to be passed ("me"), and the passer (not stated, but understood as the person to whom the request is addressed, or "you"). It may seem like the same verb, *pass*, but it is doing a different job and is thus two verbs, not one.

The way this is explained in linguistics is to say that a verb *subcategorizes* for a fixed number of arguments. The verb, you might say, comes with a certain number of ready-made slots that must be filled (they are obligatory) and others that may be filled or not (they are optional). These are part of the projection of the verb. The first of these slots, or arguments, is always obligatory: *agent*. In the same way that every sentence must have a subject to be grammatically well formed, so every action and state must have, logically, an agency. How could a little lamb be "had" if somebody did not have it?

Two other arguments figure frequently in verbal constructions (we encountered this idea before in chap. 3 but it bears repeating in this new context). The direct object of a verb, syntactically speaking, is semantically the focus of an action—that to which the acting is directed—and it is known technically in linguistics as a *patient* (also referred to as a *theme*). Any sentence whose verb subcategorizes for both an agent and a patient is called *transitive*: The link is from a doer to a done-to. A third argument that may be obligatory, for certain verbs, is called the *goal* or the *recipient* or *dative* (the construction described in our earlier discussion of ditransitivity); its syntactic equivalent is an indirect object.[11] Other arguments that a verb may subcategorize for, usually optionally, include the *beneficiary* (for whom the act is done), the *source* (from whom the object was taken), the *time* (when the act occurred or a state of affairs existed), the *location* (where the action occurred or the object was located), and the *instrument* (how, or by what means, the agent produced the action).

The complete picture of such thematic roles (as they are also called) is termed an *argument structure*. A remarkable feature is that it seems to be a constant across all languages. As Bickerton (1990, pp. 66–67) observes: "When we learn a foreign language, initially we make all kinds of mistakes. . . . In only one area do we never make mistakes, indeed our success is so complete we probably never realize how effortlessly we are 'learning.' That area is argument structure." Everybody starts with the same basic set of meaning categories, Bickerton thinks; they are universal.

AGENTIVE PROPERTIES OF LANGUAGE AND TEXT

We now come to the second of the topics we announced at the beginning of the chapter, how language mediates the act of speaking. Language is a medium. It works by the generation of a text that, after being enunciated in speech or written, becomes the instrumentality by means of which one actor can influence another. It is a crossover between subjective and objective worlds—actors and their texts—that depends for its communicative effect on the generation of a hybrid agent or actant. It is hybrid in the sense that it is both subjective (in that it speaks for us) and objective (reflecting the properties of the medium, language). It is significant that texts are both symbolic (subjectively invested with meaning) and material (an inscription in some physical base that renders them trans-scribable, that is, not bounded by the same constraints of time and space as the

---

[11]In current theory, categories such as *direct object* and *indirect object* are subsumed under a more general theory of *case*. Once again, we flag the nuance without further explanation, in the interest of keeping our discussion to its essentials.

conversation in which they were initiated. If language, in its guise as text, is part of the objective or material world, a surface for us to move on and in, then it must, when it is realized in conversation, be more than instrument: It must bring its own properties of action with it. Those properties are our topic in this chapter.

Because Chomsky is indifferent to the contexts of use of language, we need now to turn to a different tradition, that of systemic-functional grammar (Halliday, 1985) and the work it has inspired in sociological research (Hodge & Kress, 1993). Here we reconsider the ideational function of an utterance from the perspective of its agentive role in speaking: what we call its epistemic effect. What is of central concern to us is how, in the expression of someone's ideas, the object that is language comes to mediate the exchange process and to produce a "spoken"—a text—that has hybrid properties: that is us but also not quite us.

The interpretation of a sentence—how we read its meaning—involves mapping one set of structures, the syntactic (the kind we described in our discussion of the X-bar hypothesis) to another, the argument structure. It is the reverse path to speaking. We formulate sentences to convey our meaning, and we read the meaning of those we hear; that is why speech is a technical achievement. How that mapping is done, however, has many degrees of freedom. It is what turns "ideational" into "ideological" (Hodge & Kress, 1988, 1993) and transforms language from an abstract system à la Chomsky into a social instrument à la Halliday.

Consider the following sentences (suggested by a newspaper article):

1. Wild cats are overrunning Australia, and killing off many native species.
2. Australia is being overrun by a plague of wild cats who are killing off many native species.
3. There is a serious problem of overpopulation of wild cats in Australia. Decimation of many native species is occurring.
4. In Australia, many native species are threatened by an uncontrolled proliferation of wild cats, risking disappearance of many native species.

According to Halliday (1985), when you build a sentence, in some interactive or other communicative context, you have a certain number of options at your disposal. Among other possibilities, you can play with the variable of subject. The concept of *subject*, linguistically speaking, has more than one meaning. There is first what would be defined in traditional grammars as the grammatical subject or what we usually think of as Subject ("that of which something is predicated"; in Chomsky's terms, the specifier of the main verb of the sentence). *Subject* is a term that may also refer to the theme or psychological subject ("that which is the concern of the message," in Halliday's terms, but there is no equivalent for Chomsky because he is not interested in messaging). Finally, the subject may be interpreted as the Actor or logical subject (the "doer of the action," i.e., the actor or agent, part of what Chomsky designates as logical form).

In the four sentences in our illustration, there is, logically speaking, just one main actor (or agent), the *wild cats*, and one main process (or action), *killing off many native species*. That, along with the reference to Australia, is the shared ideational part of the utterance. The grammatical subject ("that of which something is predicated") is, however, different in each case: "Wild cats" in sentence 1, "Australia" in 2, "There" and "Decimation" in 3, and "many native species" in 4. The theme ("that which is the concern of the message") is similarly variable, sometimes coinciding with the grammatical subject, and sometimes not: "Wild cats" in 1, "Australia" in 2, "a serious problem" and "Decimation" in 3 and "many native species" in 4. Only in sentence 1 do the subject (grammatical subject) and theme (psychological subject) coincide. And in both 2 and 4, "Australia" is given greater prominence that in 1 or 3 by its receiving first mention, but in different ways, once as patient, once as location.

There are other differences. There is a mention of a "plague" in 2, "a serious problem of overpopulation" in 3 and "threat" and "uncontrolled proliferation" in 4. Using the word *plague* makes it sound like a natural phenomenon, with connotations of a (perhaps contagious) danger to health; "a problem of overpopulation" puts the actor/process kernel of meaning into a completely different circumstantial frame, with connotations of ecological deterioration and hints of global processes in the background, whereas "threat" and "uncontrolled proliferation" shine a different light on it: If there is a "threat" and it could be controlled and is not, perhaps someone is being irresponsible? And because the sentence begins "In Australia," we are in no doubt as to where the responsibility lies.

Making Ideological Hay

Conducting this kind of analysis is the lifeblood of a school of research that goes under the title of "Social Semiotics" (Halliday, 1978; Hodge & Kress, 1988, 1993; Kress & Hodge, 1979; Thibault, 1991). In the words of Hodge and Kress (1993, p. 9): "The world is grasped through language. But in its use by a speaker language is more than that. It is a version of the world, offered to, imposed on, exacted by, someone else." So powerful do they see the framing that language accomplishes, and so tendentious its uses in the phrasing of its speakers and writers, that they describe normal conversation as a "state of covert war" (p. 12). We normally think of putting a spin on events as something that happens in Washington or on Madison Avenue; they think we all became "spin doctors" the day we learned, early on, what a judicious choice of language could do for us.

The focus of their empirical work has been to identify the devices language furnishes to accomplish the spin. Using Chomsky's original notion of transformation, they have catalogued some of the ways a transformation can be used to highlight and hide information. One such tactic is passivization—splitting the grammatical from the logical subject. To say *Wild cats are overrunning Australia* is not the same thing as *Australia is being overrun by wild cats*: In the first instance, Subject and Actor coincide; in the second, they do not. Now the logical actor, semantically speaking, is no longer directly linked syntactically to the verb, other than by a preposition (*by*), so that the link between cause and process has been weakened. It now becomes possible to delete reference to agency (recall that subjects are an obligatory slot, arguments headed by prepositions are not) and produce a nice headline: AUSTRALIA OVERRUN! The unstated linking verb has now become *is*. No longer describing an active process, the new sentence is attributive: It enunciates a category, and the force of the action is further diminished.

Other transformations have similar effects. A favorite is nominalization. Words like *population* or *decimation* furnish examples. An effect of nominalization is to make it possible to delete, syntactically, reference to the logical actor. Although Australia may be facing decimation, the agency responsible for decimating has vanished. Another is to turn a verb into a noun, so that it now serves as the subject of another verb, as in *Decimation may occur*. *Decimation* still means killing off but the force of the word is totally different, and *occur* is a process without a specific origin in agency. Psychologically, as Hodge and Kress observe, the effect is to further dilute the salience of the event and obscure who was responsible for it. In like fashion, the cleft construction in sentence 3, *There is a serious problem*, is a way of framing the main process of cats killing off other species to render it thematically secondary, leaving unclear for whom it is a problem. Finally, in sentence 4, "disappearance" is an instance of negative incorporation where the apparent agent, "native species," is something that is said to "not appear" any more—not quite the same thing as being "killed."

There are so many ways to manipulate language to create the effect you seek. Hodge and Kress report, for example, on some of the language used by British newspapers in their coverage of the 1992 Gulf War. Britain had "Army, Navy and Airforce"; Iraq, "A war machine." On Britain's side there were "Reporting guidelines" and "Press briefings"; on theirs "Censorship" and "Propaganda." Our boys were "Professional, lion-hearts, cautious, confident, heroes, dare-devils, young knights of the skies, loyal, desert rats, resolute, brave"; theirs were "Brainwashed, paper tigers, cowardly, desperate, cornered, cannon-fodder, bastards of Baghdad, blindly obedient, mad dogs, ruthless, fanatical." Our missiles caused "collateral damage"; theirs, "civilian casualties." George Bush was "At peace with himself, resolute, statesmanlike, assured"; Saddam Hussein was "Demented, defiant, an evil tyrant, a crackpot monster." We "Took out, suppressed"; they "Destroyed, killed." These were the actual words used; whatever the facts of the situation (do we really know?) their tendentious, argumentative, rhetorical—ideological—character hardly needs emphasizing.

Language and the Construction of Reality

Hodge and Kress bring into a single focus two main ideas. The first of these is that language shapes how we see the world: what we concentrate our attention on, which features of the world-made-visible-to-us-in-language are emphasized and which are not, and what emotional value comes to be attached to the objects in the text-world landscape laid out before us. Even if you have never been to Australia, you know about cats gone wild (feral cats, they are often called), and you imagine vulnerable little cuddly furry creatures with exotic names like *wombat* (especially if the newspaper adds photo illustrations). Although Hodge and Kress do not refer to Kenneth Burke, they might well have, because Burke (1966, cited in Wess, 1966) wrote: "An 'ideology' is like a spirit taking up its abode in a body: it makes that body hop around in certain ways; and that same body would have hopped around in different ways had a different ideology happened to inhabit it" (p. 1). For Burke "only a tiny sliver of reality" is experienced firsthand, the larger picture being a construct of our symbol systems: "[C]an we bring ourselves to realize . . . just how overwhelmingly much of what we mean by 'reality' has been built up for us through nothing but our symbol systems?" (cited in Wess, 1996, p. 2).

If anything, Hodge and Kress would go farther than Burke to question whether even that "tiny sliver" of "experienced-at-firsthand reality" had not already been filtered through the selective categorization screen and compositional structures that characterize any particular language. At several points, they cite with approval the Sapir-Whorf principle of linguistic relativity which says, to cite P. Lee (1996, p. 123), that "[i]n a microexperiential sense each speaker unconsciously selects a different subset of all the possible perceivable features of the situation, this selection being a function of automatic linguistic processes which have become cognitively entrenched in the process of acquiring language." The consequences of such language dependency are far-reaching:

> The difficulty Whorf confronted was whether we, as mature speakers of a particular language or languages, can ever find a way of talking and thinking

about what experience is like prior to language acquisition. If we cannot, we are trapped within the languages we speak to such a degree that, as scientific investigation of the world around us can only take place through languages known to us, we can never feel confident that we have knowledge of the world which is not at least partly a function of our cultural construction of reality. (P. Lee, 1996, p. 92)

What Hodge and Kress add to this picture of language dominance in the way we carve up and respond to our world is the idea of discursive process. Perhaps every language is like a Stradivarius violin, so special in its properties that it stands out as unique, but a Strad was made to be played, and so is language. Language is not just a classification system and a syntax of expression. It is "an instrument of control as well as communication. Linguistic forms allow significance to be conveyed and to be distorted. In this way hearers can be both manipulated and informed, preferably manipulated while they suppose they are being informed" (Hodge & Kress, 1993, p. 6). Or as they say elsewhere (Hodge & Kress, 1988, p. 3): "Ideological complexes are constructed in order to constrain behaviour by structuring the versions of reality on which social action is based, in particular ways."

An act of speech involves two kinds of agency: the speaker and his or her motives (that Kress and Hodge associate with the exercise of power) and the language they must express themselves in (the product of centuries of development and providing its frames that structure what we can say and how we say it). You could say that the British reporters covering the Gulf War were exploiting the resources of language for their purposes, but it would be equally true to say that the exigencies of newspaper journalism dictated to them what to say.

LINKING DISCOURSE-WORLD TO TEXT-WORLD

Linguists have shown the structuring properties of language as a framer of our conceptual processes and how such properties serve to shape our individual experiential worlds, and thus secondarily, our text-world. For linguists, this is a technical issue; for sociologists, it is a moral and political one. The frontier between speaker and spoken—discourse-world and text-world—remains intact. What we now explore is a more radical idea, prefigured in our earlier discussions. The discourse-world is itself also shaped by frames as basic as those postulated by Chomsky's X-bar hypothesis—frames of meaning that also have a universal basis, although they are to be found in another area of texting and are narratively, not sententially, based. As we enter this phase of our inquiry, the boundary separating speaker and spoken becomes problematical. Here too we find a dynamic interplay of construction and frame (chap. 3), because the constructions, although englobing them, are similar in kind to those of sentence grammar. But the nature of the resulting interpretive process carries us into the heartland of organizational theory. We come back to the question of how language frames and structures not conceptual processes, but organizational ones.

Consider once again the canonical structure of a sentence, as it is visualized in X-bar theory (see Fig. 4.3 on p. 115).

The X-bar theorists seem to have unearthed an odd fact. The uppermost node in the construction they postulate as the fundamental description of a sentence is not even a word, in the usual sense, much less the sentence itself. It is an *inflection* (**I″**) that will typically appear, in the spoken sentence, as no more than an affix to the main verb, in a form such as *-ed* or *-ing*, often in combination with an auxiliary verb such as *was* or *is*. The oddity is this: The root of *inflection* is *inflect*. Something that inflects something else "changes" it, "turns" it, makes it "bend," or "veer." It is not itself a primary mover, but an influence on something else that results in a recognizable change in the latter. In linguistics, the something being changed is a verb—within the context of a sentence. So what is *inflection* doing up there in the X-bar structure, at the top of the pile, standing in for the sentence itself? Might this not lead you to suspect that there is a vital piece of the puzzle missing in the conventional X-bar representation? Is it possible that X-bar style linguists have a predilection for dealing only with orphans, or perhaps a better analogy would be homeless waifs, torn from their natural homes and left to the tender mercies of specialists in the care and treatment of language misfits? Or are linguists perhaps caught in the equivalent of an inquiry into family structure based on a sampled population of drifters?

Let us find out. To do so we need to develop some background knowledge. The inflections that we are concerned with are tense and mood. The concept of *tense* is straightforward enough (although we discover a catch): It tells us when the action occurred or will occur, or when a state existed, exists, or will exist. It is the question of mood, and its logical basis in modality, that we now want to examine more deeply.[12]

Mood and Modality

The distinction between mood and modality is a mirror image of that which differentiates syntactic structures from their semantic interpretation,

---

[12]Our principal reference is Bybee and Fleischman (1995). The cross-cultural study of mood and modality (or indeed its study at all) has tended to remain at the periphery of linguists' concerns. It occupies a very minor role in current explorations into the minimalist program, for example (cf. Abraham, Epstein, Thráinsson, & Zwart, 1996).

or logical form. Mood is a syntactic category: the grammatical expression of modality that appears in the structural representation of the sentence as an inflection (the *mood*) of the main verb, as in Fig. 4.3. They include such categories as indicative, subjunctive, optative, imperative, conditional: *She's tall, It would be nice if she were taller, You may, if you wish, Oh, grow up!, I would have come if only I had known.* Categories "vary from one language to another in respect to number as well as to the semantic distinctions they mark" (Bybee & Fleischman, 1995, p. 2). The subjunctive mood, for instance, is omnipresent in French (a headache for English speakers who are trying to learn it) and, although not exactly absent in English, is muted, hardly noticeable (*I wish you were here* not *I wish you are here*).

Modality, on the other hand, is in the domain of semantics; it pertains to a particular function of the sentence, whose common denominator, according to Bybee and Fleischman (1995, p. 2) "is the addition of a supplement or overlay to the most neutral semantic value of the proposition of an utterance, namely factual and declarative." That "supplement" or "overlay" is usually taken (Palmer, 1986) to refer to the attitude or belief of the speaker, or degree of commitment (to an action or a state). Modality is expressed in language in a variety of ways, not only by the mood of the verb but also through auxiliary verbs such as *must* or *could*, and sometimes just by intonation or phrasing. Often, knowledge of context is enough: When R says to Jeff (chap. 3) "Why don't you take them through the model?" the mood may be interrogative but people there knew that the modality was imperative (a typical strategy in fact). In other words, even when it is not expressed in so many words, modality is present semantically. It is an essential part of the meaning of the uttered sentence.

Bybee and Fleischman's description is perhaps transparent to a linguist, but it needs some clarification for those of us not immersed in linguistic thinking. One way to explain the concept is to think of it as expressing *intentionality.* According to Descombes (1996), there are two kinds of expression: natural and intentional. A <u>*natural*</u> expression is one that states a bald fact, such as "Mary had a little lamb." An <u>*intentional*</u> expression is one that says what happens when it happens, as in "It is said that Mary had a little lamb." It is the *saying* that makes it intentional; it would be equally so if we replaced *saying* by *thinking, affirming, hoping, doubting, asking, announcing,* and so on. The difference then is that the natural describes what occurs, or is, and the intentional what occurs (or is) *to someone.* Inanimate objects are not intentionally related to their world; humans are. Even when the intentional is not explicitly verbalized in the sentence in the form of a recognizable marker such as *It is said that . . .* , it is still there. (There would not be an expression *Mary has a little lamb* if somebody had not said or written it. There is no such thing as an un-said, un-written language.)

So the distinction Descombes is making is not between two kinds of sentences, but between two levels in a single sentence, one embedded within the other. One (the embedded) is always enunciated whereas the other (the embedding) is sometimes enunciated and sometimes merely intimated, expressed nonverbally, or left implicit; one, as Bybee and Fleischman put it, "factual and declarative," the other "a supplement or overlay."[13]

Halliday (1985, p. 75) explains modality this way: "Modality means the speaker's judgement of the probabilities, or the obligations, involved in what he is saying. A proposition may become arguable by being presented as likely or unlikely, desirable or undesirable—in other words, its relevance specified in modal terms." Given the reference to "speaker's judgement," it is not surprising, thus, that Bybee and Fleischman (1995, p. 3) find that "many of the functions of modality are inextricably embedded in contexts of social interaction and, consequently, cannot be described adequately apart from their contextual moorings in interactive discourse," and that "modality, as we have discovered, lends itself best to investigation in social, interactive contexts." (Halliday would agree, but so did Jeff in the example we cited earlier; he knew what R's intention was.)

Modality, to use a colloquialism, comes in two flavors: *deontic* and *epistemic* (we introduced this distinction in chaps. 2 & 3). *Deontic modality* "is concerned with the necessity or possibility of acts performed by morally responsible agents (Lyons 1977: 823), and is thus associated with the *social functions of permission and obligation*" (Bybee & Fleischman, 1995, p. 4; emphasis in original). *Epistemic modality* "has to do with the possibility or necessity of the truth of propositions, and is thus involved with knowledge and belief" (Bybee & Fleischman, 1995, p. 4, following Lyons, 1977, p. 793). A different way to say this is that the epistemic modality is about what is or was or will be, deontic modality about what should, or could, or may be, and who is responsible to see that it is: cognitive versus pragmatic, to Greimas' way of thinking.

"[M]ost linguists," according to the same authors, "understand epistemic modality as expressing the degree of a speaker's commitment to the truth of the proposition contained in an utterance" (Bybee & Fleischman, p. 4). Epistemic modality may also be conveyed in auxiliary verbs such as *may, might, could,* and *must* that serve to modulate the force of conviction by modifying the main verb; in terms such as *maybe*, as in "Maybe that *is* Mary's little lamb" (where voice intonation might be another clue); or in tags such as *I think*, or *I'm not sure*, indicating less than total certainty as

---

[13]Note that their "supplement or overlay" is equivalent to the unspoken modal proposition of a speech act, such as we described in chapter 3. They point out, however, that the unspoken part is context-sensitive.

to the factual status of the sentence. Commitment to the truth of a sentence is, after all, often a matter of degree.[14]

It follows—this is a central point in our argument—that the complement of an epistemically framed sentence (such as *I believe that . . .*) is a second sentence that makes an assertion of fact (*. . . Mary had a little lamb*). This is how Descombes defined intentionality, that is, a sentence that has another sentence as its direct object or complement.

Deontic modality focuses on notions of obligation and permission. It has as its complement, therefore, not a sentence that makes a statement of fact, but one that describes an action (where the main verb is either transitive or ditransitive, in other words). Permission is what Bybee and Fleischman (1995, p. 5) term a "socially enabling condition," with, at its root, the notion of the ability of the agent to act. Obligation has to do with future states, and it has to do with the duty of the agent to act.

Deontic is sometimes split into subcategories: agent-oriented and speaker-oriented. *Agent-oriented modality* "encompasses all modal meanings that predicate conditions on an agent with regard to the completion of an action referred to by the main predicate, e.g., obligation, desire, ability, permission and root possibility" (Bybee & Fleischman, 1995, p. 6). *Speaker-oriented* (we would prefer recipient-oriented) modality refers to "[m]arkers of directives, such as imperatives, optatives or permissives, which represent speech acts through which a speaker attempts to move an addressee to action" (p. 6).

With this background in mind, let us return to the question we posed earlier: Is the X-bar representation describing an orphan?

Consider Fig. 4.3 again. Suppose the node **I″** to be the grammatical representation of the mood of the sentence, the syntactic equivalent of its semantic modality. But if the sentence dominated by the root **I″** is logically a complement, as we have concluded, then it must be a complement of something (following X-bar logic). It must figure as a node in a higher level construction that expresses modality, even where that enveloping construction has been syntactically deleted. A sentence, in other words, has to be specified for modality. If there is no specifier, the sentence does not yet make a statement. As we pointed out earlier, ". . . had a little lamb" is indeterminate in reference until its agency is specified by adjoining

---

[14]Austin (1962) has pointed out that descriptions are never purely objective because, as statements, they always involve selective perception and are uttered for a purpose. "It is essential to realize that 'true' and 'false', like 'free' and 'unfree', do not stand for anything simple at all; but only for a general dimension of being the *right and proper thing to say* as opposed to a wrong thing, *in these circumstances, to this audience, for these purposes and with these intentions*" (p. 144, emphasis added). "The truth or falsity of a statement depends," he goes on, "not merely on the meanings of words but on what act you were performing in what circumstances."

"Mary." Similarly, we now extrapolate, "Mary had a little lamb" is not yet a sentence of English until it is specified for modality. It lacks a vital point of reference, which is the modal intention of the speaker, in the absence of which the sentence is not comprehensible as an act of speech.

This point is less salient in the case of a sentence such as *Mary had a little lamb* because it is phrased in the indicative mood, and indicative is the unmarked mood, in that no limitation of the belief of the speaker is expressed. It is what Bybee and Fleischman refer to as "factual and declarative"; there is no overt "supplement or overlay" expressed—no visible trace of the degree of belief of the speaker. But of course a mood, the indicative, is expressed. So there is always modality as there is always tense, and this is why the **I″** is the prime root of the sentence in Fig. 4.3. It is the link point with an embedding modal construction.

But if every sentence is embedded, logically, in a higher level structure that expresses mood (call it root **M″**, for purposes of exposition), then we must now inquire, following X-bar theory, what is the specifier of **M″**? The answer can only be the intention of the speaker, in the sense of commitment to a belief, desire, sense of obligation, and so on (Fig. 4.5). But intention, in the very special sense we are giving the word, is not, prima facie, thought of as a grammatical category, but as a state of the speaker. Yet this state is an obligatory component of the sentence, if the latter is to be fully grammatical.

What we seem to be saying (we are) is that the speaker is part of—embedded in—the spoken!

Although not quite as evidently, the role of tense is similarly circumscribed. Consider the sentence *Mary had a little lamb* again. It is stated in the past tense, yet the relationship of Mary to the lamb is not past-to-present: They must occupy the same time frame for there to even be a "having."

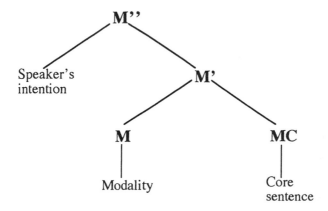

FIG. 4.5. Modalization as a component of sentence structure.

The reason the sentence is phrased in the past tense is because it is past from the point of view of the speaker. Einstein's relativity principle is not limited to physics; the tense of a sentence is an inflection that reflects the relative position of the speaker with respect to the spoken. Once again, the state of the speaker figures as an obligatory, formally embedded component within the sentence being spoken (every declarative sentence must have tense).

How are we to make sense of this? We see communication as the crossing point between subjective and objective worlds. Seen from a subjective perspective, we are individual human beings who exist independently of language. We are embodied creatures with emotions, feelings, perceptions, attitudinal leanings, and so on. Speaking is just one of many things people do in the course of their daily life, where they attempt to convey, express, or hide, their feelings, beliefs, and desires in the things they say (compare our earlier discussion of Schutz). Sometimes, they feel they have successfully communicated their feelings, sometimes not. Language is something they produce; it is outside of them—an instrument.

From an objective perspective, on the other hand, a state of mind is an obligatory node in a sentence structure—a head, in fact. Intention is not a psychological state of mind; it is a constituent of text. It is objective, not subjective. As a consequence, when people speak they automatically communicate an intention, whether they mean to or not (and thus create themselves as agents for others), because the intention, grammatically speaking, is not their real state of mind (which they can never communicate), but a functional element in a syntactic construction. Even if they do not declare a modal state, it will be there as a trace, in the uttering of the sentence. Even if they try to mask their real intentions, the latter will still be read, perhaps erroneously, but nevertheless read, because they are a part of the sentence being spoken. People may produce speech, in one sense of the term, but in another sense speech also produces them because it constitutes them as speakers with intentions, objectively. The intentions (using that term to cover all the modal possibilities) are not defined psychologically, but textually. The terms *actor* and *agent* are syntactic before they are psychological categories, and the objects of their actions are constructions in language before they are effects in the real world. They constitute themselves by being an object in a textual construction.

Linguistic Structure and Organizational Imbrication

We can use this analysis to clarify a concept we introduced earlier, that of tiling or imbrication. We have seen that the structure of the most elementary text of language—a sentence—is a multiple embedding of head–complement relationships. We suggest that this structuring principle mirrors a deeper reality, which is that of human organization. To begin with, organizations, as sentences, are characterized by objects: their states and their transformations. Second, transformations have causes, and causes are associated with (a) instrumentalities and (b) actor-subjects. Third, actions have reasons: Action and belief are modally inflected, that is, informed by intentionality. Fourth, modality is transmittable and is that which transforms speech into act by establishing the basis of belief and action, communicationally. Finally, communication is itself framed narratively, by its association with precipitating events, qualification, performance, and sanction.

This is how the parts of an organization are stitched together. Because communication is tied to objects, their states and transformations, and because objects are part of the hard, material world, communication is structured by its very dependence on the objective world. Dealing with objective reality enforces discipline. The instruments that serve to manipulate the objective world—our technology—is in turn a discipliner and an assurer of organizational stability. But if in addition our very intentionality is an objective construction enforced by the exigencies of language, it is not surprising that here too organizational stability is assured. The words of the language come with built-in scripts. The intentionality of being a doctor, a lawyer, a businessperson, a TV star, or a university professor is part of our frame knowledge. Of course, there is room for individual creativity, but not unlimited room. Language is a script for organizing; it is our storehouse of acquired knowledge about how to deal with the physical and how to constitute a social world. It is not the single words that do the job, but their imbrication in thickly imbricated head–complement networks of relationship that assures a measure of organizational stability. Each individual, and each act, is wired into place by its imbricational links.

It is this insight that we return to look at in chapter 5 when we turn to consider some existing concepts of enactment, structuration, and translation.

The Straitjacket of Language-as-Code

The point of this discussion can be summarized in a phrase: Language is a self-contained universe of sense. Descombes (1980) employs the familiar language of mathematical communication theory to explain why. One of Shannon's (1948) premises in the construction of a theory of communication as information transfer was that an obligatory prerequisite is the existence of a code, and that both parties to the communicative exchange must share in their knowledge of it. Otherwise, in the absence of an agreed code, the message has no interpretation, and thus no meaning. The code thus "precedes all its hypothetical uses, and *defines all the situations in which it can be used*" (Descombes, 1980, p. 93, emphasis added). It follows, on this logic, that "an unexpected message is impossible. The message can never entail the unprecedented or the unforeseen" (Descombes, 1980, p. 93). Only when the receiver of the message is able to compare what has been said with what might have been said does it become recognizable, and what might have been said is constrained by what the code permits saying. The code thus delimits what may be said. And because the code exists independently of the communicators, as an a priori condition of being able to communicate at all, it thus defines a field within which they may communicate meaningfully. Simultaneously, it defines a whole universe of experience that is closed to discourse because it is not covered by the code: "The message is not the expression of an experience; rather it expresses the possibilities and limitations, in comparison with experience, of the code employed, whence the difficulty of articulating the unforeseen" (Descombes, 1980, p. 95).

As Descombes says, "If language is a code, it is language which speaks each time that the speaking subject delivers a remark, of whatever kind. Speech is not a gesture which renders the meaning of the experience, 'still dumb', into verbal expression, for dumb experience has no meaning by itself. . . . It is the meaning that experience can receive in a discourse which articulates it according to a certain code—that is, in a system of signifying oppositions" (Descombes, 1980, p. 98). We are, he says, "subjugated to the signifier."

The ironical implication is that "the only way for the speaker to generate meaning is to produce a message bereft of meaning, that the code had not foreseen. . . . Non-meaning is thus the repository on which we draw in order to produce meaning" (Descombes, 1980, p. 95).

It is the issue of that "non-meaning" that we take up in Part II of the book.

CONCLUSION

We described, in chapter 1, contrasting tendencies in the interpretist literature on organization: ethnomethodological and critical. These orientations, we argued, are not so much mutually exclusive theories of communication, as they are dimensions of communication reality that need to be incorporated in a more comprehensive theory. In chapter 2, we proposed a model of communication in which such dimensions are conceptualized as constraints of two kinds: (a) those which govern the orderly conduct of interaction and which, although they regulate the organization of talk, also transcend language because they aim to sustain basic sociality—the interactive order, and (b) those which are specific to language itself and relate to its innate structuring properties. We argued that communication occurs when one dimension, that of experience, is mapped to another, that of language. In chapter 3, we explored a concept of communication as furnishing both a site and a surface for the emergence of organization: a site, because whatever organization is, ontologically speaking, it is clear that it must be realized in the interactive arena of communication for it to take on a tangible existence, and a surface because, we claim, it is language that makes the agencies and objects of organization available to us for the knowing. In this chapter, we have been exploring in greater depth a theme that was adumbrated in chapter 3: the surface that language provides to read organizational reality. We have found that language provides a base system of patterns, or constructions, that explain the emergence of agency and objects, along with categories of instrumentality, time, place, and manner, in the semantics of ordinary speech: a canvas on which we are enabled to paint the outlines of organization, and thus recognize it as it appears. It is also frame knowledge—the storehouse of Schutz' typifications—that supplies the paint by means of which to delineate the patterns by giving them figurative depth and recognizability. But as we have continued our exploration into the nature of language as constraint, as text form, language begins to appear more like a straitjacket: a tyrant, dictating to us both how we can know and experience language. This, we saw in chapter 1, is a version of the criticalist view: language the colonizer.

But is such a fatalistic vision inevitable, as soon as we consider, in a critical spirit, the role of language in human affairs? In the second part of the book, we begin a different kind of exploration, one which emphasizes the alternative perspective, that of conversation. And there we find there is reason to arrive at a very different notion of the role of language. We transfer our attention from language-as-symbol (the "code" system of which Descombes was writing) to language-as-link. The focus shifts from symbolic to subsymbolic, and as it does, our theory of organization becomes enlarged. It turns out that organization emerges in communication in more than one way.

There is a fundamental tension that divides the two modes of expression of organization in communication. On the one hand, the texts of language constitute organization as a system and thus compel us to fit our lived experience into its categories, much as molten iron is poured into a mold and given a shape. On the other hand, the conversation always transcends the fixed categories of language because, although it may be linguistically mediated, conversation is not essentially a phenomenon of language, but rather of interpersonal exchange through interaction, that is, what Goffman (1981) thinks of as a game with moves that count in the establishment of configurations of sociability and power and that exploit the fixities of the codified rules in order to produce an unlimited variety of outcomes.

The communication researcher is uniquely positioned to comprehend the dynamics of a process that is both fixed and variable: fixed in that constructions and frames of language may not be ignored, yet variable in how the interaction plays out in practice. In the second part of the book, we look at how organization has been and might be studied. We begin by looking at the ideas of three authors who have individually attacked this problem and whose works have much influenced our own, although in the end, our approach is distinct from all three. The authors are Karl Weick, Anthony Giddens, and Bruno Latour. Finally, we consider briefly a conceptualization from which we have also drawn: that of William Labov.

Part II

THEORY OF ORGANIZATION

Reinterpreting Organizational Literature

The first part of this book developed two ideas. One is that communication occurs at an intersection of two resource/constraint dimensions. The first dimension recognizes the essentially situated character of communication in a world of practical, mundane involvement in lived experience, framed by circumstances of time, place, materiality, and personhood and requiring attention—"care," Heidegger called it. People live in situations, and communication is thematically connected to them. Situations have to be dealt with and communication is one of the instrumentalities that actors call on to do so. The second dimension focuses on the principal medium of human communication, language. Language furnishes an impressive resource base for the making sense of—interpreting—experience by giving it a name and thus linking it with other places and other times. This is frame knowledge. But it also imposes formal constraints on the acting out of communicational performances. These constraints, we argued, can be traced to a deeply embedded semantics of narrative, in which the agents and objects of organizational life are not merely named, but provide scripts to be acted out. This is construction knowledge.

The second thematic thread of Part I was the extraordinary shaping role of language in how we conceive and live out our organizational world. So powerful is the influence exerted by the technology we call language that it would be easy to conclude that we are literally prisoners of our own success: less calling language's tune than dancing obediently to its rhythms. If there is something called "postmodern angst" this is it: the conviction that we have indeed, as Habermas and Deetz put it, been "colonized" from within, victims of our own verbal sophistication.

139

In this second part of the book, we explore a very different idea of how communication works, the role language plays in it, and how to think about organization. We argue somewhat as follows. The emphasis in Part I was on language as symbol system: how individuals separately make sense of their world ("think") and then transmit their perceptions to others by encoding them in a shared language of symbols (of which spoken language is the most powerful, but not the only, instance). But it is because, as Descombes pointed out, symbol systems are codes that they are also self-contained, closed systems of sensemaking, and thus exclude variety beyond that which their own channel capacity permits. But language can be seen differently, not as an instrument for interpersonal communication but as the glue of an organizational network. It is not, in this different context, merely an instrument for the transmission of knowledge, but also for its construction, in the diffuse interrelating of the laminated organizational conversational components. Such constructed knowledge is, we argue, a property of the network itself and not of any individual in it, in that no individual can formulate it with certainty. It is therefore no longer symbolic, but subsymbolic. And because it is subsymbolic, it is not inherently restricted by the closure described by Descombes, because it is no longer subject to the same rules that apply to any rational system of logic or code. The subsymbolic system of knowledge is instead an open, adaptive, learning instrumentality that develops wherever there is a distributed, locally autonomous system of intelligence. Chapters 6 and 7 are devoted to the explication of this alternative view of communication. In it, we discover that text ceases to be tyrant and is returned to its role of medium.

But if there are two kinds of knowledge, symbolic and subsymbolic, then an issue arises: How do we, individually, know what we, collectively, know, without translating the subsymbolic into the symbolic? (Obviously, we cannot.) It is in the phrasing of this question that we perceive the power of a theory that assumes an ongoing conversation/text translation to reside. In Part I, we took that crossover translation to occur at the level of the individual transaction: people in interaction making sense of their own exchanges by narrativizing them. But if conversations develop knowledge as a result of multiperson interactions in networks, then the transaction-by-transaction model of translation is no longer an adequate explanation. In chapters 7 and 8, we propose an alternative explanation, which assumes that for a kind of knowledge that has been generated by the collective interacting of an organizational group to be symbolized and thus known at the individual level, it must find a spokesperson who is authorized to enunciate it, symbolically. It is in fact in this power to enunciate that *authority* lies.

This we believe to be the most radical idea of the book: that organization is a system of collective action, which develops subsymbolic knowledge whose formulation in a conventional language of symbols is the motivation for the emergence of organizational macroactors. These actors speak in the name of the group as a whole and thus represent it, both by giving it a voice and by interpreting back to it in symbolic form what it collectively knows, at the subsymbolic level of cognition. Chapter 9 brings these alternative explanations into a single framework, acknowledging both the symbolic and subsymbolic explanations as having their own validity, although each offers an incomplete explanation of how the organization works. Our means of effecting this synthesis draws on the concept of mapping. We assume that organizational process is an ongoing reconciliation of the imperatives of the symbolic and the subsymbolic: a continuing two-way translation of conversation into text and text into conversation.

In this chapter, we consider some of the antecedents of our approach: authors who have influenced our way of thinking and whose ideas figure throughout, even when they are not explicitly mentioned. Three figures in particular are the focus of the chapter: Karl Weick, Anthony Giddens, and Bruno Latour. Each of them illustrates, in their different ways, what we take to be a "flatland" approach to the study of organization, that is, one that assumes that whatever organization is, it must be realized in the day-to-day interactions of its members. We conclude the chapter by a brief consideration of an element that is missing in each of their accounts: the issue of rights and obligations. Here we draw on the work of Labov and Fanshel (1977).

THE "FLATLAND" PERSPECTIVE ON ORGANIZATION

Established management theory treats organization as a structured entity, of which the best-known manifestation may well be the notorious organization chart. Figure 5.1, for example, is an example of how a government bureaucracy might construct an image of organization, using this well-established graphic illustration.

This concept of organization as a hierarchy of offices was given credibility in the 1920s by the great German jurist, historian, and social economist Max Weber (1923; as what he called an ideal-type of rational organization). Others in the same historical time period, such as Fayol (1925), proposed much the same idea. There are of course other more contemporary pictures of the structure of an organization. In chapter 6, for example, we consider an influential view of organizational structure as a hierarchical system of productive processes—subroutines or embedded miniprograms—which owes its parentage to cybernetics and systems theory and was first elaborated in March and Simon's (1958) *Organizations*. Current notions of reengineering are variations on that theme.

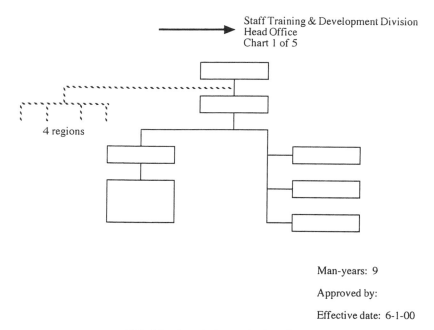

FIG. 5.1. A typical organization chart.

R. C. Smith (1993) points out a common feature of all these versions of the organization-as-entity model (as well as much of the organizational communication literature): They conceive of communication as being in or within organization, "flows," as Mintzberg (1979) put it. This is accomplished by according (at least implicitly) a privileged ontological status to organization, which is implied to have an existence autonomous of communication, in that it serves as the container for the latter.

As Orlikowski (1996) observes, one way to grasp the ontology of a theory of organization is to look at how it conceptualizes change. In the organization-as-entity view, change is seen as a transformation of structure (Fig. 5.2). In this model change becomes a transition between one stable structure, t_0, and another, t_1.

Let us term the organization-as-entity image the *heteronomous* theory of organization, because change is thought of as an effect produced by an exogenous agent or agency (person or circumstance) and no endogenous change agency is predicated (nor indeed encouraged or even countenanced).

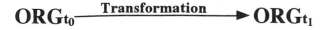

$$ORG_{t_0} \xrightarrow{\text{Transformation}} ORG_{t_1}$$

FIG. 5.2. A conventional view of organizational change.

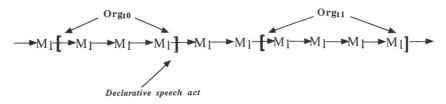

FIG. 5.3. Organization as a sequence of mediations.

The theory of organization we explore in this and subsequent chapters is based on a very different premise: that because organization emerges in communication, it is constantly evolving (a perspective that Orlikowski calls that of "situated change").

This view rejects the macro–micro assumption of two levels of reality (organization-as-entity/individuals-as-components) and instead argues that all organization must be found at a single level—a *flatland*[1]—which is invariably situated, circumstantial, and locally realized in a finite time and space, involving real people. Figure 5.3 illustrates what such a flatland might look like (the 'M' refers to the mediation of language).

Let us term this revised view the *autonomous* theory of organization (J. R. Taylor, 1995). Under this alternative hypothesis, managerial interventions are not in fact exogenous at all, but merely another locally realized, personally communicated act expressed in language (a speech act), with this special characteristic, that they are meant to be, and are treated as being, declarative (chap. 3). Because, communicationally speaking, everybody is an agent of change, the manager becomes one change agent among others (although one endowed with singular declarative powers).

The thesis of autonomy has, of course, troubling implications. As Poole and McPhee (1983, p. 195) express it: "In organizational research, we confront an undeniable paradox: People create, maintain, and control organizations, yet organizations attain a life of their own and often overshadow, constrain, and manipulate their members . . . The explanation of this complex relationship is one of the great goals of organizational studies and also one of its greatest problems."

We are, to be sure, not the first to have opted for a flatland take on organization. In this chapter, we consider some of the ways organizational theorists have addressed this issue.

---

[1]The idea of a "flatland" is a curiosity first conceived in the 19th century by Edwin Abbott (1884/1953) in *Flatland: A Romance of Many Dimensions.* In Abbott's imaginary landscape, everybody had been reduced to a two-dimensional existence (in a sense inverting Einstein's innovation of four dimensions). Latour has occasionally used the term (although we have been unable to locate the source), as we do, to emphasize his opposition to the reification of a macrostructural level of society. Our resort to the term is only metaphorical, to make a point: Obviously organizational communication is not "flat."

KARL WEICK: ENACTMENT

The first of these conceptualizations is Karl Weick's notion of *enactment*, a concept he has elaborated in his *The Social Psychology of Organizing* and in a number of articles (Daft & Weick, 1984; Orton & Weick, 1990; Weick, 1969, 1976, 1977, 1979a, 1979b, 1985, 1988, 1989a; Weick & Bougon, 1986; Weick & Daft, 1983; Weick & Orton, 1989) as well as in another book (Weick, 1995a).[2] His thinking draws on both systems theory and phenomenology. His ontology, including his commitment to the flatland position, is already revealed by his choice of title: the social psychology, not of organization, but of organizing.[3] We present an outline of his theory here; in chapter 8, we return to examine his ideas in a more critical vein.

Weick's thinking gravitates between two poles: enactment and loose coupling. The concept of *enactment* is based on an idea he has often defended: that organizations actively construct the environment that "impinges on them" and to which they then react. They "impose on that which subsequently imposes on them"; they "implant that which they later discover and call 'knowledge'" or "understanding of their 'environment'" (Weick, 1977, p. 267). This perception in turn rests on another: that what is fundamental in all human activities is the centrality of action, and specifically, action designed to control. It is the action and its consequences that become "the raw materials from which a sense of the situation is eventually built" (p. 272). The organization discovers "what it is up to" only in retrospect, as it makes sense of its own actions. Organizations thus "invest their settings with meaning" (p. 272). For the organization to even have an environment, it had to have built it; on the other hand, the way it goes about acting to control this built environment is strongly influenced by how it has constructed it mentally (or, as he says, cognitively). Yet it is only by acting that it learns about the environment. The action and its result is thus dependent on how the environment has been conceptualized, but the conceptualization is inversely dependent on what the action was. It is this mutual interdependence of action and thought—this chicken-and-egg indefiniteness of finality—that Weick is out to capture in his theory of enactment.

---

[2]For discussion of the relevance of Weick's theory to communication research, see the special issue of *Communication Studies*, published in 1989 (Weick, 1989a; Putnam, 1989).

[3]Weick (1977, p. 274): "The misplaced concreteness of talk about *the* organization and *the* environment diverts the attention of organizational theorists from crucial problems. If one asserts the existence of a mythical entity, then observers are tempted to search for its properties rather than treat its 'existence' as problematic. If it were viewed as problematic, the more crucial questions would consist of queries such as under what conditions its 'existence' is posited, what that positing accomplishes for the positer, and how people operate when they punctuate their streams of experience with other nouns than 'the external environment.'"

An analogy may help in grasping this inseparability of action and knowledge. Imagine yourself in a dark field, at night, with only a flashlight. The objects you can pick out dimly around you with your unaided sight are ambiguous: Is that just a bush, or is it a dangerous animal, crouching to attack? By turning on the flashlight, you create a circle within which things are made clear, and you can now act with some assurance. It was the initial action of turning on the light that effectively created a new environment where things become interpretable. But it is still just a circle of light, and what is outside the circle remains as mysterious as ever, until you redirect your flashlight beam to it. It is in a way roughly analogous to this, Weick thinks, that companies by their investments, scientists by their choice of experiment, governments by their adoption of regulatory policy, and so on, constitute themselves as actors in an environment. The flashlight, however, is mental: "[T]he environment is located in the mind of the actor and is imposed by him on experience in order to make that experience more meaningful" (Weick, 1977, p. 274). That is why entrepreneurs behave like entrepreneurs, scientists like scientists, bureaucrats like bureaucrats, and so on.

Weick characterizes what we have called the "circle of light" using one of either of two terms: *enacted environment* or *cause map.* By enacted environment, he means the "output of organizing," which is to say (in the terms of our analogy) the circle of light created by turning on the flashlight: that which "the organization [can] clarify and take seriously" or, to put it differently, the environment that has been "created . . . out of puzzling surroundings" (Weick, 1979a, pp. 132–3). By cause map, he means how you have understood the environment created by the flashlight to "allow [you] to interpret what goes on in a situation and . . . to express [yourself] in that same situation and be understood by others" (p. 132).[4]

Organizing processes are then merely the dynamics of enactment as they work themselves out over time: enacting (making a circle of light) in order to create a sensible environment, selecting what to pay attention to therein, consigning the result of your action to memory, and then acting again. What activates the dynamic is that the effects of enacting are never predictable, either because of what is revealed within the circle of light that has to be dealt with (because it is not as it should be), or because of what you failed to illuminate and should have (it was not the bush picked out with your flashlight that was the wild animal, but the one you did not notice). You never have a flashlight powerful enough to light up everything, and so your environment remains forever equivocal—open to more than

---

[4]Although his definition of terms is not always consistent; elsewhere he defines enacted environment this way: "Thus, an enacted environment is the residue of a sensemaking episode that is stored in the retention process as past wisdom" (Weick, 1977, p. 279).

one interpretation. In one of Weick's favorite figures of speech, it remains an environment of puns.

Organizing is thus an ongoing process "directed toward reducing the perceived level of equivocality judged to be present in enactments that are taken seriously by the organization" (Weick, 1979b, p. 133). The organization he describes is evolutionary: Change is the rule, not the exception. Structure, for him, is no more that a "frozen moment" in the life of the organization. Some responses to the environment prove to be successful, some do not, but which will succeed cannot be predicted in advance. Present organizational forms are thus the result of natural selection: things that worked in the past have been retained but those that did not were discarded.

There is no teleology in Weick's view of evolution: we are not moving forward—we are just moving! Furthermore, there is no hope of eventually arriving at a stable adapted state: organizations continue to undergo change, now, and will still be doing so tomorrow, and the day after. They will still be organizing; they are never permanently organized. The search by previous generations of organizational theorists for an underlying scientific model of management—a "one best way" or ultimate structural principle, whether contingent on properties of the environment or not—has no echo in Weick's thought: as he sees it, the only constant is change. For him, the environment is like a deck of cards that is being endlessly reshuffled, and organizations are just the way we play them. Some players win; some do not. There is no overall gain. And winning yesterday is no guarantee of success tomorrow. In Weick's (1979b) ontology, it is a Las Vegas world.

Loose Coupling

Turning from the environment to the organization, Weick's position is harder to read. On the one hand, it would seem that the concept of organization has no more substantial a basis than that of environment. Organization too is a product of enactment—something "posited": "Actors immersed in experiential streams organize and punctuate those streams by positing organizations and environments . . . [T]he last thing we want to do is define away their solutions to sensemaking by imposing for them the logical but empirically empty distinction between internal and external worlds" (Weick, 1977, pp. 273–4). He is quite clear in his rejection of the notion of an organization as a "rational" entity clearly delineated from its environment by a boundary; he describes organization's self-attribution of itself as "rational" as no more than a "facade" and a legitimation tactic or rationalizing device that, by dramatizing its efficiency, "deflects criticism, and ensures a steady flow of resources into the organization" (Weick, 1985, p. 110).

He does not even see management as actually managing the organization, but rather as managing the process that manages the organization, preoccupied not with operations but with decisions. Instead, it is the "segmented sub-units" of the organization that design the operating structures (Weick, 1985, p. 114). These segmented subunits (sometimes called subassemblies) provide the stability of organization (such as it is), and such stable units, he thinks, are very small, basically consisting of no more than "ten strong pairwise relationships" (p. 117). It is this segmentedness of organization that leads him to propose a principle of *loose coupling*. The loosely coupled communication of the organization allows local organization of activity to maintain its own adaptations (in effect to construct its own enacted environment), a significant degree of decisional autonomy, and its own identity. He sees advantages in this loose coupling: a capacity to preserve more diversity, a simpler and thus less expensive system of control, and a sensitivity to a wider range of changes in the environment. It is an image, however, that raises the question of how organizational coherence is sustained at all.

Conversation and Text: Weick's Enactment

Throughout all of Weick's writings (that cover more than 30 years) you can feel him wrestling with the "undeniable paradox" of which Poole and McPhee (1983) wrote. On the one hand, that which is real is the immediate task of sensemaking, first as individual cognitions, and second as shared understandings among people who interact with each other on a regular basis. Such sensemaking tends to be very local; this is why his "stable sub-units" are defined, practically speaking, as formed of an ongoing (largely face-to-face) conversation of people engaged in a common activity (such as a jazz band, one of his early examples), out of which, following the principle of enactment, a singular frame of understanding, or "cause map," develops (Bougon, Weick, & Binkhorst, 1977). On the other hand, his use of the terms "sub-assembly" or "sub-unit" would tell us that he also accords a kind of grudging ontological status to organization as such, although he never theorizes it in so many words (subunits are, by definition, components of a larger entity) and he remains skeptical of the conventional theorizations that one is often confronted with in management studies. His way of dealing with this ontological indeterminacy—very characteristic of Weick's thought—is to describe it as *ambiguity* (Weick, 1985, pp. 121–126). Nevertheless, he says: "A loosely coupled system is not a flawed system. It is a social and cognitive solution to constant environmental change, to the impossibility of knowing another mind, and to limited information-processing capabilities" (p. 121).

The way for managers to "reduce ambiguity to tolerable levels" is to "make meanings for people," to "act *as if* loosely coupled events are tied together just as they are in a cause map" (Weick, 1985, pp. 126–7, emphasis added).

As he puts it, citing March and Olsen (1976), organizations are a "set of procedures for argumentation and interpretation" (p. 128). It is words that "induce stable connections" to which "people can orient"; it is "labels" that "carry . . . implications for action": "[T]hat is a cost (minimize it), that is spoilage (reduce it), that is overhead (allocate it), that is a transfer price (set it)," and so on. "A significant portion of the environment," he says, "consists of nothing more than talk" (p. 128). "Raw talk," he writes elsewhere (Weick, 1977, p. 280), "is the data on which subsequent sensemaking operates. The talk—the saying, the soliliquizing—is what is meant by the activity of enactment." "Organizations talk to themselves" (p. 281) and, as they do, the organization is talked into being, almost in spite of itself.

It seems evident that Weick's view has parallels with our own. If Weick's theory has not been more influential in empirical communication studies than it has, it is because he has not himself shown how to operationalize the concept of ambiguity reduction in discourse (other than the vague programmatic pointers that we have been citing). The work of Boden, discussed in chapter 1, seems to us to have filled part of that gap and ought to generate renewed interest in Weick's evocative writings on organization. His "loosely coupled sub-groups" have become, in Boden's rephrasing, conversations, and she turns his "loose coupling" into a different image: that of the "lamination" of conversations to produce an interconnecting network of ongoing sensemaking.

Nevertheless, there is a dimension of Weick's thought—a heritage of a cybernetically inspired systems theory—that is absent in Boden's portrayal of administration as a practice of conversation-grounded interpretation and laminated accounting. The advantage he sees in loosely coupled systems is that they "preserve many independent sensing elements and therefore 'know' their environments better than is true for more tightly coupled systems" (Weick, 1976, p. 6). There is a sense, in other words, that "loosely coupled" networks know more collectively than any single one of their components can or does, management not excluded. Sensemaking, we could interpolate, now becomes less a cognitive activity located within the human brain, than a function of distributed intelligence. As we see in chapter 6, this thinking is a forerunner of the subsymbolic hypothesis, and it is, therefore, no surprise that an article Weick published in 1993 with Roberts is one of the first to outline the implications of subsymbolic knowledge for organizational research. In chapter 6, we report on work (including that of Weick) that promises to alter radically our view of the role of conversation in the construction of an organizational cause map and that poses new theoretical questions to the communication researcher.

There is one respect, however, in which our approach diverges from that of Weick: in our concept of text. As we have seen, Weick thinks that images of reality form initially as individual cognitions: The environment is "located in the mind of the actor" and is "imposed by him [sic] on experience." This starting premise leaves Weick with the task of explaining how the plethora of "mind-located" environments (or cause maps) characterizing a large and diverse population of organizational actors gets turned into a shared image of the world—a challenge he has never quite addressed, nor, practically speaking, shown how to (the topic of chap. 8). Our premise is different. It is that the environment is constituted in conversation through the generation of a text-world. It is the text-world thus brought into being that creates a situation with respect to which many people can collectively and coherently act. The reality "in the mind of the actor" is not the starting point of sensemaking, but is itself a result of collective text-making through interaction.[5] We believe he is right in marking a critical dimension of all management as the construction of a fabric of "words" (to repeat our earlier citation). What is problematical—why there is inevitably "loose coupling" in a laminated organizational conversation—is the construction of a text which is legitimated by organizational participants. It is not crucial that there be unanimity in the diverse cause maps, but it is crucial that everyone subscribe to an agreed-upon text, whatever reservations they may privately continue to entertain.[6] Only in this way can the organization retain its life-giving variety (i.e., stay loosely coupled), yet manage an acceptable degree of uniformity in its corporate interventions (a topic that we consider in depth in chap. 7). How texts come to be legitimated is thus an important issue of research, which we take up in chapter 9.

Significantly, neither Weick nor Boden deal much with conflict or hierarchy, nor is their treatment of power elaborated with any depth. This is a criticism that surely does not apply to the next author to be considered, Anthony Giddens.

ANTHONY GIDDENS: STRUCTURATION

Giddens adheres strictly to the flatland view of organization.[7] In a 1984 book called *The Constitution of Society*, for example, he contrasts two ap-

---

[5]Peirce (1950/1955) writes: "Unless we make ourselves hermits, we shall necessarily influence each other's opinions; so that the problem becomes how to fix belief, not in the individual merely, but in the community."

[6]Eisenberg (1984; Eisenberg & Witten, 1987).

[7]The theory of structuration is developed in a number of texts. Giddens presented his ideas in three books (1976, 1979, 1984). Cohen (1989) provides a comprehensive introduction. See also Held and Thompson (1989), Craib (1992), and Mestrovic (1998). For a succinct and clear summary from a communicational point of view, see Banks and Riley (1993), and McPhee (1989). For a cogent critique of Giddens' view of structuration, see Conrad (1993).

proaches to the study of organization (or society) one of which he terms functionalist/structuralist (including systems theory), and the other, hermeneutic or interpretive. Each, he thinks, overstates its case. The first (the basis of much traditional management theory) emphasizes "the pre-eminence of the social whole over its individual parts (i.e., its constituent actors, human subjects)" (Giddens, 1984, p. 1). The second (more compatible with the social psychological interpretation of organization) accords primacy to action and meaning, paying little attention to structural constraints (this is what we perceive to be the greatest weakness of Weick's approach, incidentally). The difference, Giddens says, is in the ontology: Functionalism proposes "an imperialism of the social object"; interpretivism is founded, by contrast, on an "imperialism of the subject."[8] His own challenge, Giddens says, is to transcend these "imperialisms." It is this alternative view that he calls "structuration." "I wish," he says, "to escape from the dualism associated with objectivism and subjectivism" (p. xxvii).

As does Weick, he begins with the interactive world in which the individual is caught up (it is this that makes his approach, like that of Weick, attractive to communication scholars). People's lived experience, he argues, starts as an ongoing flow of time: an undifferentiated "duration" or *durée* (Giddens, 1984, p. 3). It becomes meaningful only when it is reflexively monitored and rationalized.[9] What Giddens is getting at here is that people are caught up in a practical world of immediate involvement and action, and the only way that such a world can make sense to them is by its being transmuted into a representation of it (which is what he means by its being rationalized). It is not enough to live; to live meaningfully means to become self-conscious (this is what he means by monitoring). What people call *purpose, intention, reason,* or *motive* is an attribution resulting from our collective monitoring and rationalizing of the interactive experience. This rationalization reflexively constructs not only the subject but also the setting (the parallel with our own rationale of the manner in

---

[8]Weick can be read as attempting to liberate himself from "imperialism of the subject." In his early work, the role of individual cognition is strongly emphasized: "While the categories external/internal or outside/inside exist logically, they do not exist empirically. The 'outside' or 'external' world cannot be known. There is no methodological process by which one can confirm the existence of an object independent of the confirmatory process involving oneself. The outside is a void, there is only the inside. A person's world, the inside or internal view is all that can be known" (Weick, 1977, p. 273). Over the years, however, this salience of the subject has become less marked, as he has moved toward a more interactive view of sensemaking. We are not trying to suggest a total reversal of point of view so much as a shift of emphasis: Even in his early work he discusses socially grounded sensemaking (as, for example, in a jazz band).

[9]As we saw in chapter 3, Weick, citing Schutz, makes the identical point, that time exists as "pure duration," and its meaning emerges only in its segmentation, such a segmenting being the result of sensemaking on the part of the experiencer.

which textualization constitutes the subject, developed in chap. 4, should be evident here although, as we shall see, the textuality of representation is not central to his conceptualization). The social self is an attribution that can be traced back to consciousness of self—the result of monitoring and rationalization by means of which the person's social competence is evaluated (here Giddens explicitly acknowledges his debt to Goffman).

His theory takes the notion of agency or action as primary (he uses, he says, the terms *agent* and *human actor* interchangeably, see p. xxii, an equivalence that we do not share, as will appear as we go along). This in turn leads him into a discussion of power because power, he thinks, is an inherent property of action. To act is to make a difference, and the making of a difference, he says (Giddens, 1984, p. 14), is already "to exercise some sort of power."[10] For Giddens, there is no zero point of power: " 'Domination' and 'power' cannot be thought of only in terms of asymmetries of distribution," he says, "but have to be recognized as inherent in social association (or, I would say, in human action as such)." "Action," he says, "logically involves power" and therefore "power is logically prior to subjectivity, to the constitution of the reflexive monitoring of conduct" (p. 15).

(Notice the shift of emphasis: While both Weick and Giddens place action at the center of their theory, Weick points up the cognitive effects of action, Giddens its social effects, i.e., the establishment of a power relationship. The difference reflects, of course, disciplinary orientations: social psychology and cybernetics vs. sociology.)

Action always involves the mobilization of rules and resources. If rules and resources are the media through which power is exercised, it follows logically, that the extent of the power of an action depends on the rules and resources the actor draws on or is legitimated by. There is no reason to postulate these as ever being equitably distributed. Acting reflects the already existing distribution of resources and biases of the rules but it also constitutes society in a way that practically guarantees social inequalities (by Giddens' definition of power). The systemness of society thus arises from action, precisely because of the power relations it creates: "Power within social systems which enjoy continuity over time and space presumes regularized relations of autonomy and dependence between actors or collectivities in contexts of social interaction" (Giddens, 1984, p. 16).

Now we see the thrust of his argument. What he has committed himself to show is that the micro and the macro are already inherent in the ordinary, everyday interactive order—and nowhere else (otherwise we would slide back into dualism). That interactive order is a universe of

---

[10]The equivalence of power with action is more intuitively evident in French where the word *pouvoir* is both the term for *power* (in the usual English sense of that term) and also expresses the more neutral idea of *being able to* (or *has the capacity to* or *can*) act—a modalization of the main verb, linguistically speaking.

action where actors (as a result of their acting) have effects not only on the natural but also on the social world. Power is always being exerted to transform the natural and the social world. But the organizational issue is the scope of such power, in time and space: its capacity to affect that which is not immediately present as well as the present. If power were to be limited to the immediate sphere of interaction (face-to-face), there would be no need at all to introduce notions of macro-organization. It is because action is capable of transcending the local bounds of *this* space and *this* time—to "enjoy," as he puts it, "continuity over time and space"—that an explanation is needed. Such "continuity" supposes "regularized relations of autonomy and dependence between actors or collectivities." Interaction will always be local; the relationships of power will not.

How to explain such "regularized relations" of power that transcend the local circumscription of time and space? If we have been faithfully tracking the steps of his reasoning, it must be in the self-conscious, reflexive rationalization of action. For people to be in a relation of power involving nonpresent actors, the latter will have either to subscribe voluntarily to an interpretation of events that sustains such a relationship or to be so constrained that they have no choice but to do so. For action to have the kind of scope that enables it to transcend the bounds of the local, it will have to be recognized as having such scope. "Structure exists, as time-space presence," he says, "only in its instantiations in . . . practices and as memory traces orienting the conduct of knowledgeable human agents" (Giddens, 1984, p. 17). The exercise of power, in other words, is in the eye of the beholder.

Structure, then, is not a configuration of roles and statuses—not an organization chart such as that in Fig. 5.1—but a set of rules (and resources) that underlies "a 'virtual order' of transformative relations" with a resulting "reproduction of situated practices" allowing for "the 'binding' of time-space in social systems, the properties which make it possible for discernibly similar social practices to exist across varying spans of time and space and which lend them 'systemic' form" (Giddens, 1984, p. 17). Rules and resources are indissociable because meaningful action must mobilize both resources (as the medium of action) and rules (as the "methodological procedures" in the absence of which interaction would not be possible; here Giddens draws explicitly on Garfinkel's ethnomethodological rationale). Interaction is interpretable and has meaning because it is rule-based (a constitutive function); it is sanctionable because rules can be broken, and when they are reflexively monitored, the rule-breaker may be corrected (a regulative function). So it follows that "the day-to-day activity of social actors draws upon and reproduces structural features of wider social systems" (p. 24).

To summarize, structure is a set of rules and resources, "out of time and space," whose only materialization is in the observable practices of people (and their "memory traces"). It is, as he puts it, "marked by an 'absence of the subject'" (Giddens, 1984, p. 25). The subject comes into the picture only as the actor in some real here-and-now who, in acting and thus mobilizing rules and resources, is constituted as an agent that is recognizably social. In this way, the structure lends meaning to action (because it supports its reflexive monitoring), whereas the action once again exemplifies and reinstates the structure. It is this bifocal relationship that Giddens designates as the duality of structure. The result is a social system in which action is both enabled (the rules allow for the marshalling of resources) and constrained (the application of the rules and the mobilization of resources is sanctionable). The reification of organization—the tendency to see it as an objective entity—is no more than an effect of the reflexively interpreted rationalization of action, merely a product of ideology.

Giddens then identifies three "modalities" that he thinks of as the "dimensions" of duality (Fig. 5.4). The dimensions of structure are *signification* (whose modality is an "interpretive scheme" and which is realized in interaction as "communication"), *domination* (whose modality is "facility" and which is realized in interaction as "power"), and *legitimation* (whose modality is "norm" and which is realized in interaction as "sanction").

One other component of Giddens' formulation deserves mention (it also has echoes of Weick). The outcomes of action, he says (citing Merton), typically have unintended consequences. Outcomes are not foreseeable, nor, he thinks, can the principles of organizational evolution be reduced to formal laws. Organization may be dually self-organizing, but the path

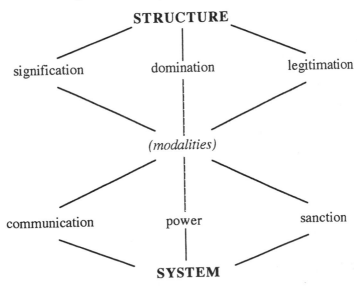

FIG. 5.4. Structure and system as linked by modalities.

its organizing takes is not scientifically predictable because it is not governed by formulable laws.

We are comfortable with the main thrust of Giddens' theory of structuration. As he does, we too see the structures of society as reproduced within the ongoing (always situated) conversation. We particularly like the tension he sets up between *system* and *structure*, in that systemness is characteristic of interaction (compare our earlier discussion of the systematics of conversation), whereas the structure is what is realized. We too see the emergence of structure as a product of a representing, and reflexively monitored, process. A similar tension motivates our distinction between site and surface. But here a difference in his theory and ours becomes evident, because it is not clear to us what he takes to be the surface of emergence of organization. His surface is no more than "practices and memory traces." But this leaves us up in the air: What, to put it in terms of our discussion in chapters 2 and 3, are the a priori forms of practice that we could recognize as organizational? And how are we to investigate "memory traces"?

What if we were to read the theory of structuration somewhat differently? Suppose we were to postulate that the structures of organization are not, first, "rules and resources" but rather are inscribed in the deep structure of the everyday texts that people generate when they enter a conversation. Every time a conversation occurred it would result in the reproduction of the system (the patterning of the discourse-world, to put it differently) and at the same time the reaffirming of the underlying structure (as a text-world), including how the world is signified, what kinds of dominance relations are recognized in that social group, and what are people's usual views of legitimation. Then, as people learned to speak their own community's language, they would in fact, secondarily, be absorbing its "rules." You cannot even use the word *judge*, for example, without having grasped what judging is, what a judge is, and in what context judges judge: That is all part of frame knowledge. The only "memory traces" involved would be those that come into play as a result of speaking (or writing). And this would emphasize a second of our points: that language is itself an extraordinary "resource" whose skilful manipulation is a way of unlocking other, more material, resources.

This, it seems to us, simplifies interpretation of Giddens' theory. Consider his view of resources. Resources are of two kinds (Giddens, 1984, pp. 16, 374): allocative and authoritative. *Allocative resources* "stem from control of material objects or of aspects of the material world." Let us take that definition and its relation to the exercise of power as uncontroversial for the moment: David's slingshot wins over Goliath's muscle (we come back to the issue of extended resource mobilization over time and distance in a later section of the chapter). It is the other part of the equation that is less clear: the authoritative resources (p. xxxi, emphasis added) "which," as he says, "*derive from* the coordination of the activity of human agents." Would it not be equally reasonable to say that the coordination of the activity of human agents derives from authoritative resources? Does not his formulation sound suspiciously circular, even tautological (especially because elsewhere he insists on what he calls a "dialectic of control" which admits that power is always at least minimally negotiable)? What is the origin of authority, in the absence of which authoritative resources can hardly be said to exist? What is the feature of the representation of action that would explain authority?

Let us now consider a second problem: Giddens' explication of rules, which, we think, exemplifies the same circularity. Rules, he says (with a bow to Wittgenstein, 1958), are related to routines, to sustained practices, have to do with how resources are employed, and imply methodological procedures (the French sociologist Bourdieu, 1980, has termed this *habitus*). They "relate on the one hand to the constitution of meaning, and on the other to the sanctioning of modes of social conduct" (Giddens, 1984, p. 18). But now the question is where does the power to constitute meaning and sanction come from? What, for example, if everyone does not share the same rule set (an entirely plausible organizational assumption, surely?

His problem, in both instances, arises from his treatment of communication. For Giddens, communication expresses no more, as a structural dimension, than what he calls signification. The exercise of power, and hence the realization of the presumed underlying social dimension of domination, is not described as a function of communication. Nor, in his model, is the application of sanctions and the realization of the underlying dimension of legitimation part of communication (Fig. 5.4).

This strikes us as a singularly unfruitful conception of communication, because it leaves Giddens without any effective means to explicate the central principles of his theory, domination and legitimacy.[11] He argues, we have seen, that power based on "authoritative resources" is associated with the "coordination of the activity of human agents." How such coordination could be accomplished other than through communication we find hard to imagine. Similarly, how legitimation could be mediated to produce, interactively, sanctions other than through communication would be difficult to conceive. As Conrad (1993) has written: "[T]he communicative processes through which these processes occur, particularly regard-

---

[11]Oddly enough, Weick's and Giddens' theories turn out to have the same blind spot, although for different reasons. Weick, by concentrating on the interpretive functions of communication, simply ignores the dimensions of power and legitimacy: They form no part of his characterization of organization. Giddens makes them his cornerstone, but by abstracting them from communication, ends up by treating the latter as no more than a medium of interpretation.

ing transformation, are left ambiguous in Giddens' model." We think this understates the case.[12]

How much simpler it would be to say that the modality which is common to signification, domination, and legitimation is the interactive generation of a text, in a situation of conversation, by means of which the structural relationships of the organization are once again realized in the systemic properties of the discourse-world thus brought into being, namely, the constitution of knowledge, power, and sanction. In this way, communication has become both the site and the surface of the emergence of society, or organization.

In chapter 3, we identified three modalities characteristic of text: the epistemic, the deontic, and the declarative. These are, we believe, the real basis of Giddens' trilogy of signification, domination, and legitimation. It is these that we should be studying, not the mysterious "rules" and "resources." We too employ the word *modality* but we see it as a function inherent in language-in-use and thus a potential field of communication study. We believe communication furnishes the primary modality by means of which sense is established, power instantiated, and behavior sanctioned.

Because of its textual basis, communication already furnishes modalities of interpretation, authoritative resource mobilization, and the application of sanctions. Among other advantages this revision of the theory of structuration offers is to relocate the domain of rule application, displacing it from individual behavior to interaction. This liberates us from what is perhaps the weakest part of Giddens' system, his notion of rules, which sounds, in the end, like a neo-Parsonian version of "internalization of norms" and leaves Giddens, as Parsons, with the difficulty of explaining conflict and change. After all, Parsons also began his theorizing with concepts of voluntaristic action, and he too, as Giddens, was forced (to get the system in) to resort to a mysterious internalization of norms.

There are other problems with Giddens' formulation. One in particular deserves mention. Conrad (1993) observes that "his ontology makes it difficult for him to incorporate collectives (for example, organizations-as-actors) as social agents into the theory of structuration" (p. 200). Here Giddens is trapped by the same initial premise as Weick: the primacy of the individual as a source of undisputed reality construction, or sensemaking. Thus, although he cites Goffman on the emergence of identity in interaction as a function of monitoring/rationalization, his decision to

---

[12]It has always puzzled us why Giddens chose to ignore Austin's insights into speech as a form of action, especially because Giddens' rival Habermas (1984, 1987) had previously constructed a whole theory of "communicative action" on it. Giddens need not have followed Habermas' interpretation (or misinterpretation) of Austin; an acceptance of speech as a siting of action would, however, have rendered the theory of structuration more operational than it is.

treat human actor and agent as equivalent leaves him no way to explain the appearance of corporate actors as effective agents, and thus renders his theory of power curiously nonorganizational and static. How, for example, do you mobilize resources to act at a distance (David's slingshot kills Goliath, even though David is not physically present or the land mine phenomenon) other than to become a corporate actor whose action is mediated by an intervening agent? It is this issue that we now take up. The theory we consider is the work of a French sociologist of scientific knowledge, Bruno Latour, the implications of whose thought far transcend the original frame of scientific practice which he, and a remarkable group of colleagues, has been studying intensely since the 1970s.

BRUNO LATOUR: TRANSLATION

As is Weick, Latour[13] is committed to enactment (his own variety, to be sure), and, as does Giddens, he situates his thinking about social organization by triangulating it with respect to theories of face-to-face interaction, such as ethnomethodology. He arrives, however, at a different view than that of either Weick or Giddens, partly, he says, as the result of a collaboration with a famous primatologist, Shirley Strum of the University of California at San Diego.

Strum and Latour (1987) distinguish between what they call "ostensive" and "performative" views of society. An *ostensive* view supposes society has a structure that makes it possible for actors to enter into it, and social actors are thus in society: part of it (as we saw, the mainstream image of management theory). In the *performative* view, by contrast, actors define, for themselves and for others, what society is, that is, it exists nowhere else other than in their performance of it. It is this second view that the authors develop. As Giddens did, Strum and Latour reject the macro/micro dualistic ontology of much of sociology. Latour, in particular, is a flatland proponent all the way.

But Strum and Latour (1987) illustrate performativity in the unorthodox way of drawing a comparison between baboon and human society. Extend-

---

[13]Latour's affiliation is with the École des Mines in Paris. (The "School of Mining," in spite of its rather pedestrian name, is one of the elite institutions of higher learning in France). There he, along with Michel Callon and others have pioneered in an approach sometimes known as "actor-network" theory. Their originality, among other factors, is in having woven threads of semiotics into their sociology, and in particular the semiotics of Greimas (whom we have described in chap. 3). From the elementary semiotic perception that subject and object are mutually defining, they have created a highly original approach to the sociology of networks, very different from that of someone like Everett Rogers, who is better known in North America. See Latour (1986, 1987, 1993, 1994, 1996; Latour & Woolgar, 1979).

ing over more than a half century, observations of primate colonies, in natural environments, such as that of baboons, have obliged primatologists to revise progressively their view of the life of our distant relatives and to recognize grudgingly its remarkable social complexity. In this contemporary account, baboons are actively constructing their social reality, "constantly testing, trying to see who is allied with whom, who is leading whom, which strategies can further their goals" (p. 788). They "perform" their social structure; they are "social players actively negotiating and renegotiating what their society is and what it will be" (p. 789). They are constantly (they "invest a great deal of time") testing, monitoring, and interfering with each other. They are not so much in a group (because that would assume the "group" existed autonomously of their performing it) "as striving to define the society and the groups in which they exist, the structure and the boundaries." Rather than being in a hierarchy, they are "ordering their social world by their very activity." Stable hierarchies develop "not as one of the principles of an overarching society into which baboons must fit, but as the *provisional* outcome of their search for some basis of predictable interactions" (emphasis added). They are the perfect exemplars, ironically enough, of the principle of the social construction of reality: "A baboon is, in our view, the ideal case of the COMPETENT MEMBER portrayed by ethnomethodologists, a social actor having difficulty negotiating one factor at a time, constantly subject to the interference of others with similar problems" (p. 790, emphasis in original). If you have ever worked in an office, and if this sounds to you too much like office politics for comfort, then you will have taken their point!

Their social life exemplifies "complexity," ours, the authors think, "complication." And the complexity of their social life mirrors that of the face-to-face human interaction of the kind that Erving Goffman first wrote about in his *Presentation of Self in Everyday Life* (1959): There is a kind of "information game" going on.

So, because in every other respect human society is radically different from that of the baboons, there must be something missing in the intersubjective account as it applies to modern society (R. McPhee, 1989, describes Giddens' theory, for example, as based on intersubjectivity; it is interesting that concepts of "rules and resources" do appear, at least superficially, to fit the baboon society Strum describes as well as they fit human society). The structuring of the human organizational frame, Latour believes, cannot possibly be an effect of intersubjectivity, because then we would never have escaped from the complexity of baboon existence and the limitations of scale it implies. The interpretive, ethnomethodological model can deal with the remarkable complexity of ordinary locally situated interactive talk (the sort of thing Boden reported on), but it fails to account for the transcendent features of contemporary social life (that is to say, patterns that hold over time and space). We are "complicated" in a way the baboons cannot aspire to.

The poor, benighted baboon is never alone socially (other than if banished from the tribe), with the result that he or she is never free from intrusion by others into his or her affairs (this is what makes his or her life "complex"). The human's world, by contrast, is full of constructed boundaries that both reduce complexity (by keeping unwanted interruptions out) at the same time as they increase complication. This is sort of like the Pentagon: on the one hand, a stunningly extended and complicated warren of corridors, offices, meeting rooms, storage spaces, laboratories, cubby holes, gyms, toilets, shooting ranges, and so on and so on (not to mention all the technology linking it to the outside world), and on the other, a place where every rank in the hierarchy is associated with its own specific barriers of access (that go to define the rank, in fact) and thus reduce complexity (this is why they have offices). Imagine a general equally accessible to every member of the U.S. Armed Forces—all of them, without exception, 24 hours a day—and you will have understood why baboons, competent members of society though they may be, do not have generals (or Pentagons), and humans do.

There would be no transcendence, Latour then argues, if, in the mediating processes of interaction, it were not possible to enroll nonhuman agents to our purposes. It is nonhuman actors that both enable and constrain because they provide the means by which actions are amplified. Thus, our own (and others') influence may be realized over greater expanses of time and space and those of others (and our own) similarly constrained: both globalized and channeled. Roman roads still handle traffic in parts of Europe, millennia after they were built, still facilitating and orienting. The enormous difference in the complication of our existence, compared with that of the baboons, is an effect of technology. Boden's organization was filled with human subjects; Latour's will be jam-packed with objects.

Latour's views need to be seen against the background of his singular take on the duality of structure/system (although these are not the terms he uses). All action takes place on the same plane, he argues, but not all actors are the same. What makes the difference is very simple: who the actor speaks for. Part of our everyday knowledge is how to distinguish between *I* and *we, he* or *she* and *they* (and in many European languages, although not English, between *you* singular and *you* plural). When an actor speaks for more than him- or herself (as a "we," in effect), such an actor speaks with an enhanced authority because it is the voice of more than one person, and thus has an extra weight. By a simple extension of the same principle, an actor who speaks for a whole group or community (the dean who says "the Faculty considers . . ."), has even more authority, and one who speaks for society as a whole (or perhaps a large organization) has the most authority of all. Such an actor has become a *macroactor* (Callon & Latour, 1981).

There need thus be no macro level corresponding to an objective society (nothing for communication to be in or within) but there may be macroactors because of the position they occupy in the organizational conversation. They speak with a different, more authoritative voice. The power of an actor is thus not explained as a property of the actor, but of the network of those who have authorized him or her to speak in their name (it is a power, evidently, that can be taken away as well as given). It is no longer the actor who is acting, but the collective network of people who speak through his or her agency: what Latour and his colleague Michel Callon call an *actor-network*. The game of power, then, is the putting together of an alliance of networked individuals for whom one speaks. Much of Latour's empirical work has aimed to show the putting together of alliances to create actor-networks as it works out in science.

But there is another logical consequence. If it is no longer the actor who acts but what is represented by the actor (who thus becomes an agent or what Latour sometimes calls an *actant*), then this "actor/actant" is no longer restricted to being human. Objects can also act in the name of a society, group, or organization: a press release, for example. This is, in essence, Latour's radical move. It is why Latour has become known for his championing of the hypothesis of subject-object symmetry. It turns out that he thinks we never act without enrolling some other agency. Let us consider why he thinks so and how this explains a central concept of his: mediation.

To act, he argues (Latour, 1994), a subject must enlist the aid of an object or objects (and perhaps other subjects), but objects are not neutral instruments (no more than are subjects). Objects come with built-in properties (often worked out over centuries of enculturation of the material world) that, because they exert an influence independently of the intentions of the subjects to which they are now joined, also affect the action. The woodsman's ax is an enabler because it opens a new potential for action, but it also dictates how it is to be employed: from what angle, with what force, using which hand—all involving skills that have to be mastered for the axer to ax. On the other hand, the ax without the ax wielder is no more than an inert artifact.[14]

---

[14]Latour (1994) cites the public debate over the limiting of access to firearms. According to the National Rifle Association (NRA), guns do not kill people, people do. The opposite argument—the materialist—holds that it is the gun that turns people into killers. In societies where guns are not easily available, the murder rate is dramatically lower than it is in the NRA's home country, the United States. Artifacts, this argument might run, come with scripts: Guns were made to kill—and they do. To the NRA it is clear: Bad people kill, good people do not; guns are nothing more than a neutral instrument. The materialist point of view

Agency, therefore—that which acts—is lodged neither in the subject nor in the object, but in a hybrid, a that-which-acts-for, thus literally becoming the agent (i.e., conforming to both of the definitions of agent offered by the dictionary: "that which acts" and "that which is empowered to act for another"). It is the agency inscribed in the hybrid resulting from the marriage of subject and object that both enables human interaction to transcend itself (future possibility), yet also constrains it (effect of the past). It is in the materiality of the enabling/constraining hybrid that time and space are spanned (we inhabit and are enabled and constrained by a constructed environment—constructed by ourselves in some previous time). Because the constituting of agency inevitably involves the recruitment of an object (in the absence of which the intention of the subject could not be realized), it is an instance of *mediation*.[15]

Latour is thus proposing that we return to first principles. What happens when we act? Break the program of action down into its parts, he suggests: intention, goal, means. After a goal is formed, and an intention is thus made manifest, then the issue is one of means. The concept of *means* is closely tied to that of *instrument*. The leap from baboonness to humanity is now illuminated: The baboon's only instrument, for the most part, is its own body; a human is able to enlist—to mobilize—a multitude of objects to enable him or her to achieve his or her purposes. But after an object is made an accessory to action (that is the whole point of technology) it has the curious feature that it can now act independently, in the absence of its human partner. Latour uses the example of a speed bump—a "silent policeman"—to illustrate. The speed bump was put there by someone with the purpose of slowing down traffic, but after it was installed, it goes on acting with no human source remotely in view.

It is this that leads Latour to postulate a principle of symmetry between subject and object. That which acts (the *actant*) is neither subject nor object in isolation but a new kind of agent, arrived at by a mediation that he calls a "translation," to produce an actant that is neither quite subjective (because, whatever the intentions of the human actor, they have been

---

reverses the presumption of causality: People become the executors of actions that their technology does not merely make available, but practically obliges them to follow. "The two positions," Latour points out (p. 31), "are absurdly contradictory. No materialist claims that guns kill by themselves. What the materialist claims is that the good citizen is transformed by carrying the gun. ... As to the NRA, they cannot maintain that the gun is so neutral an object that it has no part in the act of killing. They have to acknowledge that the gun adds something, though not to the modal state of the person holding the gun."

[15]Note how Latour has given a different meaning to Weick's enacted, or self-constructed, environment and in doing so has emphasized an inherent tension between the subjective and the objective that is absent in the earlier conceptualization: subjects can only act by the mobilization of objects but objects, per se, have no meaning in the absence of a subjective investment.

mediated and subtly transformed by the instrumentality of the object), nor objective (because the object in question is not a spontaneous occurrence in some natural nonhuman world, but has been mediated by the purposes of the user to become a new object in which are inscribed nonmaterial purposes).

The real world, where we all live, is a mediated world. "The myth of the Natural Tool under complete human control and the myth of the Autonomous Destiny that no human can master are symmetrical," Latour says (1994, p. 32), "But a third possibility is more commonly realized: the creation of a new goal that corresponds to neither agent's program of action." He calls this a *shift.* The outcome is not going to be fully predictable because, if both human and material object each have their own kind of power to act and if neither acts autonomously but they act in combination, then their joint mediation—the syncretic agency thus produced—is not fully under the control of either. Mediation is an ongoing process: as in baboon society, endlessly renegotiated, but in the human case on a greater scale of complication (multifaceted, but orderly: disciplined in a way that the baboons cannot possibly aspire to).

It is this composite actant that is the building block of human organization. The baboon's world is still one of actors in a natural environment; the human's is a domesticated natural. All human life thus takes the form of a succession of mediations, involving agents that are neither purely human nor purely material, but *hybrids*: agencies of mixed provenance. For Latour, every local world carries the actantial traces of a larger, more extended world—indeed, extending indefinitely back in time as well as in space—and it is in the mobilization of objects that the mobilization of humans—the emergence of organization—is made possible.[16]

---

[16]The essence of Latour's symmetry—and its feature he most insists on—is that it fuses Nature and Society into a single seamless web because, if it true that the nonhumans in our world all bear the mark of human purposes, the reverse must also be true: The humans similarly all have been so conditioned by the influence of nonhuman agencies that our very humanness—our modernity—is a hybrid product too. This idea is developed in depth in Latour (1992). As we have already mentioned, much of Latour's writing fits within the sociology of scientific knowledge (SSK). SSK has demonstrated to what an extent science is a hybrid enterprise, where trying to sort out what is due to nature and what to society is a thankless task because so much of what is found there is a tangled web of mediations, involving both human and nonhuman kinds of agency. Part of any scientific practice is laboratory-bound: involving the building of more and more complicated equipment where what is then discovered through research is indeed an effect of the scientists' questioning. But there is also an effect of the agency of the equipment, which has its own purposes and programs built into it and which tends to make some things visible and others not. And on the social side, what gets accepted as scientific "knowledge" ("blackboxed") depends on how many human allies have been brought on board, how the "scientific" results fit their purposes, how many human authorities can be marshalled to go along with the laboratory "findings" that the inscription and analysis of data (by the researcher) furnishes (Latour, 1987).

According to Latour, then, human interaction mobilizes constellations of objects which endure after and extend beyond the time and place of the interaction, and, as they do, serve to frame future interactions. Although this may seem like a variant of Giddens' structuration (resource use as the actualization of structure), it is fundamentally different. The originality of Latour's approach lies in his recognition that objects participate in interaction—indeed mediate it—yet at the same time, they form an integral part of a network that extends beyond the interaction, in time and in space: They continue to act even in the absence of their original subject partner. They have been, Latour puts it, "blackboxed": all traces of their original subjective investment obliterated. Therefore, there is no need to postulate a virtual structure of subjectively based rules and resources; rather, interactions mobilize objects that mediate and thus structure, reflexively, these same interactions at the same time that they surpass them.

Objects express agency and, thus, act.

LATOUR, WEICK, AND GIDDENS

Latour's performative theory of organization extends productively the range of the concept of enactment. Where Latour differs from Weick is in the emphasis he lays on the material transformation of the environment resulting from enactment. In other respects, the idea is the same. To act is to construct one's own environment by mobilizing objects, but because the material world has its own internal properties of agency independent of ours, the outcomes of action are never predictable. Our greatest strength as humans—the ability to inform the material world with our intentionality and thus shape it to our purposes—is also our greatest vulnerability. The world we have shaped—Weick's "environment"—is one that we do not completely control. In acting for us, it reinterprets us, and the resulting agency is more than medium, it is transcendence.

Latour, like Weick, rejects the macro–micro view of organization because for him the organization never actually exists (as an identifiable entity, that is). What exists is an *organizing*, an ongoing process of mediation in which the objective world where we live and interact both frames what we do and supplies us with the material for our own reconstruction of it. What we think of as organization is what is left over as a trace or a memory of yesterday's organizing. In chapter 2, we quoted Weick as saying that by the time we recognize the organization it is no longer there. What is there is our transformation of it; what makes it recognizable—re-cognizable—is precisely its no longer existing.

Latour also clarifies a second dimension of Weick's theory, that which concerns knowing: cause maps, for example. Again, the difference between the two versions is in the interpolation, in Latour's case, of materiality.

Weick thinks of knowledge as a subjective phenomenon and then has difficulty explaining how it is turned into a socially shared view of the world. Latour's work in the sociology of scientific knowledge (Latour & Woolgar, 1979; Latour, 1987) has repeatedly emphasized the role of transcription of findings, or production and validation of texts, in the context of a social community of scientists, where knowledge is turned, as he puts it (Latour, 1987), from *artifact* (the initial report, still bearing the imprint of the author or authors and only one step removed from the messy, ambiguous data of the laboratory) into *fact* (a scientific discovery now accepted by the community as established and no longer controversial). Latour's cause maps (scientific explanations), unlike Weick's, are written down, an object to be collectively viewed and judged as reliable or not. After being accepted, they are, like a black box, closed to further inspection and are merely part of what everyone knows, that is, facts.

Everything he cites as basic to science would apply with equal force to management. There too knowledge is socially constructed; there too the circulation of texts (reports, chalk talks, etc.) is a way to fix the facts. The Weickian tension between rule-governed behavior based on a known environment and open-ended cycle assemblies in the face of heightened equivocation finds a plausible explanation in the fixative properties of text, as opposed to the fluid character of conversation, and one which is closer to the communicational perspective. What Weick thinks of as rule-governed is what Latour would say had been black-boxed (and we would say texted, made procedural); the organization only reverts to open-ended recycling when the box reopens (and thus becomes conversational, rhetorical, open to argument). Latour's version of that recycling is considerably more strategic and rhetorical than Weick's (mobilizing allies, human and artifactual, developing an effective argument), and that too seems to us to have greater verisimilitude than Weick's more neutral characterization. After all, cause maps are resources too, in the context of a debate.

Similarly, Latour's explanation deals more effectively with the issue of power than does Giddens'. Neither is in disagreement with the principle that action instantiates a relationship of power, and indeed that power is an intrinsic component of action, simply because it transforms. Where they differ is in where they locate its agency. For Giddens, its locus is in the human actor, whose action is amplified in its effects by the mobilization of resources, material ("allocative") and moral ("authoritative"). But this leaves him with the difficulty of explaining how a human actor (his version of an agent), circumscribed in time and space, can act in a different time and place, where he or she is no longer present other than in the minds of the people there. Latour has no such difficulty because he never assumed an equivalence of actor and agency to begin with. For him, the intentions of the human actor have had to be mediated materially (or socially, through a human agent) so that what acts is not the first human actor, but a hybrid actant, which, whether material or social, can just as well act elsewhere as in the context of its coming to be (where it was first mobilized), so that the intentionality of the subject, now mediated, may as easily be present there as here. Someone's power is explained, Latour (1986) observes, not by what he or she does, but in what others do, that is, not by what the General does, but what the soldiers do. Then the power of an actor—the principal—continues even when he or she has withdrawn from the scene. This seems to us a more powerful version of structuration, precisely because, again, it makes no assumption as to the subjective state of the actors because they are already necessarily enabled and constrained in a material world, which bears the traces of interaction that has occurred elsewhere and at another time.

Latour's version of the structuring of society, it seems to us, has a good deal to recommend it to a communication researcher. It is behavioral all the way, with no mysterious "cause maps," no "out of time and space" structure inscribed in the "memory traces" of social members. Its whole emphasis is on transaction. And, it does deal with how organization takes form (as an actor-network) as well as with the emergence of organizational macroactors (who may be macroacting, but always in a microworld of interaction). And finally, by his emphasis on agency as the product of a translation of subjective intentionality into material form, he provides a means to explain the emergence of human organizations that transcend the local, both in showing how today's interaction is framed and constrained by the outcomes of yesterday's transactions (having been then materialized, thus rendered capable of acting now in the present) and in showing how today's interactions may be shaping tomorrow's, in virtuality.

Although Latour's theory constitutes a significant advance over previous accounts of the self-organizing communicative basis of society, it nevertheless has a limitation, and it is the same as for Weick and Giddens: a reluctance to deal with communication. Latour looks around him and sees in all the objects that surround him evidence of previous organizing (mediating): in the buildings, in the machinery, in the instruments and tools we put to use without ever questioning their ordinariness—their just being there. The material world bequeathed to us by previous generations becomes our surface of activity: where we carry on our business. But, oddly enough, he does not seem to have noticed that the language we use is part—a vital part—of that surface: that it too is a trace, a memory, of yesterday's organizing, and that it also both frames our current activity and provides us with a material to reconstruct our world. There would not be any scientific (or other) knowledge in the absence of language.

Language as Object

Latour's attitude to language is ambivalent. He has consistently emphasized the role of transcription and text in science. He understands the transactive character of social interaction. On the other hand, he is inclined to think of language as a symbol system and of language-based explanations of organization as an extrapolation of a subjectivity that he has been at pains to refute—a harkening back to an unsullied Habermasian sociality where technology is no more than a corrupting interference and not a vital principle that explains the hybrid character of modernity. Perhaps because, as a charter member of the Sociology of Scientific Knowledge, his attention has been so centered on the physical sciences (physics, biology, engineering), he seems not to have noticed that there is also a science of language, that treats it as an object, and indeed as a technology. To us, however, it appears that the same rationale of mediation he argues for in the hard sciences is at least as relevant for an analysis of human discourse.

Using his own chain of reasoning (Latour, 1994), suppose somebody (Agent 1) wants to express an idea; they are, as he puts it (p. 32), "interrupted," until they have enlisted the support of a second agency (Agent 2), namely, language, whereupon, as a consequence of the "detour," now "a third agent emerges from a fusion of the other two" (Agent 1 + Agent 2 → Agent 3), which is neither the person (the speaker) nor the instrumentality or resource (the language) but the spoken (what Ricoeur, the interpretive philosopher, 1981, 1991, would call the *dit*, the "said," not the *dire*, the "saying"). The spoken—our term for it is text—is thus an actant in just the way Latour describes: It reflects both (partly) and neither (totally) of the agencies that presided at the mediation that produced it. The moment of speaking (or writing) is that instant when subjective is transmuted into objective and the objective takes on qualities of the subjective.

Latour's characterization of organization thus seems to lack a component. Consider again how Callon (1986) and Latour (1994) picture the formation of an actor-network. Initially, there are a set of diverse actors, each with their own interests. The network begins to form when all of them are confronted with a problem that might have a common solution. This is called *problematization*. After they have recognized their interest ("intéressement") in a proposed (by someone) solution, a differentiated aligning of roles ("alignement"/"enrôlement") begins to take shape. They have been translated into an actor-network (notice again the implication of hybridization, because both human and material actors may be involved) that can now speak with a single voice, a macroactor. The essential step in the process is what is called an *obligatory passage point* ("point de passage obligé"), which is to say a recognition that a certain step is a necessary convergence for all of their (in other respects divergent) projects.

This model works rather well for the formation of organization, from Henry Ford's assembly line to Ray Krok's hamburger line. What justifies most organizations is the recognition of an obligatory passage point, or one (or more) essential process(es) that is (are) part of everyone's agenda, whatever their other differences. It is interesting that it also explains conflict and the dissolution of an actor-network when, as differences multiply, the alignment gets out of whack. But although it explains what brings the organization into being and continues to constitute its raison d'être, it is not very informative about another dimension of organization that we think of as moral. Nor, although it explains the genesis of structure, does it do a very good job of accounting for its persistence.

Suppose that we accept the Latour hypothesis of translation and the reinterpretation of Weick's enactment and Giddens' structuration it entails, but with the one condition that the texting of language is to be included as a manifestation of translation with all the conceptual baggage that accompanies that latter concept. Then language becomes an object with its own properties: a technology that has been worked over for centuries, even millennia, and that we inherit as part of our culture, as with the other mediating substances Latour has in mind. Now, if we are to be consistent, we have to buy the whole package; we cannot selectively pick those properties of language that fit with our other ideas on translation as effected by other material agencies and discard what we do not like. It's in for a penny, in for a pound.

When we do, we discover a dimension notably absent in Latour's presentation: rights and obligations. As we explore this dimension, we can begin to clarify how communication recreates organizational patterns over time and space, as Giddens proposed it must.

LABOV AND FANSHEL: RIGHTS AND OBLIGATIONS

In our three previous chapters, we considered the properties of language. We concluded that one of those properties—a vital one because it is the link between text and discourse—is modality. We found, in this chapter, that there is a correspondence between the linguistic conception of modality and the sociological equivalent identified by Giddens as the instrumentality of structuration. Gidden's intuition is well founded, we believe, provided we accept a different idea of operationalization of structuration, as conveyed by the modalities of speech. To illustrate how modality is realized communicationally, we borrow from an analysis reported by Labov and Fanshel (1977).

Their organization is very micro: a family composed of a mother and her anorexic daughter, whose recorded therapy sessions form the data source analyzed by the authors. Nevertheless, their case history example illustrates a principle that applies to large as well as small organizations: the rights and responsibilities of actors—macro as well as micro. We term it the theme of *governance.*

Their analysis is centered on exchanges such as the following (the mother has been visiting another, married, daughter and has been away from home; the two are talking on the telephone):

Daughter: *Well, when do you plan to come* **home***?*
Mother: *Oh, why-y?*

At issue is the daughter's feeling of not being able to cope in her mother's absence, and her utterance can thus, in context, be read as a request for action—specifically, a request that her mother return home to look after her. The mother's reply is neither an acceptance nor a rejection; it is a form of putting off the request of the daughter for action—one that the analysts perceive to be a socially legitimated way of turning aside a request for action, namely by interjecting into the sequence an answering request for information ("Why-y?"), a way to stall, if you like. The actual exchange thus conveys more than it says superficially: It is an oblique reference to the rights, duties, and obligations that go with the respective roles of daughter and mother.

Labov and Fanshel see in the daughter's utterance what they call a mode of argument.[17] An argument, enthymemically speaking, typically consists of a general statement or premise (that is called a *proposition*), a fact, and a conclusion. The daughter's spoken utterance refers (in its presupposition) to a fact: The mother is away from home. The unspoken premise, or proposition, which gives the utterance its argumentative force is hypothesized by the authors to be the daughter's belief that a mother's place is with her daughter, especially if the daughter has difficulty in coping. The implied (if unspoken) conclusion is that the mother should immediately return home, and it is to this (highly mitigated but still intelligible) act that the mother responds by her "Oh, why-y?". The daughter is calling on (and the mother reacting to), the authors believe, a socially sanctioned way of making a legitimate request. They call their hypothesized procedure a "Rule of Request" (Labov & Fanshel, 1977, p. 78; see also chap. 9). It is through the operation of such rules that, they believe, words are translated into actions and vice versa.

If we credit the reasoning of Labov and Fanshel, then the attempted explanation of the formation of an actor-network offered by Callon and

---

[17]Note that we are using the word *argument* here in the rhetorical, not, as we did earlier, the specialized semantic sense of formal linguistics.

Latour is too simplistic to accept unconditionally. At issue is the theory of communication to which the analyst subscribes.

Actor-network theory differs from the conventional standard theory of networks in foreseeing the possibility that what starts as autonomous nodes may, in the interaction, fuse to form macronodes, either replacing the original or adding new ones to the network. The glue that holds the macronodes together is the obligatory passage point. Otherwise, the assumption is one of symmetry—indeed, a level of symmetry that envisages objects (such as populations of scallops, in one of their famous studies) as constituting nodes in the network, side by side with the human actors. As long as the disparate interests converge, the macronode holds; when they diverge, it dissolves. It is thus a theory of coalition formation, and its ontological foundation is more psychological (people and their interests) than communicational.

We recognize coalition formation as an effect of horizontal communication. But it leaves out of account the complementary hierarchical form of communication we presented in chapters 2 and 3: one that is ditransitively constructed and grounded in narrative logic. We seriously doubt that an organization founded solely on the principle of mutual interest ("intéressement") would ever last very long because the bonds are too fragile. Let us now give an alternative, more communicational, explanation—one which mobilizes the concepts we developed in chapter 4.

Governance as a Head–Complement Relationship

According to Labov and Fanshel, patients (and presumably everyone else as well) carry into therapy (among other occasions) assumptions about "the normal course of social life" (1977, p. 55): what we have characterized as frame knowledge. They describe these assumptions, or propositions, as including what they call "status predicates." Included in their list of predicates is one that reads (p. 55):

(HEAD) X is head of a household.

But, as we saw earlier, the concept of *headness* presupposes that of a complement. The mother–daughter relationship furnishes a fair example of what manifestation such a logical couple might take in a practical world of everyday affairs. The nature of such a bond is to join two heads to form a couple in which one head is accorded precedence over the other, creating a somewhat uncomfortable, although indispensable, partnership. This is inherently a mixed motive situation. It engenders two modalities of communication: control (on the part of the head) and commitment (on the part of the complement). We might refer to this complementarity as a *governance contract.*

By *rights and obligations* we mean this: The head is responsible; the complement has rights.

What we term the *structure* of an organization is a tissue of embedded head-complement relationships, dominated by one macro head node, which is the organization itself, as an accredited actor, and the complement as its members. But from this first node there flows a whole cascade of localized head-complement couples, situationally negotiated and renegotiated on a daily basis.

Latour's Agent 1 + Agent 2 → Agent 3 formulation makes a match to the X-bar construction, providing we assume Agent 1 is head, Agent 2 is complement, and Agent 3 is the resulting X-bar node.

In a head–complement relationship, one agent takes the reponsibility for the modalization of the performance of another (just as the anorexic daughter took her mother to be responsible for her). Such modalization includes forming judgments about the nature of reality, taking the initiative in coordinating the respective responsibilities for performance of key tasks (commands and promises), and decision making. The complement position is one of petitioning. But in practice, any such relationship supposes the willing (if reluctant) participation of both agents and is thus susceptible to evolution over time as the nature of the relationship is renegotiated. If this is structure, it is never quite top down, nor entirely bottom up, but process driven, negotiable in communication.

How do such structures persist over time and space? Giddens would have us believe that it is through the learning of rules. Neither Weick nor Latour address the question at all, in so many words. Our explanation draws on our general theory of communication and, in particular, the role of text in it. Words such as *mother* and *daughter* (or indeed *manager* and *worker*) are part of frame knowledge: that which we acquire when we learn to use a language. As we saw in the previous chapter, such words come equipped with a built-in program that specifies how they will enter into a head-complement relationship. Language is thus a carrier of scripts. Even though there are two partners involved, we need not assume they bring identical scripts to the union, nor need we assume that scripts are invariable throughout the lifetime of the individuals concerned. On the contrary, we take it as given that the meaning of words is an effect of learning. Put somewhat differently, yesterday's communicational experience (recorded in text) now becomes a guide to and the basis of today's organizational frame that makes interaction (through texting) feasible. For the most part, mothers do "mothering" in much the same way they learned it should be done when they were "daughtering."

The advantage of a communicational interpretation, we believe, is that it both accounts for organizational structure and its persistence, while at the same time making allowance for evolutionary change. We know that couples such as mother–child, husband–wife, manager–employee exhibit constancies across situations, and yet are highly variable in their patterns from one society to another, and indeed over time within a given society (as Jacques, 1996, pointed out). Our assumptions about family life today, including its distribution of rights and obligations, is distinctly at variance with what was the case 50 or 100 years ago. (People often see this as loss of social coherence, but it is really something quite different, that is, a transition to a different set of assumptions, and, lexically speaking, a change in the meaning of words).

The proponents of actor-network, or translation, theory were in part reacting against the structuralist movement that dominated French thought in the 1960s. Structuralism found its justification in principles outlined in de Saussure's views on language as a system which, from a set of arbitrary (or perhaps not totally arbitrary) differences (apples vs. oranges, for example) went on to construct a paradigmatic conceptual universe of embedded categories (apples and oranges are fruit, fruit and vegetables are greengroceries, etc.). The emperor of the structuralists was Claude Lévi-Strauss, an anthropologist, and it was he (although not only he) who persuaded social scientists into believing that society itself manifests a hidden category system (kinship systems being the most plausible candidate). Management theory has generally been receptive to the idea that organization has a structure and that such structures may be planned and implemented. The problem with these approaches is that, after the structure has been revealed, there is no mechanism to explain how it might subsequently evolve other than through the intervention of a deus ex machina (a topic we develop in chap. 6). Actor-network theorists have quite properly been searching for such a change mechanism, but this leads to the difficulty of accounting for the constancies of structure. Our earlier discussion of the role of text in communication seems to offer a resolution of the difficulty. What remains to be investigated is the other side of the equation: how organizations change.

CONCLUSION

In this chapter, we have developed the themes that will preoccupy our attention in the remainder of the book. They can be summarized as follows:

- A flatland view. Each of the authors considered have agreed on one elementary idea: that there is no ontological difference between the macro and micro levels of organization. What we call "the organization" is generated in the same conversation where individual actors find their identity.

- Experience is a retrospectively monitored flow, which we make sense of by rationalizing it, or giving it an episodic character. This is essentially what we mean by the mapping of circumstance to frame knowledge and conversation form to text form. Experience emerges in our retrospective interpretation of it.

- If we accept Giddens' definition of system versus structure, then structure is instantiated in process as an effect of modalization. We differ from Giddens in perceiving the three dimensions of structure—signification, domination, legitimation—as originating in the narrative semantics of language and as being realized in the construction dynamics of interpreted action.

- Environments are an effect of enactment; they are invested with meaning. The realms of action and thought do not exist on separate planes but are dimensions of the same enacting experience; action and knowledge are co-constructed.

- The loose coupling of organizational networks creates the potential for forms of knowledge that transcend those of the individual (a dominant theme of chap. 6 and 7).

- Organizational process is marked by tension between two kinds of knowledge: that which is stored in cause maps and constitutes a residue of past experience versus that which is generated in the loosely coupled networks of ongoing conversation of people (the source of organizational variety). This is the theme of chapters 7 and 8.

- There is a fundamental difference between actor and agency: *Agents* may take the form of individual persons, but they may also be materialized in technology or represent metonymically collective actors, or macroactors. The emergence of the latter is an effect of the constitution of actor-networks, or groups of actors mobilized around a common object of concern. This is the theme of chapter 8.

- In the end, every action supposes the mediation of a material agent. Because of their materiality, such agents can act at a distance and over time. They thus serve to transcend the inherent limitations of locally situated action and thus explain the emergence of globally structured organizational forms.

- Of these agents, that which is materialized in speech and writing is of particular importance because it is in this way that head–complement relations with their attendant rights and obligations are instantiated, and in this way, the authoritative resources of which Giddens writes are made actual.

Chapter **6**

From Symbol Processing to Subsymbolic Socially Distributed Cognition

Chapter 6 initiates a line of inquiry that leads into the next three chapters and investigates organization in a new way. In this chapter, we lay the groundwork for those that follow. In chapter 5, we referred to an idea of Karl Weick's, among many others, thrown off almost casually by that fertile mind: that interconnected networks of people, in some sense of the word, know more than any of the individuals who compose them. It is this that Weick sees as the principal advantage of loose coupling. Organizations can accumulate variety, and variety is the key to expanding what we called, as an analogy, the circle of light created through organizational enacting. It is an idea that, as we shall see, Weick himself continued to explore in later work and that has taken on greater plausibility as a result of research into the bases of computing—an exploration that has shaken the field of artificial intelligence to its foundations. Our own interpretation of this hypothesis leads us in a surprising direction in chapter 7, that is, toward an exploration of the logical basis of the emergence of organization as an effective actor (or macroactor, to use the Callon–Latour term), and how such emergence can explain a key concept of Giddens' theory, namely, authority. It is this issue of authority and its consequences that then forms the topic of chapter 8.

A second objective of the chapter has an epistemological orientation. Toward the beginning of the 1900s, the father of modern linguistics, Ferdinand de Saussure, proposed, in addition to the distinction between *langue* and *parole*, which we mentioned in chapter 1, a distinction between diachronic and synchronic modes of analysis. A *diachronic* view of human language is historical in its orientation. It patiently traces the step-by-step

173

evolution of language forms over long stretches of time to discover how languages that are now quite distinct from each other, such as English and Swedish, can nevertheless be traced back to a common ancestor. De Saussure proposed an alternative, or *synchronic*, method of analysis, which emphasizes the systemic properties of the object being studied at a given point in time. By stopping the clock, as we might put it, the analyst can concentrate on those features of the object under examination that have structural stability and can thus be treated as a system. De Saussure was thus the originator of structuralism.

Contemporary linguists continue to divide along the boundary line de Saussure drew. Geneticists are similarly divided into those who are preoccupied with the creep of evolution as a historical process of accumulation of errors in the replication of genes (Jones, 1993, p. 129, estimates, for example, that "humans and chimps share 98.4 per cent of their DNA"), and those preoccupied with mapping the human genome. Again evolution versus structure. Quite evidently, the choice of perspective—diachronic versus synchronic—has real consequences in what theorists focus on and, thus, see.

This difference of perspective is characteristic of two current versions of organizational theory. The first of these images pictures organization as an information network linked to a central decision system, management. Like most 20th century characterizations of organization, it is structuralist. It takes the organization to be an object with sufficiently constant systemic properties that it can reasonably be studied synchronically, as a structured configuration of parts—people and tasks. It portrays organization as a unity-in-diversity. The organization is conceived as being made of parts that have specialized functions, all linked together in a complementary fashion, so that their collective activities not only form a sum of discrete processes but also achieve common purposes that can be explained only as a property of the whole. However loosely coupled the parts may be, they are nevertheless coupled to compose a more or less coherent totality, or organization. As Orlikowski (1996) observes, it is an image that assumes stability and visualizes change as the exceptional circumstance. This is the *symbol processing* view of organization.

The radical alternative that Weick, along with a few others, is writing about displaces the decision-making and information functions by postulating them as distributed properties of the network itself. This latter version of a network is evolutionary in a way that the former, more structural model of organization, is not. Change is not the exception but the rule (it is a flatland perspective). This view makes obsolescent the idea of an autonomous central decision maker. This is what we call a *subsymbolic*, or *distributed cognition* view of organization. However, as our investigation proceeds, we discover that this second theory has hidden within it a more complex mix of knowledge types that seems to us to call into question the very division into diachronic and synchronic as it applies to organizational research.

Although both theories of organization draw on a common well of ideas originating in the theory of computation, they nevertheless arrive at a very different, and even opposed, conclusion. One objective of the chapter is to explore the roots of this divergence. Since the 1940s or so, the theory of computation has become what might be called the dominant metatheory of a number of fields, including artificial intelligence, organizational theory, and communication theory—to the point, indeed, that it could be fairly described as a genuine exemplar of that seriously over-used term, a paradigm. A *paradigm* is a pattern of seeing so elementary that it is capable of informing many diverse intellectual activities, without necessarily being recognized as doing so (Kuhn, 1970). Earlier societies used the concept of body, organism, or machine in this way; ours, since the 1940s, has been mesmerized by the computer. Communication scholars need to be self-aware of their own tacit reliance on the computation paradigm, especially because it is now an area of intense controversy, which places its continued paradigmatic status very much in doubt.

Behind these more limited objectives there lies another, to which we return in chapter 9. We see it as important to encourage the communication researcher to be more reflective on the practice of the research craft by considering his or her own role in the constitution of organization. Our investigation into the evolving computational theory of organization points up a difference between symbolic and subsymbolic modes of intelligence, and suggests, given their mutual reflexive interdependence, a central role for the theorist of organization.

Finally, it is in these chapters that we hope to accomplish the objective of connecting the analysis of organization with the ideas presented in Part I. As we investigate the play between the symbolic/subsymbolic, we simultaneously explore the hypothesis of conversation/text form and their organization-creating constraints on communication.

SYSTEM THEORY: ORGANIZATION AND COMMUNICATION

Over the time the field of organizational communication has existed as an identifiable area of scientific research, that is, since about the mid-1960s, organization theory has been predominantly informed by a body of theoretical precepts that emerged in the previous generation, roughly from

1936 to 1956: the theory of computation.[1] The theory of computation furnishes the same scaffolding of ideas that led to the design and building of a general purpose digital computer but that event, although salient in the popular imagination, is just the tip of an iceberg (we come back to give a more adequate description of computation later in the chapter). The theory of computation does indeed underlie the making of an artifact called a *computer*, but it has wider ramifications that carry us into what might seem at first glance to be nonobvious applications, namely, organization and communication theory.

The theory of computation is currently in turmoil, as we shall see, and has branched into two theories, based on quite different (and in some respects contradictory) principles of what it means *to compute*, and thus how one might explain organization and/or communication in terms of a computational language. It is this branching that we take up in the second part of the chapter. To lead into this inquiry, we need to give a brief introduction to the conventional theory.

March and Simon: *Organizations*

The critical historical turning point in the development of the organization-as-system theory was the publication in 1958 of March and Simon's book, *Organizations*, in which they laid out for the first time a fully elaborated and explicit theory of organization as a computational system that included, although it did not highlight, a theory of organizational communication as the functional operating system for the transfer of data and instructions.

That book is one of the most—if not the most—influential management-oriented works on organizational theory ever written.[2] It is a 20th-

---

[1]1936 is the date of Turing's paper on computing machines, the first full-blown theoretical blueprint for a computer; in 1946, the first working digital computer came into operation; 1956 is the date of Newell and Simon's unveiling of the "General Problem Solver," often thought of as ushering in the age of artificial intelligence and cognitive science.

[2]We are aware of an alternative reconstruction of the history of organizational conceptualization—one which would make the sociologist Talcott Parsons the linchpin figure in the "imaginization" (Morgan, 1993) of organizations as systems. Clegg and Dunkerley (1980), for example, hold this view. However, they, in our opinion, considerably underestimate the importance of Simon and March (possibly because the latter are not sociologists?) even though they admit that Parsons is "not such a major figure as he once was" (p. 172) and that "in his work there is not a great deal of attention paid to organization analysis" (Parsons, 1960, was primarily concerned with a theory of society, within which organization figures as a component level). Similarly (and closer to home), it is evident that Farace, Monge, and Russell's (1977) early introductory text, *Communicating and Organizing*, is inspired by Parsons' "structural-functional" framework. Significantly, by the end of the 1950s, Parsons (1960) had also incorporated computational theory into his framework of social action. Nevertheless, we

century watershed. Before *Organizations*, there were two main bodies of managerial thought on organization, the so-called classical theory of administration, and the human relations school of employee motivation. After *Organizations*, there were three—or really only one, because March and Simon's had absorbed the other two. And the influence of this book is as potent today as ever. Sometimes the link is quite explicit, as in Stinchcombe's (1990) *Information and Organizations* or Boden's (1994) *The Business of Talk* or in recent articles by Pentland and Reuter (1994), Pentland (1995), Yates and Orlikowski (1992), Orlikowski and Yates (1994), and Fulk and Collins-Jarvis (1996), to take only a few examples. Mostly the connection is implicit, but genuine. The current literature on the learning organization is in some ways just a replay of ideas sketched out in *Organizations*. The implementation of computers into the workplace has been dictated almost in its entirety by the March–Simon rationale (Sachs, 1995). If their book had not been written, reengineering would not sound so plausible. And managers would not be able to so readily justify their self-image as decision makers, strategists, and planners.

This is also the book that set out the guidelines that have served as a mainstay of theory in our own field. The colleague they describe as their "collaborator," Harold Guetzkow, is, for example, one of the three earliest references cited by R. C. Smith (1993) in her review of the organizational communication literature (along with Lee Thayer and Charles Redding). Guetzkow's chapter in the 1965 *Handbook of Organization* (the latter having, incidentally, been edited by James March, one of the authors of *Organizations*) was entitled, prophetically, "Communication in Organizations."[3]

Why was the March and Simon book so influential? How did it become the accepted theory of organization, which was so plausible to its readers that it has taken on the guise of conventional wisdom, with its language absorbed

---

continue to believe that the March and Simon book, although less "Grand Theory" than Parsons, was better founded in the contemporary theory of computing systems and has ultimately been much more influential.

[3]Guetzkow drew on earlier work initiated by Alex Bavelas (1948, 1950), a student of Kurt Lewin, in which he proposed an experimental procedure for the study of message exchange in small (five person) groups. Bavelas was aware of the broader organizational implications of his research and in a book published in 1951 (Bavelas & Barrett, 1951) set out his thinking on the subject. Bavelas' ideas were given a more sophisticated systems theory exposition by a group at MIT (Luce, Macy, Christie, & Hay, 1953; Macy, Christie, & Luce, 1953). The MIT group drew on cybernetics and information theory in an elaborate mathematical treatment of the communication-in-organization idea, again, however, in the context of small-group research. During the 1950s, a flourishing experimental research expanded on the Bavelas proposal (see, for example, Shaw, 1964, for a review). Guetzkow was one of those directly implicated in this work. March and Simon were the first to place this, and other traditions of research of the time, in a fully elaborated theory of organization. Most of this other literature remained social psychological and limited to microlevel phenomena.

into the vernacular? How did it become just a part of folk science, with principles to be followed prescriptively by those who make decisions in organizations, who thus construct a fabric of practice and sensemaking that, because it is indirectly inspired by the theory, becomes in turn a confirmation of it—a kind of tautological loop that Weick calls "enactment"?

In answer, consider what these writers accomplished in the light of Kuhn's ideas on how an ordinary theory is transmuted into a paradigm, or at least reinterpreted in the framework of a paradigm (Kuhn, 1970). March and Simon did not reject previous bodies of theory (any more than modern geometry rejects the Euclidean version); their theory absorbed and superceded the earlier ones. Their theory of rationality, compared to the classical school of organization theory, was better grounded intellectually and more persuasive; it was, after all, for his work that Simon was to receive a Nobel prize in Economics. Until March and Simon made the link, there had been no way to make a connection between the macrolevel thinking of classical organizational theory and the microlevel field work findings of the human relations school of social psychology or of the empirical microsociology of organization, such as the work of Merton (1940) and his students, Blau (1955), Gouldner (1954), Selznick (1949), or Whyte (1948). So they accomplished the kind of synthesis that brings together the diverse strands of an emerging field of research.

Another of Kuhn's requirements for the emergence of a paradigm is that it provide a platform on which subsequent investigators can build a research program to carry out what Kuhn calls "normal science": The theory should be productive. On this score, the March and Simon development is exemplary. It opened many doors. Consider just one. Their insistence on the *boundedness* of human rationality meant that they conceived organizational structure and process not in mechanical, but in something closer to organic, system terms. The emphasis in the latter part of their book is on evolution, adaptation, and learning. True, they say, "communication channels may be sometimes deliberately and consciously planned" (March & Simon, 1958, p. 167) but they also develop through usage: Birds of a feather flock together. Channel usage is self-reinforcing so that the communication network emerges not only because of task needs, but also in response to social functions (as, they note, George Homans, 1950, had argued). This emerging network in turn begins to have an influence on decision-making processes, so that not only does the organization develop a mixed pattern of local rationality because of task specialization, but the global pattern of communication is itself somewhat self-organizing, as much a product of history as unadorned rationality. And once established, such patterns become self-justifying and self-reinforcing.

Here, they were sketching out in rough form the outlines of a contingent theory of organizational structure, something that we know was to emerge in the decade following the publication of *Organizations.* One can even see in their reading of organizational dynamics many of the seminal concepts that were later to be elaborated by Weick: local versus global rationality, the tendency not just to respond to the environment but to structure it in a way that simplifies response, and the centrality of sensemaking in goal-oriented work. Contemporary research literature on the ecology of organizations can be traced to its origins in this 1958 book. So can reengineering. But so, strangely enough, can a theory development of a very different order, the constructivism of a Deirdre Boden. The theory gave researchers something to chew on.

There is also a sociological explanation for the success of *Organizations*: the prestige of the authors. We have mentioned that Simon would win a Nobel prize in Economics; he was also an author of a widely cited text on administration that came out in the 1940s. In 1957, he had published a mathematically challenging book, *Models of Man*, in which, among other things, he did a fascinating take on theories of the sociologist Homans and the social psychologist Festinger, then among the giants in the social sciences. Two years earlier, in 1956, in a collaboration with Alan Newell that was sustained for 40 years, he unveiled the "General Problem Solver" (GPS) that was to be the foundation stone of the new field of artificial intelligence (AI) and cognitive science (the emphasis in the March–Simon book on problem-solving comes from here).

Truly extraordinary versatility of an order seldom seen: Simon is an icon of an era. And his colleague, James March, was not far behind. He had impeccable credentials in organizational studies and his influence was to continue in the years following the publication of *Organizations*. He coauthored (Cyert & March, 1963) another influential text on organization in the 1960s; he was, as we have already noted, the editor of the 1965 *Handbook of Organizations* and its subsequent editions. He has gone on to write extensively on decision making and learning.

Computation as the Basis of Rationality

So now let us consider what they said in this paradigm-making book.

First, as March and Simon see it, the employees of an organization are not just dumb instruments ("judgmental dopes," in Garfinkel's phrase) for carrying out a predetermined task (Frederick W. Taylor's prescription), but rational, thinking beings. They may not have perfect knowledge of their environment, nor are they exempt from the limitations of seeing things from a particular perspective or subjectively colored frame of reference. On the contrary, their choices are always taken on the basis of a limited, approximate, simplified image, or "definition," of the real situation. Their rationality, such as it is, is imperfect—"bounded." The elements of the situation that are perceived reflect the influence of psychological and sociological processes, including the employee's own activities and those of people with whom he or she is associated.

That which makes the individual organizational members rational is the purposeful manner of their reacting to events in the environment. They accomplish this by calling to mind, or "evoking," programs that have been learned at some previous time and whose performance both gives their activity shape and is an appropriate response to the event. Whatever the domain—manual labor, clerical tasks, the practice of professions such as medicine or the law—such programs can range from highly routine, where the definition of the situation is familiar and well structured, to cases where the situation is unfamiliar or ambiguous, in which case there is problem solving to be done. All organizational activities involve routine; they all call for problem solving in some situations (for discussion, see Pentland, 1995).

What is a performance program? Here is the example they give (this obviously comes from before the era of "just-in-time" management). Think of a two-bin system of inventory control. Two variables are critical: how much to order and when to order it (the latter being determined by the buffer stock or the amount that should be on hand when a new order is placed). A program might then read: When material is drawn from stock, note whether the quantity that remains equals or exceeds the buffer stock; if not, Write a purchase order for the specified order quantity.

Although not all performance programs are going to be this simple, they will usually be a variant on the same pattern: Perform an operation, take a measurement of the result, and, depending on a given criterion, either carry on with the performance as before or take alternative measures that involve a correction or an alternative course of action. It is like a computer flow chart, or what Miller, Galanter, and Pribram (1960) called a TOTE unit (Test-Operate-Test-Exit).[4]

Most behavior in organizations, March and Simon think, is governed by performance programs, more or less explicit, more or less routine. The organization as a whole is thus a "complicated mosaic" of performance program executions (March & Simon, 1958, p. 149), distributed over the population of employees and executed in parallel by them.

---

[4]In March and Simon's words: "The decomposition of tasks into their elementary program steps is most spectacularly illustrated in modern computing machines which may carry out programs involving thousands of such steps" (1958, p. 144). The computer deals with both the routine and the nonroutine: "The capabilities of computers have now been extended to many tasks that until recently have been thought to be relatively complex, involving problem-solving activities of a fairly high order" ... [such as] ... "a program that enables a computer to discover proofs for certain kinds of mathematical theorems, and a program for translating languages." (Remember, this was published in 1958; their estimation of the computer's potential was optimistic.)

Not all programs have the same value, however. Three levels can be distinguished. We have already mentioned programs for performing tasks, the basic business of any kind of enterprise—that which gives it its identity. At the next level are programs for switching, that is, rules for when to apply one program and when another. At the highest level of the pyramid is a program whose purpose is to "revise other programs, either by constructing new ones, reconstructing existing ones, or simply modifying individual premises in existing programs" (March & Simon, 1958, p. 149). Each lower level program, in other words, figures as the content of a higher. As you might expect, therefore, there is a "parallelism between the hierarchical relations among members of the organization and the hierarchical relations among program elements" (p. 150).

The intermediate-level programs constitute the control system and the coordination system of the organization. Control programs take as their input the performance outputs of lower level performances and may lead to corrective measures. Coordination programs, on the other hand, link lower level activities into sequences to produce more complicated, interconnected organizational responses. This enhanced interdependence goes hand in hand with specialization. The degree of specialization characteristic of an organization will vary depending on the predictability of the environment. It may range from relatively autonomous local self-organization to process specialization and global integration. Coordination mechanisms vary from highly planned and routinized to ones that involve considerable feedback and ongoing mutual adjustment through verbal exchanges. Coordination is more horizontal, control more vertical.

Does it not sound plausible? It should, because it has become conventional wisdom. How accurately does it portray real organizations, however? That is another issue, as we shall see.

Communication in a Computational Organization

March and Simon conceptualize communication as having two main functions: first, getting the job done (i.e., where the object of communication is the "substantive content" of work) and second, procedural matters. Communication is therefore also conceptualized as a form of programmed activity of four kinds:

1. Communication to establish, adjust, and coordinate other programs (this is the procedural dimension);
2. Communication to provide data for the execution of programs;
3. Communication to evoke the performance of a given program or to signal the starting up of an activity;
4. Communication to provide feedback on the results of activities.

(The latter three functions of communication fall under the heading of substantive content, rather than procedural matters.) The authors also recognize the reality of communication for nonprogrammed activity but treat it as a residual, or catch-all, other category.

(Note that all this communication occurs in the organization, which it is thought of as functionally supporting.)

The Centrality of Information

An organization, if it is, as they think, a system of computation, incorporates information processing at just about every point. Information, to begin with, enters the picture at the point of environmental stimulation, when the program is being evoked. They see rational behavior as involving the substitution of a model of reality for the lived experience "that is sufficiently simple to be handled by problem-solving processes" (March & Simon, 1958, p. 151). This leads them to their view of what information is. The best way to deal with the raw material of experience in all its complexity, given constraints such as time, they argue, is to summarize it, and the most evident way to summarize it is by classification. The advantage of assigning a situation to a known class is that, when this is done, an appropriate action program can be applied. After a situation is symbolically coded, the calling up and performing of the appropriate program becomes relatively routine. The whole goal of professional and vocational training is to build repertories of programs that fit known situations—situations that can be categorized. This is how we prevent the complexity of our environment from overwhelming us, and, practically speaking, how we keep the costs down.[5]

In March and Simon, information comes into play in a second way: in mediating between activities. Loss of variety is necessarily involved in the act of classifying. The raw data (which someone else might have interpreted differently) have been replaced by a summary judgment—a phenomenon known as "uncertainty absorption" (March & Simon, 1958, pp. 155, 164–166). In their words, "Uncertainty absorption takes place when inferences are drawn from a body of evidence and the inferences, instead of the evidence itself, are then communicated" (p. 165). The recipient of the information is now poorly placed to evaluate independently the well-foundedness of the judgment by embarking on an independent assessment of the raw data, so there is an issue of power involved. If you can establish the premises on the basis of which other people are now going to act,

---

[5]According to Clegg and Dunkerley (1980, pp. 264–5), March and Simon's thinking was in this respect influenced by the pragmatism of William James who emphasized the amplifying effects of habit on the carrying out of daily tasks.

because they have accepted your information—the results of your uncertainty absorption—you are exerting real influence.[6]

System Dynamics

By imagining organization to be a distributed rationality, where rationality is inherently limited in its scope, certain generic properties of organization can be made to stand out. Perhaps the most interesting is this: Intelligent action is not just boundedly rational, it is inevitably locally rational. The reason is this: Rationality is oriented to the execution of a program; programs are always specific to the performance of a certain task and are thus specialized; specialization means focusing on certain sources of information and ignoring others. The focus of attention is now displaced from the goals of the larger organization to the subgoals that come from task differentiation. Everything conspires in the direction of a circumscribed vision of the world: the natural tendency of people to "see things that are consistent with their established frame of reference" (March & Simon, 1958, p. 152), the reinforcement that comes from regular association with others whose focus of attention is similar to one's own, and the constraints of the task environment itself, which is repetitively throwing up problems of a certain kind that have to be dealt with, often urgently. So it is quite possible, even likely, that the goals that people come to follow in their own particular universe of daily challenge are different from and even incompatible with those of the organization as a whole. How such differences get worked out in practice may sometimes be solved computationally, through analysis, but where goals are not shared nor operationally comparable, then effective decisions will involve bargaining. A strictly computational solution, they concede, may not always be feasible (March & Simon, 1958, p. 156).[7]

MARCH AND SIMON'S MODEL REVISITED

March and Simon's characterization of organization, like many a rich theory, invites more than one interpretation. We offer three. Two of them

---

[6]In Weick's words (1995a), "Perrow (1986) has suggested that organizations operate with three forms of control: first-order control by direct supervision, second-order control by programs and routines, and third-order control consisting of assumptions and definitions that are taken as given. Third-order controls are called 'premise controls,' because they influence the premises people use when they diagnose situations and make decisions." This is another instance of the influence of March and Simon. For recent discussion, see Tompkins and Cheney (1985) and Cheney (1991).

[7]Their discussion of displacement of goals draws on the sociological insights of Robert Merton and his students, whose penetrating analyses of the dysfunctions (Merton's term) of bureaucracy are reviewed in some detail in chapter 2 of *Organizations*.

treat it as a stab at a literal description of real organization; one that picks up themes from preceding chapters, does not.

First (and this is how it has most often tended to be seen), their book is a sophisticated revision of the Weberian rationalist view that incorporates some of the remarkable intellectual advances of the post-World War II era, such as game theory, statistical decision theory, information/communication theory, and cybernetics. Because it takes account of situational constraints and the limited capabilities of human beings as information processors, the result is a good deal more subtle than the wooden, prescriptive formulae of earlier generations. By adopting a more relativistic position, it preserves the principle of organizational rationality while giving it some breathing room.

The criticism of this reading is that the picture they paint is still too rational by half. As we have seen, Weick in his writings on the looseness of association of the parts of an organization (that March and Simon also called loose coupling), disputes strongly the presumption of managerial rationality. One of the most astute critics of the undiluted rationalist view would subsequently turn out in fact to be one of the authors, March, whose later work strongly emphasized the happenstantial character of choice making in organizations. He likened it to a "garbage can" where many factors get mixed together in no particular order (March & Olsen, 1976; March & Weissinger-Baylon, 1986)—not particularly rational.

Certainly, for a communication scholar, it is impossible to read March and Simon's characterization of "communication" (one section of one chapter) without protesting at its lack of realism. It is too much based on the model of computer command procedures. Their remarks on uncertainty absorption and its effects on communication are perhaps compatible with our own presentation of the epistemic function of communication (chap. 3) but their ideas on the deontic dimension of command and control, by contrast, are overly simplistic: "establishing, coordinating, and adjusting programs." How this might actually occur (especially in light of Weick's remark on the limited range of management, cited in chap. 5) is left almost entirely to the imagination. The diagentive dynamics of situations of command receive no recognition whatsoever (other than as "nonprogrammed" activity). The declarative functions of management are, it is true, emphasized, and their final chapter is devoted to planning and initiating change. But a close reading of their text reveals that they concentrate on what leads up to the decision and its declaration and pay no attention whatsoever to what follows it, as if, after it is declared, change just takes place. Our own field research over the years and our reading of the literature suggests exactly the opposite: that a declared change almost never leads to the expected result, whether the domain is computerization (J. R. Taylor & Van Every, 1993) or self-managing teams (Barker, 1993).

So as a description of the rationality of *Organizations*, it is intriguing but not very convincing (not too surprising for a text now 40 years old). If we had been looking for versimilitude, it is not with this book that we would have started.

A second interpretation of their book is afforded by Boden (1994), who draws a different set of lessons from March and Simon. This is because she picks a different point of entry. We might call hers the "butterfly in a cocoon" interpretation. For her, what they are writing about is imperfect knowledge: socially and operationally situated groups, with considerable autonomy, who develop idiosyncratic ways of seeing, and processes of communication with ample room for interpretation (because uncertainty absorption hides as much as it reveals). Information exchange takes on a problematical quality. Her own book can be read as a reconstruction of ideas that they had begun to explore, but never developed fully. Under her interpretation, *Organizations* comes out not as refurbished rationalism, but as a harbinger of interpretivism. This is an interesting reading of the book, and one that can be defended, but that is not totally persuasive. The book's rationalism is more salient than its nascent interpretivism.

We offer a third way to interpret March and Simon, and it is the one that is going to be at the center of our attention in the rest of this chapter. Our reading of their book ignores the issue of its descriptive adequacy and, instead, a bit like Foucault, looks at what their text is saying, qua text, and not through it to what it purports to say. We might call this, inspired by Weick, the "map interpretation." Rather than treat their account as realistic—the more-or-less-successful constitution of a text-world—let us instead consider it as an ideational construction—a text that does not so much describe as instantiate an image of organization.

There is a reason for our doing this. Suppose the flatland view is right and there is no macro entity that we can call an "Organization." It is all micro—or, more accurately, the macro–micro dichotomy is artificial, nothing more than a construction of language. Think of an analogy. Say to yourself, there is no entity "The United States of America" other than something that keeps cropping up in some situated local conversations. Certainly, in the absence of Customs and Immigration, or some other explicit sign, you would have no clue that you had just crossed the border between, let us say, North Dakota and Manitoba. The countryside looks the same on both sides. So on what basis do people continue to treat the United States of America as real? The answer must be that they have documentary evidence of its existence: a constitution, flags, anthems, uniforms, styles of housing and clothing, city planning and architecture, people's accents, cars, maps, the Capitol and the Lincoln Memorial, TV shows, *Time* magazine and *People*, and so on and on. The signs are everywhere. You cannot miss them.

But this raises a question: Why, if there really is no macro entity called "The United States of America," other than something that keeps cropping up in some situated local conversation, do we continue behaving as if there were? The answer would seem to be that, although people's lives are lived out, always, in some locally parametrized situation, it is not always the same one. People move: They travel, they migrate, they relocate, they visit, they make pilgrimages. And when they move, they need to know where they are moving, which means having a map (a theme to which we return in chap. 9). The United States, before it was "The United States," started as a movement of people from Europe to North America. It did not become "The United States of America" until maps had been drawn, both graphic and in text, covering both the natural and the social spheres. It was less important that such maps should accurately delineate the territory than that they should exist and furnish documentary proof of the existence of the land and the people they described.

Perhaps March and Simon's *Organizations* is a map. There is some evidence that they themselves were not totally unaware of this possibility. In a short postscript (1958, p. 211), they call it "a summary of a vast mass of theorizing and (to a far lesser extent) empirical verification of theories." They call organizational behavior a "to date almost unexplored terrain" (note the significance of that word "terrain") So what they were supplying, even in their own minds, was not an accurate description of real organization but a text carrying the traces of other people's (and therefore recognizable) writing on the subject while adding something new: a metaphorical basis in a new science of computation that supplied a kind of metaphysical backbone, making what they wrote singularly credible to their colleagues. It was less important that they be right, than that they be seen to be right. By supplying an authoritative text, they constituted what Goldberg calls "frame knowledge" and Werth a "common ground" so that people could communicate with each other. Theirs was a text that would be taught in management schools and whose concepts would gradually filter into management discourse, where they allowed practitioners to make sense of what they were doing as choosers, decision makers, planners, or initiators. Their real accomplishment was to have naturalized hierarchy, that is, turned it into a mere feature of programming, an inevitability.

In a nation on the threshold of a postwar burst of unprecedented corporate growth, but the inheritor, historically, of a premise—a "self-evident truth"—that "all men [sic] are born equal," this achievement was of some importance.

It did not matter that the map was not accurate.

It seems doubtful to us that people ever limit themselves to local understanding; they also need to make sense of themselves as a collective unit. *Organizations* was a way of making sense for people. As communication researchers, it is important that we understand the role in communication of such textual structures as *Organizations.*

For people living in the second 50 years of the 20th century, the image of the computer has an extraordinary fascination; it is singularly seductive. March and Simon were the first to put that latent image power to work (Latour might call it an agency). In retrospect, their treatment of the computing analogy appears a bit heavy-handed, but its newness in 1958 meant that nobody was any cleverer than they were in detecting its weaknesses. But the theory of computation is now undergoing a revolution from the inside. In the remainder of this chapter, we begin to examine the consequences of such a turnaround and how it is (ever so gradually) beginning to influence how our present generation now maps the organization.

THE THEORY OF COMPUTATION AND ORGANIZATION

As we have been saying, the conceptual foundation of *Organizations,* and the most important thing that separated it from lesser works, was its theoretical foundation in an abstract mathematical and logical structure of statements, one of the extraordinary intellectual achievements of the 20th century, such as you would typically find in the so-called hard sciences. The development of the theory of computation, in its contemporary guise, can be traced back to papers by Kurt Gödel (who has been described as the greatest logician since Aristotle); Alan Turing (and others of his generation such as Post and Kleene) who laid out in exquisite detail a theory of effective procedures and an imaginary "machine" to carry them out; John Von Neumann who was among those who, apart from helping to design the atomic bomb, also wrote the first software for a computer, invented game/decision theory, and thought deeply about the error-correcting dynamics of neural networks; and the biologist Ross Ashby, who gave cybernetics its definitive description (and greatly influenced the thought of Weick).

Simon was to become, as we have said, a founding father of a new field—cognitive science and artificial intelligence. And he is still going strong. When the *New York Times* reported in 1996 on their first battle of wits pitting chess grandmaster Gary Kasparov against a computer program called Deep Blue, who did they interview? Herbert Simon, of course—40 years after his first publication on the subject of the General Problem Solver! So we can read *Organizations* not just as an empirically relevant theory of how large modern organizations function but as an attempt to get at a much deeper, more fundamental unity, where the cognitive organization of the human brain and the social organization of human

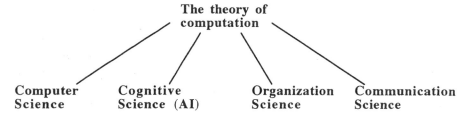

FIG. 6.1. The theory of computation as root metaphor for contemporary organizational sciences.

collective associations can be seen to manifest the operation of a single complex of abstract logical principles.[8] We could map this unity somewhat like this (Fig. 6.1):

The Symbolicist View as a Theory of Cognition

Let us now consider the symbolicist theory of computation more carefully. For this purpose, another of Simon's collaborations, *Human Problem Solving* (Newell & Simon, 1972), is a convenient source. This book served as basic text for a whole generation of cognitive scientists. (According to the preface, there may have been a first draft as early as 1956, and there was certainly a draft copy circulating by 1959, so that it was already in gestation at about the time that March and Simon were readying *Organizations* for publication.)

If the computer can serve as a metaphor for the brain it is because it has some identifiable properties that seem familiar to us. It has input and output ports that can be treated, metaphorically, as the equivalent of the body's sensors and effectors, because they can be coupled to sound and image-capture and operating devices linked to the outside world. It has the equivalent of a memory in that its internal configurations can be read as stored tokens, and the memory can be partitioned into a long-term and a short-term memory. It has a central processing unit—a brain—that can perform transformations on the stored or input tokens, and these operations can be interpreted as having an arithmetic and logical meaning. It has internal control systems that determine the routing and scheduling of the operations of storing and processing, thus serving metaphorically as analogs of the human nervous system.

---

[8]In Newell and Simon's words (1972, p. 161): "A theory of individual behavior microscopic enough to concern itself with the internal organization (neurological or functional) of the central nervous system will have a significant organizational component. A theory of organizational behavior macroscopic enough to treat the organization as a monolith will be a theory of an 'individual' ".

A symbolicist approach to computation is so-called because it is language based. It builds on a vocabulary of basic symbols, which are then operated on to produce strings (a form of text). Symbols can be thought of in two ways. Qua symbols they stand for something (an object or idea, for example). They represent (the domain of semantics). Because they are also elements that can be manipulated by combining them and performing operations on them, they can also be regarded merely as tokens (the domain of syntactics). The computer is a symbol-processing (more commonly called an information-processing) machine in the limited sense that its operations are performed on configurations of binary signals (such as 11010010) that are conventionally understood to have a symbolic interpretation. These symbols, syntactically viewed, are its version of tokens.

The operations a computer performs are of two basic kinds, both of which mimic a kind of reasoning. One such operation follows an "if-then" pattern, as in our inventory example: If inventory is less than x, then order y. This is known as a *production*, or *condition-action* pair. The other kind of operation exploits the logic of classes, in order to trace out connections in an associative network: If it is a pigeon, it is a bird; if a bird, it is a living being; therefore, to claim that there are pigeons on Mars implies that there are living beings there too. This type of operation fits the category of *logical inference*. (This is a highly oversimplified description of such sophisticated artificial intelligence languages as LISP or Prolog or C++, of course, but it will do for our purposes.)

The concept of cognition, or thinking, that underlies the symbolicist approach is thus something like the following, applied to human beings. Confronted with an experience, the individual translates it into a symbolic representation (which is now informational in that it stands for the interpreted data of experience that constitute our knowledge of the environment). That was one of March and Simon's main points in their discussion of classification. Through operations performed on the symbols, the individual comes to a conclusion as to how to deal with the environment. To the extent that logical inference is needed, this can be thought of as problem solving. The thought processes are carried on in language—not, as they point out (Newell & Simon, 1972, pp. 65–66), the surface structure of natural language but its supposed deep structure which many linguists have considered to come close to a system of formal logic.[9]

The computational theory of organization we outlined earlier is simply a working through of the implications of this theory of cognition for cooperative social systems of work. In the computational theory of organi-

---

[9]In work published in the early 1950s (with George Miller), Chomsky demonstrated that the concepts of program and grammar can be construed as an equivalence (Chomsky & Miller, 1958; Chomsky, 1957).

zation, the individual's functions are well defined: cognizers who encode the data of experience by giving them a symbolic interpretation (to produce a linguistic representation), a memory store for the recording of such symbolically encoded information, a decision maker who computes an answer to a problem on the basis of a systematic treatment of symbolically encoded information, and an operator who carries out a performance guided by a program or routine. The group exists through the interconnection of individual functions, either to coordinate program performances into a routine with subroutines, to exchange data, or to communicate executive commands having as their object changes in program, or scheduling and routing. The group's properties are the result of the communication linking individuals, this latter taking the form of symbolic transmissions, with the result that communication is an exchange of information that has been produced by individually (if boundedly) rational cognitive processes of symbolicization. The group, in effect, mediates between the individual and the organization, so that it can be thought of as constituting the network of the organization and communication as that which occurs in the network. The organization is a logically structured system of computation, imperfect because people's rationality is imperfect, but otherwise manifesting a single intentional implication in the world of events.[10]

We are at the core of March and Simon's achievement. They have supported the macro–micro thesis by translating it into programming terms. This explains for us why people have thought that communication was something that occurred in or within organization, as the oil that keeps the information-processing cylinders greased. The theory has had a powerful influence on how we conceive of organization in a taken-for-granted (as-

---

[10]We have been treating this from the perspective of what the theory of computation contributes to social science; consultation of such technically specialized journals as the *ACM Transactions on Information Systems* would show that there has been a reverse influence, in that computer scientists regularly write programs that mimic task-oriented group interaction. A typical way of doing this is to describe people in their manifestation as "workstations" (Kim, Ballou, Garza, & Woelk, 1991) where there is "execution of fairly computation-intensive applications on local data" (p. 31). This leads to a conception of a database system architecture, including both private and shared databases "such that each user owns a persistent private database and voluntarily shares part of his or her database with other authorized users" (p. 32). The databases are then operationalized in the terms of an object-oriented language to produce a network of interrelated, but distributed, concepts. This is only one of many possibilities. For example, there has been some interest in speech-act-based systems of coordination and negotiation, inspired by Winograd and Flores (1986). Here again, the image of organization is plainly computational: "[O]rganizations can be modeled as open systems that are composed of many interdependent and interconnected agents. In our view, an agent can be a person, a computed-based [sic] system, or any combination of the two, depending on how much is automated. Organizational work is distributed among these agents (i.e., employees, departments, etc.) and their effort has to be coordinated in the direction of reaching a goal" (Chang & Woo, 1994, p. 361).

sumed, no need to define) terminological language: such phrases (culled at random from papers in organizational communication presented at a conference) as "fundamental organizational processes, including sense-making, control, power relations, decision-making," "communication-related processes, including information-sharing, negotiation, exertion of power and control, sense-making, decision-making," "inform upper management and facilitate better coordination," "organizational control of work-flow," "decision processes in organizations," "flexible organizational control systems," "communication that strategically manages uncertainty," "information-sharing, coordination, control and sense-making." This is a terminology that has been naturalized to the point of insidiousness; it is in fact a language of theory, not a natural language (at least originally) but that has been forgotten. Nothing better illustrates the achievement of March and Simon than this banalization. They had fabricated a common ground for organizational research—a text of organization.

REVERSING THE FIELD: COMPUTATIONIST THEORY IN DISARRAY

But what if March and Simon got it wrong? What if the theory of computation on which their whole edifice is sited turned out to be, not a rock of Gibraltar, but shifting sand? Is it possible that, even if we were to accept that human organization is a computation system, it might not operate on the principles they thought, but on a different logic? Would we have been carried down a dead-end street?

A theory is a theory. It inevitably explains some things at the cost of leaving others unaccounted for. Over time, Kuhn (1970) speculated, the anomalies of a theory accumulate and begin to generate sufficient unease among researchers to create an openness to change. But a paradigm shift does not take place until there is a viable alternative that explains everything the older theory did and more. So, although it would be easy to cite research that pointed out limitations of the computational thesis as a metaphor for human organization, there has never been a real alternative with the depth that March and Simon aspired to and, in good measure, achieved.

Until now.

The Critique of Symbolism

Symbolism has been criticized from two quarters: researchers in cognitive science (in particular, artificial intelligence), and social anthropologists who study cooperative work situations. Although the perspectives are different, the reasons to doubt the validity of the symbolist position turn out to be much the same.

The first criticism has to do with limitations on the kind of cognition that a symbolist theory can easily explain. In their *Human Problem Solving,* Newell and Simon concentrated on "problems" such as cryptarithmetic and chess playing, showing, through the analysis of their human subjects' attempts to find solutions to logical problems, the existence of thought patterns that could be mimicked by a computer. As in many such controlled experimental situations, the internal validity was high, but the external validity was low. Outside the lab, it proved to be less easy to capture the skills of ordinary people in mundane, everyday contexts. The puzzles the cognitivist experimenters presented to their subjects were quasimathematical mazes that are especially hard for human beings but easy for computers to solve, because computers combine formal logical skills with extensive search involving memory—exactly the kind of thing ordinary people have most difficulty with. Not many of us have ever followed through the steps of a complicated mathematical proof—one of the early triumphs of the General Problem Solver, cited by Newell and Simon as early as 1956. Playing chess is another case in point, and it has turned out to be one area where the symbolist school can point to an unqualified success. But this success has led to the accusation, now leveled at the symbolist approach, that it is good at solving "toy problems" (C.-D. Lee & Gasser, 1992) but does not "scale up."

Artificial intelligence, but not people, has great difficulty accounting for context. As anthropologist Lucy Suchman (1987)—perhaps the most persistent of the socially oriented critics of symbolism—points out, purposeful activity is unfailingly situated. It occurs in a context. It is not just that people use their knowledge of context to make sense of events—that goes without saying—it is that language itself is only comprehensible in a context because of the phenomenon of "indexicality" (Garfinkel, 1967). Words take on specific meaning because people communicating in a context know where they point, or what their implicit reference is. It is not surprising that a recurring criticism of the symbolist method is that it has difficulty in processing language in real time, not an encouraging sign for a theory that prides itself on being based on the principles of the deep structure of language! The symbols of spoken discourse, unlike the language of a computer, are not fixed in their meaning because they are affected by context (something that Barwise & Perry, 1983, call the *productivity* of language-in-use). To take a trivial example, it is quite possible that a tall soccer player is shorter than a short basketball player: The word *tall* is "fuzzy."

Artificial intelligence deals with the situatedness of meaning systems, as it deals with everything, by programming in explicit background knowledge, but this soon leads to unmanageable complexity. It now seems clear, it is not that the computer, although more and more powerful, still does not have the processing capacity of the human cortex with the latter's billions of cells, but that the human brain does its computations using a different and more effective logical principle than the serial processor computer: a principle which emphasizes pattern recognition over logical operations. The computer now begins to look like a rather unsatisfactory metaphor for the brain.

Then there is the problem of learning. Computers mainly learn, according to Dinsmore (1992), by being told. To change their behavior, rules have to be explicitly added to the code of the system; the computers have to be reprogrammed. They are, he thinks, very poor at adapting or organizing themselves dynamically on the basis of experience. This becomes a devastating accusation when translated into a criticism of March and Simon's theory of organization. If the higher level programs of senior management are driven by a symbolicist computational motor, and if this problem-solving mechanism is not inherently a good learner, then for learning to occur there, one would have to exit the system and call on an extraneous and unexplained source of intelligence. In cognitive science, presumably the human programmer plays this (unacknowledged) role; in organizational science, who? The chief executive officer? A consultant? But then the theory is vacuous. In the case of learning, it explains nothing because it leads to a potentially infinite regress: Who programmed the programmer?

Another criticism of performance systems based on symbolicist computational principles is that they are very poor at coping with ambiguity, equivocality, and noisy information sources—things that are unusual, unplanned, or faulty. Again, in such circumstances, humans do much better than any equivalent symbolicist computer yet devised. Among the most unremitting of the critics of standard artificial intelligence are the adherents of what is called "fuzzy logic." In Kosko's words:

> The world of math does not fit the world it describes. The two worlds differ, one artificial and the other real, one neat and the other messy. It takes faith in language, a dose of make-believe, to make the two worlds match. I called this the *mismatch problem: The world is gray but science is black and white.* We talk in zeroes and ones but the truth lies in between. Fuzzy world, nonfuzzy description. . . . Statements of fact are not all true or false. Their truth lies between total truth and total falsehood, between 1 and 0. (1993, p. 8, emphasis in original)

He goes on (p. 17): "I don't think any human brain works with Aristotle's syllogisms or with computer precision. It's messier than that. The days of symbolic reasoning in 'artificial intelligence' are over." And, because he is able to back up his criticisms with reference to successful product development that does not follow the standard recipe, they have bite.

To sum up, there are properties of human cognition that symbolicist theory cannot seem to explain: People are quick to see patterns, they handle ambiguity well, they are capable of exercising ingenuity in unexpected circumstances, they are adaptable, they handle language effortlessly in real time and, a point to which we return, their sociability is part and parcel of their capacity to process information. Nevertheless, the design of both technology and of management systems has gone ahead on the assumption of the correctness of the symbolicist model. What happens when a technology, or a management program, which does routine tasks well, but has inferior abilities in dealing with the nonroutine, is implemented in a real-life situation where the nonroutine is routine, if we can put it that way?

We have not read a better reply to this question than that given by Weick (1985): "Existing controls are disrupted and parts of the system that had previously been self-regulating are disconnected. No one knows what is occurring and everyone knows less about the organization than they did before, because interdependencies have been made more variable."[11]

THE NEW THEORY OF COMPUTATION

An Alternative: Connectionism

According to Von Eckardt (1993), there have been two phases in the development of computation theory. From 1956 to about 1980, the Newell–Simon thesis, or the symbolicist school of cognition, predominated; since 1980, we have seen the rise of another school of thought called variously connectionism, subsymbolicism, parallel distributed processing (PDP), or neural network theory. There is now evidence that a third phase is emerging, that builds on the earlier work, but with a twist. It is founded on an assumption of socially distributed cognition (Hutchins 1995), or socially shared cognition (Resnick, Levine, & Teasley, 1991), or of a collective mind (Weick & Roberts, 1993). In the remainder of this chapter, we first sketch in very broad outline the connectionist view and then con-

---

[11]P. Sachs (1995) draws a distinction between what she calls "an organizational, explicit" view of work and "an activity-oriented, tacit" view. Her "organizational, explicit" is the one we have described as symbolicist; her "activity-oriented, tacit" is more in line with the socially distributed conception we now turn to examine (Sachs, by the way, illustrates what happens when an inappropriate system is introduced: effectiveness is seriously affected). One consequence of seeing "activity-oriented, tacit" work through the lens of a "organizational, explicit" view is that the work begins to be "invisible," its actual complexity having disappeared from view, when seen as a rational production process (Suchman, 1995).

clude by discussing the most recent development and its relevance for organizational communication research.

The connectionist version of computation differs from the symbolicist by an inversion of metaphor. The essence of the symbolicist position is that the brain is a computer. The brain is taken to be a serial information processing system that works on the pattern of a Von Neumann computer or Newell and Simon's General Problem Solver. The connectionist school has flipped this somewhat jaded analogy on its head, by designing computers that, in their architecture at least, try to imitate features of the brain's cortical structure. Their approach is loosely inspired by findings of neurophysiological research: no longer brain as computer but rather computer as brain. The switch of perspective may seem like a play on words but the results are almost astonishingly different, even though both theories still claim to be computational.

The intellectual roots of connectionism can be traced back to the same origins as the conventional school of artificial intelligence in the 1940s. One of the ideas then being put forward was that the brain has the architecture of a neural net, a densely interconnected web of brain cells (or neurons), which are active or inactive—fire or do not fire—and whose firing has an accumulating effect (which can be either excitatory or inhibitory) on their neural neighbors' level of activation. As the firings continue in sequence, they take on the look of a wave passing through the network. This patterning of network-wide excitation, it was claimed, constitutes both the memory of the brain and how it learns. McCulloch and Pitts (1943) had observed, furthermore, that the on–off (fire–do not fire) behavior of the neurons qualified them as the most simple possible of logical operators, called technically, *finite state automata*, and that, accordingly, such networks are in their own way also systems of computation, with this addition, that, as their interconnections strengthen and fade, the network's structure evolves and displays emergent behavior, and thus learns. To this picture, Hebb (1949) added a further dimension, pointing out that, as parts of the network begin to develop relative autonomy, they can be thought of as "sub-assemblies" and the brain can thus develop functional specialization (of which the left brain/right brain division is the most striking illustration), allowing for selective response to a wide variety of eventual stimuli, when faced with a complex environment.[12]

---

[12]This early theorizing led to concrete efforts in the 1950s to produce working instantiations of neural net principles. The most frequently cited is that of Rosenblatt's (1962) "Perceptron," which was capable of elementary pattern recognition. It is now generally conceded (Bardini, in press) that the reason this line of research and development was not continued had to do with politics. The symbolicist school controlled the research funds and, because the other work was inconsistent with the orthodoxy of symbolicism as enunciated by Newell and Simon, support dried up.

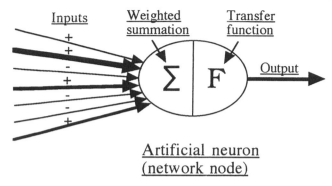

FIG. 6.2. The structure of an artificial neuron, or network unit (node).

At the beginning of the 1980s, a group of researchers at the University of California at San Diego (McClelland, Rumelhart, & the PDP Research Group, 1988; Rumelhart, McClelland, & the PDP Research Group, 1986) began a program of experimental simulations, based on a design that incorporated assumptions similar to those of the earlier thinkers. They conceived of a new kind of computing device, which had the following characteristics (Fig. 6.2): It would be composed of simple nodes from practical considerations, usually in the hundreds, but the number is not limited in principle; each node would be governed by an input–output function (F) (generally nonlinear) that took into account the prior state of the node as well as the stimulation it was receiving from other nodes joined to it by connecting links; when the sum of the stimuli attained a certain threshold (Σ) the node would be activated; a node might be influenced by many others, and could in turn influence several more; such influences might be positive (excitatory) or negative (inhibitory); and the amount of influence any given node could exert on another was determined by a weight, or degree of influence, which was the one feature of the network that was subject to change over time.

The nodes would be organized in a feedforward pattern (communication without feedback) in three layers: One group constituted the input layer that was connected to external stimuli, one group (called the "hidden" units) formed an intermediate layer, and one group made up the output layer, where the behavior of the network as a whole would be expressed and where it could be connected to a variety of activating devices (Fig. 6.3).[13]

---

[13]Note that the number of units in the hidden layer is less than that of the input or output layers. This is so that the network is forced to learn in that it prevents it from simply feeding forward, unchanged, the input pattern on a one-to-one basis. In effect, by the reduction in number, the network is obliged to recognize redundancies in the input, and it is in this sense that it has become a computer. Having learned one set of redundancies then sensitizes it to similar redundancies in other stimuli and allows it to generalize, to fill in the missing information, and so on.

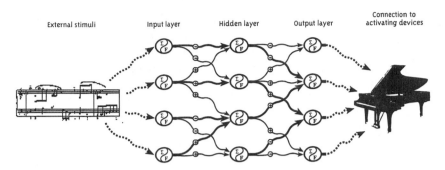

FIG. 6.3. The typical structure of a connectionist network.

The goal of the experimenters was to show that such a network can learn to recognize and to respond reliably to configurations of environmental stimuli of many kinds, and in this sense can be said to have recognized objects and events in its environment. The learning schedule involved, first, presenting the network with a pattern of some kind, and then letting the network show a response. Because initially the network connections had been established randomly, the first response would be wide of the mark. The experimenter, acting as teacher, noted whether the network had overshot or undershot and, depending on the assessment, an algorithm went into effect to automatically alter the values of the weights, first at the output, and then at the hidden level. This was called *backpropagation.* As a result, the internal connections linking the individual cells would begin to change, and the kinds of effect each was having on others would become more or less positive, stronger or weaker. After repeated cycles of this kind, it was observed that the network would settle on a stable behavior and—this was the dramatic part—that it had learned to recognize the stimulus object and would do so reliably, again and again, even when the re-presentation came much later, after it had learned other patterns as well, or even in the face of partial evidence.

As Kosko (1993, pp. 208–211) demonstrates, this network, after training, will zero in on the right response, even when the stimuli are ambiguous ("fuzzy," in his terminology).

Connectionism as a Model of Computation

The achievements of this new form of computation are quite impressive. Connectionist nets can simulate finger movements in skilled typing, can learn to distinguish between different animal species on the basis of their features, and can deal with three-dimensional objects. They can learn, it is claimed, how to pronounce English words reliably and how to form the past tense of English verbs without error (Rumelhart & McClelland, 1986).

They can detect fraud in the use of credit cards and compute nonlinear functions (Meilich, 1996). Because the same network can learn many patterns of stimuli, the individual nodes are multipurpose; the learning is not attached to the node but is a property of the configuring of the network when stimulated. As such, this kind of computer has some singular advantages, in that it is able to handle noisy, incomplete, or ambiguous information very well and can see connections between similar classes of stimuli.[14]

This is as far as we are going to go in presenting connectionism. As an approach, it has its critics, particularly among linguists who have observed its difficulty in handling language (Fodor & Pylyshyn, 1988; Pinker & Prince, 1988); as a still very young, untried movement, the jury is still out on how much it can explain. It has, however, two contributions to make to our own investigation. First, it has shown up, definitively, the limitations of the classical, or symbolicist, theory of computation. After it became clear that this newer kind of system of computation could do things—notably things that humans do—that a standard symbol processing system could not, or could only with great difficulty, then we can no longer credit the latter as being a fully adequate explanation of how people (and other species) process information or think. The March and Simon account of how people turn experience into information by an act of categorization was considerably oversimplified. Symbol processing may be one way to process information, but it is not the only one.[15]

In the words of a psychologist who can be taken as a relatively disengaged observer of the symbolicist/connectionist debate (Gardner, 1985, pp. 110–111): "The portrait of human cognition emerging from cognitive science is far removed—at least at the molar level—from the orderly, precise, step-by-step image that dominated the fathers of the field ... Human thought emerges as messy, intuitive, subject to subjective representations—

---

[14]There are hazards, of course, in this kind of speculative exercise. One instance is frequently cited among connectionist researchers. Having been trained to reliably recognize a certain kind of military tank, the system then failed to carry over its capability when confronted with a new sample of photographs. The reason: The first lot had been shot in daylight, the second at night. The system was thus recognizing not tanks, but the time of day!

[15]As early as 1966, Bateson (1972, p. 482) was arguing for "a new way of thinking about what a *mind* is." What he describes as the "essential minimal characteristics of a system, which I will accept as characteristics of mind" included: "(1) The system shall operate with and upon differences; (2) The system shall consist of closed loops or networks of pathways along which differences and transforms of differences shall be transmitted (what is transmitted on a neuron is not an impulse, it is news of a difference); (3) Many events within the system shall be energized by the respondent part rather than by impact from the triggering part; and (4) The system shall show self-correctiveness in the direction of homeostasis and/or in the direction of runaway. Self-correctedness implies trial and error." Bateson goes on to note these characteristics of mind apply "in a great many other places besides the inside of my head and yours." It is evident that this is connectionist reasoning.

not as pure and immaculate calculation. . . . Our concepts of cognition need to be considerably broadened."

SOCIALLY DISTRIBUTED COGNITION: A NEW MODEL OF ORGANIZATION

Connectionism has turned out to be a stepping stone to the most recent development in organization theory: socially distributed cognition.

To introduce this last of our themes, we need to first say a word about the main difference between a symbolicist and a connectionist model of cognition. In a symbolicist computer, there are identifiable stores of information and an identifiable unit for the processing of the stored information, such information being taken to be interpretable as symbols. There is, however, no intrinsic correlation between the patterning of the cells in the storage location and their meaning, other than that which is supplied by the experimenter. A symbol, let us say 11010011, might be given whatever arbitrary meaning the programmer wanted. In a connectionist computer, the network is at once the storage and the operational unit—there is no hierarchical distinction between the functions—and the configuration of the cells forming the network is intrinsically a representation of the object or event being recognized. It is not a symbol so much as an icon or neural picture of the thing to be represented. Information is not stored in the nodes of the network but in their interconnections. It is in the mutual influence patterns that recognition takes place; any information the node has goes into the building up of a picture.

Interpreting this as a metaphor of human organization, we would say that the individuals in the organization were not its information stores, but that it was in the ongoing interaction between members of the organization that an image of the environment was successfully negotiated, such an image being more complex than the parts that were located in the participating members of the network. It is here that the break point with neoclassical organization theory is to be found. The term that now covers this newer school of thought is *socially distributed cognition.*

One point needs immediate clarification. Socially distributed cognition is not the same as social cognition. There is an abundant psychological literature, dating back to at least Asch and Sherif, on how social circumstances affect individual thought processes. In this older literature, although the circumstantiality of reasoning is emphasized in the sense that people are sensitive to the constraints of their social situation, the locus of cognition is still the individual's head. March and Simon, for example, saw the social constraints operating on cognition as one of the factors that explains the boundedness of individual human rationality. A social connectionist view goes further, in that it sees the cognition as occurring not in but between the members of the interacting group. Information is constructed not in the brain but through a collaborative social process, and the result transcends the bounds of individual knowledge (for further discussion of the distinction, see Resnick, 1991 and Cole, 1991).

The Weick–Roberts Study

Two in-depth studies are cited here to illustrate how socially distributed cognition might work. The first is Weick and Roberts' (1993) study of what they call "heedful interrelating" on the flight deck of an aircraft carrier. Landing a plane on the deck of an aircraft carrier is not, they point out, a solitary act. The plane does not so much land as it "is recovered." Recovery involves a complex interaction involving air traffic controllers, landing signal officers, the control tower, navigators, deck hands, the ship's helmsman, and many others (not to mention the pilot). There are 9 to 10 people on the landing signal officer's platform, up to 15 more in the tower, and 2 to 3 on the bridge observing the recovery, the latter having the discretionary power to abort a landing. If there is any breakdown in the interrelating of these multiple activities, the result is disaster (and the authors of the study do report one such instance, which resulted in the loss of a plane, although, fortunately, not its crew). The tolerance for error is minimal; here is how they describe the organization of a carrier:

> . . . Imagine that it's a busy day, and you shrink San Francisco Airport to only one short runway and one ramp and one gate. Make planes take off and land at the same time, at half the present time interval, rock the runway from side to side, and require that everyone who leaves in the morning returns that same day. Make sure the equipment is so close to the edge of the envelope that it's fragile. Then turn off the radar to avoid detection, impose strict controls on radios, fuel the aircraft in place with their engines running, put an enemy in the air, and scatter live bombs and rockets around. Now wet the whole thing down with sea water and oil, and man it with 20-year-olds, half of whom have never seen an airplane close-up. Oh and by the way, try not to kill anyone. (Weick & Roberts, 1993, p. 357)

Weick and Roberts' point is that the intelligence needed to cope with such a complex, danger-laden situation could not possibly be lodged in a single person. Instead they draw on connectionist logic to explain how "complex patterns can be encoded by patterns of activation and inhibition among simple units, if those units are richly connected" (Weick & Roberts, 1993, p. 359), so that relatively simple actors (20-year-olds with no experience of flying, for example) "may be able to apprehend complex inputs," providing that "they are organized in ways that resemble neural networks." When this interconnectivity is accomplished, what Weick and Roberts call a "collective mind" emerges, with properties that are "not contained fully in the representation of any one person nor are they finalized at any moment in time" (p. 365). "This pattern of distributed representation," they go on, "explains the transindividual quality of collective mind. Portions of the envisaged system are known to all, but all of it is known to none." The collective mind is located in the process of interrelating. It exists "as a kind of capacity in an ongoing activity stream and emerges in the style with which activities are interrelated" (p. 365).

Weick and Roberts have thus demonstrated, in an original way, how organization can be explained in terms of a computational theory, yet where the image of organization that emerges is very different from older symbolicist ways of thinking. They do, however, introduce a caution on the use of the connectionist metaphor. The example of collective interrelating they have been studying differs from more ordinary situations of work precisely in its low tolerance for error and its stringent requirement of high reliability. This in turn makes it practically obligatory that those involved pay heed to what they are doing, at all times—be "heedful" (Weick & Roberts' term). Even though the system has built-in redundancy, heedlessness would invite disaster. This means that the attentive performance of the units, or cells, making up the collective social entity is pretty much assured. In a connectionist experiment, conducted in a computer laboratory, the performance of the unit-cells is guaranteed, because it is determined by a mathematical function, and such reliability is indispensable to the emergent learning of the network as a whole. In human contexts, this kind of heedfulness is far from assured, and the legitimacy of the connectionist logic, as a metaphor for human organization, is by this fact made problematical for situations where the pattern of interrelating is intermittent.

The Hutchins Study

By far the most comprehensive presentation of the social distribution of cognition thesis is to be found in a book by Edwin Hutchins, which carries the intriguing title *Cognition in the Wild* (1995). Hutchins' object of analysis, marine navigation, is practical enough, but his approach is also theoretical. He begins by drawing on an idea of the psychologist David Marr (1982), who argued that, to describe an information-processing task adequately, three levels have to be taken into account: first, what is being computed (this is what the system does and why it does it), second, how the information is represented and transformed (its code, the mapping of one reading of information or representation to another), and third, how the representation and its transformation are realized physically (a question of media).

In navigation, Marr's model translates into a operation of taking readings (such as a compass, radar, or star sightings) and then combining

them in order to arrive, through a precise computation, at a fix, which is
to say an exact determination of where the ship is on the surface of the
sea. In Marr's system, that which is computed is location; it is achieved,
on the kind of ship Hutchins was studying, by mapping observations of
landmarks to a chart; and this is accomplished by a mixture of human
and technical operations. This is one pattern. In other societies, and in
other eras than our own, navigators achieved the same result differently
(Hutchins makes a fascinating analysis of the differences between occidental and Melanesian practices of navigation). Nevertheless, the fundamental
computational constraint is the same: on the basis of a limited number of
signs, compute a location so that you will know where you are.

Hutchins then makes two radical moves. First, he asks, why do all the
steps of cognition that Marr and other psychological researchers identify
have to occur in the head? In navigation, Hutchins shows, they clearly do
not. Second, why do the steps of cognition have to be carried out only via
the medium of human wetware (jargon for brain), socially distributed or
not, when it is also clear from navigation practice that the computational
part is in the instruments that the navigators use, reflecting, as they do,
centuries of perfection of design. It is not something that the people
involved have to spend their time doing. As he puts it:

> I want the sort of computation that cognition is to be as applicable to events
> that involve the interaction of humans with artifacts and with other humans
> as it is to events that are entirely internal to individual persons. [The] theory
> of "disembodied cognition" has created systematic distortions in our under-
> standings of the nature of cognition. . . . The task of navigation requires
> internal representation of much less of the environment than traditional
> cognitive science would have led us to expect. (Hutchins, 1995, p. 118)

The moment-to-moment mundane work that navigators do is not particularly computational, even though the outcome of their collective activity
is. The computation done by the system is thus not equivalent to the
cognitive tasks performed by the members of the team. Most of the time,
the latter are serving as representational media, doing what Marr would
have thought of as the input-output of information: By taking telescopic
sightings of certain visible landmarks, the seamen on deck provide the
basic data that the Quartermaster in the cabin enters on the chart, as he
draws the sightings to compute a location. It is actually the chart that
performs the final step of calculation to establish a fix of the ship's position.

To think of this as an instance of an artifact amplifying the cognitive
abilities of the user is, Hutchins argues (1995, pp. 153–154), to miss the
point. The use of the tool is simply one step in a chain of representational
transformations that, thought of as a whole, he claims is cognition: None
of the component cognitive abilities of the people has been amplified. What

the tool of the chart has done is to represent information in such a way that the problem solution is made transparently evident. The expertise is neither in the user nor the tool, but in the process of successive representations—re-presentations—of the original data to produce an answer.

The development of technologies that fit into a socially distributed cognition is what culture is all about. "We will not understand the computation until we follow its history back and see how structure has been accumulated over centuries in the organization of the material and ideational means in which the computation is actually implemented" (Hutchins, 1995, p. 168). As he goes on to point out (p. 169): "The environments of human thinking are not 'natural' environments. They are artificial through and through. Humans create their cognitive powers by creating the environments in which they exercise those powers."

It is in Hutchins' characterization of how the team's communication works that he comes closest, in spirit at least, to a pure connectionist theory. He makes two main points. First, redundancy is inscribed in the network. The senior members of the team have themselves performed the more elementary tasks earlier in their careers and understand their constraints. This is one of the properties that distributed processing in neural networks has always been understood to possess and one of its strengths in the face of ambiguous data and error: It allows for what is called in conversation analysis the "repair" of "breakdowns" (we come back to this idea in chap. 7). Second, interaction between members of the team involves constraint, inhibitory as well as excitatory, and it is out of the piecing together of pieces of information, none intrinsically meaningful per se, that a coherent representation is constructed. As he says (Hutchins, 1995, p. 236): "Far from being a simple one-way trajectory for information, the communication is in fact the bringing together of many kinds of constraints in both bottom-up and top-down directions."

This is precisely the connectionist logic at work: a combination of feedforward and back propagation. This has radical implications for an information theory interpretation of communication: "The meanings of statements and questions are not given in the statements themselves but are negotiated by the participants in the context of their understandings of the activities underway" (p. 236). As he says (Hutchins, 1995, p. 283): "The communicative acts of the members of the navigation team are not just about the computation, they *are* the computation."

Rumelhart's View

Hutchins is not the only theorist to question an assumption that dates at least back to Descartes: that thinking goes on strictly inside the head. David Rumelhart (1992), a prime moving spirit of connectionism, seems to be arriving at a similar position. He argues this way. There are three ways we as humans deal with situations: reasoning by similarity (this situation is like one we have already dealt with), reasoning by mental simulation (calling to mind in our imagination the possible outcome of a line of action), and reasoning by formal logic (which, by the way, is what a nautical chart accomplishes). Humans (as well as connectionist systems) are very good at the first two of these strategies, but terrible at the third. We are skilled at pattern recognition, we are good at modeling the world in imagination, but not so good at abstract manipulation of complex symbolic structures such as we find in mathematics. What we are also especially good at, however, is manipulating our environment: constructing tools, creating pictures of the world around us, and drawing maps and diagrams. So our way of dealing with the kind of problem that requires complex symbol processing is to reduce it to an issue in pattern matching, at which we are good. We do this by constructing tools that do the job for us or by devising algebras that turn mathematics into a set of steps that are individually simple for us to do, and where, by our doing, we end up producing a result that our unaided brain could not have accomplished.

The symbolicist theory of cognition, if you believe this newer school of thought, had the stick by the wrong end. The computer is not a model of human cognition; it is one more instrument that we have devised to obviate the necessity of performing operations that we do not do well. Most everyday reasoning by individuals, says Rumelhart (1992, p. 72), "does not involve much in the way of manipulating mental models."

Hutchins' Critique of the Symbolicist View

In Hutchins' (1995) final chapter, he develops what he calls an "alternative history of cognitive science," in which he claims that we have all, in effect, been the victims of a con. The official view of artificial intelligence is that the computer is a model of human intelligence. Hutchins points out the absurdity of this claim. The computer is an instrument we use to perform logical, rule-driven operations on symbols (or more properly, tokens), something that is practically difficult for us to do, using the mental equipment we were born with. The intelligence is not in the instrument but in the interaction between the instrument and the person employing it. What is actually being modeled by the computer program is not the processes engaged in by a person doing that task but an abstract computation, achieved by the manipulation of the symbols, that is needed as one step in the completion of the task. "The physical-symbol-system architecture," he says (1995, p. 363), is not a model of individual cognition. It is a model of the operation of a sociocultural system *from which the human actor has been removed.* . . . The computer was not made in the image of the person.

The computer was made in the image of the formal manipulations of abstract symbols. And the last 30 years of cognitive science can be seen as *attempts to remake the person in the image of the computer*" (emphasis added).

The Revised Verdict on *Organizations*

We could extrapolate. Is it possible that attempts to model the human organization as a rational—even boundedly rational—system of production were also, in effect, a con: also an attempt to remake (not this time the individual, but organization) in the image of the computer? Perhaps they also achieved this image remake by removing the human actor. You will find nothing in March and Simon's *Organizations* that mentions owners who buy and sell companies as if they were baseball cards, chief executive officers who downsize and send operations offshore while they vote themselves humungous salaries (even when the company's profits are down), accountants who embezzle, or ambitious climbers or union leaders who profiteer. Nor will you find honest employees who do their best in trying circumstances (or people who cheat, either), office politics, or people who are deeply hurt and confused as a result of being "let go" after years of service (or people who take advantage of company loopholes). The view of the organization based on the computer metaphor would lead us to believe that the production system, modeled as an extended computer, is society; Hutchins' view would more likely be that such a production system is merely an artifact, as many others we have made in our culture, and that the real organization appears only when we re-couple the artifact with the people who use it.

CONCLUSION

Neither Weick and Roberts nor Hutchins devote much of their analysis to the social context of the computational universes they describe, other than those activities that are strictly instrumental. Hutchins does mention a Captain who does not like the door behind him to be open, even though its being closed causes a considerable inconvenience for his navigational team. And Weick and Roberts do comment on a case of executive dithering that led to the loss of a plane. But that is about all. In their own way, they are as rationalist as March and Simon were.

Perhaps because the background in both cases is the U.S. Navy with its highly disciplined social patterns of behavior, on the whole they tend to ignore social dynamics. The result is that, although their studies are a contribution to our understanding of the social construction of reality

(Berger & Luckmann, 1966), they have little to tell us about the construction of social reality (Searle, 1995).

Hutchins does have this to say about social processes (1995, p. 283): "The playing out of computational processes and the playing out of social processes are inextricably intertwined. Social moves have computational as well as social consequences. Computational moves have social as well as computational consequences." That is an intriguing remark, but it leaves us, as one says in French, *sur notre appétit*—wanting more. What does he mean? We detect a hint—ironically enough, given Hutchins' insistence on cognition as a mixed mode of personal and material—of what Latour, in his criticism of science as practice (1992), calls "purification": the tendency to divide up the world into distinct realms of material science and social science, with the material lending itself to computation and the social involving something else (never precisely specified). What, for heaven's sake, are "social processes," as distinct from "computational processes"? Is navigation only about locating oneself in a natural environment? Are we not also confronted, daily, with the necessity of locating ourselves in a social environment? And is this not also a computational activity? We would have thought so.

The studies we have been analyzing have given us new insights into what information processing is—inherently social—and what organization is—inherently computational (although what "computational" actually means is not entirely clear)—but their treatment of communication is not satisfying. They have achieved their insights (and we believe they are genuine insights) by a restriction of focus that successfully obscures from view large areas of cognition, namely, those that have to do with the representation and computation of social data. In chapter 7, we take a different view on connectionism by imagining what its network would look like if translated into the terms of an ordinary human conversation. As we work our way through this exercise, we get a better idea of the power of the theory, but we also conclude that, although it explains some things in a new (and potentially exciting) way, it is too limited to serve as a general theory of human organization.

Chapter 7

Conversation Transformed: Organization

In chapter 6, we sketched in broad outline a computational theory that claims that cognition—or at least *re*-cognition—can be caused by connecting up a network, even when the latter consists only of dumb information processor nodes. Such networks will, over a number of trials, produce a representation of rather complex environments, and thus, in one sense of the word at least, process information, or compute. Originally (McClelland et al., 1988; Rumelhart et al., 1986), this was a theory of how the equivalent of a brain (conceived of as a neural net) might think but we discovered that others—Weick and Roberts, and Hutchins—were soon prepared to go further and to see parallel distributed processing in a network not only as a metaphor for how cooperatively working groups of humans function, but also as a theory of collective organizing (at least in the small). Using data recorded in naturally occurring situations ("in the wild," in Hutchins' words), they have tried to show how groups composed of individuals with distributed—segmented, partial—images of a complex environment can, through interaction, synthetically construct a representation of it that works: one which, in its interactive complexity, outstrips the capacity of any single individual in the network to represent and discriminate events. This is a theory that says not only that people put their ideas together summatively to produce a common pool of knowledge, but also that, out of the interconnections, there emerges a representation of the world that none of those involved individually possessed or could possess.

These new ideas of how knowledge is produced and where the locus of knowledge itself is to be found (in the interconnections, not in the individual nodes) have upset, for the moment at least, the applecart of established computational and information theory with its overwhelmingly individualist and symbolicist bias. They challenge us to rethink the theoretical basis of understanding the organization/communication relationship. They invite us to pick up the theoretical gauntlet, if for no other reason than that, although the authors writing in this emerging new tradition of thought may include a section or even a chapter on communication (Hutchins does, for example), it comes as an afterthought, a belated acknowledgement that communication is central to the explanation they are setting out, but lacking any real theory of communication on which to base it.

BOTTOM-UP THINKING

In chapter 5, we found that theorists as diverse as Weick, Giddens, and Latour agree that the literature on organization has promulgated a macro–micro division (and thus has seen organization through a functional/structural lens). As against this view, these authors argue for what we have called a flatland perspective, which images organization through, depending on the author's terminology, a "performative," "interpretive," "structurational," or "enactive" lens. In the conventional view, as we pointed out (chap. 5), organizational change is a top-down phenomenon (the result of planning); to these authors, change is bottom-up: negotiated and emergent. The classical symbolicist view of computation and organization—such as in March and Simon's portrayal—is top-down, through and through. Change is programmed and the changer is a programmer, designer, or developer (their final chapter, for example, deals with planning).

Because they took a macro–micro ontological split for granted, conventional theorists of organization thus for the most part (and often with less nuance than March and Simon) bought into the top-down logic and its conception of communication. When organization is treated theoretically as a planned structure of interlinked communicational exchanges to form a pattern of exchange and a structure of relationships that conforms to computational requirements, then it enfolds—and soon overshadows—local, circumstanced communicational interaction. The local interaction comes to be seen as secondary in importance to global parameters of structure and process. Theory at the macro level has the character of a design puzzle: how to construct an efficient pattern of nodes and connections (i.e., a planned network). To the extent that communication comes into the picture, it is seen as a means to an end. In this construction, there is little room for emergent organization.

Theorists who take communication as a starting point are more likely to start from a micro perspective. Communication is a level that addresses the immediacy of interaction-mediated-by-(typically)-talk, in all its circumstantial situatedness. Organization, to the extent that it figures in discussion, is seen as, at most, a constraint and/or a resource (Giddens, 1984). The making of theory is focused on the procedures, purposes, and content of the transaction. The view is bottom-up, and exchange is the metaphor: (intersubjectively understood) interpretation or structuring, (interobjectively interpreted) mediation.

Connectionism appears to offer an alternative to the classical top-down model of organization. Superficially, at least, it seems to be claiming at least a measure of bottom-up thinking, in that it assumes spontaneous learning on the part of networks.[1] To the extent that it does, it has the advantage of social legitimacy (because it too is rooted in a scientific theory of computation) and yet it restores communication to a primary role as the locus of emergent organization. The singular advantage of March and Simon's computational interpretation of human organization was its plausibility. Is the new computational theory as plausible as the old, when its structuring principles are reinterpreted in human terms (and if so, are we seeing the first stage of a paradigm shift)?

Our approach to this question is as follows. We re-contextualize the connectionist logic by applying it to conversation using the principles of conversation analysis (CA) we have already described (chap. 1). Here we put CA theory to work by asking how well it fits with connectionist thinking. If we find a reasonable match, then it seems to us that the connectionist thesis has at least surface validity for socially as well as for neurally based intelligence.

WHAT WE WILL FIND

Organization is always realized in conversation, but it is conversation in the large as well as the small. An organization, in this sense, is a vast, sprawling, multileveled universe of talk and other linguistically supported exchanges, composed of not just one but many face-to-face (and, increasingly, via media of cellular telephone and email) exchanges. Organization is produced in the same conversational manifold that it in turn, reflexively, produces: in the conversation and nowhere else. The intelligence it displays (this is where the theory of connectionism is of value) is in the connectedness of the conversing. In contrast to the symbolicist image of organization our field has commonly preferred, we need not postulate decision-

---

[1]We are not prejudging the issue here because, as an experimenter-driven approach, its logic is still, at least in part, top-down. It is, after all, the experimenter who organizes back propagation. Our purpose in this chapter is to explore what bottom up might actually mean.

making centers, corporate planners, a hierarchy of embedded programs, or an all-knowing management, because all these functions are distributed throughout the network. There is coherence, but its basis is not classical rationality, but rather a much more dynamic and newer idea: emergence of pattern in the interconnectedness of ongoing conversation.

But the connectionist-conversationist thesis, we will conclude, is not a fully adequate communication theory of organization. Although it does provide a rich theory of organization—one that reveals organization in a new way—and although connectionism, reinterpreted in CA terms, does seem to us to have surface validity as an explanation of an aspect of organization, that is, its ability to map the environment and otherwise generate knowledge, it does not explain one vital fact: that organization is not just the scene of the action, it is itself an actor. As an entity, it has an identity distinct from that of those who participate in it. Connectionism thus provides new insights into what we described in chapter 3 as the epistemic modality but leaves unconsidered the deontic and the declarative. Organization is not just process; it is also a subject-actor, but a subject-actor of a very special kind, in that its identity emerges only in its symbolic construction, through a kind of translation into a textualized actor, given a human voice.

THE ORGANIZATION HAS TO MAP MORE THAN THE ENVIRONMENT; IT HAS TO MAP ITSELF

It is because organizational members are immersed in a larger conversation than the merely local that they must also, to move around and thrive, possess what Weick (1995a) calls a "cognitive map" of the social territory they inhabit (or what Hutchins, if he had been thinking about a social rather than a natural environment, would presumably have called a "chart"), one that provides an orientation to its salient landmarks, including those regions of the conversation that lie beyond their immediate sphere of daily transactions. This larger territory that the mapping brings into being is how organization comes to take on reality status for us (mapping, we see in chap. 9, is a form of textualization), even though the territory it portrays is not physical, but social.

The basis of organization-as-conversation is interaction; the basis of or-ganization-as-text (or map) is description, in a symbolic language. Lan-guage enters in both instances, but in different ways: in conversation as a medium of interaction (where it occurs in shortish staccato bursts of half-completed, elliptical, sentences and jointly negotiated assertions) and in text as a medium of representation (where it tends to be more elaborated, and where there is an author or authors). Text is the product of the conversational process, but it is also its raw material and principal preoccupation. Together, then, conversation and text form a self-organizing loop (J. R. Taylor 1995; J. R. Taylor et al., 1996). Because connectionism does not deal very well with the text-conversation translation, it is thus a convenient point of entry to organizational commuication theory building, but no more than that.

ORGANIZATION AS CONVERSATION

Our question in this chapter can be summarized as follows: Is it tenable to think of conversation using the metaphor of a connectionist network, reinterpreted as a social network, in the sense that the units are no longer mathematical functions or finite state automata, as in a neural net simulation of cognition-at-work (the artificial intelligence perspective), but rather are ordinary human beings whose collective communicational patterns go to make up a system of socially distributed cognition or a collective mind (the Weick & Roberts, and Hutchins perspective)? We explore the idea of a networked basis of cognition ("cognition in the wild") that is at the core of the connectionist proposal: not how people exchange knowledge through communication, but how they (assuming with Hutchins, and Roberts and Weick that they do), collectively and interactively, constitute knowledge. How plausible is this idea, where the interconnected network is thought of, differently, as an image of human organization?

Obviously, a shift of perspective is involved. Schegloff believes that the basic mode of human communication is conversation:

> In many respects, of course, the fundamental or primordial scene of social life is that of direct interaction between members of a social species, typically ones who are physically copresent.... Ordinary conversation is very likely the basic form of organization for talk-in-interaction. Conversational interaction may be thought of as a form of social organization through which most, if not all, the major institutions of societies—the economy, the polity, the family, and the reproduction and socialization of the population—get their work done. (1991, p. 154)

Reinterpreting Connectionism in a Bottom-Up Perspective

Connectionism, in the context we described in chapter 6, furnishes an experimenter's bird's-eye overview on communication. It tends to put a superficial gloss on the nuts and bolts of locally situated communication, limiting itself to only those properties of the latter that are minimally necessary to explain the performance of a network whose nodes, unlike human beings, are no more than elementary input–output functions. Because locally situated communication is our usual experience of communication, as those personally involved in it, the connectionist perspective initially seems strange—lacking in apprehension of the immediacy and subjective investment of the communication experience—but this strangeness does not make it invalid. We need to recognize it for what it is, an abstraction or model, and abstraction is often a useful tool in the building of theory (provided we bear in mind that that is what it is).

Out of all the possible properties of the ongoing process of internodal or interunit (translated: interpersonal) exchange, the connectionist, cognitive science/artificial intelligence model specifies only a few: such things as the number of connections linking units, the strength (or weight) of a given connection, its polarity (whether it is excitatory or inhibitory), and the reaction tendencies of each individual, specifically, the threshold and strength of their reaction. This network-oriented view of the conversation from above further recognizes the possibility (even the necessity) of specialized adaptations, where a unit or subassembly has become sensitized to certain features of the environment more than to others, and this differentiation will be reflected in its patterns of response.

Two other assumptions of the neural net (or parallel distributed processing) view of conversation—remember, we are engaged in a mental exercise of transposing their assumptions to a human network—are feedforward and backpropagation. Feedforward is a necessary condition for information processing to occur, in any kind of network (otherwise, it would never arrive at a decision), but there is no logical reason for the net to limit itself to feedforward; it is merely a convenient assumption in the pragmatics of the doing of a simulation. For ordinary conversation to show the property of computation, it too must have feedforward although, again, whether the interaction is strictly feedforward is not crucial.

Backpropagation is a convention among artificial intelligence researchers that, although its neural equivalent is controversial, has been adopted because it works, and because the feeling is that there must be some such mechanism in any adaptive network that is capable of learning. How the brain manages backpropagation, nobody really knows (Zipser, 1990), but it must have some such capability. To explain how organizations learn, we would also have to postulate some communicational mechanism of similar effect. What the socially distributed equivalent of backpropagation might be is a question to which we return later.

Although connectionism thus imposes very stringent conditions on communication when we apply its model of cognition to the normal human conversational context, we can still ask: Does this model become totally artificial in the transposition from one sphere of analysis to another, or are there, notwithstanding the shift of perspective, properties of interaction-through-talk that, even if phrased in a different language, are plausibly explained by and would support the network metaphor?

To answer this question, we must first invert the top-down experimenter perspective on networking and develop in its stead a bottom up, worm's-eye view of conversation-based organization, still, however, hypothesizing that intelligence is a product of interconnectivity. Fortunately, we are not the first to ask whether it makes sense to think of conversation in this way. The issue has been addressed by Emmanuel Schegloff, in a chapter of a book (Resnick, Levine, & Teasley, 1991) that bears the title *Perspectives on Socially Shared Cognition* (notice the shift of terminology, from "distributed" to "shared": seen from above, as a connectionist experiment, a network is distributed, from below, as a synthesis, it is shared).

Schegloff, as we observed earlier, is a founder of conversation analysis (among other distinctions, a coauthor along with Harvey Sacks and Gail Jefferson of the 1974 paper). He has remained one of the most disciplined and eloquent spokespersons of this school. When he takes up the question of the social distribution of intelligence, he does so with unique credentials and a special authority.

Schegloff's Conceptualization of Conversation

What are people doing in a conversation? For Schegloff, they are engaged in what he calls "the maintenance of a *world*" which is, moreover, "mutually understood by the participants as some *same* world" (1991, p. 151, emphasis in original). He thinks of this as "the achievement and maintenance of intersubjectivity." It is important for our purposes to underline that he does not mean by intersubjectivity that people have the same knowledge, or that, as he puts it, their "separate memory drums" have "identical contents." On the contrary, the challenge people face in conversation, given that the knowledge they have in their heads is not uniformly the same, is how to sustain, in spite of the interindividual heterogeneity, a shared basis of intelligence (and a collective capacity to act). For Schegloff, this is why cognition and interaction are "inextricably intertwined" (1991, p. 151). Shared knowledge, he says (citing Garfinkel), involves "a *procedural* sense of common or shared, a set of practices by which actions and stances [can] be predicated on and displayed as oriented to 'knowledge held in common'— knowledge that might thereby be reconfirmed, modified, and expanded" (p. 151, emphasis in original). What is shared is how to put the pieces together; conversation, then, is like family members doing a jigsaw puzzle over the holidays. What is important is the attainment of commonality of knowledge. Given the inevitable diversity of individual perspectives on the world, the fund of common knowledge, unlike a jigsaw puzzle, must be endlessly updated and repeatedly reestablished through interaction (cf. Werth's concept of common ground, discussed in chap. 3).

CA began as an investigation of the procedural dynamics that govern talk-in-interaction and make it more than information exchange—joint information construction, in fact. Conversation, as Sigman (1995) reminds us, is consequential: It counts, in its own right. In Schegloff's words:

> The domain of social action and interaction . . . is not a structureless medium that merely transmits messages, knowledge, information, or behavior that are planned and processed inside the skull, with no further ado. Rather, the world of interaction has its own structures and constraints. Its shape not only bears on the fate of acts, messages, and utterances once they are enacted by persons. It also enters into the very composition, design, and structuring of conduct and is part and parcel of whatever processes—cognitive or otherwise—are germane to the conception and constitution of acts, messages, or utterances in the first instance. *The very things that it occurs to speakers to express . . . are constrained and shaped by the structures by which talk-in-interaction is organized.* (1991, pp. 153–154, emphasis added)

(Note the parallel with connectionism: It is as if he were saying that firing, "the very things it occurs to speakers to express," is dependent on inputs.)

Procedurally, participants in a conversation confront a practical problem. Because conversation is mostly intelligible only if one person talks and the other listens, the issue of turns of talk is omnipresent. CA has shown, by meticulous analysis of protocols of verbal interaction, how much complicated knowledge goes into the organizing of what, at first glance, might seem to be a trivial accomplishment: turn taking. On their reading, the organization of interactive talk is actually highly rule governed. This is how the mechanics of turn-taking, of sustained coherence of sequences of successive utterances, and of the whole occasion of talk can succeed in producing a fluid, seamless flow of conversation and how intersubjectivity emerges. Because it is rule governed, it is constraining, and individuals have to learn, as part of their entry into communal sociality, how to conform themselves to the constraints. Only by mastering the constraints can they hope to have their contributions to the conversation paid attention to. Schegloff's way of saying this is to claim that "the basic natural environment for sentences is in turns at talk in conversation" (1991, p. 154).

Before we go on with our presentation of the theory of conversation Schegloff is presenting, let us note, in parenthesis, a similarity and a difference between the connectionist and CA views of internodal (or interpersonal) linking through the process of communication. The similarity is the assumption of structural constraint operating on the exchange process; the difference is in the assumed origin of such a constraint. By *structural constraint* the connectionist means the pattern of weights (which in turn determines the emergent configuration of links); the weights are typically set at random by the experimenter at the beginning of a simulation and undergo change following the dictates of an algorithm that feeds back (backpropagates) information on the success or failure of the network. For the CA analyst, the constraint is intrinsic to interaction maintenance and coherence. The weight is built in.

Yet, at another level, they are saying something quite similar. Cognition is accomplished as a property of interaction, and the interaction is rule governed. The difference in this conception comes from the connectionist assumption that constraint has an extraconversational basis in the exigencies of network structuredness to produce a collective response (this is why we call theirs a top-down view of the network); in this respect, the connectionist position is not totally at variance with March and Simon's characterization of communication, which also was premised on an overriding organizational imperative (the power to program). CA assumes constraint has an intraconversational basis, that arises as a consequence of the inherent difficulty posed by the turn-taking imperative (this is why it is bottom up).[2] The difference of perspective will not matter in an essential way, providing that the intrinsic constraint properties result in a behavior that satisfies the extrinsic requirements of the network, and vice versa. That is the question that we are exploring.[3]

The Reconstructive Nature of Talk-in-Interaction

One of the central tenets of CA is the principle of what is called the "organization of repair" (Schegloff, 1991, p. 155). As we turn to consider Schegloff's comments on the relevance of this principle to the social sharing of knowledge, we recommend that you ask yourself, as we are doing, whether there may not be an essential correspondence between organization of repair and what has been called in the connectionist literature on cognition (for example, Johnson-Laird, 1988; McClelland & Rumelhart, 1981) "the reconstructive nature of human memory." McClelland and Rumelhart's explanation is built on the supposition that different nodes have different parts of the answer (parallel processing is occurring) and that easy and immediate identification is made possible because the pattern of excitations and inhibitions manifested in the internodal interaction both (a) point in the correct direction (that is the excitatory part) and (b)

---

[2]But later, in our discussion of Boden, we question whether it is ever strictly bottom up.

[3]Again, it is worth reiterating the originality of an approach that starts from communication, as opposed to ending up with it. Social science originated either in sociology or in psychology, so that what seemed most real was either the structures of society or intrapersonal dynamics. Communication came to be seen as either that which is done in society to make it work, or that which people say and do to others, among other things they do. One approach sought for laws in (a) the constraints of social structure, the other in (b) the constraints of individual behavior, so that neither recognized the existence of constraints that were neither social nor psychological, but interactional.

point away from the wrong direction (that is the inhibitory part). Our speculation is that the CA organization of repair is fulfilling a similar role, again to produce a joint answer that is the product of the separate knowledges, and not just their sum (in other words, social memory is also reconstructive in its nature).

Certainly, it is here in the organization-of-repair principle that Schegloff perceives the source of the emergence of socially shared cognition (1991, pp. 157–158): "The ordinary sequential organization of conversation thus provides for displays of mutual understanding and *problems therein*, one running basis for the cultivation of the talk and conduct in the interaction" (emphasis added). Identifying and correcting "problems" in the interactive production of understanding is, we think, a way of being what a connectionist would call inhibitory. The excitatory part is the "display of understanding."

Repair is necessitated whenever there is a problem in shared understanding (sometimes called a trouble in the CA literature), creating the risk of divergent understandings and leading to a "breakdown of intersubjectivity." Sometimes it is in the turn where the trouble, or potential trouble, occurs that the repair is initiated, as in the following extract of talk (reprinted from Boden, 1994, p. 184, who notes, incidentally, that this is often a preferred strategy because it allows the speaker to retain the turn):[4]

> **Peggy:** What- what is happening is that (0.5) a census is being taken for ev- *by- on* every shift.
> (0.8)
> So it's not a specific *mi*dnight census (.)
> count
> (0.6)
> 'Mean they *call* it the midnight census but it's not actually (.) being counted (0.3) at midnight. .h: So it's being counted at three-thirty
> **Lucy:**   ⌈Hm hmm⌉
> **Peggy:** ⌊On one ⌋ shift, it's being counted at eleven o'*clock* on another one, and in the *morn*ing as well. (0.4) Sometimes- ideally (0.4) all these re- reports should add up (.) to the (.) total census, but sometimes there's a *prob*lem with it. (0.4) Problem occurs when . . .

---

[4]The following conventions occur in the transcriptions that follow. Numbers in brackets indicate a gap in tenths of seconds; a dot in parentheses indicates an almost imperceptible gap; italics or underlining indicate emphasis; brackets are used to indicate overlap or simultaneous speech; an "h" prefixed by a dot indicates an inbreath, without a dot an outbreath; colons indicate that the immediately prior syllable is stretched, the number of colons indicating the duration of the prolonged syllable; expressions such as "hm" indicate back-channel continuation signals.

In this instance, it is Peggy who voluntarily opts to clarify the evident confusion that could be created by her mention of a "midnight census" that was not, in point of fact, taken at midnight.

Another common pattern is found where the hearer breaks in to clarify a point, as in this imaginary sequence:

A: Yeah, well I'll be back on Friday, and ⌈uhn . . .
B: ⌊You mean this Friday?
A: Right, yeah that's right, *this* Friday . . .

It is the third pattern, however, that is the focus of Schegloff's attention in his discussion of shared cognition: what he calls "third position repair." Third position repair is found when the initiator of a sequence has realized that the conversational partner has misunderstood, and a correction is necessary, as in this exchange between two women roommates living in Los Angeles, one of whose boyfriends, Stuart, is about to move from the East Coast to be closer to her (reprinted from Schegloff, 1991, pp. 160–161):

M: What' Stuart have to say.
N: Didn' I tell you?
M: No::,
N: He's <u>coming</u>
M: Oh that's righ⌈t
N: ⌊Yeah he's <u>coming</u> he's <u>coming</u>
M: Oh that's right, ⌈he's going to Berkeley
N: ⌊Yes.

As Schegloff points out, this sequence bears on the issue of intersubjectivity, or socially shared cognition, in more than one way. It is both about getting to an immediate understanding of what N (the source of the news) is conveying to M and about establishing, retroactively, what they know in common or had already established. This is surely an instance of "reconstruction of memory," the difference from the connectionist network variety being that now it is a socially shared memory. And, the reconstructive process is a mixture of excitation and inhibition.

As we would expect, given Schegloff's bottom up viewpoint on conversation, his conclusion emphasizes the sharing of perspectives that conversation makes not only possible but also inevitable. A conversation, for him, is an "understanding display" device, where understandings may be problematical and engender clarification activities to achieve intersubjectivity (which he takes as a synonym for socially shared cognition). But, although his initial starting point on the conversational exchange is so different from the connectionist (as interpreted by Hutchins or Weick & Roberts), the conclusion he draws is remarkably compatible. He too rejects the individualistic, psychologistic Western tradition of the single, embodied, minded individual who constitutes an autonomous reality in favor of a conception that treats understanding of the world and of one another is an achievement "in an inescapably social and interactional context" (p. 168). As he says: "Interaction and talk-in-interaction are structured environments for action and cognition, and they shape both the constitution of the actions and utterances needing to be 'cognized' and the contingencies for solving them" (Schegloff, 1991, p. 168).

What we have been trying to establish is not that the connectionist and CA positions are reducible, one to the other, but something more modest: that, at least on a preliminary reading of them, what they are saying need not be taken to be a priori irreconcilable, always providing that we take account of their different purposes and methods. But CA, in the version we have been discussing, has usually not had much to say about how individual conversations interactively combine to produce large scale organization, or institutionally complex agglomerations of socially shared memory/cognition. Just as we found the connectionist movement suggestive in the light it might possibly shed on the microworld of ordinary conversation, so we are intrigued by what CA, with its insistence on the structuring organizational constraints that inhere in the conversational exchange itself, might have to contribute to our understanding of the macroworld of large organization.

Again, we do not need to speculate. We can draw on Boden (1994) to provide an explicit answer to the question because this is precisely the issue, as we have seen in chapter 1, that she set out to address.

FROM THE "BUSINESS OF TALK" TO THE "TALK OF BUSINESS"

Although Boden has rooted her view of organization in ethnomethodology and exploits the insights of CA, she has also been critical of the latter. Because of its procedural focus, she says, the context of talk-based activities was initially ignored, with the effect of "bracketing out the issue of *who* was speaking to *whom*, *where* and *why*, in the interests of learning *how* they were doing so" (Boden, 1994, pp. 74–75, emphasis in original). So, although she subscribes to the notion of local construction of even the most elaborate of social entities, she is prepared to enlarge the circumference of inquiry to take account of context: ". . . the recursive features of both talk and its organizational context *matter*—to the talk, as well as to how the organization is created and sustained through talk" (pp. 74–75).

Accountability

Central to Boden's argument, as to the ethnomethodological position generally, is the concept of an account, and it is here that the link with
connectionism is to be found. The word *account* is used in more than one
way, and each of those uses is vital. To begin with, *accountable* means being
responsible for one's acts: You are accountable in the sense that you are
expected to be able to render an account of your actions—to justify them.
Behind this lies the assumption that people are agents, in that behavior
is informed by purpose and involves a moral responsibility. In their collaborations, "human beings must—as a central condition of existence and
even survival—treat each other as reasonable and competent, as well as
reasonably compliant and cooperative. This 'reasonableness' is what I mean
by agency" (Boden, 1994, p. 14). Never mind the official mechanisms of
organizational accounting. Presenting an account of your activities that
will pass the muster of your mates is already a subtle form of socialization
that can be in its way a more effective bondage than the most authoritarian
of systems. It is one of the essential disciplines that enforces the social
strain of intelligence as connectionism postulates.

The word *account* is also used in a second way. People make accounts
of many things, not just of their own actions, for example, stories, narratives, and explanations. They describe others' actions as well as their own,
and the way they do this *accounts* (a third sense of the word, i.e., to explain)
for the production and expectation of "agency in immediate and distant
others who, *through their actions*, constitute the organizations and institutions
of their society" (Boden, 1994, p. 14, emphasis in original). This is how
the facticity of a matter-of-fact world is created, a world that both opens
up opportunities and instantiates constraints on action. It is in this way
that the continuity of experience is accomplished, as current actions (and
inactions) are made to "retrospectively mesh" with earlier actions and
future projects (p. 21).

The accounting process, mediated by language, is thus crucial not only
to how people interpret their social world (their organization, for example), but also to the constituting of the organization as such: There is no
organization other than that which is the product of the accounting process. And the making of accounts, Boden believes fully as strongly as
Schegloff does, is fundamentally a social achievement of talk-in-interaction.
"Cognition," she says categorically, "is not an 'individual' matter'" (Boden,
1994, p. 20). Rationality, she thinks, is not a psychological, but an "interactionally bounded phenomenon" (p. 21). Meanings "do not occur as
isolated cognitive phenomena in the heads of atomized individuals; they
are constructed interactively and under quite pressing conditions of time
and space" (p. 18).

So the organization becomes a "real and practical place" (Boden, 1994, p. 15) only as the consequence of a recurrently generated ongoing conversation, multiply laminated, a world of "telephone calls, meetings, planning sessions, sales talks and corridor conversations" by means of which "people inform, amuse, update, gossip, review, reassess, reason, instruct, revise, argue, debate, contest, and actually *constitute* the moments, myths and through time, the very *structuring* of the organization" (p. 8). What started as turn-taking ultimately ends up as "turn-making":

> Social agents take the general framework of turn-taking and make it work for them as talk—for their immediate needs, topics and tasks, as well as operating in terms of their relevant identities and shared goals . . . In this way, the structuring properties of turn-taking provide the fine, flexible interactional system out of which institutional relations and institutions themselves are conjured, turn by turn . . . The business of talk, in the technical sense, is thereby transformed into business that gets done *through* talk. (pp. 73–74)

LAMINATION OF CONVERSATIONS

Does conversation analysis successfully scale up to explain the organization as a network with cognitive properties such as those identified by the connectionists?

Conversations as a Connectionist Network

A connectionist network, it will be recalled, had three categories of units: input, hidden, and output. In a socially constituted connectionist network, all the units are people, and all the connections are conversational. Presumably anybody might be an input (although it may be, as social network research would suggest, that some people revel in the input role and become regular liaison figures). Whoever serves as input, CA assumes that (a) people's experience of the environment, and hence the stimulation to which they are exposed, is seldom, or never, the same for any two people, and (b) even if it were, people do not necessarily record the same impressions when confronted with the same stimulus. This is the whole point of intersubjectivity, or social sharing of cognition: No single individual can claim definitive knowledge of the environment. On this score, the presuppositional basis of CA is compatible with that of the cognitivists. All that we require is that the stimulus be such that its different facets are registered multinodally at the level of input, that is, that it be multiplexed.

Multiplexing constitutes a principal advantage of the connectionist explanation of cognition over a more traditional symbolicist one. The reason for this (and it applies, as far as we can tell, equally well to networks composed of people as to those built of mathematical functions) is that such networks are sensitive to nonlinear stimuli. As Weick (1979b, 1985) has repeatedly emphasized in his analysis of management rationality, environments are equivocal. He likens environmental stimuli, as actually experienced both by individuals and organizations, to puns. This equivocality of the experienced world, as we saw earlier, now has a name in mathematics and systems development: *fuzziness*. In Kosko's (1993, p. 12) words: "Up close things are fuzzy. Borders are inexact and things co-exist with nonthings." (Things that coexist with nonthings is close to what Weick means by "equivocal.") The symbolicist approach is to give a state of the environment a name (i.e., a symbolic identity) and then to manipulate the name syntactically, assuming that, after a semantic equivalence has been established to the real world, computation is context-free—basically, as with mathematics. But, if the world is in fact gray, not black and white—an equivocal environment of puns—this is problematical. As Kosko (p. 15) puts it: "Language, especially the math language of science, creates artificial boundaries between black and white. Reason or common sense smoothes them out. Reason works with grays."

The advantage of a multinodal (or multiperson) image of the environment is that it retains the shades of gray. What is recorded as the sum of the individual experiences of the environment is both variable (and may even be contradictory) and redundant, or overlapping. It is, in other words, nonlinear. It is this nonlinearity that underpins the claim of a connectionist theory of cognition to explain learning. If, through its inputs, the network has a multifaceted, equivocal image of the environment registered in its nodes, then through interaction, depending on how internodal interdependencies evolve, it can generate different interpretations of the environment, and even then it is not stuck with them because subsequently it can progressively adapt them by reshaping the pattern of connections (an idea which comes very close to Weick's, 1979a, explanation of enactment). A symbolic model of cognition, to claim that it is learning, would have to go back and change its representation of the environment by giving it a new name; a connectionist model never loses its potential for change because, as Schegloff put it, it does not assume "identical contents" in its separate "memory drums." What it assumes is procedural structural stability, by means of which a multiplexed representation can be made to generate a variety of interpretations, depending on how the separate funds of knowledge are dynamically interconnected. Such a network knows more than it says it knows. What it says is contingent on the existing configuration of connections; what it also knows is inscribed in the virtual configurations, that could eventually link nodes differently to say something different.

The patterns of interconnections are formed in the hidden units of the network. Much of CA work is so focused on the interpersonal encounter, with the organizational context bracketed out of view, that the englobing interconnections are invisible. The network has vanished, perceptually speaking. By comparison, we find Boden's characterization of organizational process, although deeply imbued with the CA philosophy, quite compatible with the connectionist view (always bearing in mind that we are thinking network, not the mechanics of local interconnection). Listen to how she describes the hidden layer (in older sociological treatments of organization, it was often literally hidden in the sense of being ignored):

> People in organizations talk everywhere, in large formal meetings planned weeks and months in advance or in emergency sessions of one kind or another. They talk in small informal meetings, crammed into one another's office, or at staff meetings and production meetings in large windowless rooms with coffee machines in the background. They talk in plush conference centers or in the back of noisy taxis. They talk on the phone—constantly, or so it would seem. They hang out in doorways, hovering on the boundaries of each other's territories, exchanging not just pleasantries and football scores but urgent news and stale stories, new jokes and hot gossip . . . They talk not so much up and down the hierarchy in the strict steps suggested by organizational charts, but all over the place—up, down, and most creatively laterally—weaving news and information, sniffing for smoke, watching for trends, catching the quickness or monotony of the moment. (Boden, 1994, p. 76)

There are some obvious differences here from a typical connectionist laboratory simulation network. For one thing, the nodes tend to be more numerous; in practice, connectionists prefer smallish collections of nodes, usually numbering in the hundreds, whereas the kind of universe Boden has just described might easily go to thousands. But connectionism is compatible with any size of network. For another, there is more laterality and feedback than you would normally find in a connectionist simulation (even though this additional complexity is not excluded in principle in the connectionist theory). Although neither of these conditions is essential to connectionism, her description of how an organizational conversation unfolds in the large is nonetheless, as far as we can see, compatible with the connectionist view. We are further encouraged in this view by what she describes as "the laminated effect of meeting upon meeting" (Boden, 1994, p. 91). As she describes it, there is feedforward in a natural human organizational net, as well as in an artificially constructed one: "Organizational decisions are *talked* into being in fine yet layered strips of interaction" (p. 91, emphasis in original). This is important: A measure of feedforward is an essential condition of connectionist computation because, without it, there would be no output.

As the previous quote would indicate, Boden's view of output is centered on the idea of decisions. Trying to identify the decision, in the conventional sense of the term as a cut-and-dried choice of one well-defined option among others, is usually not easy, because decision making, as every other conversational activity, is a procedure of interaction. Many meetings have as their focal point the taking of a decision, but most of the time the decision is not actually made there. Either it has already been made, and the meeting is to validate it conversationally (rubber-stamping), or the decision is to call another meeting, perhaps of a subcommittee to whom the decision is delegated. It is not that decisions do not get made; it is just that the moment of their taking may not be easy to pin down, so much does the decision making shade over into what she calls "the politics of information" (Boden, 1994, p. 84–7): "Generally, while formal meetings have the appearance and, no doubt, shared sense of democratic decision-making in action, the actual day-to-day decisions in organizations are not typically accomplished in large formal settings, however much they may be recorded in official documents or the power-packed boardrooms of media portrayal."

So, as we see the comparison, the conversation view of the organizational network does recognize the input/hidden/output distinction, but with the difference that the boundaries separating the functions are considerably more fluid than in an artificial intelligence simulated organization. This does not invalidate the sense that there is a homomorphism—a profound similarity of pattern—involved. The connectionists discovered that a network of units can be said to know something that none of the units individually knows. Knowledge, they argue, may be subsymbolic, which is to say not enunciated in language, but a property of the connections linking the actors in the net and not something the latter individually know. If this principle holds for human sociability, it means that human societies know more, or at least something different, from their members, such knowledge arising out of the conversation. Is it possible that there are two kinds of knowledge, subsymbolic and symbolic, and if there are, what are the implications for organizational communication? It is to this question that we now turn our attention.

WHY ORGANIZATION-AS-CONVERSATION IS NOT ENOUGH

The image of organization as a conversation is thus seen to have considerable appeal, both theoretically and empirically. Nevertheless, it is not a fully satisfactory explanation of what we know about organized life, not even of connectionism as a theory of organization. Let us see what it fails to account for.

Recall once more how a connectionist simulation works. A programmer initially configures a network of units (the units are actually mathematical functions) into a densely interconnected, randomized pattern of links. A stimulus is presented, the network responds, and the programmer evaluates the result (undershoot/overshoot). Either by employing the instrumentality of an algorithm (backpropagation) or by manually reconfiguring the values, the programmer gets the net to reconfigure itself, as instanced by its altered interconnection weights, then re-presents the stimulus. This recycling goes on until a criterion performance is attained (often after many runs). In this model (with the programmer factored in), the human actor (called a teacher) is an essential component in the learning loop. As we have seen in chapter 6, some quite remarkable results have been registered following such a protocol.

The attractive feature of this picture of organization to the organizational communication scholar, we have been suggesting, is the correspondence of distributed network and conversation. But before we leap too hastily to this conclusion, let us look again. We have just been saying things like "the programmer factored in" and "the human actor is an essential component in the learning loop." These little incidental remarks should stand out for us like flashing lights. Theories consist not only of the formal statements in which they are enunciated but also are always embedded in a presuppositional frame, which, because it is a frame, we tend to ignore. But we ignore it at our peril. Nowhere is this more true than in the case of connectionism. Let us consider why.

In a connectionist experiment, the participating actors are divided into two classes: (a) those that form the nodes of the network (input, hidden, and output) which cannot make interpretations framed in normal language (because they are merely mathematical functions), and (b) that person (or those persons) who can, and who thus gets to play the role of interpreter and teacher—the programming expert(s). What the theory explicitly asserts is limited to (a); what it presupposes is (b). In an ordinary human organization of the kind Boden describes, there is no teacher (or perhaps it would be more accurate to say that everyone is potentially a teacher, because anyone could, in principle if not in practice, step into the role of the experimenter/programmer who reads off, i.e., makes a symbolic interpretation of, and evaluates what the network knows, to teach it how to do better). We, as the experimenters in a connectionist simulation, can all talk; the nodes in our networks cannot.

The Achilles heel of connectionism from the outset and the point at which it is most vulnerable to counterattack from the symbolicists is the assumption that cognition can be uniquely explained as the output of a connected network of dumb (although efficient and mathematically precise) units of elementary computation. Linguists, even as they admit the validity of the connectionist achievement at the level of pattern recognition, nevertheless insist that it fails to take account of the syntactic subtleties of

natural language and, in particular, the mastery of the rule-governed grammar the latter supposes (see in particular Coltheart, Curtis, Atkins, & Haller, 1993; Pinker & Prince, 1988; Prasada & Pinker, 1993).[5]

We leave that argument to the linguists and their allies, the critics of
connectionism within the cognitive science community. We are concerned
with another aspect of language that the connectionists gloss over too lightly
for our taste: not its syntactics, but its pragmatics. The connectionist
assumption poses, for us, a logical problem, that arises out of our understanding of the communication structure their research paradigm illustrates.

Suppose it is possible that the network, authentically, knows the environment because, in the way it is configured, it can generate in its output
a quasi-iconic representation of it (by computing the concealed regularities
or, to once more quote Kosko, 1993, "sensing the fuzzy patterns in the
data"). Then—and here is the catch—how can we know what it knows
until its knowledge had been framed in a statement (in language, that is)?
How could it itself know what it knows? And if you do not know what you
know, can you be said to really know it?[6] Or, as Weick likes to ask (1979b,
1995a): "How can I know what I think until I see what I say?"

In an AI simulation, the programmer tells us what the network has
learned; that is why there is a literature on connectionism—books and
articles in considerable proliferation, whole issues of the journal *Cognition*—all reporting on the acquired knowledge of the networks. The networks, however, do not produce representations of the environment that
are symbolic: They are subsymbolic. It is the scientific descriptions of them,
written by the researchers, that are symbolic. Yet, in the absence of symbolization, there would be no communication to us readers, and we would
never have known about parallel distributed processing and its cognitive
possibilities. (Could it be that, as has happened before, the reported results
of connectionist experiments have tended to underplay the importance

---

[5]It it not only linguists who have reservations as to the limited capacities of connectionist
nets. Dinsmore (1992, p. 18) writes, for example: "Clearly, connectionist networks with
significant cognitive abilities will have to be far more complex than the simple computational
models that now exist. But as models become more complex, they will become more opaque
(recall also that connectionist networks are for the most part trained, not programmed). For
this reason connectionist models cannot dispense with higher-level functional abstractions
that summarize large parts of the network structure or behavior." For more upbeat views on
the potential of connectionism, see Seidenberg (1992, 1994). For a readable summary of the
arguments pro and con, see Bechtel and Abrahamsen (1991, chap. 6).

[6]This is a point made by Searle (1984) in a criticism of what he called "strong AI." He
used the analogy of the "Chinese Room" where there sat an individual, without any knowledge
of Chinese, who nevertheless, by following rules written in English and using them to compose
strings of Chinese symbols, could actually fool the casual observer into thinking the "answers"
to the questions being submitted were those of a native Chinese speaker. Searle's critique—his
rejoinder to the famous Turing test of intelligence—is based on a confusion he perceives in
AI between syntactics and semantics.

of the presence of the programmers and the computations that they were themselves doing?)

Significantly, artificial intelligence is the study of cognition, not communication.

Identity and Voice

Watzlawick, Beavin, and Jackson (1967), following Bateson, made a distinction between two modes of representation that they termed "analog" and "digital."[7] The term *digital* was not felicitous, because what they in fact had in mind was knowledge that was encoded in language (not necessarily in binary digits, or bits); their distinction, nevertheless, takes on extra meaning in the present context, if we read *analog* to mean subsymbolic and *digital* symbolic. Subsymbolic cognition would then be one that captures in its representation the contours of the stimulus, by configuring its parts in a way that produces a resemblance (and thus deals well with nonlinear phenomena, as we have learned). After the configuration is accomplished, it remembers, in the sense that in the future it will recognize the pattern of the stimulus, even in the presence of noise and even when detail in the image is missing. To this extent, it knows the environment more faithfully than a symbolic representation ever could, because one property of language is to introduce edges and clarity of boundary, even though the actual environment remains fuzzy. Language categorizes, "typifies" (in Schutz's term), and makes distinctions whose roots are not just semantic, but syntactic: such as subject, verb, object, adjective and adverb. Syntax is a rule-based structure of the language, not of what it represents.[8]

The connectionist network knows without being able to say what it knows, because its output still has to be interpreted, read, and stated. Reading and stating is what the programmer (or teacher) does. The net-

---

[7]A similar distinction is developed by Dretske (1986).

[8]According to Leach (1964, pp. 34–35): "I postulate that the physical and social environment of a young child is perceived as a continuum. It does not contain any intrinsically separate 'things.' The child, in due course, is taught to impose upon this environment a kind of discriminating grid which serves to distinguish the world as being composed of a large number of separate things, each labeled with a name. This world is a representation of our language categories, not vice versa. Because my mother tongue is English, it seems self-evident that bushes and trees are different kinds of things. I would not think this unless I had been taught that it was the case." Leach sees in this carving up of the world the origin of taboos. If, he argues, "it is crucially important that the basic discriminations should be clear-cut and unambiguous" and if, on the contrary, "[o]ur uninhibited (untrained) perception recognizes a continuum" then the obvious solution is to suppress from perception the parts of the continuum that separate the things. Hence, the necessity of taboos—nonthings that cannot be recognized because they have no name, even though they exist: homosexuality in a homophobic society, for example, or the eating of household pets, in societies with pets.

work, as such, has no voice—and nothing to say if it did have one. It can produce intelligible sounds, to be sure, but nobody, least of all its teacher, would take them to be a statement of what the network believes, wants, or feels. The network does not publish its results, if for no other reason that that it did not know they were results. It is the experimenter who gives the network its human voice (is there any other kind?).

Having a voice, then, implies more than the ability to enunciate recognizable sounds of language (which the network can manage); it implies having an identity. It is through speaking, being heard, and in having recognized that what you said was your statement that making your knowledge communicable is accomplished. In the absence of this ability, there would be no human conversation, no socially distributed cognition.

We could be tempted to conclude, on the basis of persuasive arguments by analysts such as Schegloff and Boden, that what constituted the network as an organization (or, vice versa, the organization as a network) was its being a conversation, and, furthermore, that the very idea of socially distributed cognition necessarily depended on the talk-in-interaction of the conversation. This would be equivalent, in terms of the presentation of chapter 2, to recognizing the constraint of conversation form (as generative of organization) and ignoring that of text form. We now want, not to reject (because we are in agreement with it, as far as it goes), but to qualify, their view.

Conversation as formal constraint is one way to look at an organization. It is even a powerful generalization, because it explains how structure emerges out of process, whether that structure be cognitive or social. It is an imaginative way of making the organization/communication link. But it does not explain the organizational phenomenon we have just drawn attention to, how the organization comes to have an identity and a voice to say what it knows. For that level of analysis, we would have to take account of text form—the symbolic, as well as the subsymbolic, the digital as well as the analog.

The Constitution of Corporate Actors

The point we are making is so obvious that we believe this is why it frequently escapes attention. You can verify our claim by inspecting any newspaper, any day. Here, for example, are just a few of the expressions we gleaned from a casual reading of one day's issue (March 27, 1996) of the *New York Times*: "the Federal Reserve, by fighting inflation so aggressively in recent years, has kept the economy from growing," "the Communist Party's new embrace of the Russian church," "the organization that represents Federal judges across the country today denounced a plan ... the organization said such authority posed a threat," "the House and Senate approved different versions of the bill," "businesses here [Nebraska] fight over workers the way most companies fight over customers," "the United States Agriculture Department said it would increase the number of cattle brains that are routinely tested," "today's criticism from the Judicial Conference . . . ," "Amnesty International said . . . ," "opposition groups characterized . . . ," "U.S. confident," "the [British] Government blames . . . ," "Pakistan is rethinking . . . ," "Washington has recently condemned . . . ," "with Dole's star on the rise, his town hopes . . . ," "Judges' group condemns . . . ," "Chrysler sues (The Chrysler Corporation today took legal action)," and this is just a partial sample from one day's paper.

We can take it for granted, surely, that behind the bald statement of position of each of the organizations in question (Federal Reserve, Communist Party, Judges' group, House and Senate, Nebraska businesses, United States Agriculture Department, Judicial Conference, Amnesty International, opposition groups in Bahrain, the United States, the British Government, Pakistan, Washington, Dole's home town, Chrysler Corporation) there was a conversation that made a computation of the situation and, through whatever messy, hard-to-track, "garbage can" (March & Olsen, 1976) process, finally arrived at an output, or decision, that reflected properties of the stimulus, as well as the computing it made to arrive at a position. There was an organization-as-conversation, in Boden's sense, or (for a connectionist) distributed parallel processing, behind the announced view of the organization. But, we do not have access to that conversation or that parallel processing; we deal with the organization differently, as a node in our conversation (conveniently mediated by the *New York Times*, as it happens). A shift of perspective has occurred. The mediation in question is what we call *textualization*. It is a crucial step toward explaining backpropagation in human organization, and how such organizations, unlike the connectionist network of the laboratory, not only organize, but self-organize—learn without a teacher, in other words.

BACKPROPAGATION: THE LEARNING ORGANIZATION

Textualization occurs when the network—which, being a network, may know but has no voice to say what it knows, nor any way to translate its knowledge into a symbolic form that could be voiced—states its knowledge (or rather has it stated for it). Textualization of cognition supposes a transformation from subsymbolic to symbolic, from analog to digital. The reason that this transformation explains backpropagation is that it allows for the emergence of agency, and, without agency, the organization would never have a voice and thus never exist as an actor.

Agency

Consider again those fragmentary excerpts from the daily newspaper we just cited, this time from the point of view of the verbs that are used. For convenience, we have grouped them under three headings, attitudes, actions, and statements, each with three possible valences, positive, neutral, and negative.

Attitudes:
- Positive:
  approve, embrace
- Neutral:
  hope, is confident
- Negative:
  No examples found

Actions:
- Positive:
  will increase
- Neutral:
  keep down [the economy, but in the interests of controlling inflation]
- Negative:
  fight [against], fight over, sue, take action [against]

Statements:
- Positive:
  say (3 different mentions)
- Neutral:
  rethink
- Negative:
  denounce, criticize, blame, condemn, characterize

What these verbs all have in common is an attribution of agency to the organization that figures as the subject of the sentence: it thinks, it acts, it does, it says, and so forth. At the risk of belaboring the obvious, we do not normally think of a conversation as having the capacity to act—to have the will, the skill, and the instrumentalities that are the hallmark of acting. A conversation is just talk-in-interaction (Schegloff's phrase); it is not talk-as-action. Agency has to be lodged in someone with the "heedfulness" of a purposeful actor (Weick & Roberts, 1993). To the extent that an organization is conversation (or distributed parallel processing, if you prefer that terminology) it cannot be an agent. Yet, we see that it is an agent, at least to the journalists of the *Times*—and we presume to pretty much everyone who reads that paper, too.

Boden observes, with justification, that, logically, organizations cannot act. As she says (1994, p. 56): "Organizations do not *act* or *do* anything, people do" (emphasis in original). Yet, as we have seen, they do act, they do do things. Is this a contradiction, or is there an explanation, and, if so, what is it?

As we see it, no contradiction is involved, but a confusion is, and it is to be found in the way we use the word *agency*. The dictionary commonly admits two principal readings. On the one hand, agency means action, power, or instrumentality. This power-expressed-in-acting, or instrumentality, is what the verbs we have just been enumerating attributed to the respective corporate actors they qualified. On the other hand, agency means acting for somebody else, or on someone's behalf (J. R. Taylor & Cooren, 1997). Here is the point. The ability of an organization to realize itself in action comes about because it has found an agent (or more properly, an agent has presumed, and been recognized as having the right) to speak for it—where *agency* now has the second dictionary meaning of acting for somebody else. There has to be a spokesperson to mediate the transformation of the organization from the talk-in-interaction of a conversation to actor-in-a-conversation: the person who speaks in the name of the organization (Boden's point). And that occurs at the moment of textualization of the organization's collectively computed knowledge.

Textualization confounds the levels of individual and network (and sheds, as we shall now show, a somewhat different light on one aspect of Boden's analysis, the fusing of personal and organizational agendas). It is also the key to understanding a puzzling aspect of group life, its self-organizing character (J. R. Taylor, 1995). It is here that we perceive the mutual interdependence of conversation and text: Conversations, although they are the locus of the generation of knowledge, nevertheless need to know what they know, and this is only possible in the translation of their collectively generated knowledge into an (imperfect) textual rendering of it, which then has to be, once again, recognized in the interpreting processes of the network—truly an instance of what Hofstadter (1979) terms a "strange loop."

The Confounding of Levels

Networks, as the connectionist literature reminds us, may contain what Hebb (1949) called "sub-assemblies": configurations of units that develop specialized functions within the network. A sub-assembly might be thought of as a mini-organization. As such, because it also has an interpretable output, it too could take on a voice. The *New York Times* of March 27 refers, among other actors, to the United States of America, Washington, the White House, the House and the Senate, and the U.S. Department of

Agriculture. If we were to consider this collection of names from the organization-as-conversation point of view, we would predict considerable lamination, that is, conversations within conversations—a hierarchization of the conversation to produce: (United States of America > (Washington > ((the House and the Senate) + (the White House > the U.S. Department of Agriculture)))). But through textualization, all these actors are brought down to a level playing field (a flatland): character actors in our organizational conversation.

Nor do we need to stop there. Individual nodes, in the connectionist view, may also have specialized functions. The same newspaper, if we had chosen to go further, mentioned many individual actors (many of whose role identities have changed since 1994), such as: Alan Greenspan (Federal Reserve Bank chairman), Gennadi A. Zyuganov (Communist leader), Bill Clinton (President), Bob Dole (Senator/presidential candidate), Sheik Isa bin Salman Al Khalifa (Bahrain leader), John Major (British Prime Minister), and Daron Woelk (who runs his family's jewelry store on Main Street of Senator Dole's town of origin, Russell, Kansas). Each of them is individually, if we credit the connectionists' view of how the brain works, a parallel distributed processing—an internal conversation of neural cells—which then takes on a voice.

Boden makes frequent reference to the importance of the individual actor and to the playing out of the organization, always at the local level, through his or her interactions. Again, she is making a valid point, but it too needs to be qualified. In reading her quite detailed analyses of the encounters of organizational actors (and, in particular, a meeting of university officials, to which she devotes an entire chapter), it is very evident that all those present have constantly in mind that they speak for a subassembly of the institution that forms their particular conversational envelope, their bailiwick: Provost's office, Faculty, Financial Department. As conversational actors, they go even further, from time to time freely evoking the larger agenda of the University as a whole (and even of the State), by interpreting its position, making themselves its putative spokesperson, associating (and thus justifying) their own agenda with its. In this way, by proxy, the organization, which speaks for all the people in the organization as its collective intelligence, is nevertheless also vicariously present in the conversations that go toward its own constitution: It becomes, in the person of its spokespersons, simultaneously the whole and a part (or, rather, participant).

Conversely, the person who gives voice to the organization is both in the organization (as one of its individual nodes) and not in it (as the voice who speaks in its name). Although the organization, constituted as an actor through the good graces of a human agent, speaks for everybody, because it alone is the repository of their collectively and interactively shared knowledge, it is now simultaneously turned into a special pleader for one particular interpretation of the collective mind. The organization is the conversation, as we have seen, but, through its textualization, it is also in the conversation. It is this paradox that the connectionist literature fudges by pretending that the experimenter is not part of the network but is instead apart from it.

This confusion of levels is the consequence of what is called a *syncretism*. The individual who is speaking, Boden's Dean let us say, is speaking for himself, as someone with personal ambitions, but he also aims to speak for the organization of which he is merely a part. This is a powerful and potentially troubling phenomenon because it goes against the grain of many of our unspoken assumptions about the roots of personal identity: It leaves very much open to doubt whether an individual identity can ever be fully abstracted from the organizational. Every person is always being both actor and agent. An organizational actor is one where the actor, as agent, speaks for someone else, namely, the collective network; an individual actor speaks only for him- or herself. The distinction sounds clear enough in the abstract, but it turns out to be less so in practice.[9]

What we have called a confusion and a seeming paradox is the real reason for the remarkable richness of conversation that Boden describes with acuity. It makes every interaction a complex dance of identities and an exercise in organizational hermeneutics. It is one of the clear ways in which human conversation differs from a connectionist network, in that the identities (if you could even call them that) of the latter's units stay individual. They have no capacity to speak for anyone but themselves. In

---

[9]The notion of a *self* is considerably more problematical and culture-dependent than we are usually accustomed to acknowledge, especially in North America, with its prevailing individualistic ideology. Kondo (1990) reports on the view of self in Japan, very different from that in North America. A U.S. anthropologist of Japanese extraction, her field work took her to Japan, where she discovered that her physical resemblance to the Japanese people she was with, her fluency in the language, and the resulting habit of treating her as also Japanese, was at odds with her own sense of herself, as a U.S. citizen. The tension was felt more acutely because of the very different way self is seen in Japan: always in a matrix of social relationships (as daughter, wife, coworker, superior, etc.). There is, significantly, no exact equivalent in Japanese for the pronouns *I* and *me*: You do not say "I think" but, for instance, "Daughter thinks." In a very different context, that of West Africa, de Medeiros (1994) also reports that the occidental concept of a self is quite foreign to an African, for whom the self includes parts of the world that we would attribute to the environment, either social or physical: one's family and domicile, for example. In his work, which is concerned with standards of medical care, the North American habit of treating the individual as an isolable physical entity appears bizarre to an African, because his or her conception of self does not attach the same significance to the boundary of the skin and, therefore, treatment of sickness is perceived in quite a different way. It is our perception that we have, in the West, materialized the notion of the self, and thus forgotten to what extent it is part of the construction of sense through the use of language which, as Leach pointed out, segmentalizes the world in a culture-specific way (see note 7).

a human net, this constraint is no longer operative—a consequence of textualization and the agency it makes possible. But, although this is a striking difference between human conversation in all its complexity and the austere networks of the programmers, it is not, we believe, the most important difference. Even given textualization and its effects, human conversations also develop emergent knowledge, and are collectively computational (as Boden's characterization of decision makes evident), fully as much as their software equivalents. However much more complex the details, the pattern is the same. The real difference lies elsewhere—in how backpropagation occurs.

Backpropagation as Organizational Change

Neural net research took off when an algorithm was worked out that would systematically change the weights of the interconnections to reflect the relative success of the net-as-a-whole back to the unit level. Resetting the weights by an algorithm is *backpropagation*. Some such feedback procedure is of the greatest importance in explaining how a network can learn. Without learning, the organization is an inert object, lacking in adaptability; with learning, it takes on the alternative meaning of organization, as organizing—and, more important still, self-organizing.

No one would quite claim that the AI backpropagation algorithm is a replica of how the brain comes to modify its synaptic patterns of interconnection. The justification for an algorithm, in simulation circles, is its utility. When we discuss backpropagation in the human organizational context, we look for an effect that is equivalent to that which the connectionists call backpropagation, but we assume that the mechanism will be different.

The connectionist premise, translated to our own sphere of inquiry, is not that learning—the effect—is the consequence of changes in the individuals (a common error in the voluminous literature on organizational learning), but rather in the configuring of their interrelations.[10] Learning occurs when the pattern of interconnection changes, and the presumption we explore is that such a change process has an inherent dynamic, or at least a built-in logic or impetus. So there are two questions: Does backpropagation make sense in the organizational sphere? and How does it come about there?

---

[10]We are not trying to say that individuals do not learn, but that in the context of an organization what they bring to the conversation is constrained, and that the originality they manifest is often characterological. Nevertheless, the premise of individual variety is a necessary condition for the functioning of a distributed system of intelligence. This is one of the more attractive features of the conversational approach, in that, unlike the model of a rationally programmed organization, variety is not only consistent with, but essential to, an intelligent organization. Engeström (1990) reports on what happens when the network is deliberately structured to impede distributed intelligence. The results are not pretty.

With respect to the first of these questions, recall briefly what it is we are looking for. Neural net research assumes that the units, or sub-assemblies, make a specialized contribution to the collective sensemaking process: Each brings its own component-specific sensitivity to particular aspects of the environment. That sensitivity is constant; it is the stimuli and the interconnecting links joining the nodes that are variable. Making due allowance for the difference in scale, this seems a plausible assumption to make in the human context as well. People have reasonably stable tendencies to react in certain ways, to see things in certain lights, to make certain interpretations of what they have experienced, and their interventions in conversation tend to become predictable.

A further assumption of connectionism is that when two units interact frequently, their tendency to interact increases: The link gets stronger the more successful their jointness becomes. As this happens over many sub-assemblies, the network eventually settles on an interpretation of a field of stimuli (it has learned), and its future tendency will be to assimilate ambiguous—sometimes even contradictory—data to what it has already worked out interactively. A bit of a conversational rut becomes evident (overlearning, perhaps?): the same people talking to the same people, coming to the same conclusion each time in the face of variable stimuli. This means that for learning to now occur, in the face of a pronounced tendency to retain what has already been achieved, the connections have to change. New conversational partners mean new ways of putting people's individual knowledges together and, from this, an evolution in the collective consciousness. Where, before, the strength of a given connection had been growing, it now shrinks as other links take over. The network reconfigures. Do organizations actually learn in this manner?

Again, Boden supplies evidential support for the hypothesis, as well as sketching out a possible line of explanation for it.

The first relevant concept is that of an *agenda*. Organizational actors are certainly individuals, each with their own idiosyncratic traits of character and personality, but they are nevertheless organizational: They voice an interest (which is to say that of a sub-assembly). Agendas have a certain built-in constancy, whoever speaks for them: Chairs of university departments, to take but one example, face common budget-crunch problems, curriculum problems, dealing-with-faculty-and-student-problems, keeping-on-the-good-side-of-the-Dean problems, keeping-up-with-your-research-and-publication problems, and so on. The result is a surprisingly limited degree of freedom of choice of agenda, so that departmental chairs' behaviors show considerable redundancy, even when one occupant of a chair is replaced by another. And much the same thing is true of all the other people in the university network, from President to Dean to student representative. Organizational units, like connectionist network units, have some constant properties that are repetitively reflected in the way they enter into the organizational conversation.

Secondly, none of those agendas can be realized without entering into interaction with a variety of other people. Suppose there is a position—a line—that you as Chair want to fill. This involves budgetary approval by the Dean, and there you are in competition with other departments and programs for the limited pool of financial resources the latter controls. This means phone calls, office visits, meetings. Some people support your position (excitation), some people oppose it (inhibition). Then, you have to bring your own faculty to agree with what you are trying to do (and you can be sure, if it is a faculty of more than three, some will favor one policy, others another, and faculty members—in other respects usually the nicest of people—can turn obdurate and noisy, when it comes to the choice of a new colleague). And, of course, yours is not the only agenda in play; Deans have their objectives, as do faculty members, Provosts, students, support staff, the personnel department, the alumni office, and so on. Now, says Boden, the interactions multiply, sometimes one on one, sometimes in small groups and task forces, sometimes in meetings and faculty assemblies. As they do, a kind of computation begins to take shape, out of which decisions not so much are taken as emerge. A familiar pattern of hiring new staff once again can be discerned, as can all the other patterning that delineates the usual profile of a large, modern North American university.

At the fine-grained level of a conversation analysis, such as Boden reports on, you can actually detect the interplay of units taking shape to produce a joint outcome that is neither A nor B, but AxB—A times B. Each of these interactions, in turn, to use Boden's terminology, "laminates" the interaction, rolls it up into others, and "collects people and activities" (Boden, 1994, p. 151), so that the departmental pattern is transformed progressively into a faculty pattern, then into a university pattern, and then into an institutional pattern, typical of a whole population of organizations, that is, universities. She calls this process (p. 140) "the nested and embedded nature of organizations in action." The process is exactly what we would expect, if we were taking the connectionist theory seriously. Along the way, the strengthened connections that index learning will be found: "The coalitions of organizations are thus managed in the flux of talk. But they are also stable and familiar groupings that persist across time— through more talk" (p. 151).

So where does backpropagation come in?

The answer is easy. The actors look after it themselves. They act as agents for themselves and also for the organization. To function at all well, it is not enough for organizational actors to stick to their last, to "respond to the moment"; they also have to be sensitive to the larger context that embeds their own, to "attend to the larger picture," as Boden (1994, p.

137) puts it. If you are Chair, you should keep your weather eye open to the University's budgetary situation, because, if you do not, you may be in for an unpleasant surprise. You should know something about university (and the larger sphere of state and federal) politics because, otherwise, you will not understand the new regulation on hiring practice as it relates to special categories of sex or ethnicity. The characteristic form that back-propagation takes in human organizations, then, is information. Part of what you do as agent is work toward an agenda; part is seek out the information you need to bring your activities into line with the larger, organizational, agenda. You need to know "what's up." Seeking information is part of the reason the connections in an organizational network keep changing. As the organizational agenda moves from one preoccupation to another, so does the relevance of information sources. But, the information itself may provide an impetus to seek new associational links, to form new alliances, and to enter new coalitions.

If seeking information is a function of getting access to the broader organizational agenda, then the teacher in a human organization, as opposed to a connectionist net, is itself embroiled in a conversation, and in fact the teacher is not a single individual but a conversational process, out of whose textualizing there emerges, progressively, a perception of the organizational text and, hence, of what has been learned.

This is one of the ways organizations really learn. In most cases, it is a slow process because the strength of established patternings is a powerful inertial force. But it is still not a complete theory of backpropagation, because it still only describes intraorganizational processes. Organizations, however, are also institutionally framed. We need to explain not only, as Boden does, how the environment is read within an organization, but also how organizations come to have transcendent properties—how it is, to take just one example, that universities are so like each other, with individual idiosyncracies but broadly much the same, certainly on the North American continent. To explain this, we need to delve further into the notion of organization-as-text.

ORGANIZATION-IN-TEXT

The Historical Context

To set the stage for this final piece of the theoretical puzzle, we need to take a step backward, logically and in time, to consider what lies behind the idea of socially distributed cognition, or group mind. How did Weick and Roberts's or Hutchins's working groups come to exist in the first place, in the established context of the U.S. Navy? The concept of a group mind, or a collective consciousness, is not original to Weick and Roberts, or to Hutchins; it already figures prominently in the thought of a French sociologist of the late 19th, early 20th century, Émile Durkheim. In one of his later works, *The Elementary Forms of the Religious Life* (Durkheim, 1915), he speculates on the principles that might explain the construction and maintenance of a community in the socially and geographically distributed aboriginal society of Australia, and the role totems (lizards, ants, frogs, etc.) play in such a construction.

Durkheim reasons somewhat as follows. Through society, people are enabled to accomplish things they could never manage individually (one is reminded of Weick & Roberts's description of the feverish activity on an aircraft deck, or Hutchins's vivid portrayal of what happens when the power is cut off in a large naval vessel as it enters harbor). Because of this, collective endeavors have a coercive effect on people's behaviors, the flip side of enabling, you might say. But this enabling/coercing society has no voice of its own, and thus no existence and no way to enable or coerce, until it is given one (does the thrust of Durkheim's argument sound familiar so far?). The capacity of the speaker to give voice to society in such a way that it will command respect and be obeyed depends on the extent that such a voice can claim moral authority. It then takes on what he thinks of as a kind of "psychic energy."

Where does the moral authority come from? The answer is that it is conveyed not only by the voice but also by the representation it gives voice to. For the speaker (or the writer) to be recognized as not just the voice of one individual but the voice of all, he or she must represent the collective knowledge authentically—get it right.[11] Then we, as its members, know "it is society we are listening to" (Durkheim, 1915, p. 297). How do we know the representation of society's knowledge is authentic? Because, says Durkheim, "opinion" says it is. And what is opinion? Answer: the collective sharing of a common representation—that which is collectively, not individually, known. And so the circle closes: If opinion is the chicken, representation must be the egg. But note that it all depends on getting the representation right. And that occurs in the communication linking the voice of society to its listeners, the assembled members of society (Durkheim, because he is writing about the context of an orally communicating

---

[11]Note the double connotation of *representation*. Like *agency*, it points in two directions: (a) as a faithful statement or description of something, and (b) as speaking in the name of some agency (as in sales rep). The distinction has to be pointed out, because we normally take a person speaking to be doing both: saying something about something, and doing something by such saying (see Cooren & Taylor, 1997; J. R. Taylor, 1993; J. R. Taylor, Cooren, Giroux, & Robichaud, 1996). We typically (or ethnomethodologically) fuse speaker and spoken into a single idea; the sociology we examine here is concerned with prying them apart.

society, makes no reference to the role of media in "assembling" the community of listeners).[12]

There is a correlation here:

Voice of society relates to the **Community of listeners** as **Representation** relates to **Opinion**.

Or we might write the correlation this way:

Voice of society/Community of listeners

<=>

Representation/Opinion.

One dimension (voice of speaker, ear of listener) is conversational; the other (representation, opinion), textual. The first dimension constitutes the bringing of the community into a state of collective identity (i.e., organizational existence) as a pragmatic occurrence (its realization in the practices of communication); the second dimension constitutes the realization of collective identity as a semantic or ideational occurrence (its conceptual realization: the output of the network). The linking of the dimensions through the voicing of a representation is a rhetorical occurrence: the capacity of the speaker to speak to her audience in the latter's role as a collectivity—to convince it that what it is hearing is its own opinion. The success of back propagation is now seen to be contingent not only on effective agency (speaking for) but also on the construction of an authentic representation. Vice versa, of course, the success of a representation is contingent on its efficient communication because representations, as Durkheim points out, that are not reiterated in their communication rapidly lose their force. We would say that, in the absence of the conversation, the text is lost (but, of course, what makes the conversation organizational to start with is its realization of the text). No conversation without text; no text without conversation.[13]

---

[12]Rothenbuhler (1993a, 1993b) sees this piece of Durkheim's as an early attempt at a communication theory of organization that was not entirely successful because the communication part had not yet been worked out. We consider that as a plausible interpretation, although we are less sanguine as to whether the communication theory has been fully clarified in the interval.

[13]As Prelli (1989, p. 12) observes, for the 5th century Greek sophists, such as Gorgias, "there is no separate 'reality' apart from what people are induced to believe through the persuasive power of language." It was the politically conservative Plato who poured scorn on the democratic relativity of the sophist position. Aristotle distinguished between theoretical (as in his *Analytics*) and practical argument (explored in his *Topics* and *Rhetoric*). Over the years (and it is still true today), the logic of analytics has tended to seem more scientific than the argumentative strategies of rhetoric with its connotation of emotionalism and its essential situatedness. But if, as the connectionist literature has begun to suggest, knowledge is inherently a distributed phenomenon, then the apparent solidity of analytic logic is in fact an illusion: What passes as knowledge is in fact backpropagation.

Oh, and one other point. Why is a totem a sacred symbol? Not, says Durkheim, because of its religious significance, but because it stands as an image of the society itself. Different totems identify different tribes, clans, and moities, and so help to maintain their distinctive identity as actors in a larger conversation that has no intrinsic boundaries to demarcate one group from another (other than comparative frequency of interaction, which may or may not correlate with perceived identity—and it is perceived identity that counts). We use flags, logos, and trademarks.

The representation is how the society knows what it collectively thinks; the totem is how it recognizes that it collectively is.

The Modern Context

We are entitled, in retrospect, to be sceptical of a description of Australian aboriginal society written by an armchair anthropologist sitting in Paris, basing himself on secondhand reports produced by observers with a less than perfect knowledge of the aboriginal language and no doubt filtered through the screen of some interesting attitudes and prejudices. But, of course, Durkheim's subject was not really aboriginal society at all, but his own. So let us give him the benefit of the doubt and delve further into the intriguing relationship of the speaker to the representation (or text). How does a text/representation come to be generally accepted as authentic? How is it validated, no longer in aboriginal Australia, but in the context of contemporary organizational society?[14]

The answer cannot be a simple transposition of Durkheim's analysis because, in the modern context, the social configurations do not lend themselves to the assembling styles of a simpler world, where every member of the group may be copresent and the sense of community is still integral. We have tried to make clear that, on the connectionist hypothesis, the representation by a speaker of the knowledge generated by the network supposes an act of faith, for the same reason that symbolically encoded knowledge constitues necessarily a reduction in variety when the translation from subsymbolic occurs. To the extent that opinion refers to collectively, not individually, generated knowledge, it cannot ever be definitively stated, not even on the basis of a total census (precisely because the procedure of the census ignores the role of connectivity, which is to say, communi-

---

[14]Textualization, as we tend to think of it, does not, superficially, seem to fit the mold of a fully oral culture such as that of the aborigines. Yet we should not be hasty in making this judgment. To the Australian native, the entire landscape is a text: Every feature of it has a meaning, and when the aborigine goes on a long walkabout (that may last weeks or even months), he or she "sings" the landscape, because the territory is its own map. For a wonderfully evocative picture of how landscape is made textual in this context, see Bruce Chatwin's *Songlines* (Chatwin, 1987).

cation). But if this is true for the pretender who claims to be the voice of society, it is equally true for the community of listeners who have the role of sanctioning the authenticity of the voice who speaks for what all know, even though none separately does. The listener too is linked to a distributed/shared network opinion by a representation so that, ironically, in the realization of society by its being given an identity (through the voice of its agent) the germ of its fragmentation is simultaneously planted (through the disparity of representations arising in the speaker-to-hearer encounter). It is this dialectic that we explore in chapter 8, and, in particular, how the process is stabilized through textualization in its different manifestations.

CONCLUSION

We have taken three steps. First, in the final part of chapter 6, we outlined one theory of the organization of human intelligence, connectionism. Second, in this chapter we have considered the implications of treating this general theory of cognitive organization as a specific theory of human organization (which would imply, among other things, that human organization is a form of intelligence—an implication we were prepared not only to tolerate but also to expand). In the third step, we broadened our focus to look at the experimental context differently, taking organizational account of the (not normally emphasized) presence of the simulator and his or her part in the computational cycle. When we made this shift of perspective, we made a discovery about connectionist theory: that its published accounts make the researcher distinct from the object of study, and so project an image of a network where one of the vital nodes, the teacher, is treated differently from the others. The significance of this is that the teacher-node is also the writer-node, so that, as we take a more comprehensive view of subsymbolic cognitive science, we find there is actually symbolization going on, not in the network, but in the act of describing it. Such symbolization, however, is an intrinsic not an extrinsic part of how the network functions; because the teacher was already a writer before he or she took on the task of teaching and will be afterwards too, the published results leave something out: why the experiment was being undertaken in the first place and how it fit into the agenda of the researcher in the context of his or her organizational conversation.

In the sociological literature on science, as we discover in chapter 8, this is seen as a typical move, which Latour (1992) calls "purification." The transition from subsymbolic to symbolic is what he refers to as a "mediation" or a "translation." It is because of this hybrid intermixing of subsymbolic and symbolic in fact and its separation in the published texts that Latour claims there is purification at work. It is, he says, the distinguishing characteristic of the modern world.

We believe this finding provides the basis for a general theory of organization. We claim that the subsymbolic/symbolic dialectic is a fundamental reality of all organization. As applied to the domain of human interaction in communities of people, we think of it as the interplay of conversation and text. Through conversation, collectively interacting individuals produce an emergent knowledge, which is not merely the sum of their joint contributions but arises out of the dynamics of interconnection (as CA, and not just connectionist artificial intelligence, confirms). This knowledge is not something in the abstract, but part and parcel of their doing something together as a collectivity that they could not have accomplished severally, much as Hutchins or Weick and Roberts described it. But, for the network of interacting people to learn, collectively, there must be backpropagation to the individuals as to how the collectivity is doing. In human society, even in an authoritarian society, there is no teacher to do this in the manner described earlier because the collective knowledge, by definition, transcends the individual so that no one individual can claim absolute perspicacity. Instead, in human organization the teaching function is inscribed in the conversation itself, but it is mediated in a particular way that Durkheim had already outlined. The collectivity speaks through a spokesperson, or persons, who gives voice to a representation through the production of a text. Representations claim authority in many ways; one of these, as we see shortly, is science. The methods of science objectify knowledge, thus removing from its spokespersons the taint of personal interest. Other fields use other sources of authentication to convince opinion that the representation being presented is acceptable. For example, citing the Bible used to be the most common authentication; appealing to prejudice, authority, or custom are other usual strategies. Representation, in this reading, is part of rhetoric because the text must be authenticated, or not, by processes of collective opinion (and we are back into the conversation).

The actual process is a good deal more complicated than this summary portrayal would suggest because the making of representations and the writing of texts goes on at many levels of the organization, and one process gets, as Boden puts it, "laminated" into another, to generate a global interactive and representational tissue held together by information flows. All this goes on around agendas, and it is the agendas, focused on getting a representation right, that give structure and form to the otherwise sprawling, incoherent interactive mass. Our only quarrel with Boden's way of characterizing agendas is in her insufficient emphasis on the role of text making and text evaluating. You could read her book and imagine a paperless office because, although she from time to time does mention a report, she does not emphasize it or its role. Her concern is with talk. This is not our experience of organization; our work would suggest that organizations take written texts very seriously, sometimes to the point of immobilizing themselves (Giroux, 1993; Cooren, 1995a, 1995b). Without texts, no authority: After all, the words *authority* and *author* have the same root!

Chapter 8

Reenacting Enactment

In chapter 7, we began by exploring one idea of emergence-of-organization-in-communication, which conceptualized conversation as a network of interconnected nodes characterized by feedforward and backpropagation. We found that, although it may indeed be plausible to believe that conversation, thought of this way, has properties of a collective mind (Weick & Roberts, 1993) or distributed intelligence (Hutchins, 1995), such a theory has no way to explain the ability of an organization to act. We argued that, for it to be enabled to perform the role of an actor (as it is universally assumed to do), its knowledge must undergo two transformations: first, to be textualized so that it becomes a unique representation of the (otherwise) multiply distributed understandings in the network, and second, to be voiced in the person of someone who speaks in the name of the network and its knowledge. But this latter step (to become what Callon & Latour, 1981, call a macroactor) in turn supposes another, where the voice of the network must now be recognized by the network (otherwise, it is still not an organizational, but merely an individual, text, and therefore lacking in authority). The author of the text must be demonstrated to be the network, not merely its spokesperson. The speaking and the spoken of the collective knowledge of the network are thus a product of conversation, in that they reflect its virtual understanding as the generative source. But, in transforming the network's collective knowledge into a form susceptible to being communicated, a translation has occurred (from analog to digital), where the conversation has been successively turned into a text, and then voiced. Yet in its very voicing, the text must in turn, for it to be even recognized as text, be made a contribution to an ongoing conversation.

It is this cycle that has, logically speaking, neither a starting nor an ending point, and that we conceive to be the communicational basis of organization. In this chapter, we explore the implications of this mutual interdependence in greater depth. Our chosen vehicle is a reexamination of the theory of enactment, which we have already encountered briefly in chapter 5. The theory of enactment provides a convenient illustration because it too links knowing and acting as indissoluble dimensions of behavior—the two faces of a single coin. But as our investigation proceeds, we discover that the conversation/text cycle has rendered problematical one of the cornerstones of much organizational theory, namely, the environment-system distinction. We discover a profound ambiguity in Weick's thinking, this time with respect to a further dichotomy, namely, the management-employee distinction, which is also seen to have a dubious logical foundation within the context of a communication theory of organization.

WEICK AND ENACTMENT

Karl Weick, as we have already said, has over the years consistently been one of the most influential writers in organization theory, at least among those who study organization with a managerial orientation. Unlike many of his compeers, he also has been through the years a frequent collaborator with researchers in organizational communication by participating in conferences and coauthoring published articles (for example, Weick, 1983; Weick, 1989a; Weick & Browning, 1986). He had a key chapter in Putnam and Pacanowsky's (1983) landmark book that launched interpretivism in organizational communication studies. Johnson's (1977) introductory text was inspired by his work, and in 1989, *Communication Studies* devoted an issue to a retrospective look at his thinking. He was a special speaker to Division IV (organizational communication) at the 1996 International Communication Association annual conference in Chicago. He has had a potent impact on the field. For our purposes, then, Weick's thinking serves as a convenient entry point to the theme of this chapter (and chap. 7), which is how the organization comes to be constituted as an actor with a point of view and identity that transcend that of any of its members, singly.

Perhaps the most intriguing of the many concepts this fertile intellect has contributed to the research community is that of enactment (chap. 5). As the term itself would suggest, the core of the idea is that knowledge, information, and understanding never occur outside a context of acting, and that people, singly or in collaboration, are not bystanders, passively observing the world around them, but participants, actively shaping what they in turn respond to. Weick invites us, thus, to abandon our habit of regarding knowledge as a static commodity, something to be jealously hoarded and traded, and instead to think dynamically of an interpreted world seen from a point of view—that of an actor.

We, as many others, happily acknowledge our debt to Weick; it is evident at many points in this book. The notion of enactment underpins our principal thesis, in that we too conceptualize organizational life as a product of ongoing enactment. Nevertheless, we have to confess to a malaise with the manner in which he has explicated the idea. It seems to us that, when push comes to shove, he draws back from the logical deduction of his own theory; he hesitates at the brink, as someone who talked up a November swim but was actually the "last one in." This chapter is about how and why our view differs from his. He says the environment is enacted; we claim that the enactment of the environment is merely incidental to the most fundamental enactment of all, that of the organization itself. And we argue that the divergence of perspectives can be traced to how his view of communication is at odds with our own at a critical juncture: the role of agency.

The first problem we face in embarking on a discussion of the differences between his theory of enactment and ours is that Weick is an almost discouragingly prolific author, and, even more of a complicating factor, his ideas on enactment have not remained fixed through the years. Weick, in his own words, prefers theorizing to theory (1989b, 1995b)[1] and it troubles him not at all if some inconsistencies creep into his published work, because that is the whole point of enacting—trying it on for size. He sees his role as a generator of creative thinking, not as a grand theorist in the Talcott Parsons tradition. Nevertheless, the idea of enactment has been a relatively constant pole in his conceptual map of the organizational universe, and we are not going to be concerned here with the finer nuances of the theory. The broad sweep is what interests us. For clarity of exposition, therefore, we focus on two articles, written in collaboration with Richard Daft (Daft & Weick, 1984; Weick & Daft, 1983), somewhat after the publication of Weick's 1979 book, *The Social Psychology of Organizing*.

In these articles, Weick and Daft outline a theory of organizational sensemaking that is in significant ways a further elaboration of Weick's ideas in the 1979 publication. The presentation of the enactment thesis is mediated by a concept that the authors call an "Interpretation System" (we hear echoes of a similar idea in Boden, and, of course, that was what we were describing in chap. 7). In this chapter, we first examine what we perceive the authors to be saying, and then we draw a different picture of enactment. Their description of enacting is shown to be itself an enactment and one that is the essence of our theory of the enactment of organization. As we do, we pick up on the themes we developed in chapter 7. This leads

---

[1]In his words, "methodological strictures that favor validation rather than usefulness . . . weaken theorizing because they de-emphasize the contribution that imagination, representation, and selection make to the process, and they diminish the importance of alternative theorizing activities such as mapping, conceptual development, and speculative thought" (Weick, 1989b, p. 516).

into a discussion of the limitations of any computational theory of organization. Finally, to conclude our analysis, we briefly summarize what we believe to be the main reorientation of Weick's ideas on enactment since the publication of these earlier reflections, and, in particular, his more recent book, *Sensemaking in Organizations* (1995a).

THE CONCEPT OF AN INTERPRETATION SYSTEM

The authors introduce both articles with a description of the old parlor game Twenty Questions.[2] They are attracted to this metaphor of the enacting organization because in Twenty Questions there may be an answer, but it is not evident to the person that has been picked to be the questioner.[3] The significance of this, say Weick and Daft flatly (1983, p. 71; Daft & Weick, 1984, p. 284), is that "[o]rganizations play 'twenty questions'" too. Organizations "have limited time and questions," they "strive for the answer (discovering what consumers want that other organizations do not provide)," they "presume there is an answer to the puzzle," they "query the environment (with samples, market surveys, test markets)," and they "try to find an acceptable answer."

We draw the reader's attention to a point we made in chapter 7, that is, that verbs such as *play, strive, presume, query, try,* and *have* (i.e., *have* in the context of "limited time and questions") are required grammatically, in English, to take a subject whose main noun is marked for agency, and, more specifically, human agency. So the (implicit) assumption here is that organizations are agents and can act as such, just as humans can.

In the paragraph that follows, however (Weick & Daft, 1983, p. 72), the language changes. "All of these activities," it now transpires, are "*in* organizations" (emphasis added) and involve "people" who "are trying to interpret what they have done, define what they have learned, solve the problem of what they should do next." Individual human limitations on information processing are now invoked (including a reference to March and Simon's 1958 book, discussed earlier). So, it seems that, although it is the organization that enacts the environment (and the main thrust of the articles is precisely to show that organizations differ systematically in their enactment patterns and strategies, and that their "effectiveness" in doing so can be

---

[2]As they explain, the Daft & Weick, 1984, paper, entitled "Toward a Model of Organizations as Interpretation Systems," is an "extension" of the Weick & Daft, 1983 article, "The Effectiveness of Interpretation Systems"; it repeats, textually, whole sections of the earlier paper while emending and adding others.

[3]Later in each of the papers they introduce a modified version of Twenty Questions where there is no answer to start with; it emerges as a result of the questioning (see also Weick, 1985). This is their way of pointing out that the reality out there is not a given; it too is emergent.

evaluated, and even, perhaps, measured), the actual activities of making sense are done by people. Weick and Daft have thus set themselves a challenge: how to reconcile two logically distinct levels of analysis. Although it is the organization that acts, it is people who do the sensemaking. Yet acting and sensemaking are indissociable—merely, as they will show, different aspects of enactment.[4] How can this be?

A first step toward resolving this puzzle, Weick and Daft propose (1983, p. 72), is to define a presuppositional starting point for thinking about organizations. If, as they admit (and even emphasize), organizations are "vast, fragmented, elusive, and multidimensional," it follows that the investigator is obliged to make an ontological assumption as to the basic nature of organization (the word "ontological" is ours, not theirs, but that is the sense of their observation). To adopt a perspective (however limited or faulty it may eventually turn out to be) means seeing through a lens. Are organizations, they ask rhetorically, "input-output systems, resource allocation systems, collections of human beings with needs to be met, growth and survival systems, tools in the hands of goal-setting owners, coalitions of interest groups, transformation systems" (p. 172), or what?[5] The choice matters, because on it depends not only what the observer will focus on, and, having thus enacted, actually see, but also whether it explains how an organization can be an actor. As we discover, their choice leads them into difficulties.

The rationale for their chosen perspective on organization is an idea of Kenneth Boulding's (1956). He proposed that theories of organization can be classified according to the degree of "system complexity" they postulate (notice that an implication—and we come back to it later—follows automatically: by adopting Boulding's 7-level classification, the authors have made a commitment to enacting organization as a "system"!). Each level on the scale of complexity alters how we abstractly view organization. Views range from level 1, being merely a framework (a "container," in effect), to level 2, a clockwork (organization as machine, to use Morgan's, 1986, terminology), to level 3, a control system (a cybernetic and computer metaphor), to level 4, an open system (organization as organism, with processes and structures that are contingent on context), to level 5, a

---

[4]See Weick (1979a, pp. 131–132): "We have used the terms *enacted environment* and *cause map* to refer to retained content. Each phrase captures a slightly different nuance of what is retained. We have used the label *enacted environment* to emphasize that meaningful environments are outputs of organization, not inputs to it. . . . We have used the label *cause map* as a second means to characterize retained content to emphasize that retained content is organized and stored. . . ."

[5]A very similar point was being made by Morgan (1986) at about the same time: that to even talk about an organization means having an image of it, such images being most frequently grounded in a metaphor. An organization is patently not an object in the usual sense of something to be physically apprehended by the senses.

growth system (what would now be considered the ecological view of organization), to level 6, a differentiated system (with "specialized information reception, nervous system, choice processes and multiple, ambiguous
goals," much like what March and Simon described), to level 7, a symbol
processing system (with "high-order human characteristics: self-awareness,
symbolism, meaning").

Their choice turns out to be level 6: a differentiated system. The reason
they choose this image of organization is that, for them, a differentiated
system can also be shown to be an "interpretation system," or one where,
for someone interested in assessing organizational effectiveness (as they
are), what can be observed is how the environment is interpreted, what
the decision processes are, how information is managed, and how consensus around goals is accomplished. (Because the subject matter of their
papers is the effectiveness of organizations, they need to develop a rationale
for selecting certain measurable variables of organizational performance
to explain such effectiveness. The relative ability of organizations to turn
information into decisions meets this criterion.) The emphasis is on computation—reading an environment on the road to action. But, as we also
have discovered, the term *computation* means different things to different
people.

What then is their version of a differentiated or interpretation system?
It turns out that, taking into account differences in jargon, Weick and Daft
now describe a system characterized by parallel distributed processing—a
connectionist network, in effect.[6]

The Virtual Connectionism of the Weick–Daft Model

Here are what Daft and Weick (1984) call their "working assumptions"
about the nature of organization, conceived of, alternatively, as a
differentiated or an interpretation system.

Organizations, like connectionist networks (the "like" phrase in this
sentence and the ones that follow is our editorial interjection), have inputs
from ("process information from") an environment. They develop mechanisms "capable of detecting trends, events, competitors, markets, and technological developments relevant to their survival" (p. 285).

---

[6]It seems reasonable to us to see these two articles as constituting a transitional phase in
Weick's thinking and, perhaps, in the theory of organization more generally. Terms such as
decision processes, information management, choice processes, information reception, and *goal consensus*
are throwbacks to the established computational view of organization that March and Simon
had described 25 years earlier. It is not unusual for a new theory to still be cloaked in the
language of the older. In these two articles, and in other work that was shortly to follow,
Weick's seems to be evolving to a different view, and it is thus not surprising to find in his
later 1993 paper with Roberts an explicit adoption of the connectionist theory (as we saw in
chap. 6).

Organizations, like connectionist networks, cope well with nonlinear, fuzzy stimuli:

> The interpretation process is more interpersonal, less linear, more improvisational, and more subject to multifinality than organization scholars realize. Effectiveness in a differentiated system may include the ability to deal with equivocality, the ability to coerce an answer useful to the organization, the ability to invent an environment and be a part of the invention. Interpretation systems try to make sense of the flowing, changing, equivocal chaos that constitutes the sum total of the external environment. *People in organizations try to sort this chaos into items, events, and parts that are then connected, threaded into sequence, serially ordered, and related to one another.* In the course of interpretation, *individuals, and perhaps the organization as a collective, develop cause maps.* (p. 78, emphasis added to point up the connectionist language, with this difference that where the latter school use the word "representation" Weick and Daft speak of a "cause map")[7]

While individual human beings are the ones who actually send and receive information, and "in other ways carry out the interpretation process," organizations, like connectionist nets,

> do not have mechanisms separate from individuals [authors' note: for "individuals" read "nodes of the network"] to set goals, process information, or perceive the environment. Yet . . . it is assumed that *the organizational interpretation process is something more than what occurs by individuals.* Organizations have cognitive systems and memories. . . . Individuals come and go, but organizations preserve knowledge, behaviors, mental maps, norms, and values over time. *The distinctive feature of organizational level information activity is sharing.* A piece of data, a perception, a cognitive map is shared *among managers who constitute the interpretation system.* Passing a startling observation among members, or discussing a puzzling development, enables managers *to converge on an approximate interpretation.* Managers may not agree fully about their perceptions, but the thread of coherence among managers is what characterizes organizational interpretations. *Reaching convergence among members characterizes the act of organizing and enables the organization to interpret as a system.* (p. 285, emphasis added to point up the parallels to the cognitive science literature on parallel distributed processing)

Organizations, like connectionist nets, develop sub-assemblies. "Organizations can be conceptualized as a series of nested systems, and each sub-system may deal with a different external sector" (p. 285).

---

[7]Note the allusion here to the possibility of a collective cause map, an idea which, as we have seen, is given much more emphasis later in Weick and Roberts (1993) and Weick (1995a). We examine in greater detail in chapter 9 some of the ways the notion of a cause map has been used. Weick himself has been ambivalent on the issue.

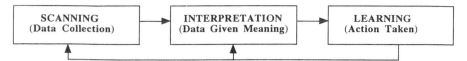

FIG. 8.1. The structure of an interpretation system (from Daft & Weick, 1984). Republished with permission of Academy of Management, PO Box 3020, Briar Cliff Manor, NY 10501-8020. *Toward a Model of Organizations as Interpretation Systems* (Figure), R. L. Daft and K. E. Weick, *Academy of Management Review*, 1984, Vol. 92. Reproduced by permission of the publisher via Copyright Clearance Center, Inc.

Organizations, like connectionist networks, have outputs. "Strategic-level managers formulate the organization's interpretation. When one speaks of organizational interpretation one really means interpretation by a relatively small group at the top of the organizational hierarchy. . . . Upper managers bring together and interpret information for the system as a whole" (p. 285).[8]

Organizational information processing, as in connectionist nets, is feedforward. "Many participants may play some part in scanning or data processing, but the point at which information converges and is interpreted for organizational level action is assumed to be at the top manager level. . . . Below the vice presidential level, participants are not informed on issues pertaining to the organization as a whole" (p. 285).

Organizations, like connectionist nets, learn, and because of this they develop distinctive organizational configurations of sensemaking. "Organizations differ systematically in the mode or process by which they interpret the environment. Organizations develop specific ways to know the environment. Interpretation processes are not random" (pp. 285–286).

At one point (Daft & Weick, 1984, p. 286), they draw a picture of the system they have in mind (Figure 8.1).

All you have to do to reinterpret this graphic representation as the diagram of a connectionist net (Fig. 6.3) is to substitute input units for "scanning," hidden units for "interpretation" and output units for "learning." The equivalence falls out (Fig. 8.2). The computational part (hidden units) is the mechanism of interpretation, or where the data are given meaning. Inputs and outputs are links to the environment. The output is simultaneously enacting ("action taken" by the manager) and retention ("learning" in the network). The input is at one and the same time proaction ("scanning") and information registering ("data collection"). The left-

---

[8]We flag this point for the moment, because it is part of the interpretationist theory we find most problematical. We return to discuss it in greater depth later. It is, incidentally, another area where Weick has sometimes been ambivalent.

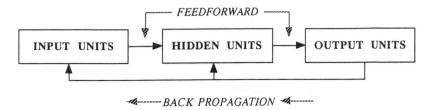

FIG. 8.2.   The structure of a connectionist network.

to-right arrows index feedforward; the right-to-left arrows presumably do the same for backpropagation (i.e., the effects of learning).

In one respect (and an important one), however, Weick and Daft go beyond the connectionist model; without quite contradicting it as far as we can see, they nevertheless point to a gap in its conceptualization of learning. This is in their discussion of enactment.

Enactment

The difference between a Weickian organization and any of the many cognitive science versions of a connectionist net is that the former, but not the latter, is involved—up to its neck, you might say—in action. Connectionist nets do not strive, question, discover, find, presume, query, or try (although we presume their teachers may); organizations do, because unlike mere networks, they are actors—agents, not just instruments. Making sense—an interpretation—is not an accomplishment in a vacuum, it is not just context-free networking. Organizations make interpretations because they "must" (Weick & Daft, 1983, p. 74). In a typical outpouring of Weickian rhetoric (similar phraseology crops up in other papers of his), the authors expand on the cogency of the "must." "Managers literally must wade into the swarm of events that constitute and surround the organization and actively try to impose some order on them. Organization participants physically act on the environment, attending to some of it, ignoring most of it, and talking to other people to see what they are doing" (p. 74).

The structure in this "swarm of events" is not just perceived (an environment is always multiply readable); it is "*imposed* on the apparent randomness" (emphasis added) because in the absence of imposition, interpretation could not occur (you might recognize a pattern, but its relevance to action would not be clear, and anyway, given the multidimensionality of organization, several plausible versions of the pattern would likely be in competition, with no clear basis for deciding among them). So, interpretation does not mean simply recognizing a pattern (the connectionist preoccupation) but implies a rather more complex sequence that consists in, first, being confronted with a world; second, fabricating a pattern of response to fit it; third, manipulating the environment to make it conform to the pattern; and only then, fourth, recognizing in the environment the echoing lines of what one has constructed. If it works (if the environment is compliant), a structure in the environment has been identified, or recognized; if it does not, then we are on our way back to the drawing board. "Only by testing our interpretations back on 'the' environment can we know whether they are reasonable" (Weick & Daft, 1983, p. 75; note the use of the word "reasonable," rather than *right* or *true*).[9]

A connectionist network, by way of contrast, could never know anything, until its teacher told it what it knew. As Weick is frequently quoted as saying, "How can I know what I think until I see what I say?" In other words, thinking is not knowledge until it has been textualized (notice the curious choice of the verb *see* rather than *hear* in the aphorism—the "what I say" must have been made text, in the generic sense of that term, before it could be "seen").

Interpretation is a process of "developing models for understanding, of bringing out meaning, and of assembling conceptual schemes" (Weick & Daft, 1983, p. 74). These "models" or "conceptual schemes" (i.e., maps) are less mental than practical; maps are for going places, doing things— more part of activity than of idealized cognition. They record where we have been on the way to where we are going. They are, in that sense, quasihistorical: a retained history that can "clarify either a tangible present outcome or a future outcome that has to be imagined" (p. 75). They index, not explain, learning (but as Hutchins, 1995, points out and Latour emphasizes—although it is interesting that Weick and Daft do not), not necessarily one's own learning, because learning may be a cultural not just a personal achievement, a heritage of previous generations.

What Weick means by "learning" here, then, is not merely a reconfiguration of mental causal connections in the head (for one thing, the cause map of the organization-as-actor could not be, by definition, in anyone's head), but "a new response or action based on the interpretation" (Daft & Weick, 1984, p. 286). It is "a process of putting cognitive theories into action." Furthermore, as we read the authors here, the response is an organizational, not an individual, response: It is the organization that is "striving," "discovering," "presuming," and so forth. The "act of learning" is not limited to what goes on inside some individual learner, but must also be outside, part of the organization. It is first and foremost an act that "provides new data for interpretation" (Daft & Weick, 1984, p. 286)— an organizational interpretation, that is. In other words, the learning is in

---

[9]This basic line of argument can be found in a quite different literature, associated with the names of two Chilean neurocognitive researchers, Maturana and Varela (1987). For an analysis of tendencies in Varela's thinking on organization, see J. R. Taylor (1995). We come back to Maturana's ideas later in the chapter.

the relationship to an environment that emerges out of the organization's active manipulation of it.[10]

The Performative Character of Knowledge Development: Science as Enactment

Weick's theory of interpretation, first and foremost, as enactment and only secondarily as recognition and retention has recently been reaffirmed in a quite different literature, that which deals with the sociology of scientific knowledge (SSK). Because the concept of enactment is such an important theme in this chapter, and because it runs against the grain of our deeply embedded habits of Western thought about organization, we take a brief detour into the SSK literature (and, more specifically, a contribution to it by Pickering, 1995). By showing that enactment is a central feature of scientific practice (which we usually take as our measure of rational objectivity), then we can show that it is even more plausibly the appropriate model in the more patently subjective universe of ordinary organizational life. But there is another motive at work on our part. This literature emphasizes a dimension that is curiously absent in Weickian thought—the materiality of enactment.

It is convenient (if somewhat oversimplified) to see the contemporary schools of sociologists of science as taking off from Thomas Kuhn's (1970) classic study of the evolution of science, already noted in chapter 6. In this study, he persuasively demonstrated that the practice of science does not simply boil down to a patient accumulation of discoveries and facts by means of which the true nature of the world is progressively unveiled, but that, on the contrary, science is characterized by spurts, whose inspiration comes from the acceptance of a temporarily dominant metaphor, root idea, or persuasive (and pervasive) image of nature (that he designated a *paradigm*), around which the activities of normal scientific investigation cluster. If you decide at some point that the world is round (when the previous consensus was that it was flat), and if enough people buy your idea, especially those with resources to do something about it, you are in all likelihood going to set the stage for a whole century of circumnavigating

---

[10]It is perhaps important to reemphasize that Weick is ambivalent on the issue of maps-in-the-head versus collective maps at this point in his thinking (and perhaps later too). Although the sections we are citing here lean toward the reality of an interpretive system (i.e., collectively generated through interaction), other pronouncements of his on the question could be cited to support a more individualistic view (see, for example, Bougon, Weick, & Binkhorst, 1977; Weick, 1977; Weick & Bougon, 1986). Our purpose is not to criticize this vacillation, because we perceive it to be evidence of a deeply held intuition on Weick's part that we find particularly sensitive to the micro–macro issue, but rather to build on it constructively by pointing to an eventual solution.

seafarers, who can, one after the other (assuming that the voyage does not end on the reefs of some foreign shore), return to report triumphantly that, indeed, it is round! A new map starts to take shape as the explorers progressively fill in the interstices. The paradigm has focused their activities, centered their attention on certain features of the world, and, of course, distracted attention away from others that might have just as plausibly been taken as subject matter.

A growing body of empirical sociological investigations has now documented, rather convincingly in fact, this historically contingent scientific susceptibility to paradigm fascination (note, incidentally, that, for the sociologists, Kuhn's description of paradigm has itself been turned into a paradigm—a sociological one).

But SSK has gone much further. It has become evident that the practices of science are thoroughly social, and not inconsiderably political. What is taken to be scientific fact starts, as Latour (1987) puts it, as a laboratory artifact, where the traces of its making in an all too fallible scientific fact factory are still visible and the chances of the discovery's survival are quite problematical, given scientists' proclivity to indulge in controversy (Gilbert & Mulkay, 1984). Whether the initial hypothesis makes it to the status of a scientifically validated fact is not determined just by nature (on the basis of objective experimentation) but at least as much by society. Scientific validation comes, specifically, by accreditation within the scientific community, with everything which that implies, both positive, in the sense of error-correcting peer review, and negative, in the sense of error-perpetuating or error-amplifying peer review, not to mention the intervention of outside granting agencies, with their agendas, recruited through skillful promotion by scientific entrepreneurs in search of the big research grants and the prestige that goes with them. Subjected to the sociological spotlight, science comes to look less and less like the paragon of cool, responsible objectivity that we once credited it with being, and more and more like other, less simon-pure domains of human endeavor, with which we are all too familiar, wherever politics rears its ugly head.

Pickering's (1995) book is an extension of this literature, or, perhaps more properly, a corrective to what risked being a one-sided picture. It is not that he is on a crusade to refurbish the tarnished reputation of science, but rather, he wants to remind us that the latter is not altogether social either. We need to recall, he reminds his sociological colleagues, that the material world has not gone away, and it too needs to be taken account of. And this is where enactment comes in.

Pickering begins by drawing a picture of two contrasting images of how we acquire knowledge. The first of these, the conventional image of science, centers on the idea of representation (remember, this is also the theme of the cognitivist literature, whether symbolicist or connectionist). In the representational view, the task is to produce a description of nature that corresponds to "how the world really is" (Pickering, 1995, p. 5). The challenge is to faithfully reproduce characteristics of the object under study in one's recordings of it. This is pretty much what is generally meant by *cognition*. In such a story of how science works, Pickering says, "scientists figure as disembodied intellects making knowledge in a field of facts and observations"; they become "shadows of themselves" (p. 6). Reading a scientific article is likely to make you aware that all the language is couched in the passive tense, as if the experimenter had happily been present—like Chauncey Gardiner in the film *Being There* ("I like to watch," he said)—at the moment nature revealed its true self: took off the veils, in effect. The triumph of SSK has been to show otherwise, that the scientists' motives, prejudices, and social/political situation are as much a part of what they find as any objective traits of the world they study.

As against the conventional representative view of knowledge development, Pickering argues for a different conception, which he calls a *performative* image of science. Let us begin, he says, by thinking of the world differently, not as something to be factually observed, voyeuristically keeping our distance from it to preserve our scientific virginity, but instead as something filled with agency. Why does he say "filled with agency"? Because, like it or not, we also are material beings and vulnerable to the world as it acts on us. We are not just "disembodied intellects," but organisms who cope with everything from hurricanes to flat tires to sleeplessness on a hot night to tax bills in April. The way to look at science, then, is to see it as "a continuation and extension of this business of coping" (Pickering, 1995, p. 6).

Where Pickering goes beyond giving us just another, somewhat tardy, version of enactment is in his emphasis on the centrality of machines to how scientists perform as human agents in their ongoing interaction with material agents. How scientists, that is, human agents, deal with the material world of agency is through the construction of machines, that is, instruments, "that, as I shall say, variously capture, seduce, download, recruit, enroll, or materialize that agency, taming and domesticating it, putting it at our service, often in the accomplishment of tasks that are simply beyond the capacities of naked human minds and bodies, individually or collectively" (Pickering, 1995, p. 7). (He is talking science here. He could equally well have been referring to the kind of organization Weick and his colleagues are most preoccupied with; if we substituted the word *managers* for *scientists*, Pickering's observation would apply with equal force.)

After we admit the performative character of science we have to take account of time, because, as Pickering puts it, material agency is not predictable: It is temporally emergent in practice; not known in advance. There is, he thinks, something like a "dance" of agency:

As active, intentional beings, scientists tentatively construct some new machine. They then adopt a passive role, monitoring the performance of the machine to see whatever capture of material agency it might effect. Symmetrically, this period of human passivity is the period in which material agency actively manifests itself. Does the machine perform as intended? Has an intended capture of agency been effected? Typically the answer is no, in which case the response is another reversal of roles: human agency is once more active in a revision of modelling vectors, followed by another bout of human passivity and material performance, and so on. (Pickering, 1995, pp. 21–22)[11]

This dance, he says, takes the form of a dialectic of resistance and accommodation, "where resistance denotes the failure to achieve an intended capture of agency in practice, and accommodation an active human strategy of response to resistance, which can include revisions to goals and intentions, as well as to the material form of the machine in question and to the human frame of gestures and social relations that surround it" (Pickering, 1995, p. 22). He calls this the "mangle of practice."[12]

Scientific practice never starts from zero, but from "imaginatively transformed versions of its present," a process he calls "modelling" and that he thinks of as based on metaphor and analogy (Pickering, 1995, p. 19). "Modelling," he says (p. 19), "is an open-ended process with no determinate destination." It builds on machines as they now are—the inherited savvy, as Hutchins (1995) also pointed out, of the culture in which we find ourselves. But "from a given model—say a particular functioning machine—an indefinite number of future variants can be constructed. Nothing about the model itself fixes which of them will figure as the goal for a particular passage of practice" (Pickering, 1995, p. 19).[13]

Existing culture is thus, to use Foucault's term, "the *surface of emergence* for the intentional structure of human agency" (Pickering, 1995, p. 20,

---

[11]In effect, Pickering's "dance" is a version of Weick's "double interact" model of communication: act-react-adjust.

[12]A *mangle* is an old-fashioned device, in Pickering's British usage, for squeezing out the water from garments that have just been washed. In the North American lexicon of this book's authors, it would have been called a *wringer*. He uses the term to emphasize the unpredictability and messiness of science as a practice. It would certainly apply with equal force to management.

[13]In his book, he traces the path in physics research that led from cloud chamber to bubble chamber. Both are means to track the path of rare, small, and temporary particles of great theoretical and practical interest to physicists. They cannot be perceived directly, but, become visible by passing through a tank full of vapor (somewhat as the path of a high-altitude jet can be followed by the vapor trail it leaves behind it). The cloud chamber is the predecessor of the bubble chamber. Pickering's point is that the latter was one possible innovation growing out of the former, but in tracking its development, it becomes clear it was not an inevitable one: It depended on the "mangle of practice."

emphasis in original). Because of its open-endedness, "the world of the mangle lacks the comforting causality of traditional physics or engineering, or of sociology for that matter" (p. 24).

He could have added management science, we think. Weick would have.

A Critique of Weick–Daft's Theory of an Interpretation System

Let us return to Weick and Daft's conceptualization of an interpretation system, but now in a more critical vein.

The main lines of their argument went this way. They start with a premise, that an organization is a "differentiated system," which implies two things: (a) from differentiation, we conclude a "multiplicity" of information sources, choice processes, and goals (and one might add "interests" to their list), and (b) because it is nevertheless a system, it must therefore exhibit a behavior sufficiently coherent that it can be discussed using the language of action we have cited from their papers. Thus, the premise implies that an organization is simultaneously a many and a one: differentiated (and thus characterized by what March and Simon called "subgoals" that are not necessarily in line with management goals), yet also systemic (and thus made capable of unified action).

Weick and Daft's thesis is that it is the interpretation system that transforms the many into the one and explains how "information about the external world must be filtered and processed into a central nervous system of sorts, where choices are made" (1983, p. 74). Interpretation, they say, "is the process of translating these events, of developing models for understanding, of bringing out meaning, and of assembling conceptual schemes" (p. 74).[14] The critical component of an interpretation system is the process: translating, developing, bringing out, assembling. Out of this process, the organizational interpretation, that is, "choices," "conceptual schemes," will presumably emerge.

Well, as the Saturday puzzle section of the weekly newspaper might phrase it, "What's wrong with this picture?"

The answer is, it turns out, plenty! In fact, in both articles (and, as far as we can make out, in both Weick's 1979 book and in most of Weick's writings since then), the question of how that "translating, developing models for understanding, bringing out meaning, and assembling conceptual schemes" actually takes place is begged. If one were a bridge player, one might suspect the authors had pulled off a finesse. If they were magicians, you might conclude they had pulled a rabbit out of the hat.

---

[14]The same sentence can be found in Daft and Weick (1984, p. 286) with one difference: Significantly, after "assembling conceptual schemes" the phrase "among key managers" has been inserted.

The problem emerges right away. Immediately following the description of an interpretation system that we just cited (and in a section entitled "Characteristics of interpretation systems"—not, it should be noted, characteristics of [qualifier] "interpretation" but of [noun] "systems") we read: "*Organizations* must make interpretations. *Managers* must literally wade into the swarm of events that constitute and surround the organization and actively try to impose some order on them" (p. 3, emphasis added). Whoa! Who is making the interpretation, the organization or the managers? We thought that the substitution—managers for organization—was what had to be explained. By what sleight of hand did the managers get to be, without explanation, the organization? (And which managers? The "key" managers, presumably, but what is a key manager? And then, do not the other managers' interpretations count? If not, why have they been included in the first place?)

They are not unaware of the difficulty (Daft & Weick, 1984, p. 285): "Organization theorists realize that organizations do not have mechanisms separate from individuals to set goals, process information, or perceive the environment." So it cannot be the organization that makes the interpretation, can it? And in fact, reading on in their paper, the way interpretation is described makes it sound very much like what individual people (not organizations) do: construct a reading; utilize special knowledge, sympathy, or imagination; translate from one language to another; write histories; think about an event; see in the present what they had seen before; search for confirmatory stimuli; construct a picture; describe; explain; and so on. Yet, they also know (it was a part of the initial premise) that the managers have differentiated perceptions of "the environment" (organizations are "complex, fragmented, elusive, and multidimensional"). So why, without ever saying how differentiated perceptions had turned into an organizational interpretation, is most of the rest of the paper about the organization dealing with its environment and not (other than glancingly, from time to time, and without explanation) about the managers conjoining their differentiated interpretations in a process of choice making and assembling of a conceptual scheme to produce an organizational interpretation?

The Reification of Organization Via the Reification of the Environment

The language of the main body of analysis of both papers is overwhelmingly slanted in the direction of reification of the organizational agency. We have made a small analysis of the phraseology (Fig. 8.3), as it occurs in Daft and Weick (1984).

query
obtain answers about
build up interpretations about
find ways to know
interpret
relate to
interpret
scan
process information from
develop specific ways to know
passively perceive
actively intrude into
may obtain knowledge about
ORGANIZATIONS assume the analyzability of   **ENVIRONMENT**
assume to be concrete
create
have beliefs about
search for an answer in
accept whatever information they are given by
accept as given
are informal and unsystematic in their interpretation of
depend heavily on
vary in their beliefs about
construct their own
tend to display enactment behavior
send carefully devised measurement probes into
perceive as objective and benevolent
are open to a variety of cues about

FIG. 8.3. The language of organizational interpretation in Daft and Weick (1984).

In both articles, broad generalizations are drawn about not managerial but organizational behavior and personality, in terms that are frankly derivative on the psychology of personality. The organization is portrayed as having a "style," which may be "glancing, enacting, staring or discovering." It is "active or passive, intrusive or non-intrusive, directed or undirected."

Now it might be plausible to suppose that a small group of very senior managers could become so closely knit that they could develop a collective style that could, by a slight stretch of the imagination, be compared to the personality of an individual, but not, surely, a "vast, complex, fragmented, elusive, multidimensional" differentiated organization.

A short circuit has occurred: The organization has been reified. The reification is indexed by a curious wordplay in the Weick/Daft texts that centers on their use of the term *environment*. The frequency of this mention (or an equivalent such as "external environment" or "the external world") in both articles is remarkable. In Daft and Weick (1984), for example, you have page 284, 5 mentions; page 285, 11 mentions; page 286, 8 mentions; page 287, 17 mentions; page 288, 29 mentions; page 289, 11 mentions; and so on (we stopped counting at this point).

What is going on here?

The answer seems to be in how they are putting the concept of enactment to use. Enactment, in Pickering's performative view of scientific practice, implies an interaction of agencies. Although Weick does not usually employ the word *agency*, an interaction of agencies seems a fair description of his idea of enactment as well (Weick, 1995a, p. 34, "People create their environments as those environments create them."). *Agency* is a neutral term until it is qualified. You can choose, as both Weick/Daft and Pickering do, to make one of the agencies human, and the other nonhuman, or undefined (it is not an obligatory choice: you could logically also have human-human (and nonhuman-nonhuman?) interactions and that would still be a form of enactment, but these are not the usual subject matter of either the physical or the managerial sciences, at least not when the latter are concerned with environmental enactment). The point is that by distinguishing human from other, both Weick/Daft and Pickering have introduced a marking of the agency pair.[15] One agent, the human, becomes primary (unmarked); the other, secondary (marked). Pickering argues for a relative (mitigated, not total) parity of agency; in the way they phrase their discussion, Weick and Daft assume that human agency has a status that is clearly of a different order from the material or undefined complement. As they portray it, the distinctive property of human agency, in contrast with environmental, is that it is interpretive: It processes information and arrives at an interpretation, expressed in action.

There is a further choice to make in enactment theory. The human enactor could be an individual or an organization; again the theory is not specific on the details of its own applicability. For it to be applied, there is a commitment to be made. But can it be said that organizational equals human, in respect to the key qualification of being capable of interpretation? Can an organization think (process information, arrive at an interpretation) like an individual human? If not, can we legitimately attribute to it full agentive rights? This, is seems, is where Weick and Daft hesitate and why they sometimes say it is the organization who enacts and, sometimes, the managers.

It is worth pausing here for a moment to delve further into this vacillation on their part, because the differing view of agent status is where our theory branches off from that of Weick and Daft. We do not believe that the attribution of agency depends on inherent characteristics of either the individual human or the organization. Its source lies elsewhere, in the discourse of communication (chap. 3 and 4). The dilemma that confronts Weick and Daft is nonexistent in our theory. We believe that we are nearing

---

[15]Markedness was discussed earlier. It marks an asymmetry in a category, where one member or subcategory is taken to be somehow more basic than the other (or others). The unmarked member is the default value—the member of the category that occurs when only one member can occur and all other things are equal.

in this discussion the essential distinction of communication research from other branches of the social sciences—its disciplinary specificity.

The Dualist Matrix and Its Heritage

The issue we have just outlined has deep philosophical implications that can be traced back to the very beginnings of modern Western science. Since the 17th century, European thinking has been fundamentally dualistic in its orientation. The dualism can be stated (baldly) as a vacillation between what have appeared to thinkers in the occidental tradition to be the main possible reasons for believing in a real world: materialism/realism (the hard physical, material facts of something out there whose existence we cannot deny), and idealism (described as "that which we can be dead sure we know is that we know because it is mentally present to us—a something in here"—in Descartes' words, *cogito ergo sum*, "I think therefore I am"). What seems impossible to deny, in the dualist universe of sense-making, is the existence of a material environment—a rock-hard out there to which we are joined by our body (or perhaps of which our body is part)—and/or a knowing being that is present to itself—an ineffable but experienced in here—a mind. Everything else seems derivative on these essential ontological certainties of an out there and an in here. And, of course, a thinker can lean one way or the other: be more or less materialist, more or less idealist, or seek a reconciliation. The great debates now sweeping the field of cognitive science, for example, are over the question as to whether the in here, that is, mind or spirit, may not in the end turn out to be just another out there, that is, a brain that is no more than a physical neural net, or hardware (or, as the phrase goes, "wetware"), with software added (Von Eckardt, 1993; Gardner, 1985; Churchland, 1988).

Weick's theory of enactment tends toward idealism because it plays with the idea, to a greater or lesser extent, that the out there is in fact a reflection of the in here. His theory of enactment is marked, ontologically, by an assumed primacy of the interpreting mind—that, for the most part, of the individual. As we have seen, although he toys with increasing frequency with the notion of a group mind, he is clearly not entirely comfortable with it.[16]

The problem of dualism, a product of the spectacular growth of the physical sciences that began in the 17th century and has continued without abatement, is that there is no place in it for society. Is society (and therefore

---

[16]In this respect, his evolution has a parallel in the conceptual history of another highly productive and original U.S. thinker, John Searle, whose philosophy starts from a concept of intentionality that has a good deal of similarity with the views of Weick, and who has gingerly begun (Searle, 1990, 1995) to dip his toe into the pool of collective intentionality (by which he also means "group mind").

organization) a material out there? Obviously not. Is it a psychical in here? The "not" is just as obvious. So, what is it?

This is Weick and Daft's conundrum. They are committed by a dualist ideology, heritage of the well-established science of psychology, to a belief in the unquestionable fact of the individual human being. They are committed by their premise to the existence of organization, and so organization must become a primary agency—that which, like Pickering's scientist, acts on something. But, to a dualist, individual and social (organizational) are incommensurable planes of existence. Pickering has the easier road. Because his actors are individuals (or small teams of scientists), he does not have to explain organization-in-the-large (other than as an incidental effect of practice) nor does he have much difficulty characterizing what is to be acted upon (a bubble chamber in a physicist's laboratory, for example, certainly something quite concrete and recognizable). Dualism is not threatened. He can afford to be a bit relativistic.

Weick and Daft, however, are caught on the horns of dilemma, because their principal actor ("the organization") is "vast, complex, fragmented, elusive, and multidimensional" and their secondary actor ("the environment") resembles "puzzles found in puns, poems, dreams, abstractions, and foreign languages" (Weick & Daft, 1983, p. 75). Not much of either an in here or an out there in this odd marriage of circumstance. Where have the agents gone? (No agents, no enactment.)

Because they are unable to say, other than programmatically, how the multiplicity of actors making up the organization is turned into a single systemic agency, their way around this difficulty is to multiply, many times over, references to "the environment" and, by so doing, rhetorically justify the twin assumptions of (a) the existence of an organizational actor who deals with it and (b) an enactment cycle where the dealing goes on. Yet, in their articles, their characterization of "the environment" is at least as vague as that of "the organization," and maybe even more so. It is, they say, more or less "analyzable," "concrete," "subjective," "difficult to penetrate, or changing," "rationalized," "subject to discernible, predictable uniformities in relationships among significant objects," and so on (and note that these characteristics of the environment are in fact attributions about it, and subjective at that, couched in the language of the putative organizational cognizer, presumably the manager). This is not surprising because, in enactment theory, we already know that the environment may be nothing more than a projection of the organization. But then, the argument is totally tautological. Because an actor must act on something, the existence of an environment becomes a logical necessity for organization to exist as an actor (theory of enactment) and, therefore, we postulate its existence; but the justification for the belief in an organization is that it is what makes it possible to deal with the environment.

The information content of this formulation is nil. With no actorial theory of organization (a differentiated system is not, by definition, an actor) small wonder the authors return from time to time, with evident relief, to the managers and their interpretations. At least, they are real! The must be; they are human.

ENACTMENT REENACTED

As did Weick, sociologists in the SSK tradition of research have come to the conclusion that science is shot through and through with enactment. What scientists discover about the world out there (empirical phenomena) is highly contingent on the in here (their theoretical predilections) that they were projecting on it. To a considerable extent, then, science is self-confirmatory, in precisely the way Weick has been claiming management is (making due allowance for Pickering's important reservation with respect to the importance of material as well as human agency). But the SSK researchers make a move that Weick does not. Somewhat nervously, and with nothing like full unanimity, they have turned the enactment telescope on themselves, thus recognizing that while science is enacting the material world, sociologists are enacting the social world, and they too may also be discovering in their research garden the Easter eggs of knowledge that they themselves had planted there not long before (Ashmore, 1989).

We have already observed that Weick's favorite aphorism (which he uses to vividly illustrate what he means by enactment), "How can I know what I think until I see what I say," has an implication: Something said can be seen. "Sayings" that can be seen are what we think of as texts. As it turns out, the SSK research fully confirms the accuracy of Weick's play on words, in describing how enactment occurs in a scientific laboratory. The classic study in this tradition is Latour and Woolgar's (1979) *Laboratory Life*.

The Importance of Other People "Seeing What You Say"

Imagine yourself, as Latour and Woolgar do in *Laboratory Life*, entering a large, contemporary research center or laboratory, not as an expert but as a naïve visiting anthropologist who, coming from afar, has just arrived in a totally foreign setting, where everything appears exotic and anything might turn out to be important (or not). In other words, set aside for a moment all the knowledge and prejudices you implicitly share with your informants because you, as do they, live in the modern United States, and you both even may have gone to the same university together. Play the part of the innocent outsider for a bit, and try to see things as a total stranger might. What would you perceive first?

Well, say Latour and Woolgar, the thing that would practically hit you between the eyes is that everybody is endlessly writing things down. It is not that they all write the same things down; there seem to be, in fact, two classes of writers. In one room, filled with elaborate equipment, there are people identified as technicians who stare at screens, pore over print-outs, examine dials or markings on some piece of equipment, and then transcribe what they see into scribbles on a paper: traces (figures and graphs, typically). In the other room, where the scientists are (you have learned the names by now), the equipment is different: computers and word processors, for the most part (and these days, faxes and e-mail, we presume). Here, the source of what these people read is different: They scour journal articles, underline things, copy parts, cut and paste. And then, they write articles themselves.

From time to time, the two kinds of writers meet, and the first group, the technicians, communicate to the second group, the scientists, the results of their transcribing. And then this gets incorporated into the production of the articles.

That is what you would actually see as a naïve outsider for whom these activities do not yet have any deeper meaning. At the heart of the scientific enterprise is the making of representations and not just any kind of representations: The object is to produce texts.

Why are texts so important in the enactment of the physical world?

It cannot be because they are a way for you (the isolated scientist in the home context of the lab) to "see what you say." Let Button et al. (1995) explain why not:

> One can argue that the purpose of language is to *express* thought, and that speaking is thus the vehicle for the public expression of thought. But why should individuals *need* to express their thought aloud? It cannot be that when they hear what they say they then know what they are thinking! If one genuinely accepted the point about the purpose of speech being the expression out loud of thought, then one would need to add the suppressed presupposition, which is that they need to speak to express their thought to *other people.* (emphasis in original, but we would have added it if it had not been there!)

In the scientific community, those "other people" are the scientific community (or at least that part of it that is relevant to the particular researcher's field). The texts endlessly being generated are not for domestic consumption, but for the market—the scientific market. That is how the scientific community comes to be a community, through its commerce in texts.[17]

---

[17]Shapin and Schaffer (1985) and Latour (1993) trace the scientific version of this pattern of objective demonstration leading to the writing of a textual description of it to a 17th century innovation by a physicist named Boyle: an experimental procedure made possible

In management science, the "other people" are those who belong in management science. That is why management science is a community of discourse. In an organization, the "other people"—those to whom one addresses memos, meeting agendas, trip reports, draft communiqués, clippings, and so on—are the other people in the organization. That is also how an organization comes to be an organization. Enactment enacts more than the object of the action; it enacts the actors as well! It constitutes them as a society.

Weick's version of enactment is truncated. He leaves something out, that is, the essential communicability of the act of interpretation—not a two-way but a three-way relation involving an actor, an interlocutor (the community who "sees what you say"), and an "environment." As we saw in chapter 3, this is what Newcomb (1953) calls an A-B-X system. Putting the "organization" in the A position, and the "environment" in the X position, as Weick and Daft do, leaves us with a puzzle: Who goes into the B slot? Weick and Daft give no answer. Or at least not in so many words. But wait—perhaps they have given it, not by stating it but by enacting it.

Consider the Weick and Daft's papers, not in the light of what they say, but rather in terms of what they are doing in saying what they are saying. They are, as the scientists Latour and Woolgar observed, writing papers— texts. They enact their environment by doing so. They analyze data, record observations by making traces, read the literature in which other people report the results of similar activities, talk to their graduate students and research assistants, draft outlines, and so on. They are an interpretation system composed of, for the moment, two individuals (plus involved associates, journal readers, editors, etc.). Their environment is both material and symbolic. It is constituted of all the organizations they study, in all their pristine materiality—and who, having been influenced by management science, come to mirror the latter's expectations. If Weick and Daft are thus the A in Newcomb's system, because they produce the text that enacts the environment, X (and in doing so, coincidentally, enact themselves), then who is the B? Obviously, we are; you are. Everybody who reads their papers is—not to mention those who did not actually read the papers but have heard about them, as you just have.

---

by the invention of a vacuum pump. With the help of a vacuum pump, it becomes possible to show phenomena that would otherwise be invisible. To make the showing persuasive to a larger community, Boyle invited reliable witnesses to his laboratory who could attest to the existence of a fact that they had seen with their own eyes. In this way, says Latour, "he invented the empirical style that we still use today" (Latour, 1993, p. 18). And, Latour goes on, "we witness the intervention of a new actor: . . . inert bodies, incapable of will and bias but capable of showing, signing, writing, and scribbling on laboratory instruments before trustworthy witnesses . . . Endowed with their new semiotic powers, the [nonhumans] contribute to a new form of text, the experimental science article" (p. 23).

We too have been enacted. And who are we (we hardly know each other, after all; we may even collectively be "vast, complex, fragmented, elusive, and multidimensional")? Could it be that we are the organization? And would this imply the organization had been an agent in the enacting process from the very beginning? Then, there is nothing to explain: the enactor, the environment, and the organization were all cocreated in the same enactment; none of them preceded the others, and, thus, none could have been the progenitor of the others.

This is not conventional systems thinking. But it is communicational thinking.

Cognitive Domains

One way to mutilate the concept of enactment, we claim, is to forget the B. But, to treat the enactment process differently, as now only an A-B event (with the X fading from sight) is equally, in our view, an inauthentic abridgement.

Weick has not written at all extensively on his theory of communication, but in his 1979 book (see also Weick & Bougon, 1986; Weick & Browning, 1986) he described a notion that he called a "double interact." When the behavior of one person is contingent on that of another(s), he would call such an interlocking an *interact*. A *double interact* occurs when "an action by actor A evokes a specific response in actor B (so far this is an interact), which is then responded to by actor A" (Weick, 1979b, p. 89). This characterization of communication is, of course, hardly unique to Weick; it bears a striking resemblance to what is described by conversation analysis researchers, such as Schegloff, as an adjacency pair. However, we argue, it is an unproductive way to think about communication for an organizational communication scholar (as Boden seems to have realized). A reflection on the practice of science by the Chilean researcher Humberto Maturana (1991) makes clear why we should not lose sight of the "X" any more than we did of the "B."

Maturana observes first that science is a human activity, which, as any other, exists "in the domain of human relations" (Maturana, 1991, p. 30). But because "all human activities are operations in language," this means that science is a part of, to use his phrase, "languaging." The motivation of the scientist (he calls it "emotion" and thinks of it as desire or passion) is, above all else, to explain. An explanation, whatever the area of life concerned, is a reformulation of an experience in terms of other experiences. What sets science apart (as it sets apart many shared worlds of experience) is its constitution "as a particular domain of explanations" (p. 30). (Notice that he is identifying the practice of science, not first by what it does but rather by how it reports what it does—what kinds of "explanations" of experiences it will admit.)[18]

He then goes on to lay out the criteria for a proper "scientific explanation." To be an authentic explanation, the report of the scientist must be that of an observer who (a) presents an experience ("phenomenon") in terms of what he or she did to experience it ("praxis of living") in such a way as to make it experiential by what he calls other "standard observers" (what is to be observed, in effect), (b) reformulates that experience "in the form of a generative mechanism that others could employ to generate the same experience" (experimental procedure, in effect), (c) deduces (we would use "extrapolates") from the operation of the generative mechanism just described other experiences that could be explained by it (in other words, hypothesis development and theory testing), and (d) reports what was actually experienced (the result, in effect). Only when the steps have been fully and correctly carried out will the report count as an explanation.

Any of us would recognize in his (somewhat labored) description the usual form of a scientific report.

What Maturana is doing here, however, is much more radical than that. He aims to tie together the three parts of our A-B-X triplet so tightly that they cannot possibly be pried apart. On the one hand, there is an enactment of an A-X relationship (this is what he has just been describing as how to be in a relationship to an environment that counts as scientific), and he insists throughout on its enactive character. It is worth citing him at length on this point, because it is fundamental:

> [W]e human beings constitute nature with our explaining, and with our scientific explaining we constitute nature as the domain in which we exist as human beings (or languaging living systems). Scientific explanations and statements are not validated through a reference to nature, but nature is operationally constituted (known) and expanded as we constitute it as our domain of experience as living systems through our scientific explanations of our experience with elements of our experience. (Maturana, 1991, p. 44)

As he says further: "[S]cience has nothing to do with a notion of truth that is independent of the criterion of explanation that constitutes a scientific statement or explanation" (p. 44).[19]

---

[18]There are striking parallels in Maturana's thought with that of Wittgenstein and, in particular, with the latter's idea of "language games" (Wittgenstein, 1958; Kripke, 1982).

[19]A more skeptical reading of the constituting of a scientific explanation, such as you would find in the SSK literature, would interpret scientific procedure slightly differently, even as it recognizes, as Maturana does, its constructive nature. To illustrate, let us for a moment return to our imaginary anthropologist, immersed in a contemporary laboratory and trying

On the other hand, the A-X relationship is not just individual, it is social
(A-B):

> It is the conversations in which we are immersed as we do science that
> determine the course of science. And this cannot be otherwise because
> whatever we human beings do arises in our operation as such in our domain
> of experiences through the continuous braiding of our languaging and our
> emotioning that is all that we human beings do. Therefore, we do not find
> problems or questions to be studied and explained scientifically outside
> ourselves in an independent world. We constitute our problems and ques-
> tions as we flow in our praxis of living, and we ask the questions that we in
> our emotioning desire to ask. (Maturana, 1991, p. 41)

It would be tempting to see in this citation an argument similar to that
which is often given in the field of psychology and pedagogy called *social
cognition,* namely, that people's behavior and beliefs are strongly influenced
by their immediate social surroundings. Again, it is worth reiterating that
this is not what Maturana is about. His reasoning is more radical than that;
it is institutional, that is, organizational:

> [M]embership in the community of standard observers does not depend on
> the individual ability of making reference to an independent objective reality
> that the standard observer as a living system cannot do, but on the *consensual
> participation in the domain of scientific explanations.* Accordingly, only those
> observers who can participate with other observers, and to their complete
> satisfaction, in the realization of the criterion of validation of scientific ex-

---

to make sense of what is seen. As the anthropologist thinks about what he or she is observing
a little more deeply, he or she concludes (the course on Durkheim has left its imprint) that
these people are writing down a representation, not of what the connectionist network knows
(like a connectionist teacher in our previous discussion), but more generally of what Nature
knows! The experimenters are behaving, it might occur to the anthropologist, a bit like a
medium in a séance who asks questions of departed relatives and, when the inevitable knocks
on the table are heard at the climax of the séance, is able to say what the relatives meant to
convey. After all, the only evidence the technicians have to go on is an equivalent of knocks:
The phenomenon itself being studied remains in the domain of the occult. Nevertheless, it
is not the medium whose voice participants in the séance hear, but the dear departed's.
Who, when the departed speaks in the language of knocks, could possibly doubt the
authenticity of that representation? We have operationally established communication with
the other world. (The trick, we all know, is to set up the equipment correctly, so that the
departed's voice can be heard: lights out, everybody's hands on the table, concentration, a
respectful silence—and patience, plus a certain credulity on the part of the clients). Similarly
in science: The role of the technician is to record the signs of a natural (as opposed to
prenatural) phenomenon. We are not trying to parody Maturana's characterization here but
rather to reinforce a central point he is making: that science, as other human enterprises,
is constructive—a hermeneutic, in which ambiguous signs must be made meaningful by
inscribing them in a regular practice, whose outcome, a text, is plausible because the practice
is seen to have roots in a legitimacy that is socially sanctioned by an established community.

planations and, furthermore, accept this as their *only criterion of validation for their explanations*, are scientists (standard observers) and members of the community of scientists. Those observers who, for one reason or another, cannot or would not do this are either discarded as standard observers or scientists by the members of the community of scientists under the claim that they are bad observers, or they are not considered at all. (Maturana, 1991, p. 33, emphasis added)

What exactly is Maturana saying (in his lumbering, leaden prose)?

First, science, no more than any other field of human endeavor, is not a gateway to reality: It is enactive through and through. Its objectivity comes not from any special insights it has into the true nature of reality, but from the disciplined character of its conversation. That conversation of so-called "standard observers" admits certain ways of giving explanations (we could substitute the term *interpretations* for "explanations") and excludes others. The basis for admitting or excluding, however, is not any inherent characteristic of the linguistic formulation (this is not a theory of rhetoric, in the usual sense), but of the enactive practices of the explainer, the evidence of which must be visible in the explanation, or interpretation.

Because the development of knowledge is in this way tightly constrained by the community of all the other "standard observers," Maturana calls science (as he would call any other such community of people who share a similar constraint on what counts as an interpretation) a *cognitive domain*. But note that in employing the word *cognitive*, at no point does he make any attribution whatsoever to mental representations. What is always at issue is the communicative practices of members of a given community:

> The use of scientific explanations by the members of a community of standard observers to directly or indirectly validate all their statements defines and constitutes science as a cognitive domain that defines as a scientific community the community of those observers that use it ... [S]cience is not different from other cognitive domains because it is defined and constituted as all cognitive domains are, namely, as a domain of actions defined by a criterion of validation or acceptability used by an observer or by the members of a community of observers to accept those actions as valid in a domain of actions defined by that very same criterion of acceptability. (Maturana, 1991, p. 39)

We exist in language, he thinks, and that means that our experiential domain is closed—one "from which we do not and cannot come out"—but that is a limitation only if "we think that we should be able to refer to an independent reality" (Maturana, 1991, p. 47). What constitutes liberation for humans is that we generally do not, any more than scientists do, identify with only one cognitive domain, but with many domains, and such participation in many conversations allows us to think creatively, to see unexpected connections, and to develop innovative explanations. The tent of language may be closed, but there is a three-ring circus going on in it.[20]

Maturana has thus provided the missing piece in the Weick/Daft puzzle of how a manager's enactment of the environment and interpretation could be, simultaneously, an individual and an organizational enactment and interpretation. When he or she (the manager) is so enacting the environment, he or she does so as the managerial equivalent of Maturana's "standard observer" in a community (the community of managers), except that the motivation of this community, unlike that of science, is not observing/explaining but interpreting/enacting. The resulting enactment now may become a reaffirmation of both a personal and an organizational identity. We have pointed out in chapter 7 the double connotation of the word *agency*: acting, and acting for. When the manager, in his or her capacity as a standard enactor in his or her community of standard enactors (defining a cognitive domain), enacts in the name of the organization and when the explanation of how he or she does so is seen by the community to conform to its criteria of authentic enacting, then the manager has in fact acted in the name of the organization and is seen to have been mandated to so do; the organization has itself acted—by stipulation. Now, the organization exists in two senses: as an explicit enactor through its agent, the manager, and as a community of standard enactors, in the absence of which the enactment would be undefined and thus not ever exist as enactment.

Of course there are implications:

1. *All* communication is organizational (communication is not superimposed on, but embedded in, practices which it makes transparent to other members of the practicing community).

2. The identity of members of the organization is coemergent with that of the organization itself and contingent on the existence of a cognitive domain within which the enacting gives rise to identities (peo-

---

[20]What does not emerge clearly in Maturana's account is the dynamics of the scientific conversation. To be sure, inclusion in the select conversation depends on having shown oneself to be a "standard observer," that is, someone who can conduct research according to the community's norms. But what this bland characterization hides, that the SSK literature now highlights, is the other, more political side of the scientific enterprise: its contests among contending schools of thought, its personal ladder climbing in the hierarchy of prestige, its considerable entrepreneurial practices of fund raising and center building, and so on. The stakes can become very high indeed, and scientists are, in the end, very human. Bearing this in mind makes it easier to generalize from Maturana's description to other, nonscientific domains.

ple need an organization and the mandates it makes possible because otherwise action would be without meaning).

3. Communication is not a strictly symbolic phenomenon, but also has a necessary material basis in the enaction of what it reports without which the communication would not be authentic.

4. The "languaging"—the support of communication—is itself an enactment, accomplished through interaction, in a conversation of people who are jointly part of a cognitive domain.

Language is not a transparent medium, but a surface of emergence.

The Surface of Emergence

Pickering has used a term he borrows from Foucault (see our discussion in chap. 2): a *surface of emergence*. As Pickering (1995, p. 20) describes it, a surface of emergence, in science, is the existing culture of enactment, including what is already said to be known in the scientific community, and its material practices of experiencing (Maturana's "criteria"). In the absence of such a surface, the "explanations" of which Maturana wrote would be nondecipherable, and enactment would block. In Pickering's words: "Existing culture . . . is literally the surface of emergence for the intentional structure of human agency" (p. 20).

Pickering's (1995) preoccupation is with what we have called the A-X dimension, because he wants to show the interactive play ("dance," he calls it) of human and nonhuman agencies as a "dialectic of resistance and accommodation" (p. 22). Weick and Daft's characterization of the organization/environment enactive cycle fits this pattern as well. The managerial surface of emergence would then be defined as that combination of acquired understanding of the world, along with the technologies (both human and material) by means of which management is enabled to render visible the agency that is only virtually present in the environment until it has been enacted. But, there is a second surface of emergence that is of vital importance to both scientists and managers, that of the A-B dimension. You could read Maturana and imagine the scientific community as structureless, an undifferentiated field of "standard observers," held together by an ongoing "conversation." You could also read Weick and Daft and, although the word *managers* is mentioned often throughout the text, the reality of hierarchy is but barely alluded to in passing. But we know that both communities of scientists and of managers live in highly structured universes of interlocked identities, differentiated by status, reputation, authority, and power. The internal dynamics of organization have their own surface of emergence, and it is to be found in language, which is also, in its own way, an acquired knowledge and a technology.

LIMITS OF THE COMPUTATIONAL METAPHOR

One reason we chose to analyze the two Weick and Daft articles was the premise of organization as a differentiated system that they started from. We have shown that their translation of this model as an interpretation system echoes the same interrogation that we explored in chapters 6 and 7: Is organization a socially distributed cognition, or a computation? To conclude this chapter, we attempt to give a reasoned answer to our earlier questioning of the applicability of the computational model to describe complex organization. To do so, we focus on two necessary conditions for organization-as-computation to occur, namely, feedforward and backpropagation (Fig. 8.2). The issue is one of scaling up.

Do Interpretation Systems Scale Up?

In a connectionist network of intercommunicating nodes, feedforward is a logical and backpropagation a practical necessary property for the net to effectively act as a computing device. Feedforward is assured by the configuring of nodes into input, hidden, and output. Backpropagation is made possible by an algorithm that systematically alters interconnection weights. In a classical, symbolicist network, feedforward is guaranteed by centrally controlled routines of scheduling and routing of information flows (think back to our discussion of March & Simon in chap. 6). Because nodes have no enactive degrees of freedom in this kind of net (computer hardware being the prototype), there is no need for backpropagation; learning is accomplished exogenously by reprogramming (as we saw). In the socially distributed information processing networks described by Hutchins and by Weick and Roberts, feedforward was structured by the exigencies of the task and by member specialization; backpropagation occurred through interpersonal interaction (particularly evident in Hutchins' description of the crisis on a ship that had lost electronic control over steering just as it entered port). Weick and Roberts advanced a further hypothesis: that computational efficacy declines in the absence of heedfulness, which is to say uniform member concentration on the task at hand.

In the absence of feedforward and backpropagation (or their equivalents), the computational model of organization is not applicable. Are large, complex organizations appropriately modeled as cognitive (or interpretation) systems, with a computational capability? This is the question that sat in the background of our earlier discussion of models of organizations that justified the communication-in-organization metaphor. We suggest the answer is "no."

Earlier in the chapter, we flagged an observation by Daft and Weick (1984, p. 285) to the effect that "the point at which information converges and is interpreted for organization level action is assumed to be at the top manager level . . . below the vice presidential level, participants are not informed on issues pertaining to the organization as a whole."

The last half of this statement strikes us as obviously true, namely, that, below the vice presidential level, participants are not informed about issues as they appear to senior management (we take the phrase "pertaining to the organization as a whole" to be a euphemism for senior management's concerns). That seems uncontroversial enough. It is the other assumption we have difficulty with: the convergence of information and its "interpretation for organization level action . . . at the top manager level."

Our experience of organization suggests something quite different: that the upper levels of management are just as ill-informed about the lower levels as the lower levels are about the upper. Suchman (1995), as we have noted, calls this managerial ignorance of its own enterprise the phenomenon of "invisible work."

The prolonged effort in North American sociology and management theory to read the organization as a single cognitive, or computational, system strikes us as misguided, a movement animated not by thoughtful observation of organizational life but by ideology. How can we be certain? Well, we have it on good authority: Karl Weick!

There is, he says, "less to rationality than meets the eye":

> There are growing doubts about the importance of formal rationality in organizations. . . . The complaint is not that rationality is ill-conceived but, rather, that the conditions under which it works best are relatively rare in organizations. . . . Organizations use rationality as a façade when they talk about goals, planning, intentions, and analysis, not because these practices necessarily work, but because people who supply resources believe that such practices work and indicate sound management (Pfeffer, 1981, pp. 194–196). The appearance of rational action legitimates the organization in the environment it faces, deflects criticism, and ensures a steady flow of resources into the organization. (Weick, 1985, pp. 109–110)

And the notion of anything approaching a unified system is suspect:

> Not only do theorists qualify any reference they make to rationality, they also avoid the define [sic] article "a" or "the" when referring to an organization. No organization is monolithic, yet continued references in the literature to "the organization" often suggest otherwise. People persist in referring to *the* organization due to a combination of failure to discount for hindsight bias, casual sorting of organizations into undifferentiated categories, routine aggregation of individual survey responses to create nominal organizations, and preoccupation with central tendencies (the mean) rather than dispersion (variation). . . . Organizations are seen as more unified actors than they are, operating in more homogeneous environments than exist,

and capable of longer lines of uninterrupted action than in fact they can mobilize. (Weick, 1985, p. 112)

In fact, he says, stable segments in organizations are quite small (Weick, 1985, p. 116).

Not very computational.

What are they then? It seems to us, as it seems to Durkheim (and Weick as well in some of his writings) that organizations are in fact rhetorical constructions, talked into being in the unceasing interdimensional translation of representations (texts) validated, or not, in the flowing stream of the laminated conversations of the organizational members. It is this image and how it is worked out in the organizational discourse that forms the matter of chapter 9.

AN AFTERWORD ON WEICK'S EVOLUTION

It is hazardous to select for attention one or two texts from a considerable and constantly growing corpus of work that spreads over 25 years. The hazard is particularly great when the author in question is Karl Weick, because he is eclectic in his sources, wide-ranging in his theoretical interests, and chameleon-like in his adaptability. The two articles we chose to analyze mark about half way along the strip map of enactment that is Weick's own career. We might seem to have been unfair in concentrating on them to the relative exclusion of other later ones (although it might be noted that he himself, in a late book, chose the second of these articles as one out of only four self-references to be included in a list of what he calls "important resources for organizational sensemaking"). Rather than enter any further defense for what was patently a rhetorical strategy on our part, to fix a reference marker that would allow us to counterpoint, and thus clarify, our own position (somewhat as Hutchins reports Melanesian navigators do), we conclude this chapter by a brief commentary on the 1995 *Sensemaking in Organizations* version of enactment.

This book seems to us to index two evolutions in Weick's thought. First, the emphasis on the sociability of sensemaking is more marked than ever. It is not that it had been totally absent before: The article on the Utrecht Jazz Orchestra that he coauthored with Bougon and Binkhorst (Bougon, Weick, & Binkhorst) in 1977 already showed a preoccupation with collective sharing of individual cause maps, but there was still a certain ambivalence in his thinking about the crossover from individual to group that was still there in the later 1986 article coauthored with Bougon. That seems to have disappeared. On the other hand, the evolutionary systems theorizing of *The Social Psychology of Organizing*, so very evident in 1969, and still present in 1979, if less predominantly so, in this book is a tune that is played more softly with the mute in. In its place, collective sensemaking, interactively realized, has come front and center.

What is missing, as we see it, is an understanding of the organization as a communicational construction or an awareness of the institutionalizing of human society that accompanies organization with its many internal contradictions and tensions, an aspect of organization that Max Weber, good jurist that he was, at least hinted at. Systems are still interlocked behaviors, for Weick: double interacts. Sensemaking is a way station on the road to a consensually constructed, coordinated system of action. At no point are inherent contradictions in organizational structure and process even remotely evoked.

Nor does he yet respond to the question we posed at the beginning of this chapter, although he does hint at an answer. In both a 1990 article and the 1995 book, Weick cites Chatman, Bell, and Staw (1986) as saying:

> When we look at individual behavior in organizations, we are actually seeing two entities: the individual as himself and the individual as representative of his collectivity. . . . Thus, the individual not only acts on behalf of the organization in the usual agency sense, but he also acts, more subtly, "as the organization" when he embodies the values, beliefs, and goals of the collecitivity. As a result, individual behavior is more "macro" than we usually realize. (Weick, p. 23)

This comes very close to what we also are saying, but Weick does not take the idea any further. A return to the source article of Chatman et al. (1986) is of little help, because the citation is taken from the conclusion of their essay where it is little more than an afterthought, because the body of the article makes no reference to representativity, or "acting on behalf of." That Weick would have retained the afterthought sufficiently to use it in at least two of his later texts may well be a signal of a change of direction in his thinking. We hope so.

Why "In"? Of Maps, Territories, and Governance

There is a danger in emphasizing, as we do in this book, the role of language as the site and surface of organizational emergence. We risk losing sight of the situational reality of all communication. One of Giddens' many useful distinctions contrasts practical and discursive knowledge. *Practical knowledge* is the kind of skills people use to get on with their lives in everyday contexts of involvement. It stays for the most part below the level of consciousness. It is tacit. It is part of just doing what one is accustomed to do. *Discursive knowledge,* as the term suggests, is what has to be talked about: forefronted in active consciousness, usually because there is something to be dealt with that needs to be talked through. Most knowledge, Giddens thinks, is of the practical kind. Discursive knowledge is highlighted only when our involvements in activities of various kinds necessitate a rise to the level of communication. Communication, therefore, is always about something: It is invariably situated—in conversation and in life circumstances.

Giddens makes another useful distinction. He thinks about involvement in spheres of activity in terms of how we go about mobilizing resources of various kinds to deal with the world we are in. He distinguishes between allocative and authoritative resources. *Allocative resources* are the objects of the material world that we put to work in one way or another to satisfy our needs. *Authoritative resources* are the people whom we are able to enlist in the fulfillment of our purposes. Obviously, the mobilization of authoritative resources calls upon our mastery of discursive knowledge. It is the object of communication to marshal human resources, typically on the way to dealing with the kind of allocative resources that call for collective action.

Latour's particular contribution to this vision of practical involvement in a world of activities is to observe that the best way to mobilize the resources of the material world is to reconstruct that world so that our purposes are realized automatically. The objects of our attention, as reconfigured in a way that incorporates our purposes, become themselves agents who go on acting even when we are not present. They become the products of an absent human intentionality that was first made manifest somewhere else or at some other time. They are an organization that has been frozen by its inscription in material form and thus given a permanence that transcends the strictly local. It is in this way that we differ from the apes, he thinks, because they have no means to freeze organization; they are always back at point zero, obliged to mobilize the allocative resources in their world, all over again, themselves, without much aid from authoritative resources.

There is organization that has been frozen into material artifacts all around us: in our houses, our offices, our transportation systems, our banks, and our governments. It is the structuring of the physical world that channels our activities to give them a form that perpetuates organizational mobilizations originating somewhere else, at some other time. It is called our culture.

The whole thrust of technology is to structure the material world to fit today's organizational imperatives. When structured, it achieves what Latour thinks of as "black-box" status: no longer very salient in our minds (just part of the infrastructure) and not easy to change. Nowhere is this better illustrated than by the so-called "Y2K" problem: code that was inscribed in computer systems at a time when the third millennium was no more than a vague shadow on the distant horizon that threatened our welfare as a functioning economy on January 1, 2000. A trivial piece of code is involved, one that, in principle, any graduate of any good computing school could fix in a minute, but because it is hardwired into the systems of whole nations, takes billions of dollars to repair.

Latour's point is well taken, but he is talking about frozen organization, the residue of yesterday's organizing. Our concern is with the emergent organization and that, it seems to us, is revealed in communication. Nevertheless, the same impulsion, to freeze today's organization so that it channels tomorrow's spheres of activity—constraining as it enables—is still to be observed. The instrumentality making it possible to shape conversations elsewhere so that they fit the exigencies of a conversation here is textualization. It is in the hardwiring of text that resources are mobilized to realize an emergent organization of dimensions that goes well beyond the locally bounded worlds of our primate cousins.[1]

---

[1]Engeström (1990) argues that there are contradictions in every society and that they drive change. The contradictions can be traced back to the superposition of one historically located logic of work on another (the example he uses is the evolution of the medical pro-

This final chapter is an exploration into how people go about textualizing in ordinary organizational contexts. We see it as a form of mapping.

THE IMPORTANCE OF MAPS

Prior to the American Revolution, the British Government in London embarked on a determined effort to construct a comprehensive map of its territories in North America. After the revolution, other ambitious campaigns were undertaken to map the country, this time originating out of the new U.S. capital, Washington. It seems that maps are important to administrators.

One obvious reason for a map's importance is that it expands the horizon beyond the local. On the British Government's 18th-century passion for mapping, for example, G. Taylor offers this explanation:

> Perhaps [the] value [of a large-scale map] was more imaginative than utilitarian. The commissioners of the Board of Trade lived an ocean away from the colonies, and depended on letters sent by colonial officials as their primary source of information about North America—letters that took at least a month, and often much longer, to arrive in England. Their knowledge of the colonies was consequently very spotty, and needed to be supplemented by a healthy dose of imagination ... Maps played an important role in this process of imaginative reconstruction. A picture of British possessions in North America gave the British Empire a concrete form, allowing royal officials to survey their territories as if they were a chessboard on which various pieces—settlers, armies, commodities—could be played. Maps, in other words, could be used to stand in for the territory. What is more, cartography reduced the continent to a manageable size, giving royal administrators a sense of mastery over regions that they had never seen and people whom they had never met. (1996, pp. 2–3)

The British colonies, G. Taylor points out, were really a "paper empire" stitched together by communications. Having a map meant the administrator could control dominions in America from afar: plan military campaigns, organize new settlements, and so on. The orders of the administrator in London, based on the map, would be carried out (approximately) by agents in America, and so "... the imperial system of communications

---

fession from general practitioner to the technical specialized teams of today). Our interpretation of the phenomena he refers to is to see it as an encounter of frozen with emergent organizations that in communication takes the form of a dialogic of text (which inscribes inherited organizational imperatives) and the conversation (which is today's living organization, discursively realized). We call it a *dialogic* but it could reasonably be argued that it is a *dialectic*.

allowed officials to alter reality to fit the image of the map. Thus maps were a form of political discourse that not only described the world, but also served to change it" (G. Taylor, 1996, p. 4).

This chapter is about maps, but maps of a special kind—maps of organization. The thesis we develop is as follows: The organization as a whole (as opposed to smallish work groups) is not best thought of as a system, computing environmental information to produce a collectively, though imperfectly, that is, boundedly, rational representation of its environment, such as March and Simon (and to some extent Weick and Daft) proposed. The organization, to our way of thinking, is something quite different. It is a territory, a partly physical, partly social life space occupied by a diverse population of workers, managers, and other interest groups, each with their own (interconnected, to be sure) agendas (which may involve computing). Maps are an indispensable instrument for the governance of the territory—a representation that comes with an agenda. Maps, then, are for governance. They delineate territories, and territories need maps for them to even be territories.

If you spend much time in a large organization, you are tempted to conclude that its preoccupation is not so much with organizing as with reorganizing. Writing the map of the organizational territory—rewriting it would be more accurate—seems often to be the principal activity of organization. Every time you read in the business section of the newspaper that some company is "restructuring its operations," you are hearing the distant thunder of a storm of mapmaking.

What is at stake for management is not primarily the development of a strategy for dealing with the environment (that is merely a convenient rhetorical legitimation of the exercise of authority) but, as a sociologist of maps such as Wood (1992, p. 42) puts it, the "control of social processes." "[C]artography," he says, looked at in a historical context, "was primarily a form of political discourse concerned with the acquisition and maintenance of power" (p. 43)—something like Deetz's corporate colonization.

For power to be exerted in the many-tentacled octopus of a giant multinational corporation or a sprawling government department, the territory has to be mapped so that it can be, as G. Taylor put it, "imaginatively grasped": made real. The modern manager, as the 18th-century manager, is short on detailed knowledge of what occurs at the actual day-to-day working world of his or her employees (which, in Suchman's 1995 phrase, become literally invisible), and long on imagination. He or she too needs a map—a game board to move the pieces around on.

The mapping of the organizational territory may facilitate the exercise of stewardship for those in charge, but it also encourages willing obedience by those who are not, because the map is how they too fix their location, where they occupy their piece of the world and organize their lives. Power, as Latour (1986, p. 265) argues, "is explained not by the actions of the person who is obeyed, but of those who obey."[2] It is not only Hutchins' navigators who must use a chart to locate themselves.

When rendered objectively present to everyone through their materialization in a map, the lineaments of a universe of activity are sketched and given meaning. Communication can now occur in organization: If there were no map, there would be no territory for the communication to be "in" because there would also be no place for the communicators to be in. An organization, as an empire, must be constituted imaginatively.

Our image of the territory of the organization is much like the one Boden described: a diffuse, inchoate, laminated conversation, involving multiple crossings from one verbal interaction to another, bringing into play a complex pattern of agentively charged motives and relationships. In the absence of a map, such a topography of talk, in and of itself, has no overall meaning to the people involved in it. It is the map that locates members on the emergent organizational surface and provides them with a guide to navigation, that is, points to possible routes to follow to get from where they are now to where they want to go. By extending the imaginative grasp of the organization well beyond the local conversation, by situating that conversation in the larger intercourse of the organization-as-a-whole, a capacity to navigate is enabled. The map is not a portrayal of reality, it is reality for those who use it, because it summarizes the acquired understandings, culturally inherited, that enable the enactment of the present.

The organizational conversation—where the daily interaction actually takes place—is, pragmatically, always situated, inevitably local. For the totality of all the organizational conversations to constitute more than a disjointed collection of disparate exchanges, they must come to be seen to exist on some common, shared surface. It is the textually constructed map of the organization that provides this surface—the indispensable foundation of the conversational universe. Yet, because the map itself is a product—it had to have been authored—it is not only the basis of the laminated conversations, but also their main object. The relationship of territory to map and map to territory, Wood (1992) concludes, is reflexive. To us, that is the reflexivity of conversation and text manifested in a different guise. Only the map can stitch the territory together; only the text can stitch the conversations together.

---

[2] " 'Power' is always the illusion people get when they are obeyed; . . . they imagine that others obey because of the masters' clout without ever suspecting the many different reasons others have for obeying and doing something else; more exactly, people who are 'obeyed' discover what their power is really made of when they start to lose it. They realise, but too late, that it was 'made of' the wills of all the others" (Latour, 1986, pp. 268–269).

SOME GENERAL PROPERTIES OF MAPS

Before we look at the specifics of organizational maps—texts—it is useful to have in mind some characteristics of maps in general. We see the following properties as essential:

1. Maps are artifacts: They had to have been made by someone. Maps are not the world, but a representation of it, a construction. Because they are constructed—must have been constructed—they had to have had an author (a mapper), a subject (that which is being represented or mapped) and a theme (that aspect of the territory that is being paid attention to, or what is focused on among the myriad other aspects of the terrain that could have been selected for showing on the map). Because the universe to be represented is always mediated by its being seen through the agency of someone (the author), "maps, all maps, inevitably, unavoidably, necessarily embody the authors' prejudices, biases and partialities" (Wood, 1992, p. 24).

2. Maps are facts: They enable; they afford us reality. Why, given their inevitable bias, are maps so potent in their influence over us? Because, says Wood, they offer us "a reality that exceeds our vision, our reach, the span of our days, a reality we achieve no other way" (Wood, 1992, p. 4). As he says, "every map facilitates some living by virtue of its ability to grapple with what is known instead of what is merely seen, what is understood rather than what is no more than sensed" (p. 7).

3. If maps are both artifacts and facts, it is because the author can vanish. The irony is that for a map to be at all convincing, it must present a plausibly objective view of the territory. If the interest of the maker is too patently obvious, the map lends itself to controversy. For it to work, the author must disappear from view,

> for it is only to the extent that this author *escapes notice* that the real world the map struggles to bring into being is enabled to materialize (that is, to be taken for the world). As long as the author—and the interest he or she unfailingly embodies—is in plain view, it is hard to overlook him, hard to see around her, to the world described, hard to see it . . . *as the world.* Instead it is seen as no more than a version of the world, as a *story* about it, as a *fiction*: no matter how good it is, not something to be taken seriously. As author—and interest—become marginalized (or done away with altogether), the represented world is enabled to . . . *fill our vision.* (Wood, 1992, p. 70)

(We recall here what we reported Maturana as saying about the importance of being a "standard observer": To be a standard observer is one way to avoid the accusation of subjective interpretation—to escape notice).

4. Maps become factual by recording what is known. What we are saying here is similar to the point Pickering makes, namely, that the surface on which we live out our existence has been constructed over time out of an accumulating body of interpretations that are culturally inherited, which, by recording what is already known (past), provide a sensible surface for current intentional activity (present). Maps record, not objective properties of the physical topography, but our interpreted understandings of them in a way that facilitates our acting purposefully, to exploit and avoid, take this road or that, "to link the territory with what comes with it," in Wood's phrase. This surface of inherited interpretations is the real world—the enacted world. The author vanishes when the map is so faithful a reconstruction of what is known that its reconstructive nature is no longer evident.

5. Maps are not really about objective features of the landscape, but about ownership, possession. "What is at stake," Wood (1992, p. 21) says, "is not latitude and longitude . . . , but . . . *ownership*: this is what is being mapped here." Maps are not just representations of a physical topography; they are social. They do not so much identify locations as "*create ownership at a location*" (p. 21). It is not merely that maps inevitably manifest a bias, that of the selective perception of the mapmaker, but that the bias is typically conveniently aligned with the purposes of the maker and/or his or her patron or clientele. Maps work by serving interests. The map may be an object of social construction, but its motivation is, in the end, political.

6. If the interests are too flagrantly perceptible, the map no longer works as a map. Wood calls this the dialectic of the "culturalization of the natural" and the "naturalization of the cultural." For the cultural content of the map (its hidden interest) to be naturalized, so that the map comes to appear to be a transparent image of the territory and not just an interpretation of it, the natural content of the map must first be culturalized into existence: its traits identified, named, and inventoried (naming is crucial). It is in this way that mapping, by making things nameable, is also a way of creating the basis for collectively sharing a space. When named, locations can begin to take on properties we would think of as social, economic, or political—part of frame knowledge.

7. Maps are always in the process of reconstruction. The map is never quite finished. Existing maps, as telephone directories, are always slightly out of date, because they record what was true yesterday, not what is happening right now. They are, in effect, culturally inherited surfaces—a basis to work on, an "instrument," something to put to work, not drawn once and for all, but constructed and reconstructed (Wood, 1992, pp. 182–183).

8. Making a map is not enough; for it to take on authority, it has to be socially validated. Authorship does not take place in a social vacuum. It would not be a map, nor would the author be an author, unless it was

recognized as a map (our A-B-X point of chapter 8). The validation of an organizational map is negotiable (although not everyone participates in the negotiating process on an equal basis) if only because of the property of mapness that says it must be fact, and not just artifact. In the case of an organizational map, the conversation that leads to its negotiated construction is management in the raw. If there is something that could reasonably be termed a "representation system," then this is it: The enactment of an environment of which Weick and Daft wrote was merely a step toward the fundamental enactment—that of the organization itself as a territory.

THE ORGANIZATIONAL MAP

So now the question is posed: What would an organizational map be like? We suggest that it differs in at least three ways from the kind of map that Wood and other cartographically oriented researchers are dealing with:

1. It explicitly portrays a primarily social, not physical, topography. It is true that large, contemporary organizations have a geographical component, and so one feature of organizational maps would be the location of the head office, branches, factories, overseas outlets, and so on, but, basically, the map we are interested in is one centered on the valued possessions and transactions of human action. It is the textualization of the objects and roles that we described in chapter 3.

2. It deals with events, not just with places. If it is to delineate the thoroughfares of organizational action, it has to take account of time.

3. It is typically inscribed in either written text or is part of people's tacit frame knowledge (not, unlike ordinary maps, expressed graphically to represent iconically the topography of a certain region).

In spite of these differences, there are also important similarities:

1. As are ordinary maps, organizational texts must be authored by someone. Texts may begin as artifacts (stories, accounts, explanations, excuses, projects, etc.). But, as other maps, they also have to be recognized as fact, and so authorial effacement is a necessary step to recognition of map status. They must thus stop being someone's story, and become merely the truth. This is achieved to the extent that such textual maps are recognized as successfully conveying what is known (compare this with our discussion in chap. 8 of the relationship between organizational voice and representation).

We have no doubt every individual develops his or her own idiosyncratic maps of the organization—other animals than humans are mappers too

(Tolman, 1958)—but theirs are not the organizational map. For it to be an organizational map, a map has to have been, as Wood emphasizes, made "natural"; in Latour's (1987) imaginative construction, no longer merely an artifact (made by someone), but a fact (part of what everybody accepts as true, even when it disadvantages them to do so, as Deetz pointed out). In the absence of such naturalization, the organization would not exist; as administrators have always known, maps are not merely useful, but are an essential instrument of governance. If the map collapses, the state or the organization will not last because the territory has lost its coherence.

2. As with maps generally, what is actually involved is ownership. To describe an organization as being made up of turfs is more than an analogy. The organizational map (or maps) is about the identities of people, the objects they have and/or transact, the perimeter of their responsibilities and powers. Secondarily, therefore, it is about access: where to go for what.

3. It is not only topographical maps that carry the trace of an interest or interests; organizational maps are also instruments of power and means to constrain and to enable: ideologies. That they depend on a textual, not a graphical, support technology is a relevant, but not essential, criterion: a consideration of pragmatic, not logical, importance.

4. Finally, organizational maps, as other maps, have to be socially validated. They are thus negotiable within limits and in certain contexts—the definition of what constitutes a context of negotiation being itself one element of the map. The organizational map maps its own genesis—how it has been and is to be mapped.

DIFFERENCES BETWEEN OUR VIEW AND OTHER
THEORIES OF CAUSE MAPS

We are not the first to have exploited the concept of organizational maps. As noted in chapter 8, there is already an established management literature on what are termed, alternatively, causal maps, cause maps, or cognitive maps. However, we have found this body of work of limited utility for our own purposes, precisely because it fails to address the considerations we have been outlining. It is not grounded in a communication theory of organization.

The literature stems from another article by Weick that he coauthored in 1977 with Bougon and Binkhorst (Bougon, Weick, & Binkhorst). They posit three fields of study: one, psychological, that is concerned with the mind-brain problem; another, traditionally organizational, that deals with the organization-environment problem; and a hybrid, part psychological, part organizational, that takes as its subject, as they put it, the "mind-environment problem" (Bougon, Weick, & Binkhorst, 1977, p. 606). This new branch of study (which they have made their own) is termed "cognitive organization theory."

What cognitive organization theory is about is made clear in a second article Weick published the same year (Weick, 1977). In it, he explains that the usual assumption of open systems theory of a clearly delineated frontier separating organization from its environment with inputs and outputs is not well founded. Categories such as external/internal and outside/inside might make logical sense, he says, but they do not correspond to anything in the empirical world, which remains not just unknown, but unknowable: "There is no methodological process by which one can confirm the existence of an object independent of the confirmatory process involving oneself. The outside is a void, there is only the inside. A person's world, the inside or internal view is all that can be known. The rest can only be the object of speculation" (p. 273).

The environment, says Weick, "is located in the mind of the actor and is imposed by him on experience in order to make that experience more meaningful. It seldom dawns on organizational theorists to look for environments inside of heads rather than outside of them" (Weick, 1977, p. 274). What we need to be sensitive to then, he says, is how raw data are unitized (bracketed and separated), labeled, and then transformed into a "network of causal sequences" that he designates a causal map (p. 275). This is the enacted environment. Because it drives everything else, "how enactment is done is what an organization will know" (p. 277). The environment is merely the "*real*-ization" of the ideas in people's heads: "Sensemaking is largely solitary in the sense that structures contained within *individual* minds are imposed on streams of *individual* elapsed experience that are capable of an infinite number of *individual* reconstructions" (p. 296, emphasis in original). It follows, therefore, that the proper object of study of an organizational researcher is not the organization-environment relationship, because that would reveal the researcher as a victim of misplaced concreteness, or a reifier, but the ideas in people's heads about it.

In operationalizing the concept of causal, or cause, map (the terms are used interchangeably), the authors were inspired by then popular causal analysis statistical techniques (Axelrod, 1976; Blalock, 1969, 1971; Boudon, 1967; Boudon & Lazarsfeld, 1966; Maruyama, 1963). Multivariate correlation/regression constructions lend themselves to attributions of cause-effect relationships—patterns of interconnected events—and it was this feature that seems to have attracted Weick and his collaborators' attention. A cause map now becomes, hypothetically (and for purposes of research), a network of interconnected variables.

As in chapter 8, we are left with an unresolved issue: If sensemaking is individual, if environment is merely a projection of the individual's making sense of the flow of experience, and if there is no distinguishable boundary separating environment and organization (other than that which results from individual enacting), then how are we to understand the idea of organizational maps (or indeed of organization itself)? Weick thinks (1979a, p. 149) that the organization, taken as a whole, is characterized by multiple cause maps of reality, more or less loosely coupled; but if organizational maps are "multiple," and if, as they say (Weick & Bougon 1986, p. 102): "Organizations exist largely in the mind, their existence takes the form of cognitive maps," then how did we know there was an organization to be mapped? Is not the logic circular? Is not the organization as unreal—as imaginary—as the environment?

Weick's emphasis on individual sensemaking has been remarked on by others (e.g., Eden, 1992)[3] and, as we saw in chapter 6, Weick himself has since moved away from the solipsistically tinged hyperbole of his 1977 article to embrace a more collegial concept of group mind. There have been a number of attempts to track the link from individual mappings to a collective image of the environment. Eden, Jones, and Sims (1983) propose the construction of an aggregate map, obtained by merging and overlaying individual maps. Matrices of "group cause maps" have been developed, using as data the individual maps of all participants, on the basis of which a valency vector is computed (Axelrod, 1976; Bougon et al., 1977; Komocar, 1985; Masuch, 1985; Weick, 1979a). Bougon (1992) has suggested a "congregate cognitive map." R. I. Hall (1984), in tracking the natural logic of policy making, measures maps of individual departmental members to show the evolution of a firm's policymaking over time. Other research has aimed to elicit group collective maps through a modified interview-based technique (Langfeld-Smith, 1992; Langfeld-Smith & Lewis, 1989). Walsh and Fahey (1986) and Walsh, Henderson, and Deighton (1988) have investigated negotiated belief structures; they propose that knowledge mappings that define the group's collective structure are aggregated through negotiation, argument, and interaction. The values of the organizational cause map have also been measured as a consensus arrived at through group discussion, using Delphi or other related techniques (Nelson & Matthews, 1991; Roberts, 1973).

Although this work has attempted to close the gap between individual and collective cognizing, it is still focused on (a) individual managers trying to make sense of (b) an environment. As a result this work remains psychological in its orientation. However, although the kernel of Weick's idea of individual maps (and collections of individual maps) has been respected,

---

[3]"Clearly cognitive psychology is about the thinking processes and learning of an individual and yet maps are used in the field of management as something which can relate to groups, organizations and even industries" (Eden, 1992, p. 262).

TABLE 9.1
Differences Between Communication and Cause Map Views

Communication View	Cause Map View
Maps link locations.	Maps link variables.
Locations are tied to ownership.	Variables express causes and effects.
Maps reflect interest of maker.	Enactor is affected by, affects variables.
Maps are "authored" (public).	Maps are in people's heads (private).
Maps speak to collective reality.	Maps speak to *individual* reality.
Maps are materialized, made "real."	Maps are inferred by the researcher.
Maps are instruments of governance.	(The issue of governance is not raised).

the enactment part of his rationale has disappeared. The focus is now on how successfully the environment is represented in the managerial image, but the reality of that environment is no longer questioned. The phenomenological perception is lost; the revised logic of inquiry is positivistic. The issue of what an organization is never arises, and communication is put back in its box, as that which goes on in organization, as no more than a kind of interindividual map collector.

Table 9.1 summarizes some of the differences between a communication and a cause map view of maps.

How are we to interpret these differences? In the communication view, the map is what provides an image of a surface (fabricated out of a cultural inheritance of legitimated understandings) and thus gives that surface a meaning that it would not otherwise have. It is available to many people; it is a tool they may all indiscriminately, if selectively, use to guide their locomotion from one location to another in the course of their activities. The degree to which it is universally recognized as a properly constituted objective representation of the territory determines the extent to which it has the status of map, as opposed to merely a personal (and interested) interpretation. In the cause map view, the map provides an image of the underlying causal pattern of a flow of events that is constructed by, and of interest to, an individual or individuals and serves him or her or them as a guide for taking action. The extent to which such an image is in fact shared is problematical, universal acceptance not being a criterion for "mapness" in this theory.[4] But, if the authority of the map is limited to

---

[4]It is interesting that the most frequently cited reference in the cause map literature, other than Weick, is an article written by a psychologist, an experimenter using rats as his subjects, Edward Tolman, in 1947/1958; the irony of basing a theory of managerial cognition on the model of the rat's cognition does not seem to have been remarked on. Of course, the rat's map is in the head (or in their muscles), but then rat organizations, although complex, lack what Latour (Latour, 1994; Strum & Latour, 1987) calls the "complication" of the contemporary human social worlds. Rats do not need Rand McNally maps, or their equivalent, to navigate their worlds; people in the modern world do.

the territory it constitutes, and if the territory describes no more than the experience of a single individual or collection of individuals—assuming the "real" organization/environment to be merely a "personal construct" (Eden, 1992, citing Kelly, 1955)—then the issue of maps' role in governance is rendered irrelevant. And, if there is no governance, there is, by implication, no organization to be governed. Hence, the extraordinary silence in the cause map literature on questions of authority, the exercise of power, and the maintenance of control.[5]

In his 1995 book, Weick makes little use of the concept of cause map. We can find only one reference to it, and there he emphasizes the narrative basis of cognition: "[A] good story like a workable cause map shows patterns . . ." (Weick, 1995a, p. 59, emphasis added). Similarly, in a 1990 article, he says that powerful stories engender "virtual texts," which function like "a stock of maps" (Weick, 1990, p. 217). Beyond that the concept has been largely abandoned.

Let us now consider how it might be employed differently in the conduct of research, taking a communicational view.

SUMMARIZING OUR PRINCIPAL ASSUMPTIONS

We have been developing a number of conclusions in previous chapters. They can be summarized in a set of premises:

1. Premise 1: What we are concerned with in a communicational analysis is to explain how people constitute themselves as a society which, conceptualized as an organization, implies that people are themselves objects to be transformed. Society-as-organization is a constrained field of action, in which some agencies are subordinated to others (coordinated, to employ a well-known euphemism, or controlled, to use another).

2. Premise 2: All action is local, situated, circumstanced, micro, never per se macro. Communication is grounded in interaction and, whether it occurs among humans or primates, it is constrained by the protocols of interaction that we have called conversation form. Interaction necessitates a "systematics" (Sacks, Schegloff, & Jefferson, 1974). Conversation is "the primordial scene of social life"—the invariable site of the emergence of organization.

Human communication differs from that of all other species in that its medium of exchange is, above all, language. We adopt the convention of treating all strings of language, whether spoken or written, as manifestations of text. Human interaction must thus conform to a second type of

---

[5]Cheney and Tompkins (1988) remark on the silence of positivist social science generally on the question of power.

constraint (absent in primate communication), that of text form. All forms of organization that transcend the local suppose a mediation effected by language. Metalocal organizational phenomena, such as universities, can only be understood by taking into account text as well as conversation form. Text then may be thought of as a surface of emergence allowing for the agencies of organization (in the large) to be made present even when they are physically absent (in the small), indeed, even when they are no more than conventionally legitimated abstractions of language.

3. Premise 3 (which follows from Premise 2): Only people really act intentionally; organizations do not (that is a fiction). If, however, we are to understand a concept such as *university* (because, although real in its way, it is never a locally situated and figurally identifiable actor or object), we cannot assume that *agency* and *actor* are mutually defining (as Giddens did, and much of the literature still does). The self-expressing intentional action of an actor is one manifestation of agency (uniquely so when the agency is one's own self), but not the only one. The agency expressed by an actor is not always his or her own. He or she may be acting for some absent principal, not necessarily an individual person—it could be corporate. Furthermore, as Latour argues (chap. 5), agency may be inscribed in material artifacts who then act, in the sense of communicating agency, although not in the same way individuals do. In both cases, organizational analysis means look-ing through the actor who (or which) is experientially present—human or material, professor or campus—to the absent agency it expresses (oth-erwise, we will never get to the university). That the agency of an actor is problematical is an effect of language; as we saw in chapter 4, the subject-agent function is a construction of language that finds its expression in the latter's texts—given reality in the voice of a human speaker, but derived from the constructions of language which inform speech with its meaning.

4. Premise 4 (also related): Organization that transcends the local is only possible because of mediation (borrowing from Latour his interpre-tation of that term, described in chap. 5). Mediation is what makes it possible for one conversation to be present in another, in that the traces left by the first remain to mediate action in the second by reproducing agency there. "Traces" imply materialization. We have argued that language is itself a material basis of communication (the most important, although not the only one, because any object may have a symbolic role and thus convey intention).[6] Language, spoken or written, becomes the common

---

[6]Although, it should be noted, Latour claims that physical configuration of the material world has real, not just symbolic, effects in channeling and amplifying behavior: Speed bumps communicate symbolically but they also literally slow traffic down. To some extent, the same can be said for language when it is inscribed in texts (by using the plural of that word we mean to emphasize its physical materiality, as something to be stored and replicated for distribution).

property of more than one person because it is produced as a physical signal or a graphic sign (being "in common" is the basis of communication). As for materials of all kinds, we therefore need to take account of the properties of the medium. This we have tried to do (particularly in chap. 4).

One of those properties is names. The macroacting university can be present in a local micro conversation because it can be named there. A second property of language is that names may be fitted into propositional constructions, so that the university may not only be named in a local conversation, it may express its intention there in the modal indices of the spoken or written sentence (assuming that it has found a voice to enunciate the intention that the sentence communicates). After that has occurred, and assuming that the expression of intention has been "up-taken" (to use Austin's term), then a relationship has been established that is simultaneously local and nonlocal (not to mention extending over time as well). You can now, for example, work for the University (or any other organization).

5. Premise 5: When people travel outside their own familiar locality, which they know like the back of their hand, they need—use and make—maps. Through the mediating capacity of language to join conversations into networks of larger associations than the strictly local, the equivalent of a territory is created. Maps and territories are mutually defining. The map does not only record the salient features of a territory but also creates a topography that is recognizable as a socially, as well as geographically, configured space. By analogy, the multiply laminated universe of human conversation is an incoherent wilderness until it has been territorialized by the constitution of an organizational map where the parts have been given a name. The territory to be mapped, however, is not land, but conversation, so that its features are agentively charged episodes, not a landscape of fields, forests, towns, and lakes; it must be temporally, as well as spatially, parametrized for the mapness to be discernible. The territory to be settled and improved is not land, but action. Without a map there can be no boundary to the territory, no configuration of it, no governance, no organization.

6. Premise 6: The organizational map is inscribed in text. It is here that the properties of the material of communication, language, become important. We claim that the essential mapmaking property of language is narrativity. Narrativity supplies generic patterns that translate into the narrative program that underlies the recounting of social events: that which lends structure to the particular and the specific by giving it a form that is semantically interpretable as having a basis in text form. Action, as Schutz pointed out, must be typified to be recognized.

When we delved deeper into the generic forms of narrative, we found that human action—that which is to be mapped—may be situated along

two dimensions: that of opposition and alliance (a contest for the possession of valued objects) and that of hierarchy (that which is concerned with
competence, its acquisition and evaluation, or sanctioning). On the dimension of opposition, the universe of actors present in the conversation
to be mapped (the organizational network) is divided into helpers and
opponents—us's, and them's.[7] On the dimension of hierarchy, actors are
principals and agents: those who manipulate and sanction, on the one
hand, and those who perform, on the other. Here, linking the constative
or epistemic plane (where the principal-agent is located) with the performative or deontic (where the agent-subject is located) supposes the
existence of a fiduciary contract: a trust relationship involving you's and
me's.[8] Only when such a trust relationship is sealed (or at least stabilized)
can agency be delegated, organized, directed, manipulated, judged, and
rewarded. The organizational map thus has both a polemical (opposi-
tional) and a moral (trust) dimension.

7. Premise 7: The principal-agent relationship, because it supposes the
subordination of one agency to another, works only because the principal
is ultimately not only some individual, but also society speaking in and
through the voice of some individual. We described this in chapter 8 as
an A-B-X relationship, where, if A is the doer and X the done, B is the
community that serves as A's interlocutor and ultimate sanction for doing,
even though its only voice—and its implied agency—is (as it must be)
expressed in the speech or writing of a human actor (who may, on occasion,
be, reflexively, the actor him- or herself, in self-critical mode).

If the map portrays not so much topography as ownership, as Wood
claims, then individual ownership of some space of the territory—turf—is
contingent a priori on there being a territory that is collectively owned.
Private ownership is institutionally tolerated ownership. In a narrative interpretation, ownership is equivalent to the attaining of subject status,
commissioned and sanctioned. In the absence of a naturalized map and
the community that it speaks to and for, competition to possess the object
of value always risks degenerating into open warfare and the dissolution,
or at least fragmenting, of the polity.

8. Premise 8: Because of its centrality to sensemaking and the legitimacy
that the existence of a naturalized community furnishes, the making of

---

[7]As before, we signal our discomfort with the term "helper" as a translation of Greimas's
term "Adjuvant"; a better term might be "ally" or perhaps "abettor," "champion," "mediator,"
"patron," or "friend in need." What we are trying to emphasize here is that a basic narrative
function of this kind may have many surface realizations. The term "helper" has connotations that
are too narrow, but it is hard to know what better term to use, because the direct translation
"adjuvant" does not work in English in quite the way "Adjuvant" does in French.

[8]If the sender-receiver relationship is accomplished in the person of a single individual,
there is, of course, no need to talk of organization.

the organizational text is inherently a social event. A text is not even recognizable as a text in the absence of a ditransitive, diagentive transaction (a text that is not read, cited, or used, is not yet a text). The assumption of the cause map literature that maps are first produced by individuals as an act of independent cognition and then shared, is to have misunderstood the process of cognition, which is already inherently social (chap. 6). It is to invert the normal order of things. For the reasons we have just been outlining, all maps have to be legitimized—naturalized—for them to justify the subordination of the individual to the collective principle of ownership. Because they describe areas of interest—turf—the legitimization process is singularly delicate; it supposes what Maturana (discussed in chap. 8) called a "domain of explanations" or "cognitive domain" or "conversation of standard observers." It is this field of boundaried discourse that we have been calling society—not some more abstract all-encompassing entity. Society, in other words, is constituted in the same arena of talk as individual identities and the objects of their value-marked attention. It is not just at the level of turn-taking protocol, such as Sacks et al. (1974) described, that there must be due process. The map only works by exteriorizing cognition (or is it the other way around: cognition is an interiorization of the conversation?). It is in the processes of legitimization that the reality of authority emerges: who, finally, gets to write the map (who is the author)?

9. Premise 9: Although all maps, not just the organizational ones we have been talking about, are already on the way to obsolescence even as they are being drawn and thus need to be continually redone, the organizational map is singularly dynamic. Because it describes interactive events, not a noninteractive topography, its updating never stops. As technologies and product popularity change (people are hired and fired or quit) and social and economic conditions fluctuate, so, with each event, do organizational spaces expand and shrink. The text-world must be endlessly renewed (as Boden, whose work we described in chap. 1 & 7, has so well described). Ownership, linked to the necessary attainment of subjecthood as well as objecthood, is in evolution. Turf grows and erodes. The necessity of legitimation derives from the interestedness that arises from the occupation of an organizational territory, the transformation of locations into turf, and the fact of competition for limited resources that is restrained only by the transcendent interest in maintaining the integrity of the territory as a whole, in the face of external threats to it.

10. Premise 10: The organizational text or map is reflexive in a way that ordinary maps are not: Its own making is an event that must figure as an element of itself. We investigated this reflexivity in our examination of the link from discourse-world to text-world (chap. 2 & 3). The text-world is a product of the discourse-world, yet it englobes the latter by giving it meaning. The making of the text describes a world, but it also is a world, and the world it describes is itself.

Obviously, how map writing goes on will vary from one organization to another, and from one sector of enterprise to another, depending on their local culture, institutional constraints, and history. In the remainder of this chapter, we consider how these abstract principles might work in actual practice in one such context. We look at a process typical of at least one organizational environment, that of the university: an evaluation (what Greimas called a "sanction"). Our chronicle of events (which reflects our own strategy of mapping, to be sure) offers an interpretation that is illustrative and meant to be no more than illustrative.

BECOMING RECOGNIZED
ON THE ORGANIZATIONAL MAP:
A DEPARTMENTAL EVALUATION

The case we have in mind is a typical sequence of events that is reproduced in many universities in one form or another: the statutory evaluation of a department or program. Doing departmental (and other) evaluations is part of the ritualistic ongoing reconstitution of the university as an open and responsible institution—a guarantee of excellence and fairness. The evaluation we describe has nothing special to mark it from others. As we present it, everyone will play their part good-humoredly and responsibly. It is this very ordinariness that we want to emphasize. The making—enactment—of organization, we mean to show, is a part of its everyday business. Of course there are horror stories, but here we want to focus on the usual process of mapmaking, in a milieu that will seem familiar to many readers: his or her own university. We thus present a case study that is not really a case study at all, but a reconstructed-in-imagination set of events that comes as close to conforming to average practice as we can make it, based on how the sequence, as we have seen it played out over the years in more than one context, in more than one role (as student and then professor in evaluated departments, as external on-site evaluator for someone else's program, as chair of a department undergoing evaluation), typically unfolds. It is a synthesis of several experiences, resembling them all without pretending to portray accurately any single one. We are going to be telling the story of an evaluation, not presenting the results of an actual inquiry—a story (really, an overlay of stories), that is, we are not presenting a history.

The example should illustrate the premises that we have just outlined:

- subordination of agencies (reconstitution of the hierarchy);
- expression of corporate and collective agencies through the voices of individuals in local circumstances;

- text as the surface of emergence for the appearance of agency and the means by which one conversation is made present in another;
- parts of the map named (naturalized) and their intentions given expression (culturalized);
- governance made visible to participants: delegation, direction, sanctioning;
- legitimization and sanctioning involving a community of standard observers;
- rapid obsolescence;
- the attainment of subjecthood (and objecthood);
- reflexivity.

Our chronicle should likewise illustrate the principles of communication we developed in Part I of the book. We look at how each of the actors use frame knowledge to turn their perception of the departmental circumstances into a coherent image of the existing situation: what they choose to name, what they highlight, what they perceive to be the relations between actors and their objects, and how wide they draw the horizon of their description. This is the epistemic dimension of communication. In their interpretations, each of the actors modalize the state of the department as they see it. Following the analysis of Greimas, we assume that a variety of images will emerge, depending on the ways they draw the line between reality and appearance: What some present as evident reality, others will perceive to be no more than appearance.

Similarly, we are sensitive to the deontic dimension: how, as the ritualized sequence of steps of the evaluation proceeds, the different actors negotiate the ditransitive interpretations of their respective interventions in order to come to an understanding of their underlying head-complement statuses within the stabilized hierarchy of a modern university.

In addition, the case study of evaluation should highlight one aspect of mapmaking that we have not yet much touched on: the role of inscription on paper, hard-copy, as opposed to verbalized, text. Although all text, including speech, presupposes materialization, some forms of materialization are more durable and portable than others. Writing things down, and circulating the resulting texts is not the same as speaking, precisely because the traces that are thus produced have more permanence, that is, have the capacity to fix a decision of opinion by giving it solidity. They can also communicate intentionality is a more diffuse way—via publication. In our society, in spite of the electronic revolution, paper continues to occupy a unique role as medium of organizational exchange. Written text serves to modulate the processes in significant ways that need to be attended to.

Our procedure is to track the process in which our imaginary department is caught from beginning to end, over a four-year period, basing our
analysis strictly on the texts that are generated, and the other formal and
informal occasions that stitch them together. We focus on a single feature:
how the territory of the department is progressively given definition and
how it comes to be successfully mapped.

The Sequence of Events

Our chronicle begins in the spring of 1990, when the department was
informed officially—by an internal memo (written text, signed by the
Provost)—that its turn had now come to be submitted to an objective,
neutral evaluation of its performance, as every program in the university
is periodically required to be by the statutes of the institution. It is a modest
communication department: 12 full-time professors in all, not counting
sessional lecturers. Graduate studies figure largely in its curriculum;
undergraduate, somewhat less. It is located in a large, state-supported
university in a modest-sized city, with a thriving communication industry
located in a nearby metropolis.

During the fall semester, the department produced a document that
offered, as required by established practice, a self-evaluation. When a draft
of the report had been completed, one of the regular departmental meetings was turned into a forum to discuss its content and form. With the
proposals of the faculty members incorporated into the document, the
report was ready. In December, it was submitted to the Provost's office, as
the office responsible for the organization of the process (with copies to
the appropriate Faculties of Arts and Sciences and Graduate Studies).[9]

Early in 1991, the Provost named the members of an "Internal Review
Committee" to whom responsibility for the evaluation was delegated. Their
task was not to conduct the actual evaluation but to verify that it was done
according to rule. The committee was chaired by a professor from a Faculty
other than that of the department, with three other senior professors
drawn from three established departments in the same Faculty (Arts and
Sciences) who might be sympathetic to the interests of the field of communication but who had no previous personal (nor any professional) connection with it. The secretary of the committee, and its official guide and
custodian, was a senior official in the Provost's office.

After preliminary meetings to acquaint itself with its duties, the Internal
Review Committee organized a visit to the department at the beginning

---

[9]To avoid confusion, we write "faculty" (lower case) when referring to members of the
department, "Faculty" (upper case) when referring to the administrative body of which the
department forms a part. Terminology typically varies from one university to another.

of April, in which the view of the Chair as to who should be invited as external evaluators was solicited. Other members of the department and student representatives were then asked to give their opinions. Following this meeting, the Internal Review Committee chose external evaluators, and its meetings were then suspended, pending submission to it of the external examiners' report.

Two outside evaluators were approached. The first was a research-oriented professor at a very prestigious university; the other, a bit less senior, the chair of a department of communication in a smaller (and less prestigious) university, better known for its undergraduate programs and emphasis on the development of professional skills than for research. Both agreed to act.

On June 1, the sitting chair resigned, after 6 years of service, and was replaced by a new chair.

During the summer, both examiners established informal contact with the new chair by telephone (and in one case as the result of an informal chat at an academic conference they both happened to be attending). In September, just after the beginning of the new school year, the two members of the External Examining Committee arrived for an intensive 2-day site visit. They interviewed the chair at length, probing her personal perception of the situation and her view of the most urgent needs of the department (in informal as well as formal discussions, incidentally). They met the assembled members of the department, held interviews with students currently enrolled, and met with a sample of representative alumni. They spoke with office staff and visited the technical facilities of the department. They dined with the Chair, off the record. And then, they went away.

Six weeks later, they submitted their reports, individually. The University would have preferred a single, joint report, but factors of distance and disparity of perspective made that practically impossible. One of the reports was critical of the department (the one coming from the prestigious university); the other was not—or at least less so.

Over the following month or so, the chair, aided by members of the department, produced an extensive, carefully documented (with statistics) response to issues raised by the External Examiners, including an attempted synthesis of the two reports, which were quite contradictory on some key points. This was then submitted to the Internal Review Committee with copies to the two concerned Faculties (Arts and Sciences, Graduate Studies).

In March 1992, the Internal Review Committee met to consider and, eventually, adopt a draft report with recommendations jointly composed by its chair and its secretary. When it had been accepted, it was submitted to the Provost, with copies to the Department, to the Faculty of Arts and Sciences, and to the Faculty of Graduate Studies. The departmental chair was invited to respond briefly to the Review Committee's report (which included the examiners' reports as appendices), which she did shortly afterwards, in generally favorable terms, following a rather spirited faculty meeting discussion. She accordingly signaled a number of points where the department felt nuances of interpretation needed correcting. At its April session, the University Senate formally took cognizance of the Internal Review Committee's report (but took no other action), along with those of several other program evaluations then also in progress.

In June 1992, the members of the department held a study session to consider implications flowing from the report and to what extent its recommendations were realistic.

In January 1993, after inter-Faculty discussion, although without further consultation of the department, the Faculties of Arts and Sciences and Graduate Studies jointly issued what was termed an "Action Plan" in which they reviewed the results of the exercise until that point and proposed the lines of departmental response they saw being necessitated by it, particularly in rethinking its priorities of development. At the end of February, officers of the two Faculties, including both deans and associate deans, met with faculty members of the department to present the conclusions of the Action Plan orally and take note of the departmental reaction. The department was now invited to propose what actions it intended to take to follow-up on the Action Plan.

In June 1993, another departmental day-long study session was devoted to discussion of the results of the evaluation and its recommendations.

In September, the Dean of Arts and Sciences announced his resignation with the result that the autumn session was preoccupied with an election to replace him and the assistant deans who had served under him. In the absence of a Faculty interlocutor, departmental action on the follow-up to the Action Plan was suspended. In January 1994, a new dean was named and took office.

In March 1994, the Department submitted a carefully documented and rather elaborate response to the Action Plan, with specific proposals for follow-up on the actions recommended by the Faculties. In April, the new dean agreed to include a visit to the monthly faculty meeting to discuss the situation as it then stood (the latter having by now been transformed considerably in numerous respects, both at the level of the department, through new hirings, and the university, as the result of a state election followed by a change of government and a budgetary cut in allocations to higher education). In June 1994, the mandate of the departmental chair came to an end, and a new chair was named.

The evaluation was now, for all practical purposes, finished. The result was felt to be positive by all the parties involved. Although the process had occupied the best part of 4 years, this duration, in our experience, is not unusual; in a university, the pace of events is sometimes deliberate!

Initial Observations on the Process

Let us step back momentarily to see how we can make sense, in a preliminary way, of the organizational meaning of this sequence. Two features stand out immediately. There is first the duration of the evaluation process: more than 4 years in all. Given that there are more than 25 programs in the Arts and Sciences Faculty (and it is only one of several Faculties), all periodically evaluated, the implication is that this activity is a very important part of university life. This conclusion is rendered even more salient by another phenomenon, namely, that the final Action Plan rarely leads to much in the way of concrete results, and the final reports tend to gather dust. It would seem then that it is the process itself, and not its product, that is important.

A second feature of the evaluation process is the number of people who are, in one way or another, involved: students, professors, chair, office staff, deans and vice-deans, members of other departments and Faculties, the University Senate, the Provost's office, and colleagues from other universities. Why such a diversity of participants? We suggest that there is here illustrated the working through in practice of Wood's principle of naturalization of the organizational map. What is obvious from the most casual analysis of the process is the elaborate precautions to prevent any attribution of personal bias. The Internal Review Committee, whose evaluation is final, is made up of apparently objective outsiders to the department; the External Examining Committee is composed of supposedly unbiased outside experts; the Provost is merely the organizer of the sequence; the report must be formally passed by the Senate; two Faculties are collaboratively involved in preparing the Action Plan, each with its own quite distinct agenda; and the Department has numerous occasions to make its position known.

The naturalization that is occurring has, in turn, two facets: the diversity of agencies that enter into the making of the assessment (to guarantee its authenticity), which in turn speaks to the range of voices that subsequently may be said to have sanctioned the process (guaranteed its legitimacy). These people have not only participated in making the organizational map where the department is now relocated; they now also know features of the map they did not know before. Mapping did not just describe the territory (although that was the apparent function); it created (or at least extended) the territory.

Beyond these general comments, there is already evidence of the communicational principles we have been developing in this book. There is first the issue of the hierarchy of agencies. Three levels of institutionally defined actant or organizational agency can be identified: the Provost's office, the Faculties, and the Department. They are interlinked by what we termed in chapter 3 ditransitive exchanges. The object of value (the embedded proposition of the ditransitive) that supplies the focus of all the exchanges is a performance: that of the department, as a center of research and teaching. At issue is its competence in performing its mandated role in the university (i.e., the object of the embedding proposition of the ditransitive). Both the Provost and the Faculties assume both an epistemic and a deontic primacy of authority in their communications: the Provost through its delegated agencies of internal and external examiners, the faculties through its Action Plan. There is a hierarchy at work. The Provost's judgment takes precedence over the Faculties', and the Faculties' over the department's. All three of the organizational objects we identified in chapter 3 can be found: instructions and requests that serve to bring about a certain state of affairs (initiating the process, inviting the examiners, calling meetings, and so on), opinions and interpretations that serve to construct a collective image of the factual state of the world (inscribed in several texts), and declarations (the Provost's striking of committees and naming of examiners, the Senate's formal receiving of the report of the Internal Review Committee, the examiners' and the Faculties' pronouncing of a judgment on the department, and the department's own announcement of its intention).

We are, in other words, observing the emergence of an organization—a university—in the ongoing conversational exchanges of the participants. Now let us consider a bit more closely how the text that constitutes the Department in its recognized organizational materialization (its location on the map of the university) was gradually produced, in a series of laminations involving different interpreters and interpretive instances (administrative bodies). We look at how the objects and subjects of the organization are constituted as recognizable points on the map.

As you read, we invite you to put yourself in the place of the different actors (as Wood pointed out, there are always interests involved); for example, look at the department's own version of itself as an actor through the eyes of (a) the internal and (b) the external evaluators (recalling the latter's different perspectives). Then, think of how it must appear to the Provost and to each of the Deans, again recalling that each of these bodies is a budget center, an academic administration, and an arena for the playing out of academic politics. Remember that in each case the issue is how to place the program and the department on your map as university professor or dean or provost or communication expert (which means finding a place on it for a program you are looking at attentively, possibly for the first time). Obviously, these already existing maps will start from different premises. In the case of the internal reviewers, the department has to be situated with respect to other disciplines in the same university. Does it occupy a clearly delineated turf? What are its natural affinities? Is it scientific, humanistic, or technical? If it is a social science, what are its links with sociology, psychology, anthropology, and so forth? How does it stack up in size, viability, and prestige with other programs? What are its prospects for growth? And so on.

For the external evaluators, the global map on which they are locating this program is different. The department now has to be situated with respect to other universities, in the United States, in Europe, and, ultimately, in the world. Now different criteria come into play. What branch or branches of the discipline is it developing? How does it compare in teaching performance with other programs you know about? How does it compare in research and publication? What is its reputation like? Is it more research-oriented or is it centered on professional training?

Deans and Provosts think about competition among different programs for scarce resources. They think about such things as prestige, or student enrollment, or even personal ambition.

Be as unsympathetic as you like. That is part of the rules of the game.

The Department's Story: The Department as Mapped by Itself

Stories, to cite Bruner citing Labov, begin with a precipitating event. According to page 1 of the departmental self-evaluation, the precipitating event in the world of communication is "the proliferation of new technologies: satellite, cable, fiber optic, microelectronics, laser disks, cd-roms, etc." This explosion of technological innovations is said to be a major "factor of change in contemporary society." Because communication is involved in every walk of life and is integral to the conduct of every profession and because it is the wellspring from which we draw our shared images of the world and how we sustain our social structures, the transformation of communication technologies is modifying our society, our organizations, and our way of living. Such a transformation thus presents a challenge that every society must address. More to the point, it imposes the agenda of a Department of Communication. Because it is precisely by and in the processes of communication that such technologies take on an existence and how they exercise an influence on society, its structures, and its images of the world, the task of the communication researcher is to develop models of change that take account of the human, as well as the technological, component.

Sound good? You could have written it yourself? Let us go on then.

Many communication departments concentrate on professional training in communication skills (a veiled reference to a rival program); this department has chosen to place at the center of its priorities the scientific study of communication and technology (the University administration is very research oriented). Recognizing the broadly interdisciplinary interest in this subject area (the Faculty favors interdisciplinarity), it has drawn freely on the models and methods of other disciplines: psychology, history, linguistics, computer science, sociology, economics, law, and so forth, but it also has remained sensitive to the need to develop its own theories and approaches, a task rendered all that much more necessary and difficult by the fact that communication science is a relatively recent addition to the family of social sciences.

The report then includes 3 pages that describe in summary the principal orientations that derive from this preoccupation, namely, specializations in mass media technologies and in organizational communication. It then develops some background material on the founding and historical evolution of the program. It was, it says, the University that accepted the principle of establishing a program in communication science, a decision subsequently ratified by the Board of Regents (thus implicitly having received State approval). Each of its programs, undergraduate and graduate, was assessed and approved separately by decisional bodies within the University and was then formally adopted by the Senate.

[Precedent is important in organizations; maps do not start from zero.]

In the 15-year interval since its foundation, student enrollment has grown steadily year by year, and applications for admission are now running ahead of the department's capacity to meet them. At the undergraduate level, the department has attempted to reconcile two objectives: a measure of training to prepare students for a professional career as communication specialists working for enterprise, and an adequate scientific formation to enable students to go on to do graduate work. In addition, courses in communication have proved very popular with students from other disciplinary majors, so that course enrollment is uniformly high (thus imposing, it is hinted, a strain on the Department's limited resources of personnel and equipment). Graduation of communication majors has nevertheless been sustained at a satisfactory level. Graduate programs, both Master's and Doctorate, are research oriented, and in fact the Department regards its own strength as primarily in its development of research. Applications for the programs are at a satisfactory level, and the number of those completing the Master's degree has continued to be uniformly high. Because the doctoral program was introduced recently, there are no equivalent figures on the proportion of those graduating, but the prospect for future graduates appears positive. One notable fact in this respect is the proportion of foreign students that are apparently being attracted to the doctoral program, which speaks to the excellence of the preparation it offers for a career in teaching and research.

Research activities are described as "in an expansionary period." As measured by the number of grants obtained, the increase in research activity in recent years is actually quite dramatic, although it is noted in passing that much of the growth was due to the success of a single professor's fund-raising ability (the retiring chair). Overall, it is claimed, the result has been that graduate students are integrated smoothly into ongoing research programs, are adequately funded, and are offered assistantships in ideal working environments. Much of this research is in cutting edge fields of technology and is thus attracting considerable interest from the communication industry who, it now appears, is prepared to support projects financially (a consideration of some importance to University administration).

There is a section on characteristics of the faculty: relatively young compared to others in the Faculty and with very diverse backgrounds. Their research interests also reflect a very wide spectrum of concerns, from technology (seen from a number of perspectives) to mass media to organizational processes to traditional societies and their ecology. A brief mention of the level of publications in national and international journals follows, along with a section on attendance at conferences and seminars. The Department, it is noted, has itself been involved in organizing conferences with international participation.

Other sections follow: on sessional lecturers and their role (an important and much appreciated contribution), office staff (laboring under a heavy work load occasioned by the endless processing of paper that the University administration requires), budget (adequate), physical space (crowded), and equipment (seriously underfunded, even dangerously obsolete). The report then offers a comparison between its own situation and other programs with whom it is to some degree at least in competition, strongly emphasizing its own devotion to research as compared with the others' focus on practical training, and argues for the necessity of remaining competitive with them by increasing the resources of the Department. The vitality of the field as a whole, it claimed, is hardly in doubt, because communication is a growing area, both politically and economically; the issue is thus to remain in the running. A brief section then follows describing the national scene of communication studies, and how this program fits into it (modest in size, but realistic in its objectives).

Finally, the report includes a section on student life, which is described as lively, with enthusiastic participation in student newspapers, daily get-togethers over lunch in their quarters furnished by the department, as well as access to well-equipped working facilities.

The report ends on a positive note, summarizing the department's successes in the development of both teaching and research, its attractiveness to students, and its active role in the outside communication community. It notes that revisions of the department's programs have been subjected recently to external review, with positive results. It concludes by a brief mention of three possible issues: an overextended teaching staff (especially given recent successes in obtaining research grants which, although gratifying, adds to the work load), inadequate space to accommodate the growing research activity, and the difficulty of keeping up with increasingly complicated administrative procedures.

The remainder of the document is taken up with appendices (curricula, course descriptions, curricula vitae, etc.). All pretty much what you would expect.

The Departmental Modalization of Its Situation

Let us briefly review how the Department's story goes. Historically, it says, the University (first actant) accorded a mandate to the Department (second actant), entitling it to enter into competition with other departments offering communication programs (the notion of competition reoccurs at several points in the document). We could say that two organizational agencies had thus been (mutually) constituted, and a contract established between them. The nature of the relationship is ditransitive: The *competence* necessary to the receiver's (the Department's) performance of its task (budget, space, etc.) is conditional on the according of it by a sender (the University). The University is enabled to express its intention by the intervention of a number of macroactors: Provost, Faculties, committees, program evaluators, who have all been part of the establishment of the contract at one time or the other. The performance itself is justified epistemically in the document by the existence of a (vaguely described but plausible) threat to society, namely, technological innovation. The inference here is that the Department's performance is part of an assumed larger role (mandate) of the University in its relationship with society as a whole (development of knowledge). The Department-subject has, it says in its own defense, successfully carried out its mandate, with the aid of some helpers (other departments and programs with whom it has organized joint activities or from whom it has borrowed theories and methods), research granting agencies, sessional lecturers, and its student body. It has thus, through its performance, demonstrated its competence and merits, it claims, an extension of its mandate.

Notice one interesting feature of the report. At no point (other than in its description of student activities) does it offer any indication that there are organizational forces at work in the department or a life involving intrafaculty relationships, nor does it offer any evidence of a history of departmental self-organizing processes. Suppose this had been a department notoriously riven by internal divisions and personality conflicts (it happens); how would you know? The answer is, you would not (unless you already did), because the format of the evaluation constrains the departmental voice to speaking, not as a conversation or network, but as an actor in the larger (laminated) conversation of the university as a whole (the point we were making in chap. 7).

The External Evaluation: The Department as Mapped by Others

Now let us hear from the external examiners. First, the practice-oriented visiting expert. Let us call him A.

A begins his report by expressing some reticence at passing judgment on respected colleagues. He then reviews in a couple of pages what he knows of the founding of the program and the emphases of its various components. His analysis settles on the undergraduate program, and he remarks on what he perceives to be an anomaly there. On the one hand, the department proudly flags its adherence to the principle of favoring the development of scientific research; on the other hand, it also claims to be preparing its students to be ready for the job market. Although politely phrased, the evaluator now says in effect "Make up your mind!" If they are to step out into a competition for scarce jobs, new graduates will need a preparation at least as sound as that offered by other universities, and this does not mean primarily knowledge of the "theory and methodology of scientific research." He admits to having been particularly impressed by the encounter with alumni of the program who, although manifesting their loyalty to and affection for the department and its faculty, nevertheless would prefer to see a more hands-on training, including at the master's level, better adapted, in their opinion, to a changing environment. The department, he observes, is poorly equipped in facilities and equipment for the teaching of media skills. The situation, he goes on, is made even more problematical by the reliance on sessional lecturers for all of the practical courses, and even some of the more theoretical ones. None of the faculty have been recruited out of a previous career in practice, with the result that they have few personal links with people in the industry—a situation that strikes him as unhealthy, because communication, he argues, is inevitably an applied field that needs to keep abreast of media developments. His judgment: a program that is attempting more than its modest means allow it to accomplish and a faculty that, however excellent its caliber individually, is too small, is not sufficiently practice-oriented, and is working with facilities that do not meet the minimum acceptable standard for a state-of-the-art education in media skills.

On the topic of the scientific achievements of the faculty, he is impressed by the more than adequate funding, by the quite elaborate research facilities, and by the regularity of publication of departmental researchers. His main reserve is that more could be accomplished in publicizing these accomplishments. At the level of administration, he finds a competent staff, a capable chair, and a well-run program, but also some evidence of incipient administrative overload.

On the whole, the report is upbeat. His main recommendations are an increase in the size of the faculty, a more realistic policy in training graduates to enter the job market, better technical facilities, and a higher profile of the departmental image, both in the community and academically.

Now let us consider B's report (B is the research-oriented evaluator).

B also begins by evoking very briefly the history of the department, but he does so in a way that sows a doubt. If the Department has grown as slowly over the years as it has ("deliberate" is his word for the pace of development), is this a sign of a less-than-enthusiastic commitment on the part of the university administation to the program? It is a question that he leaves open for the moment, but we soon discover its motivation. His first impression of the department, he says, was positive: established programs at every level, a decent amount of research activity, a reasonably satisfied student body, in short, a "reasonably sound department"(notice the language: "decent," "reasonably satisfied," "reasonably sound"). It turned out to be, he says, "a program better than I had expected, nothing to be ashamed of," on a par with the bulk, if not the elite, of such programs, taken across the university spectrum. However, he says (and it explains his earlier interrogation of the deliberateness of growth of the department), "on closer examination and analysis, some noticeable trouble spots appeared."

In a nutshell, what he found was "a substantially large and varied program with a relatively small, compact faculty." The gap ("blatant imbalance," in his words) was being filled by an overly great reliance on part-time teachers and sessional lecturers. His report now turns into a sort of "Is this any way to run a railroad?" scold. Is this situation, he asks, being encouraged by the university administration for economic reasons, that is, more students being taught by less-well-paid instructors? If so, the administration "should be ashamed of itself" for masquerading as an institution "in search of excellence" and then doing university training on the cheap (on the grounds, perhaps, that it is "only communication, after all"?). Or, is it the departmental faculty itself that is to blame, because its members are reluctant to "get their hands dirty" or to be dragged away from their ivory tower of pure research? Or, is it merely a kind of implicit collusion involving both administration and faculty, producing inexpensive instruction for academic goodies? Or, more plausibly, is it that the situation just happened through drift and inattention, "because nobody was diligently watching the shop"? Whatever the case, "it is time," the evaluator intones, "to cut out the nonsense," and "to find a proper solution."

It is not surprising, given the background of this evaluator, that B now turns his attention to the ambitions of the department to become known as centered on research. As he does, he offers a peek into the internal dynamics of the department (which both its own self-evaluation and A in his report had scrupulously avoided). B declares that he had been agreeably surprised (because he had not expected it) by the visible signs of active research underway in the department. It is, however, he notes, "unevenly distributed" among faculty, and this leads him into some more general observations on the noticeable imbalance in the contribution individuals are making to the department, especially in the research area. A handful of people are active, soliciting grants, attending conferences, and publishing, but others are lagging behind. This is not, he concedes, an "uncommon" pattern, but in the present context it constitutes an additional burden on an already overloaded faculty. Overall, then, the evaluation of the research side is positive, although the rate of publication does not seem to match well, he thinks, with the level of activity, and the journals it seeks an outlet are not among the most prestigious.

There is a passing reference to the obsolescence of the media equipment and facilities. The report then finishes on an exercise in situating the department on a scale of excellence, from the elite universities to the junior colleges: "how it stands up against other institutions of its kind." His conclusion: it is typical of "middle-level" universities, if smaller than many of them. The department turns out to rate the equivalent of a B+, in his estimation: as he had said, "a program better than I had expected to find."

What Is Reality, What Appearance?

As Greimas would have predicted, the sanctioning exercise has turned into a kind of debate over what is reality, what merely appearance. Specifically, what the department presented as reality has been turned into a misleading impression (especially by B).

The Reaction of the Department to Its External Evaluation

The chair of the department now confronts the challenge of replying to reports that, although they are characterized by mixed messages, nevertheless invite at least damage control, so negative are some of the observations contained in them. Both have castigated the undergraduate program, and at least one has given what might be described as lukewarm praise of the research program, the department's pride and joy. Both have reservations as to the external image of the department, in the eyes of its external reference groups (although for different reasons, and with different reference groups in mind). Comments of this kind are enough to sow the seeds of doubt in the minds of the internal judges. Because it was she who (when consulted by the outgoing chair) selected the evaluators, and she who spent the most time with them during their site visit (and before), we might reasonably presume that the chair will not be taken entirely by surprise by what she reads. Her task now becomes to produce an interpretation (hers) of an interpretation (really two of them, those of the external examiners) of yet another interpretation (the original self-evaluation of the department, supplemented by oral testimony at the time of the site visit). The examiners told a story of confusion of objectives (A) and dereliction of duty and mediocrity (B); she is going to have to generate a metastory to top theirs.

She begins by emphasizing the initial openness of the department to an evaluation, because it came at a strategic moment of departmental consolidation following a fairly lengthy period of program expansion. The Department had anticipated, she wrote, constructive advice on its future development from wise, experienced academics with impeccable credentials. The actual reports had turned out to be a letdown because, even though they raised a number of important issues, they offered little positive advice. Certainly, the site visit had been well organized and thorough, and so the results were especially disappointing. In retrospect, it seemed that the problem arose from the disparity of perspectives of the two individuals, which prevented them from engaging in a constructive dialogue between themselves. This is, of course, always a risk, in that communication, like law or medicine or psychology, is a crossroads where professional practice and scientific research intersect. As it happened, the gulf in their views of the field made it impossible for them to come to a common reading. Given the failure of the evaluators to produce a single synthesis of their observations, the chair proposed to offer her own integration of the reports.

The chair then summarized their joint observations under two headings: strengths and weaknesses of the department. Under "strengths" she listed these:

- An established program, "nothing to be ashamed of";
- A competent, well-trained faculty;
- A satisfied student body;
- An abundance of research activity, well funded;
- Regular publication of research results;
- A smoothly operating administration;
- Adequate working space agreeably furnished.

On the strengths, she notes, both evaluators were in agreement. Under "weaknesses," she listed these:

- Too great a reliance on part-time sessional lecturers;
- Seriously inadequate technical facilities;
- Insufficient promotion of the department's excellence, in part because its publications tended not to be found in mainstream journals;
- Lack of contact with the communications industry;
- Uneven participation and contribution within the department;
- Mixed motives in the direction the undergraduate program was taking;
- The standing of the department.

Here, she observed, there was less unanimity.

(It is worthwhile to take just a moment to reflect on the discursive strategy adopted by the chair. By supplying the missing synthesis of the external examiners' reports, she has set up her response to their interpretations as a dialogue where she gets to play both parts: theirs and her own. As she expands on their observations, by either reinforcing or correcting them, she is in fact rewriting the whole evaluation, effectively putting her own spin on it. Unless she accomplishes this turnaround, the evaluation may be perceived to be decidedly negative.)

The expansion on the theme of strengths is brief. Using graphs she has developed based on university-supplied data, she sketches the rapid growth of the program during 5 years in grants and contracts, in number of students enrolled, and in the size of the graduating class. What is all the more remarkable, she points out, is that this has been achieved, not, as the evaluators' reports seem to suggest, by the theoretical, on-paper 12 faculty members but, counting absences for a number of motives (which she again documents), many fewer, often no more than 7 or 8 members in any given year. So, she emphasizes, if it is a program that works, that responds to students' needs, that maintains research activity, that is indeed "nothing to be ashamed of," then this has to be seen against the background of the pool of limited resources provided to make all this happen. As we shall see, this is the theme she is going to reiterate under several headings, and it is one that was already present in the external reports, although framed differently. In fact, her task can be seen as one of reframing: Do not (for the most part) argue with the findings of the evaluators, but frame them differently, so that they take on a new significance.

Most of her attention is now directed to the weaknesses identified by the evaluators.

On the issue of overreliance on part-time teachers, she notes first the reluctance of the university to open promised positions, or even to permit hiring where the line had already been granted on paper. She then develops a detailed statistical analysis, again based on official university data, to show that the per-individual performance of members of the department has been higher than all other social science departments in the Faculty (and in some cases dramatically higher) on every institutionally recognized criterion of performance: number of students per professor, rate of growth over a 5-year period, number of students whose thesis projects require advising, and so forth. To take one sample statistic: The number of students per full-time professor is running at close to 30; the average for other social science departments is no more than 18. Obviously, this speaks to a serious imbalance (and note that it is not open to question, given the official source of the data). If this imbalance has left undergraduate studies too much in the charge of part-timers, it has to be recalled that the supervision of theses and dissertations cannot easily be delegated. Again, the figures speak: the highest rate of master's graduates of any social science program and the heaviest advising load, roughly 11 per professor if both master's and doctorate programs are counted (by far the heaviest in the Faculty). So, she concludes, the external examiners were absolutely right in their conclusion, but the explanation is hardly that professors have been reluctant to "get their hands dirty." In fact, given the multiplicity of their tasks—putting together programs, teaching, soliciting research funds, publishing—the members of the faculty had surely earned, she expostulates, bouquets, not brickbats. The finding of the examiners was thus right, but their analysis was diagnostically superficial. The solution is surely obvious: give the department the human resources it minimally needs to meet its responsibilities (and the part-time problem would solve itself).

She then turns to the issue of equipment and facilities. Again, she is in total agreement with the evaluators, that the situation is at least as bad as they have described. Again, the problem is in the insufficiency of resources accorded to the program by the administration. She then describes a low-cost solution to the problem, one that would resolve the underdevelopment of facilities without a large capital expenditure (which she knows is unlikely to be forthcoming) while simultaneously reflecting the evolution of the priorities of teaching in the direction of interactive technologies (because the latter make little demand on space or heavy equipment). This, she points out, is how to respond to the criticism of evaluator A, because her proposed shift of emphasis is very much in line with industry developments.

Now she has to deal with the references to the image problems of the department, and again, her manner of doing so is to develop a basis of statistics and other factual data. It is on this one issue that she challenges the accuracy of the evaluators' information. To answer A, for example, she cites a whole list of collaborations where professors in the department have been actively called upon to advise and do research with institutions in both private and public spheres. She concludes that the department's critic has simply been in error (possibly because he did not understand the situation?). On the issue of publications (the point raised by B), she gives the result of an analysis which shows a steady rate of about an article and one half per professor per year, which she says is about the norm for the field. As to the smallish number in prestigious mainstream journals, in part, she says, this has to do with the specialized fields some members of the department work in, with the result that they tend to gravitate toward publications that are not usually identified as communicational.

On the issue of uneven participation of members of the department, her response is indirect. She agrees with evaluator B that the important thing is to recruit people of quality, but she presents this in the light of future hirings. To answer his attempted ranking of the department on a national scale of prestige, she allows herself (the only place she does) to make light of his analysis and to substitute her own, which she claims is more accurate (and less pretentious).

Having responded to her critics, our author now turns her attention to future prospects. She again makes reference to the statistics that show the vitality and popularity of the program (number of students, graduates, etc.). She then presents a clearer description of the principal orientations of the program than had been given in the original departmental report, situates each of the professor's activities within the larger picture, and, finally, addresses herself to recommendations (noting that neither of the external examiners had done so). She recommends a considerable increase in the full-time teaching staff (a minimum of three new lines), a renewal of the technical facilities (in line with the clarified priorities of the program), a beefing up of the practical dimension of student teaching (in response to the criticism of A and in line with the proposed emphasis on interactive communication), and greater concentration of the research teams and greater openness to inter-departmental collaboration (not a theme in the external evaluations, but a current preoccupation of the Faculty).

From Epistemic to Deontic: Changing the Basis
of the Evaluation

At one level, the chair's report is just one more reading of the situation, better documented by statistics. At another, however, it is a challenge to the university administration, and this carries us into the domain of a construction grammar: It will have to be answered. Using evaluator B's quite blunt assessment of the Faculty's failure to "mind the shop," the chair has now turned her epistemic assessment into a demand for action. We return to this transposition shortly.

How the Internal Review Committee Read the Various Texts

Now it was the turn of the Internal Review Committee to take center stage. They began (surprise! surprise!) with a summary of the history of their own role, including each of the steps each participant had taken up to the present. They regretted that the External Committee had in fact not behaved as a committee but had submitted two individual reports that reflected (and here the echo of the departmental chair's explanation is quite clear) distinctly different orientations within the discipline of communication. They then commented on the "well-documented" response of the department, which, they pointed out, had added essential information to the initial self-evaluation, and to which they then returned at several points in the remainder of their report. Their report then summarized the main lines of departmental history, ending with a number of recommendations. In their recommendations, they (a) confirmed their understanding of the developmental priorities of the department as stated in the response to the external examiners, (b) proposed that future developments strongly reinforce those chosen orientations, (c) recommended that the necessary resources (including professorial) be accorded to the department to carry out its mandate, (d) counseled the department to improve its performance in publication, (e) proposed that it undertake a revision of its courses to assure that they were concordant with departmental priorities, and (f) advised the Faculty to address the issue of inadequate technical facilities.

On reception, the department confirmed that it had taken account of the report and was in agreement with its conclusions. (The chair, in particular, must have felt she had dodged a bullet.)

Shortly afterwards, the committee confirmed its recommendations in a summary report presented to the Senate: confirmation of the mandate of the department (its orientations in teaching and research), enhanced publication, renewal of the technical facilities, and increase in the teaching staff.

At this point, the evaluation as such was complete. Clearly, the map had been revised to include a larger span for the Department in the territory of the University. Now the step remaining was to persuade the university to give substance to the committee's recommendations.

Coming Out of the Evaluation Process

Let us return to consider more carefully the transition that has now been effected from the modality of being (establishing the apparent truth of a state of affairs) to the modality of doing (communicating about actions intended to transform a state of affairs). The binding of a hierarchical relationship assumes that one partner to the exchange is the doer (the one lower on the totem pole) and that the other is the knower (it is the possession of knowledge that confers authority). How such relationships function in practice, however, is not simple, because knowledge is not easy to compartmentalize. The irony, in fact, is that the superior is seldom in a position to actually know what the subordinate knows. The authority relationship is then contestable on the grounds that management's perception of the situation is distorted, and so its assumption of authority is ill-founded. One common institutional solution to a difference of opinion on the facts (or to avoid such a difference arising) is to turn to a third objective party for arbitration (in effect, constituting an A-B-X triad, where the A-X relationship is referred to an external arbiter, B). We have been describing one such process of evaluation as it sometimes occurs in a university setting, but in other contexts there are similar patterns. Large organizations resort to audits or to hiring consultants who have sufficient prestige and autonomy that they can be said to deliver an unbiased judgment on the facts. The object of this calling on a third party is to disambiguate the hierarchical relationship by supplying the managerial side of it with an interpretation of the situation, generated from without, that it can now use as its basis of authority. It is able to call on a text, and it is the objective authorship of such a text that confers on management the mantle of authority. The map of the organization has been naturalized. As Wood pointed out, there are power relations inscribed in maps.

There is a catch, however. Consider the evaluation of external examiner B. It is true that he passed judgment on the performance of the department. But, he was also passing judgment on the university administration, chiding them for having failed in their duty to "mind the store" and insinuating that their lack of "diligence" was motivated by worse than greed: indifference. Similarly, although the chair's response can be read as a spirited defense of her department and its faculty members, it also has some of the character of what Labov and Fanshel (1977) call a *challenge*: a veiled accusation verging on a complaint—that the administration has failed in its responsibility to live up to its side of the bargain by starving the department of justified resources.

Hierarchies are not one-way, top-down systems of command, or control systems, of the kind March and Simon described in their book—not even boundedly rational ones—but two-way relationships. Governance is a contract, exacting a mutuality of commitments and responsibilities, not coordination, or control, or command applied from the top, as the literature has so often presented it. This is a point that is so important that it justifies a digression to clarify what is involved, before we conclude our evaluation tale. We need to understand what a "challenge" is (such as the chair was addressing to the Faculty) and how it can be dealt with (as we shall see the Faculty doing shortly).

The Transactive Character of Governance

Labov and Fanshel (1977), whose work we discussed briefly in chapters 3 and 5, observe that a given act of speech may vary in the force with which it is expressed. It may be softened (mitigated) or emphasized (aggravated). They cite the example of a command. The unmarked form of a command, linguistically speaking, is the imperative, for example, *Come home!* (their account, it will be recalled, is based on a therapy session where the anorexic teenage daughter is complaining about the absence of her mother, who is visiting a married sister). Use of the unmodified, or unmarked, imperative is, however, often deemed to be socially unacceptable, because it tends to be seen in most societies, in normal interactive circumstances, as rude, provocative, and calculated to provoke a conflictual episode (there are, of course, institutionally sanctioned exceptions, as for example at an army boot camp). More often, the command comes out quite differently, as a request, a suggestion, or a hint (or if there has been aggravation, as sarcasm).

In order to capture the common feature linking all of these different acts, namely, the attempt by one person to get another to do something (what we have called the deontic dimension), Labov and Fanshel (1977, p. 77) propose a category that they call a *Request for Action*. To make their idea clear, they postulate a Rule of Requests, which they define as follows (p. 78):

RULE OF REQUESTS

If A addresses to B an imperative specifying an action X at a time T, and B believes that A believes that

    1a. X should be done (for a purpose Y) *[need for the action]*

      b. B would not do X in the absence of the request *[need for the request]*

    2.   B has the *ability* to do X (with an instrument Z)

    3.   B has the *obligation* to do X or is willing to do it

    4.   A has the *right* to tell B to do X

then A is heard as making a valid request for action.

Now we can interpret the chair's response as a (mitigated) request for action on the part of the Faculty (add faculty positions, renovate the technical facilities, etc.). On her interpretation of the external evaluators' reports, it is clear that she considers her request to be valid: the *need for action* has been documented (condition 1a); the Faculty of Arts and Sciences (which controls the budget) will not act unless petitioned (condition 1b: *need for the request*); it has the *ability* to act (condition 2); it has the *obligation* to act and may even, she knows by now from informal conversations, be willing to act (condition 3); and the character of the evaluation process itself has been such as to justify the Department telling the Faculty to act (condition 4: the *right* to make the request).[10]

We should make clear again that Labov and Fanshel introduce their rule of requests in the context of their discussion of the situation of a dependent, a daughter, and her relationship with the principal source of authority in her life, her mother. They are talking about interpersonal relations in the context of a family unit. Nevertheless, we believe that the principle applies with equal force in more diffuse institutional contexts, involving organizational communication, for the reason alluded to by Callon and Latour (1981): Even macroactors have to conform to the rules of interaction. It is, in other words, a general rule of governance that those in the position of dependency have rights (and, vice versa, that the governors have responsibilities).

A request is thus to be understood not only as the skilled performance by a communicationally competent speaker of an established conventional procedure (making the request in an appropriate manner) where the actor has the appropriate institutionally defined characteristics (the chair is the authorized spokesperson for the department) but also, in the transactive logic described by Labov and Fanshel, as involving rights and obligations that are inscribed in the nature of the social relations concerned. This is what we take to be, from a communicational perspective, the definition of an organizational hierarchy, written into the practices that people subscribe to and follow, even though they are not necessarily formulated in an explicit code: a hierarchy of organizing and not of organization.[11]

The making of a request for action, Labov and Fanshel observe (1977, pp. 87–88), has a very potent effect: "In ordinary, face-to-face interaction, the only way in which a request may be refused with reasonable politeness is to give an accounting: an unaccounted refusal can lead to a break in

---

[10]Note that Labov and Fanshel's four conditions underpinning a request for action are in conformity with Greimas's view of modal objects. A request for action is thus a communication, as the latter defined it.

[11]At an even more fundamental level, we perceive the transaction to be an instance of an agent/beneficiary relationship (J. R. Taylor, 1993). By implication, the beneficiary is in the position of having to petition the agent (a "request for action"), which leaves the agent in a power position. The playing out of an organizational hierarchy thus takes the form of concrete transactions, in that such power must in turn be justified.

social relations." Even delaying or putting off a response is enough to justify a complaint, which has the effect of questioning the competence of the governing authority.

Competence, then, is a two-way street: diagentive, not just ditransitive. In the context of governance, complementary performances are required and, as we argued in our discussion of Greimas, performance always, in narrative logic, presupposes competence. Governors, as fully as the governed, must be qualified—be competent and be seen to be competent. And, their qualification can be challenged (within limits, and where the circumstances warrant).

Suppose the Faculty does not want to accede to the request; does it have an out (other than to admit its incompetence)? The answer turns out, if we take Labov and Fanshel as our guide, to be "yes." According to them there is more than one effective way to politely put off (not refuse) a request for action. One such is to counter with a request for information. This produces a hypothetical embedded sequence of action which unfolds in this way:

DEPARTMENT: *Request for action*
FACULTY: *Request for clarification (i.e., more information)*
DEPARTMENT: *Response to request for clarification*
FACULTY: *Response to request for action*

The Faculty, in other words, may put off the request for action by the Department for the moment, with a promise that, when the desired clarification has been given (a report taking the form of a project in response to the action plan, for example), action will be forthcoming.[12]

The Action Plan

The Internal Review Committee submitted its report in March; the Action Plan of the two Faculties, Arts and Science and Graduate Studies, appeared at the end of January, the following year, a full year after the chair's response to the external examiners. It nevertheless clearly takes the form of a response to the department's challenge. It begins with the habitual

---

[12]One of the reasons many administrators prefer sending memos and written reports to engaging in direct verbal confrontation is that they hope they can thus avoid some of the constraints that conversational conventions impose. Managers often hope that authority need not be negotiated, but may be merely transmitted. The result, all too often, is incomprehension, alienation, and institutionalized forms of conflict. It would be interesting, in this respect, to reconsider some of Merton's original notion of the dysfunctional consequences of bureaucratic management (Merton, 1940); it is a discussion that goes beyond our present purposes, however.

review of developments up to the present. It then centers its attention on the objectives of the undergraduate program, where, it says, its reading of the Department's strategy for developing its major seems to indicate a lack of clarity in what are its fundamental orientations. What is immediately evident is that this is a theme barely evoked by the external examiners (and then only by A), introduced by the chair in her letter, and reiterated by the Internal Committee. Now it is accorded priority. There is, of course, a simple explanation. In the interval from March to January, there have been numerous conversations and meetings between department and Faculties. New ideas have been circulating, new people have become involved, new projects have been bruited (as the Action Plan remarks, "Recently, we have been told about a new idea that the Department is considering, and we wonder how this project fits into its the overall objectives"). (One of the principles we argued for earlier in the chapter was rapid obsolescence of organizational maps. We suggest we are seeing here the operation in practice of the principle.) Given this "indeterminacy," the plan then recommends "that the Department conduct a further review of its strategy of development and examine how projects such as the aforementioned relate to it, and that it submit a full report on its investigations to the Faculty at the end of the current calendar year."

The request for action has now been met with a request for clarification. The request for action has not been refused, but effectively delayed.

We need not pursue the plan further, except to observe that the same pattern is repeated several times in the course of its analysis: recognize the importance of an issue, assure the department of Faculty's willingness to address the problem, request the department for further information or clarification. On the two main challenges enunciated by the department, the technical facilities and the need to increase the size of the faculty, it has this to say: (a) the University must make available the necessary funds to modernize the audiovisual facilities, and the Department should now, in collaboration with the Faculty, draw up a detailed plan to that end; and (b) the Faculty recognizes the urgent need to augment the teaching staff of the Department by the addition of new positions, and such an increase in resources will be studied when the Department has submitted its revised plan for the future strategy of development of its programs of teaching and research, as outlined earlier.

In point of fact, the decision had already been taken; what we are looking at in this action plan is the ongoing renegotiation of a governance relationship—a delicate balancing of commitments and challenges in the sustaining of what has sometimes been called a "moving equilibrium." In this renegotiation, the written texts play a crucial role in repeatedly fixing, but only for the moment, the state of the organization and thus providing an objective landmark whose existence provides the necessary fulcrum for the next rebalancing of the negotiated relationship.

Enactment: Stitching Together Text-World and Discourse-World

Weick's essential insight has been that doing and seeing are part and parcel of the same enactment of organization. It is we that distinguish between them in our theorizing of them; by Nature, they form an indissoluble unity. In the metaphorical language of mapping, this is equivalent to saying that (a) writing (re-writing) the map and (b) navigating the territory are merely two alternative ways of describing what is essentially one single, seamless reproduction of the organization in discourse. In our story of visiting experts, the external examiners, we emphasized their role as generators of a text(-world), but, if we had enlarged the canvas a bit to the larger interuniversity scene, we would have seen them differently, that is, as contributing to a discourse-world in which they were playing the part of "distinguished professors": an absolutely essential component in the constitution of such a universe of discourse (along with deans, departmental chairs, and students).

Let us now, in concluding our chronicle of an evaluation, take a tiny peek into the living organization, to see how text-world and discourse-world (as we called them in chap. 3, following Werth) constitute each other and, as they do, reconstruct the discursive environment in which organizational members find their social and cultural life-space. We are going to briefly listen to one of the Faculty deans speaking to the Department, giving his interpretation of the Action Plan's meaning and implications. Again, we should make clear, to avoid a false impression, that this is a synthetic reconstruction of how such an intervention might go, based on notes of actual sequences, but in no sense pretending to be an accurate transcription of any single one. We have broken it into paragraphs in order to facilitate interpretation and comment.

The Dean's Statement

1. I am not thinking about the issue of communication policy that was raised in the Action Plan—I think that has already been clarified—but I am thinking about a theme that you evoke several times in your own reports, which is the importance of linking up media and computerization in today's environment.

2. We perceived there to be a recurring preoccupation in the documents you have written, and it concerned the applied, practical aspects of communication; it is something that recurs over and over in all of the reports that we have been looking at.

3. Now, from this perspective, it seems clear to us that the department has already decided on its preferred options, and we mean to respect that choice: basic research, primarily, avoiding research that is too technical, too applied in the technical sense;

4. But at the same time it seems to us that the field of communication studies is going to be inevitably biased toward problems arising from the practical evolution of communication systems and the professional concerns that arise from them, which implies to us that, for your more academic projects, your research projects, it would be reasonable to think of a research approach that has something of the character of an intervention, an approach that would be more relevant to the evolution and the overall trends of the field of communications as a whole and that might have repercussions on teaching and course development as well as on the conduct of research.

5. I do not want to exaggerate the importance of this, of course, but even at the level of graduate studies, there was something in what you wrote that appeared to us to be a thread, a tendency that we could not ignore and with respect to which it would make sense for us to develop a dialogue with you to see exactly what we could jointly accomplish.

6. And so, the Faculty recognizes this tendency in your thinking and considers that reorienting your development priorities and the academic activities that go along with them would allow you to aim to attain a level of performance that would be more satisfying, without your falling into the trap of an oversimplified approach or artificial projects either in basic or applied research, but instead thinking of projects that would be solidly academic in their scope, based on this challenge.

7. This does not mean necessarily creating a professionally oriented master's program; it does not necessarily mean that at all. It might just involve some adaptation of the current program of courses and course content that you offer.

8. It is something to think about.

9. It would not mean trivial research; it would not mean only practical research; it would not mean strictly local research; it would not at all mean research lacking in a critical perspective.

10. At our university, there are a number of research centers and groups who are active in this kind of applied research, in research directed to these kinds of problems, of which we are all proud, and which have es-

tablished a solid reputation in their field. I am thinking of the center on transport policy, I am also thinking of the new research center we are in the process of setting up in the university centered on questions of race relations, I am thinking of research groups in the area of adult education that are very well established.

11. Inasmuch as there are already, in this context, models of doing research that we consider to be very significant and that permit practitioners, even in a scientific context, to produce both basic research as well as applied research, or at least that supports applied research, this is something then that seemed to us to be consistent with a reorientation of your own development priorities, in a way that links up media and the new information technologies. It is the kind of direction that would allow you to move ahead, in that way, on both of the priorities that you have opted for.

12. This is how we see it, and it is the basic position of the Faculty, which proposes to you that you clarify your orientations in terms of your development priorities and that you consider a reorientation of your priorities in the direction I have indicated.

13. This is not a new idea for you, it is this same theme of media and computer technologies, it is something that we find over and over in your own documents, the documents you produced in your department. Thus, we consider that there is an opportunity here to do, an opportunity to be grasped rather, and that it is up to us to arrive at a concrete proposition as to how you would like to proceed.

14. We are fully ready to discuss with you the different hypotheses this might entail.

15. We consider that this project is not yet ripe, that the project will still need to be developed, and we are fully ready to discuss with you the different forms it might take, what program instruments might be most relevant to the attainment of these objectives, and how they might be integrated into your other activities.

16. And, so, we could begin to look at what are the resources, the human resources you might need, what resources in the way of equipment, computing, audiovisual supports might be required.

17. It is because of this that we would hope that in the relatively near future you might be able to see if there was a project there to be developed, a path to be taken.

18. And so, in a way we are just sending the ball back to your court, because it has to do with things that grow out of your preoccupations, so that what we are basically doing here is to ask you if there is not something that you want to do, concretely, that we would be ready, for our part, to help you develop.

We have no intention of entering into a detailed analysis of this statement. We introduce it to illustrate how text-worlds—a constative dimension of communication—can be stitched together with discourse-worlds—a performative dimension—to form a seamless web of discourse.

The Constative or Epistemic Interpretation From the Dean

The first point to note is that the statement is all of a piece. There is one theme (the evaluation of the department), the addresser-addressee situation is constant throughout (Dean to members of the department), there are numerous grammatical indications that the parts of the statement are meant to be interconnected: "that has been clarified" (referring back), "a second preoccupation" (so there must have been a first), "from this point of view" ("this" refers back), "and so" (a logical connective that joins two statements), "but at the same time" (a sentential connective again), and so on. Although spoken, it thus has the properties of a text.

Second, it is a text that corresponds to a genre, that of argument: It makes a case for a position. It is thus a text of a particular kind, one that draws on many well-established rhetorical principles (Walton, 1996): argument from example, argument from commitment, argument from analogy, and argument from precedent. It is built around a central chain of reasoning (Fisher, 1988) that, as paraphrased, has this general enthymemic form (Fig. 9.1):

Most of the statement is directed to fleshing out the premises and expanding on the conclusion. The statement being made here, then, is not a simple assertion of fact (although assertions of fact are made in the course of the argument) but a structure of discourse that conforms to the contours, in a general way, of a discursive logic. Underlying the superficial

---

<u>Major premise</u>: *There are fields of study that are logically applied in their research/teaching, at least in part*

<u>Minor premise</u>: *Communication is such a field*

<u>Conclusion</u>: *Communication should be applied in its research/teaching, at least in part*

FIG. 9.1. The core of the Dean's argument.

structure of argumentation is a coherent semantic base, which is not so much a matter of the locutions it contains, per se, as of their unspoken presuppositions, or what Werth (discussed in chap. 3) calls a "common ground."

Labov and Fanshel (1977) see all speech as being embedded in what they call "fields of discourse." There is, Labov and Fanshel argue, a set of perceptions and a style of address that characterize the different kinds of situations in which actors commonly find themselves. The Dean's statement is a case in point: It has all the earmarks of academic talk in a context where considered politeness (and thus many marks of mitigation, such as "it seems," "it would be reasonable," etc.) is taken to be required. Even when other related fields of discourse are not ostensively present in a situation with its own presumptive discourse base, they are still present as external points of reference (cf. Goffman, 1981). Any act of speech thus has more than one point of reference and more than one level of meaning. Figure 9.2 indicates what we take to be some of the fields of discourse that are present in the Dean's statement (including that in which the interaction is unfolding).

Each of these fields is characterized by certain underlying assumptions, of which the following appear to us to be central (we are summarizing from the text):[13]

- Communication-as-practice: is applied, practical, somewhat technical, professional, in evolution (links between multimedia and computers/information technology);
- Research: includes policy research, may be basic or applied, if applied may be too technical or too practice-oriented, may be too locally based and lack critical perspective, may, however, be properly interventionist if applied to certain kinds of problem (there is a form of research that permits both practice-oriented and basic research);
- Field of study: biased toward problems related to the practical evolution of communications at the professional level and a research approach having the character of an intervention appropriate to the communications field;
- Programs of teaching: may be professionally oriented, must be integrated;
- Department: has preoccupations; writes reports related to projects and activities; chooses and clarifies options, orientations and priorities;

---

[13]Note that each level of embedding is associated with a subject/object relationship: researchers take communication as their object, a field of studies has research as its object, and so on.

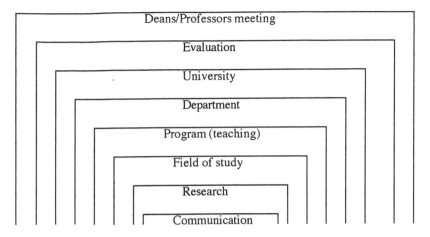

FIG. 9.2. Several fields of discourse implied by the Dean's statement.

attains objectives; orients development; creates and adapts programs; develops projects, concrete instruments, and propositions; links programs to priorities; integrates programs into its diverse activities; grasps opportunities; has resources, both human and physical; and collaborates with the Faculty;

- University: has research centers and groups that are interventionist in spirit;
- Evaluation: asks questions resulting in identification and clarification; writes and produces reports that have themes, threads, and tendencies and that are seen, looked at, and not ignored;
- Deans/Professors meeting: am (not) thinking about (of), it is clear/seems to us/is reasonable/would be wise/implies/does not (could) mean, we are proud/consider/are ready/would hope/ask/ send back the ball.

Again, we wish to make no special claim to have uncovered the hidden semantic structure of the Dean's text-world. We have simply tried to group some of the words used to illustrate that there is a structure of frame knowledge. What is notable is that, in this particular fragment of discourse, there is no outside reference to anything other than another discourse situation. Nothing that is said lends itself to a simplistic true/false analysis; if things are true, they are communicationally so, not objectively, in the hard science sense. We are thus confronted with a veritable palimpsest of embedded speech situations: communication (as media) is a discursive practice in and of itself, research is a discursive practice that studies communication, teaching is a discursive practice that passes on the knowledge accumulated in research, departments are discursive realms that organize teaching and research, university administration is another discourse situation that takes as its objects departments, and evaluation is still another discursive universe whose object is all of the above. The hierarchical organization of the levels of discourse that appears to underlie and support the Dean's statement seems to indicate that this is (at least for the Dean) what academia is—a pyramid of discourses.

It is this feature of the organization that emerges in communication that we have referred to in chapter 3 as imbrication (tiling): a stabilized overlay of head-complement relations that constitutes the map of the organization, its essential structure, which is found in the conversational dynamics of its members.

If there is a hierarchy here, it is, in Hofstadter's (1979) terms, a "tangled hierarchy" (or "strange loop"), that is, one where systems turn back on themselves: universities study media; media report on universities—a nice reversal of subject-object relationship, depending on the context.

The Performative or Deontic Implication of the Dean's Intervention

There are, in the whole statement, only two instances that conform strictly to Austin's (1962) characterization of a performative as having a semiofficial character or Searle's (1989) view of a declarative as self-referential and executive. In both cases, the sentence begins "The Faculty . . ." ("The Faculty recognizes that tendency and considers that the realignment of your development orientations . . .", "The Faculty proposes that you clarify your orientations . . ."). Everywhere else, the Dean employs words such as *I, we* or phrases such as *it is clear* when he is expressing a view. By changing to the formula "The Faculty," he emphasizes that what follows is being said as an officer in whom the authority of his institution has been vested, and that therefore what he is now saying is said with the meaning of a performative; it has the force of a declarative (Searle, 1989, 1995). His has become the voice of the organization known as "the Faculty," now given corporal (and corporate) expression. As a "certain person" in "certain circumstances," following a "conventional procedure" (all terms we borrow from Austin, as described in chap. 3), he is entitled to render an official judgment, and by his pronouncement a state of affairs has been created that the department may not safely ignore. As Benveniste (1966) points out, it is an essential property of a performative that it be self-referential, which is to say that it be itself the reality to which it refers. By enunciating the judgment of "the Faculty" in the appropriate context of conversation such a judgment is given existence as a concrete reality. It is made real. The carrying out of a dean's role supposes the existence of a context that all recognize, but in its accomplishment, it recreates its own context.[14]

It is here that the text-world and discourse-world are stitched together.

This is as far as we need to pursue the departmental evaluation. It got its positions (but not its new equipment). It eventually submitted the report the Faculty had demanded, but, by the time it did, the situation had changed so drastically that the report had become irrelevant. As Woods said, maps quickly become obsolete.

WHAT IS AN ORGANIZATION?

What is an organization?

We can perhaps sum up the idea we have been developing in this book in this way: *An organization is a form of life.* It is a structuring of the social and cultural world to produce an environment whose forms both express social life and create the context for it to thrive.

If an organization is a form of life, then this is how we should study it. Henri Atlan (1979) introduces his book, *Entre le Cristal et la Fumée* (*Between the Crystal and the Smoke*, which we noted in chap. 1), in this way (our translation):

> Living organizations are fluid and mobile. Every attempt to freeze them—in the laboratory or in our descriptions of them—reduces them to one or another form of death. . . . The biologist D. Mazia . . . described his efforts over many years to isolate a cellular structure that plays a particularly important role in the mechanisms of reproduction. Because of its instability

---

[14]It was an error of many interpretations of speech act theory, and one of the reasons it has drawn such criticism, to imagine that it is sentences marked as performative that are the carriers of the performative spin. It is more than the saying *I will* or *I hereby name this child George* that accomplishes the acts of marriage or baptism; there is a whole conventional procedure that surrounds the act of speech and that must be competently carried through for the act to convey authority. The same principle applies to making an official judgment, as deans do. The procedure must be respected. It is important not to seem arbitrary, but, rather, to show that one has behaved judiciously. One has to first demonstrate that one has received and examined the appropriate documents, that one has taken cognizance of what was in them, that one has analyzed them critically, that one has come to a (motivated) assessment of their content, and that one has now arrived at a judgment. Whether the judgment thus made meets approval is of no consequence to the carrying out of the procedure, because it is in the realm of the perlocutionary effect, and not that of the illocutionary force of the performance. Austin's concept of the *uptake* of an utterance, although it is indispensable to the achieving of an illocutionary effect, is not sufficient: performance is not limited to single statements, but also applies to more complex speech events, such as making and communicating a judgment.

the structure continually eluded him by changing its form, and when he had finally succeeded in fixing it, it was dead. All cellular organization is thus composed of fluid and dynamic structures. (p. 5)

As Atlan points out, this does not mean we cannot study the living cells of organization, biological or social/cultural. It does, however, mean rethinking how we do so.

The life model favored by Atlan (and many others who study the principles of self-organization) is that of an oscillation (his term) between two opposite notions of, on the one hand, repetition, regularity, redundancy, and, on the other, variety, unpredictability, complexity—two ingredients that, as he says, "co-exist within dynamic organization." The outer limit of repetition/regularity/redundancy is the modular physical structure of a crystal, that of variety/unpredictability/complexity the chaos of smoke (hence, the title of his book).

What we have been arguing in this book is that there are opposite poles in the spectrum of communication as well, and the space between them is where we must look for the emergence of organization. Those poles are text and conversation: text because, in its own way, it fixes a state of the world (sometimes, as in religious or great creative literature, for centuries and even millennia) and lends itself to faithful reproduction; conversation because its outcomes are never quite predictable and, unless rendered by recording into a texted equivalent, are as evanescent as smoke.

We perceive the processes of organization to be a restless searching to fix its structure through the generation of texts, written and spoken, that reflexively map the organization and its preoccupations back into its discourse and so, for the moment, produce regularity (they have, and intend to have, a function of regulating). It is the existence of such texts and the text-worlds they constitute that makes the organization visible and tangible to people (so that they can, as Weick puts it, see it). Yet the production of a text is inherently a social event (there must be a reader as well as an author, a hearer as well as a speaker, for it even to be a text), and so the production of a text-world is simultaneously the production of a discourse-world, realized in conversation. But if the text-world is reflexively itself, in its other guise as discourse-world, its very production is an event within that discourse-world that, by definition, renders the text obsolete in the very act of its own generation. As authors as different as Weick and Derrida have pointed out, the organization is never actually present to itself, because in the act of making itself present—presenting itself to itself—it has changed, and so the achievement of itself as an entity is indefinitely deferred (Derrida's term).

The task of the organizational communication researcher is to study that process—to understand something of its dynamic. The biologist studies the physical transformations that result in both the reproduction of pattern and the evolution of variety that are, between them, the characteristics of this form of life. The communication research studies the processes of discourse—of "languaging," as Maturana describes it—that form the plane on which text and conversation meet and where organization emerges. It has been our task in this book to suggest some of the lines such an investigation might take. We have tried to show that the forms of organization are already immanent—dormant, but waiting to be wakened—in the narrative semantics that form the base structure of language. But, once given substance in the conversations of organization, such patterns are no longer a property of the language as thought and spoken by an individual, but are constitutive of a relation binding individuals to each other in a bonding that is inherently unstable and endlessly subject to renegotiation. It is the folding-back-on-itself process that such a renegotiation leads to that is our subject matter.

And, of course, the researcher must always bear in mind that his or her research report is also a text and must again struggle to be validated in the conversation of the research community for it to act as an effective agent of persuasion. This is a counsel we as authors of this book have had to bear in mind ourselves.

References

Abbott, E. (1953). *Flatland: A romance of many dimensions.* New York: Dover. (Original work published 1884)

Abraham, W., Epstein, S. D., Thráinsson, H., & Zwart, C. J.-W. (Eds.). (1996). *Minimal ideas: Syntactic studies in the minimalist framework.* Amsterdam and Philadelphia: John Benjamins.

Alexander, J., Giesen, B., Munch, R., & Smelser, N. (Eds.). (1987). *The macro-micro link.* Berkeley: University of California Press.

Althusser, L. (1969). *For Marx.* London: Allen Lane.

Ashmore, M. (1989). *The reflexive thesis: Wrighting sociology of scientific knowledge.* Chicago: University of Chicago Press.

Atlan, H. (1979). *Entre le cristal et la fumée* [Between crystal and smoke]. Paris: Editions du Seuil.

Austin, J. L. (1962). *How to do things with words.* Oxford, England: Oxford University Press.

Austin, J. L. (1970a). Other minds. In J. L. Austin, *Philosophical papers* (2nd ed., pp. 76–116). London: Oxford University Press. (Originally published in 1946 in the Proceedings of the Aristotelian Society, Suppl. Vol. xx)

Austin, J. L. (1970b). *Philosophical papers* (J. O. Urmson & G. J. Warnock, Eds.). London: Oxford University Press.

Axelrod, R. (1976). *Structure of decision.* Princeton, NJ: Princeton University Press.

Banks, S. P., & Riley, P. (1993). Structuration theory as an ontology for communication research. In S. A. Deetz (Ed.), *Communication yearbook* (Vol. 16, pp. 167–196). Beverly Hills, CA: Sage.

Bardini, T. (in press). *The personal interface: Douglas Engelbart and the genesis of personal computing.* Stanford, CA: Stanford University Press.

Bargiela-Chiappini, F., & Harris, S. J. (1997). *Managing language: The discourse of corporate meetings.* Amsterdam and Philadelphia: John Benjamins.

Barker, J. R. (1993). Tightening the iron cage: Concertive control in self-managing teams. *Administrative Science Quarterly, 38*(3), 408–437.

Barwise, J. (1989). *The situation in logic.* Palo Alto, CA: Center for the Study of Language and Information, Stanford University.

Barwise, J., & Perry, J. (1983). *Situations and attitudes.* Cambridge, MA: MIT Press.

Bateson, G. (1972). *Steps to an ecology of mind.* New York: Ballantine.

Bavelas, A. (1948). A mathematical tool for group structures. *Applied Anthropology, 7,* 16–30.

Bavelas, A. (1950). Communication patterns in task-oriented groups. *Journal of the Acoustical Society of America, 22*(6), 725–730.

Bavelas, A., & Barrett, D. (1951). An experimental approach to organizational communication. *Personnel, 27,* 366–371.

Beach, W. A. (1995). Conversation analysis: "Okay" as a clue for understanding consequentiality. In S. J. Sigman (Ed.), *The consequentiality of communication* (pp. 121–162). Mahwah, NJ: Lawrence Erlbaum Associates.

Bechtel, W., & Abrahamsen, A. (1991). *Connectionism and the mind.* New York: Blackwell.

Bennett, A. (1990). *The death of the organization man.* New York: Morrow.

Benson, J. D., & Greaves, W. (Eds.). (1985). *Systemic perspectives on discourse.* Norwood, NJ: Ablex.

Benveniste, É. (1966). *Problemes de linguistique générale* [Problems in general linguistics]. Paris: Gallimard.

Berger, P., & Luckmann, T. (1966). *The social construction of reality: A treatise in the sociology of knowledge.* Garden City, NY: Doubleday.

Bickerton, D. (1990). *Language and species.* Chicago: The University of Chicago Press.

Birdwhistell, R. L. (1952). *Introduction to kinesics.* Louisville, KY: Foreign Service Institute.

Birdwhistell, R. L. (1970). *Kinesics in context: Essays on body motion communication.* Philadelphia: University of Pennsylvania Press.

Blalock, H. M. (1969). *Causal inferences in non-experimental research.* Chapel Hill: University of North Carolina Press.

Blalock, H. M. (Ed.). (1971). *Causal models in the social sciences.* Chicago: Aldine.

Blau, P. M. (1955). *The dynamic of bureaucracy.* Chicago: University of Chicago Press.

Boden, D. (1994). *The business of talk: Organizations in action.* Cambridge, England: Polity Press.

Boden, D., & Zimmerman, D. H. (Eds.). (1991). *Talk and social structure: Studies in ethnomethodology and conversation analysis.* Cambridge, England: Polity Press.

Boje, D. (1991). The storytelling organization: A study of storytelling performance in an office supply firm. *Administrative Science Quarterly, 36,* 106–126.

Bormann, E. G. (1983). Symbolic convergence: Organizational communication and culture. In L. L. Putnam & M. Pacanowsky (Eds.), *The interpretive perspective: An alternative to functionalism* (pp. 99–122). Beverly Hills, CA: Sage.

Boudon, R. (1967). *L'analyse mathématique des faits sociaux* [The mathematical analysis of social facts]. Paris: Plon.

Boudon, R., & Lazarsfeld, K. (1966). *L'analyse empirique de la causalité* [The empirical analysis of causality]. Paris: Mouton.

Bougon, M. G. (1992). Congregate cognitive maps: A unified dynamic theory of organization and strategy. *Journal of Management Studies, 29*(3), 369–389.

Bougon, M. G., Weick, K. E., & Binkhorst, D. (1977). Cognition in organizations: An analysis of the Utrecht Jazz Orchestra. *Administrative Science Quarterly, 22,* 606–639.

Boulding, K. (1956). *The image.* Ann Arbor: University of Michigan Press.

Bourdieu, P. (1980). *Le sens pratique* [Practical knowledge]. Paris: Les Éditions de Minuit.

Bresnan, J. W. (1976). On the form and interpretation of syntactic transformations. *Linguistic Inquiry, 7*(1), 3–40.

Browning, L. D., & Henderson, S. C. (1989). One-way communication transfers in loosely coupled systems. In J. A. Anderson (Ed.), *Communication yearbook* (Vol. 12, pp. 638–669). Newbury Park, CA: Sage.

Brugman, C. M. (1988). *The syntax and semantics of "have" and its complements.* Berkeley and Los Angeles: University of California Press.

Bruner, J. (1991). The narrative construction of reality. *Critical Inquiry* (Autumn), 1–21.

Bühler, K. (1990). *Theory of language: The representational function of language*. Amsterdam and Philadelphia: John Benjamins. (Original work published in 1934)

Burke, K. (1966). *Language as symbolic action: Essays on life, literature and method*. Berkeley and Los Angeles: University of California Press.

Button, G., Coulter, J., Lee, J. R. E., & Sharrock, W. (1995). *Computer, minds and conduct*. Cambridge, England: Polity Press.

Bybee, J., & Fleischman, S. (1995). *Modality in grammar and discourse*. Amsterdam and Philadelphia: John Benjamins.

Callon, M. (1986). Some elements of a sociology of translation: Domestication of the scallops and the fishermen. In J. Law (Ed.), *Power, action and belief: A new sociology of knowledge?* (pp. 196–229). London: Routledge & Kegan Paul.

Callon, M., & Latour, B. (1981). Unscrewing the big Leviathan: How actors macro-structure reality and how sociologists help them to do so. In A. V. Cicourel & K. Knorr-Cetina (Eds.), *Advances in social theory and methodology: Towards an integration of micro- and macro-sociologies* (pp. 277–303). London: Routledge & Kegan Paul.

Campbell, D. T. (1986). Science's social system of validity-enhancing collective belief change and the problems of the social sciences. In D. W. Fiske & R. A. Schweder (Eds.), *Metatheory in social science: Pluralisms and subjectivities* (pp. 108–35). Chicago: University of Chicago Press.

Carnap, R. (1959). *The logical syntax of language*. New York: Littlefield, Adams.

Caton, C. (Ed.). (1963). *Philosophy and ordinary language*. Urbana: University of Illinois Press.

Chang, M. K., & Woo, C. C. (1994). A speech-act-based negotiation protocol: Design, implementation, and test use. *ACM Transactions on Information Systems, 12*(4), 360–382.

Chatman, J. A., Bell, N. E., & Staw, B. M. (1986). The managed thought: The role of self-justification annd impression management in organizational settings. In H. P. Sims & D. A. Gioia (Eds.), *The thinking organization* (pp. 191–214). San Francisco: Jossey-Bass.

Chatwin, B. (1987). *The songlines*. Harmondsworth, England: Penguin.

Cheney, G. (1991). *Rhetoric in an organizational society: Managing multiple identities*. Columbia: University of South Carolina Press.

Cheney, G., & Tompkins, P. K. (1988). On the facts of the text as the basis of human communication research. In J. A. Anderson (Ed.), *Communication yearbook* (Vol. 11, pp. 455–481). Newbury Park, CA: Sage.

Chomsky, N. (1957). *Syntactic structures*. The Hague, Netherlands: Mouton.

Chomsky, N. (1965). *Aspects of a theory of syntax*. Cambridge, MA: MIT Press.

Chomsky, N. (1972). *Studies on semantics in generative grammar*. The Hague, Netherlands: Mouton.

Chomsky, N. (1993). A minimalist program for linguistic theory. In K. Hale & S. J. Keyser (Eds.), *The view from building 20: Essays in linguistics in honor of Sylvain Bromberger* (pp. 1–52). Cambridge, MA: MIT Press.

Chomsky, N. (1995). *The minimalist program*. Cambridge, MA: MIT Press.

Chomsky, N., & Miller, G. A. (1958). Finite state languages. *Information and Control, 1*, 91–112.

Churchland, P. M. (1988). *Matter and consciousness*. Cambridge, MA: MIT Press.

Cicourel, A. V., & Knorr-Cetina, K. (Eds.). (1981). *Advances in social theory and methodology: Towards an integration of micro- and macro-sociologies*. London: Routledge & Kegan Paul.

Clegg, S. R., & Dunkerley, D. (1980). *Organization, class and control*. London: Routledge & Kegan Paul.

Cohen, I. J. (1989). *Structuration theory: Anthony Giddens and the constitution of social life*. New York: St. Martin's Press.

Cole, M. (1991). Conclusion. In L. B. Resnick, J. M. Levine, & S. D. Teasley (Eds.), *Perspectives on socially shared cognition* (pp. 398–417). Washington, DC: American Psychological Association.

Coltheart, M., Curtis, B., Atkins, P., & Haller, M. (1993). Models of reading aloud: Dual-route and parallel distributed processing approaches. *Psychological Review, 100,* 589–608.

Conrad, C. (1993). Rhetorical/communication theory as an ontology for structuration research (Commentary on Banks and Riley). In S. A. Deetz (Ed.), *Communication yearbook* (Vol. 16, pp. 197–208). Newbury Park, CA: Sage.

Cooper, R. (1989). Modernism, post-modernism and organizational analysis 3: The contribution of Jacques Derrida. *Organization Studies, 10*(4), 479–502.

Cooren, F. (1995a). *Énonciation, médiation et organisation. Proposition d'un modèle transformationnel des actes de langage.* Unpublished doctoral dissertation. Montreal, Canada, Université de Montréal.

Cooren, F. (1995b, May). *A proposal for a transformational grid for speech acts: The problem of mediation.* Paper presented at the 45th Annual Conference of the International Communication Association, Albuquerque, NM.

Cooren, F. (in press). *The organizing property of communication.* Amsterdam and New York: John Benjamins.

Cooren, F., & Taylor, J. R. (1997). Organization as an effect of mediation: Redefining the link between organization and communication. *Communication Theory, 7,* 219–259.

Cooren, F., & Taylor, J. R. (1998). The procedural and rhetorical modes of the organizing dimension of communication: Discursive analysis of a parliamentary commission. *The Communication Review, 3,* 1–2, 65–101.

Craib, I. (1992). *Anthony Giddens.* London: Routledge.

Crozier, M., & Friedberg, E. (1977). *L'acteur et le système* [The actor and the system]. Paris: Éditions du Seuil.

Cyert, R. M., & March, J. G. (1963). *A behavioral theory of the firm.* Englewood Cliffs, NJ: Prentice-Hall.

Czarniawska, B. (1997). *Narrating the organization: Dramas of institutional identity.* Chicago: University of Chicago Press.

Daft, R. L., & Weick, K. E. (1984). Toward a model of organizations as intepretation systems. *Academy of Management Review, 9*(2), 284–295.

Dawkins, R. (1976/1989). *The selfish gene.* Oxford, England: Oxford University Press.

Deetz, S. (1992). *Democracy in an age of corporate colonization: Developments in communication and the politics of everyday life.* Albany: State University of New York Press.

Deetz, S., & Kersten, A. (1983). Critical models of interpretive research. In L. L. Putnam & M. Pacanowsky (Eds.), *Communication and organizations: An interpretive perspective* (pp. 147–171). Beverly Hills, CA: Sage.

Derrida, J. (1988). *Limited inc.* Evanston, IL: Northwestern University Press.

Descombes, V. (1980). *Modern French philosophy.* Cambridge, England: Cambridge University Press.

Descombes, V. (1996). *Les institutions du sens* [The institutions of meaning]. Paris: Les Éditions du Minuit.

Devlin, K. (1991). *Logic and information.* Cambridge, England: Cambridge University Press.

Dewey, J. (1944). *Democracy and education.* New York: The Free Press. (Original work published in 1916)

Dietz, J. L. G. (1990). A communication oriented approach to conceptual modelling of information systems, *Lecture Notes in Computer Science 436* (pp. 441–460). Berlin: Springer-Verlag.

Dietz, J. L. G. (1994). *Modelling business processes for the purpose of redesign.* Paper presented at the International Federation of Information Processing (IFIP) Technical Committee 8 (TC8) Open Conference on Business Processing Reengineering (BPR), Sydney, Australia, July.

Dinsmore, J. (1992). Thunder in the gap. In J. Dinsmore (Ed.), *The symbolic and connectionist paradigms: Closing the gap* (pp. 1–23). Hillsdale, NJ: Lawrence Erlbaum Associates.

Dowty, D. (1991). Thematic proto-roles and argument selection. *Language, 67*(3), 547–619.

Dretske, F. I. (1986). *Knowledge and the flow of information.* Cambridge, MA: MIT Press.

Drew, P., & Heritage, J. (1992). *Talk at work.* Cambridge, England: Cambridge University Press.

Dreyfus, H. L. (1991). *Being-in-the-world: A commentary on Heidegger's Being and Time, Division 1.* Cambridge, MA: MIT Press.

Durkheim, É. (1915). *Elementary forms of the religious life: A study in religious sociology* (J. W. Swain, Trans.). New York: Macmillan.

Durkheim, É. (1933). *The division of labour in society* (G. Simpson, Trans.). New York: Macmillan.

Durkheim, É. (1938). *The rules of sociological method* (G. Simpson, Trans.). Glencoe, IL: The Free Press.

Durkheim, É. (1951). *Suicide: A study in sociology* (J. A. Spaulding & G. Simpson, Trans.). Glencoe, IL: The Free Press.

Eden, C. (1992). On the nature of cognitive maps. *Journal of Management Studies, 29*(3), 261–265.

Eden, C., Jones, S., & Sims, D. (1983). *Messing about in problems.* Oxford, England: Pergamon.

Edmondson, W. (1981). *Spoken discourse: A model for analysis.* New York: Longman.

Eisenberg, E. M. (1984). Ambiguity as strategy in organizational communication. *Communication Monographs, 51*, 227–242.

Eisenberg, E. M., & Witten, M. G. (1987). Reconsidering openness in organizational communication. *Academy of Management Review, 12*(3), 418–426.

Engeström, Y. (1991). *Learning, working and imagining.* Helsinki, Finland: Orienta-Konsultit Oy.

Farace, R. V., Monge, P. R., & Russell, H. M. (1977). *Communicating and organizing.* Reading, MA: Addison-Wesley.

Fayol, H. (1925). *Administration industrielle et générale* [Industrial and general administration]. Paris: Dunod.

Fillmore, C. J. (1968). The case for case. In E. Bach & R. T. Harms (Eds.), *Universals in linguistic theory* (pp. 1–88). New York: Holt, Rinehart & Winston.

Fillmore, C. J., & Kay, P. (1993). *Construction grammar.* Unpublished manuscript. University of California, Berkeley.

Fillmore, C. J., Kay, P., & O'Connor, C. (1988). Regularity and idiomaticity in grammatical constructions: The case of *Let Alone. Language, 64*, 501–538.

Fisher, A. (1988). *The logic of real arguments.* Cambridge, England: Cambridge University Press.

Fodor, J. A., & Pylyshyn, Z. W. (1988). Connectionism and cognitive architecture: A critical analysis. *Cognition: International Journal of Cognitive Science, 28*, 3–71.

Fogelin, R. J. (1996). Wittgenstein's critique of philosophy. In H. Sluga & D. G. Stern (Eds.), *The Cambridge companion to Wittgenstein* (pp. 34–58). Cambridge, England: Cambridge University Press.

Foucault, M. (1972). *The archeology of knowledge* (A. M. Sheridan Smith, Trans.). New York: Pantheon. (Original work published in 1969)

Fulk, J., & Collins-Jarvis, L. (1996, May). *Mediated meeting technologies as uncertainty reduction tools: A comprehensive review of theory and research.* Paper presented at the meeting of the International Communication Association, Chicago.

Gardiner, Sir A. H. (1951). *The theory of speech and language* (2nd ed.). Oxford, England: Clarendon Press.

Gardner, H. (1985). *The mind's new science: A history of the cognitive revolution.* New York: Harper Collins.

Garfinkel, H. (1967). *Studies in ethnomethodology.* Englewood Cliffs, NJ: Prentice-Hall.

Giddens, A. (1976). *New rules of sociological method.* London: Hutchison.

Giddens, A. (1979). *Central problems in social theory: Action, structure and contradiction in social analysis.* Berkeley and Los Angeles: University of California Press.

Giddens, A. (1984). *The constitution of society: Outline of the theory of structuration.* Cambridge, England: Polity Press.

Gilbert, G. N., & Mulkay, M. (1984). *Opening Pandora's box: A sociological analysis of scientists' discourse.* Cambridge, England: Cambridge University Press.

Giroux, N. (1993). *Changement stratégique dans une institution: Le cas Visa Desjardins* [Strategic change in an institution: The Visa Desjardins case]. Montreal, Canada: Gaëtan Morin.

Goffman, E. (1959). *The presentation of self in everyday life.* New York: Doubleday Anchor.

Goffman, E. (1974). *Frame analysis.* New York: Harper Colophon.

Goffman, E. (1981). *Forms of talk.* Philadelphia: University of Pennsylvania Press.

Goldberg, A. E. (1995). *Constructions: A construction grammar approach to argument structure.* Chicago: University of Chicago Press.

Gouldner, A. W. (1954). *Patterns of industrial bureaucracy.* Glencoe, IL: The Free Press.

Gregory, R. L. (1966). *Eye and brain: The psychology of seeing.* New York: McGraw-Hill.

Greimas, A. (1987). *On meaning: Selected writings in semiotic theory* (P. J. Perron & F. J. Collins, Trans.). Minneapolis, MI: University of Minnesota Press.

Greimas, A. J. (1993). Préface: Les acquis et les projets [Preface: Accomplishments and prospects]. In J. Courtès (Ed.), *Sémiotique narrative et discursive* (pp. 5–29). Paris: Hachette.

Grimshaw, J. (1979). Complement selection and the lexicon. *Linguistic Inquiry, 10*(2), 279–326.

Gruber, J. S. (1967). Look and see. *Language, 43,* 937–947.

Guetzkow, H. (1965). Communication in organizations. In J. G. March (Ed.), *Handbook of organizations* (pp. 534–573). Chicago: Rand McNally.

Habermas, J. (1984). *The theory of communicative action, vol. 1: Reason and the rationalization of society* (T. McCarthy, Trans.). Boston: Beacon Press. (Original work published in 1981 under the title *Theorie des Kommunicakativen Handels*)

Habermas, J. (1984). *The theory of communicative action, Vol. 2: Lifeworld and system* (T. McCarthy, Trans.). Boston: Beacon Press. (Original work published in 1981, *Theorie des Kommunicakativen Handels*)

Haley, J. (1976). *Problem-solving therapy.* New York: Harper & Row.

Hall, E. T. (1959). *The silent language.* Garden City, NY: Doubleday.

Hall, E. T. (1966). *The hidden dimension.* Garden City, NY: Doubleday.

Hall, E. T. (1976). *Beyond culture.* Garden City, NY: Doubleday.

Hall, R. I. (1984). The natural logic of management policy making: Its implications for the survival of an organization. *Management Science, 30*(8), 905–927.

Halle, M. (1973). Prolegomena to a theory of word formation. *Linguistic Inquiry, 4*(1), 3–16.

Halliday, M. A. K. (1978). *Language as social semiotic.* London: Edward Arnold.

Halliday, M. A. K. (1985). *An introduction to functional grammar.* London: Edward Arnold.

Halliday, M. A. K. (1996). On grammar and grammatics. In R. Hasan, C. Cloran, & D. Butt (Eds.), *Functional descriptions: Theory in practice* (pp. 1–38). Amsterdam & Philadelphia: John Benjamins.

Halliday, M. A. K., & Fawcett, R. P. (Eds.). (1987). *New developments in systemic linguistics: Vol. 1. Theory and description.* London: Pinter.

Halliday, M. A. K., & Hasan, R. (1985). *Language, context, and text: Aspects of language in a social-semiotic perspective.* Oxford, England: Oxford University Press.

Handel, W. (1982). *Ethnomethodology: How people make sense.* Englewood Cliffs, NJ: Prentice-Hall.

Harris, Z. S. (1963). *Discourse analysis reprints.* The Hague, Netherlands: Mouton.

Harris, Z. S. (1965). *String analysis of sentence structure.* The Hague, Netherlands: Mouton.

Hasan, R., Cloran, C., & Butt, D. (Eds.). (1996). *Functional descriptions: Theory in practice.* Amsterdam and Philadelphia: John Benjamins.

Hasan, R., & Fries, P. H. (Eds.). (1995). *On subject and theme: a discourse functional perspective.* Amsterdam and Philadelphia: John Benjamins.

Hawes, L. C. (1977). Toward a hermeneutic phenomenology of communication. *Communication Quarterly, 25*(3), 30–41.

Hebb, D. O. (1949). *The organization of behavior.* New York: Wiley.

Heidegger, M. (1959). *An introduction to metaphysics* (R. Manheim, Trans.). New Haven, CT: Yale University Press.

Held, D., & Thompson, J. B. (Eds.). (1989). *Social theory of modern societies.* Cambridge, England: Cambridge University Press.

Hempel, C. G. (1959). The empiricist criterion of meaning. In A. J. Ayer (Ed.), *Logical positivism* (pp. 108–132). New York: The Free Press.

Heritage, J. (1984). *Garfinkel and ethnomethodology.* Cambridge: Polity Press.

Hodge, R., & Kress, G. (1988). *Social semiotics.* Ithaca, NY: Cornell University Press.

Hodge, R., & Kress, G. (1993). *Language as ideology* (2nd ed.). London: Routledge.

Hofstadter, D. (1979). *Gödel, Escher and Bach.* New York: Basic Books.

Homans, G. (1950). *The human group.* New York: Harcourt Brace Jovanovich.

Husserl, E. (1964). *The idea of phenomenology* (W. Alston & M. Nakhnian, Trans.). The Hague, Netherlands: Martinus Nijhoff.

Husserl, E. (1976). *Logical investigations:* Vols. 1 & 2 (J. N. Findlay, Trans.). London: Routledge & Kegan Paul.

Hutchins, E. (1995). *Cognition in the wild.* Cambridge, MA: The MIT Press.

Jackendoff, R. (1972). *Semantic interpretation in generative grammar.* Cambridge, MA: MIT Press.

Jackendoff, R. (1977). *X Syntax: A study of phrase structure.* Cambridge, MA: MIT Press.

Jackendoff, R. (1990). *Semantic structures.* Cambridge, MA: MIT Press.

Jacques, R. (1996). *Manufacturing the employee: Management knowledge from the 19th to 21st centuries.* Thousand Oaks, CA: Sage.

Jakobson, R. (1962). *Selected writings.* The Hague, Netherlands: Mouton.

Johnson, B. M. (1977). *Communication: The process of organizing.* Boston: Allyn & Bacon.

Johnson-Laird, P. N. (1988). *The computer and the mind.* Cambridge, MA: Harvard University Press.

Jones, S. (1993). *The language of genes.* London: Flamingo.

Kim, W., Ballou, N., Garza, J. F., & Woelk, D. (1991). A distributed object-oriented database system supporting shared and private data bases. *ACM Transactions on Information Systems, 9*(1), 31–51.

Kiparsky, P. (1982). Lexical morphology and phonology. In I.-S. Yang (Ed.), *Linguistics in the morning calm* (pp. 3–91). Seoul, South Korea: Hanshin.

Kockelmans, J. J. (1967). *Phenomenology.* Garden City, NY: Doubleday.

Kockelmans, J. J. (1984). *On the truth of being.* Bloomington: Indiana University Press.

Komocar, J. M. (1985). *Participant cause maps of a working setting: An approach to cognition and behavior in organizations.* Evanston: University of Illinois Press.

Kondo, D. K. (1990). *Crafting selves: Power, gender, and discourses of identity in a Japanese workplace.* Chicago: University of Chicago Press.

Kosko, B. (1993). *Fuzzy thinking: The new science of fuzzy logic.* New York: Hyperion.

Kress, G., & Hodge, R. (1979). *Language as ideology.* London: Routledge & Kegan Paul.

Kripke, S. A. (1982). *Wittgenstein on rules and private language.* Cambridge, MA: Harvard University Press.

Kuhn, T. S. (1970). *The structure of scientific revolutions (2nd ed.).* Chicago: University of Chicago Press.

Labov, W., & Fanshel, D. (1977). *Therapeutic discourse: Psychotherapy as conversation.* New York: Academic Press.

Lakoff, G. (1987). *Women, fire and dangerous things: What categories reveal about the mind.* Chicago: University of Chicago Press.

Lambrecht, K. (1994). *Information structure and sentence form: A theory of topic, focus and the mental representation of discourse referents.* Cambridge, England: Cambridge University Press.

Langacker, R. W. (1991). *Foundations of cognitive grammar: Vol. 1. Theoretical prerequisites.* Stanford, CA: Stanford University Press.

Langendoen, D. T. (1969). *The study of syntax: The generative-transformational approach to the structure of American English.* New York: Holt, Rinehart & Winston.

Langfield-Smith, K. M. (1992). Exploring the need for a shared cognitive map. *Journal of Management Studies, 29*(3), 349–367.

Langfield-Smith, K. M., & Lewis, G. P. (1989). *Mapping cognitive structures: A pilot study to develop a research method* (Working Paper 14). Melbourne, Australia: University of Melbourne, Graduate School of Management.

Latour, B. (1986). The powers of association. In J. Law (Ed.), *Power, action and belief: A new sociology of knowledge?* (pp. 264–280). London: Routledge & Kegan Paul.

Latour, B. (1987). *Science in action: How to follow scientists and engineers through society.* Cambridge, MA: Harvard University Press.

Latour, B. (1993). *We have never been modern* (C. Porter, Trans.). Cambridge MA: Harvard University Press. (Original work published in 1991 under the title *Nous n'avons jamais été modernes: Essais d'anthropologie symmétrique*)

Latour, B. (1994). On technical mediation—philosophy, sociology, genealogy. *Common Knowledge, 3*(2), 29–64.

Latour, B. (1996). *Aramis or the love of technology* (C. Porter, Trans.). Cambridge, MA: Harvard University Press. (Original work published in 1993 under the title *Aramis ou l'amour des techniques*)

Latour, B., & Woolgar, S. (1979). *Laboratory life: The construction of scientific facts.* Princeton, NJ: Princeton University Press.

Layder, D. (1994). *Understanding social theory.* Thousand Oaks, CA: Sage.

Leach, E. (1964). Anthropological aspects of language: Animal categories and verbal abuse. In E. H. Lenneberg (Ed.), *New directions in the study of language* (pp. 23–63). Cambridge, MA: MIT Press.

Lee, C.-D., & Gasser, M. (1992). Where do underlying representations come from? A connectionist approach to the acquisition of phonological rules. In J. Dinsmore (Ed.), *The symbolic and connectionist paradigms: Closing the gap* (pp. 179–203). Hillsdale, NJ: Lawrence Erlbaum Associates.

Lee, P. (1996). *The Whorf theory complex: A critical reconstruction.* Amsterdam and Philadelphia: John Benjamins.

Leiter, K. (1980). *A primer on ethnomethodology.* New York: Oxford University Press.

Levinson, S. G. (1983). *Pragmatics.* Cambridge: University of Cambridge Press.

Luce, R. D., Macy, J. J., Christie, L. S., & Hay, D. H. (1953). *Information flow in task-oriented groups* (Tech. Rep. No. 264). Cambridge, MA: MIT Research Laboratory of Electronics.

Lyons, J. (1977). *Semantics.* Cambridge, England: Cambridge University Press.

Macy, J. J., Christie, L. S., & Luce, R. D. (1953). Coding noise in a task-oriented group. *Journal of Abnormal and Social Psychology, 48,* 401–409.

March, J. G. (Ed.). (1965). *Handbook of organizations.* Chicago: Rand McNally.

March, J. G., & Olsen, J. P. (1976). *Ambiguity and choice in organizations.* Bergen, Norway: Universitetsforlaget.

March, J. G., & Simon, H. A. (1958). *Organizations.* New York: Wiley.

March, J. G., & Weissinger-Baylon, R. (1986). *Ambiguity and command: Organizational perspectives on military decision making.* Marshfield, MA: Pitman.

Marr, D. (1982). *Vision: A computational investigation into the human representation and processing of visual information.* New York: Freeman.

Maruyama, M. (1963). The second cybernetics: Deviation-amplifying mutual cause processes. *American Scientist, 51,* 164–179.

Masuch, M. (1985). Vicious circles in organizations. *Administrative Science Quarterly, 22,* 606–639.

Maturana, H. R. (1991). Science in daily life: The ontology of scientific explanations. In F. Steier (Ed.), *Research and reflexity: Self-reflexivity as social process* (pp. 30–52). Newbury Park, CA: Sage.

Maturana, H. R., & Varela, F. J. (1987). *The tree of knowledge: The biological roots of understanding.* Boston and London: Shambahla.

McClelland, J. L., & Rumelhart, D. E. (1981). An interactive activation model of context effects in letter perception: Part 1, an account of basic findings. *Psychological Review, 88,* 375–407.

McClelland, J. L., Rumelhart, D. E., & the PDP Research Group. (Eds.). (1988). *Explorations in parallel distributed processing: Vol. 2. A handbook of models, programs and exercises.* Cambridge, MA: MIT Press.

McCulloch, W. S., & Pitts, W. (1943). A logical calculus of the ideas immanent in nervous activity. *Bulletin of Mathematical Biophysics, 2,* 115–133.

McPhee, J. (1997). A mother's name. *The New York Times Magazine,* Sunday, Feb. 25, p. 68.

McPhee, R. D. (1989, May). *Structure, agency and communication: Linking micro- to macro-analysis.* Paper presented at the meeting of the International Communication Association, San Francisco, CA.

Medeiros, N. de. (1994). *Culture sanitaire et décodage de messages télévisés de santé chez les Fon du Sud-Bénin* [The culture of medical care and the decoding of television messages about public health in the Fon community of southern Bénin]. Unpublished doctoral dissertation. Montreal, Canada: Université de Montréal.

Meehl, P. E. (1986). What social scientists don't understand. In D. W. Fiske & R. A. Shweder (Eds.), *Metatheory in social science* (pp. 315–38). Chicago: University of Chicago Press.

Meilich, O. (1996). *Neural network applications in social science research.* Paper presented at the special conference on Organizational communication and change: Challenges in the next century, University of Texas, Austin TX, February.

Merton, R. K. (1940). Bureaucratic structure and personality. *Social Forces, 17,* 560–568.

Meštrović, S. G. (1998). *Anthony Giddens: The last modernist.* London: Routledge.

Meyer, M. (1993). *Questions de rhétorique: langage, raison et séduction* [Questions of rhetoric: language, logic and seduction]. Paris: Librairie Générale Française.

Miller, G. A., Galanter, E., & Pribram, K. H. (1960). *Plans and the structure of behavior.* New York: Holt, Rinehart & Winston.

Mintzberg, H. (1979). *The structuring of organizations.* Englewood Cliffs, NJ: Prentice-Hall.

Morgan, G. (1986). *Images of organization.* Beverly Hills, CA: Sage.

Morgan, G. (1993). *Imaginization: The art of creative management.* Newbury Park, CA: Sage.

Nelson, R. E., & Matthews, K. M. (1991). Cause maps and social network analysis in organizational diagnosis. *Journal of Applied Behavioral Science, 27*(3), 379–397.

Newcomb, T. (1953). An approach to the study of communicative acts. *Psychological Review, 60,* 393–404.

Newell, A., & Simon, H. A. (1972). *Human problem solving.* Englewood Cliffs, NJ: Prentice-Hall.

Orlikowski, W. J. (1996). Improvising organizational transformation over time: A situated change perspective. *Information Systems Research, 7*(1), 63–92.

Orlikowski, W. J., & Yates, J. (1994). Genre repertoire: The structuring of communicative practices in organizations. *Administrative Science Quarterly, 39,* 541–574.

Orton, J. D., & Weick, K. E. (1990). Loosely coupled systems: A reconceptualization. *Academy of Management Review, 15,* 203–223.

Oxford dictionary of current English, The concise (6th ed). (1976). Oxford, England: Clarendon Press.

Palmer, F. R. (1986). *Mood and modality.* Cambridge, England: Cambridge University Press.

Parsons, T. (1960). *Structure and process in modern societies.* Chicago: Free Press.

Peirce, C. S. (1955). *Philosophical writings of Peirce; selected and edited by J. Buchler.* New York: Dover.

Pentland, B. T. (1995). Grammatical models of organizational processes. *Organization Science,* 6(5), 541–56.

Pentland, B. T., & Reuter, H. H. (1994). Organizational routines as grammars of action. *Administrative Science Quarterly, 39,* 484–510.

Perrow, C. (1986). *Complex organizations (3rd ed.).* New York: Random House.

Pesetzky, D. (1990). *Experiencer predicates and universal alignment principles.* Unpublished manuscript. Cambridge, MA: MIT Department of Linguistics and Philosophy.

Pfeffer, J. (1981). *Power in organizations.* Boston: Pitman.

Pickering, A. (1995). *The mangle of practice.* Chicago: University of Chicago Press.

Pinker, S., & Prince, A. (1988). On language and connectionism: An analysis of a parallel distributed processing model of language acquisition. *Cognition: International Journal of Cognitive Science, 28,* 74–193.

Pollard, C., & Sag, I. A. (1987). *Information-based syntax and semantics I: Fundamentals.* Palo Alto, CA: Stanford University.

Poole, M. S., & McPhee, R. D. (1983). A structurational theory of organizational climate. In L. L. Putnam & M. Pacanowsky (Eds.), *Organizational communication: An interpretive approach* (pp. 195–219). Beverly Hills, CA: Sage.

Prasada, S., & Pinker, S. (1993). Generalization of regular and irregular morphological patterns. *Language and Cognitive Processes, 8,* 1–56.

Prelli, L. J. (1989). *A rhetoric of science: Inventing scientific discourse.* Columbia: University of South Carolina Press.

Propp, V. (1958). *The morphology of the folktale* (L. Scott, Trans.). Publication Ten. Bloomington, IN: Research Center in Anthropology, Folklore and Linguistics, Indiana University. (Original work published in 1928 under the title *Transformacii volshebnykh skazok*)

Putnam, L. L. (1983). The interpretive perspective: An alternative to functionalism. In L. L. Putnam & M. E. Pacanowsky (Eds.), *Communication and organizations* (pp. 31–54). Beverly Hills, CA: Sage.

Putnam, L. L. (1989). Negotiation and organizing: Two levels of analysis within the Weickian world. *Communication Studies, 40*(4), 249–257.

Putnam, L. L., & Pacanowsky, M. E. (Eds.). (1983). *Communication and organizations.* Beverly Hills, CA: Sage.

Rappaport, A. (1953). *Operational philosophy: Integrating knowledge and action.* New York: Wiley.

Récanati, F. (1991). *Les énoncés performatifs* [Performative speech acts]. Paris: Editions du Minuit.

Reichenbach, H. (1947). *Elements of symbolic logic.* New York: Macmillan.

Reichenbach, H. (1949). *The theory of probability: An inquiry into the logical and mathematical foundations of the calculus of probability* (E. H. Hutton & M. Reichenbach, Trans.). Berkeley and Los Angeles: University of California Press.

Resnick, L. B. (1991). Shared cognition: Thinking as social practice. In L. B. Resnick, J. M. Levine, & S. D. Teasley (Eds.), *Perspectives on socially shared cognition* (pp. 1–20). Washington, DC: American Psychological Association.

Resnick, L. B., Levine, J. M., & Teasley, S. D. (Eds.). (1991). *Perspectives on socially shared cognition.* Washington, DC: American Psychological Association.

Ricoeur, P. (1981). *Hermeneutics and the human sciences* (J. B. Thompson, Ed. and Trans.). Cambridge, England: Cambridge University Press.

Ricoeur, P. (1991). *From text to action* (K. Blamey & J. B. Thompson, Trans.). Evanston, IL: Illinois University Press.

Roberts, F. S. (1973). Building and analysing an energy demand signed digraph. *Environment and Planning, 5,* 199–221.

Rosch, E. (1973). Natural categories. *Cognitive Psychology, 4,* 328–50.

Rosch, E. (1978). Principles of categorization. In E. Rosch & B. B. Lloyd (Eds.), *Cognition and categorization* (pp. 27–48). Hillsdale, NJ: Lawrence Erlbaum Associates.

Rosch, E. (1981). Prototype classification and logical classification: The two systems. In E. Scholnick (Ed.), *New trends in cognitive representation: Challenges to Piaget's theory* (pp. 73–86). Hillsdale, NJ: Lawrence Erlbaum Associates.

Rosell, S. A. (1999). *Renewing governance: Governing by learning in the information age.* Toronto, Canada: Oxford.

Rosenblatt, F. (1962). *Principles of neurodynamics—perceptrons and the theory of brain mechanisms.* Washington, DC: Spartan Books.

Rothenbuhler, E. W. (1993a). Argument for a Durkheimian theory of the communicative. *Journal of Communication, 43*(3), 158–163.

Rothenbuhler, E. W. (1993b, November). *Reading Durkheim's* Elementary Forms *for communication theory.* Paper presented at the meeting of the Speech Communication Association, Chicago.

Rumelhart, D. E. (1992). Towards a microstructural account of human reasoning. In S. Davis (Ed.), *Connectionism: Theory and practice* (pp. 69–83). New York: Oxford University Press.

Rumelhart, D. E., McClelland, J. L., & the PDP Research Group. (Eds.). (1986). *Parallel distributed processing: (Vol. 1). Explanations in the microstructure of cognition.* Cambridge, MA: MIT Press.

Sachs, P. (1995). Transforming work: Collaboration, learning and design. *Communications of the ACM, 38*(9), 36–44.

Sacks, H. (1989). Harvey Sacks—Lectures 1964–1965 (G. Jefferson, Ed.), *Human Studies, 12*(3/4).

Sacks, H., Schegloff, E. A., & Jefferson, G. (1974). A simplest systematics for the organization of turn-taking for conversation. *Language, 50,* 696–735.

Saussure, F. de. (1966). *Course in general linguistics.* New York: McGraw-Hill.

Schank, R. C., & Abelson, R. A. (1977). *Scripts, plans, goals and understanding.* Hillsdale, NJ: Lawrence Erlbaum Associates.

Scheflen, A. E. (1965). *Stream and structure of communicational behavior.* Philadelphia, PA: Eastern Pennsylvania Psychiatric Institute.

Scheflen, A. E. (1973). *How behavior means.* Garden City, NY: Doubleday.

Scheflen, A. E., & Ashcraft, N. (1976). *Human territories: How we behave in space-time.* Englewood Cliffs, NJ: Prentice-Hall.

Schegloff, E. A. (1991). Conversation analysis and socially shared cognition. In L. B. Resnick, J. L. Levine, & S. D. Teasley (Eds.), *Perspectives on socially shared cognition* (pp. 150–170). Washington, DC: American Psychological Association.

Schutz, A. (1962). *Collected papers:* Vol. 1. The Hague, Netherlands: Martinus Nijhoff.

Schutz, A. (1964). *Collected papers:* Vol. 2. The Hague, Netherlands: Martinus Nijhoff.

Schutz, A. (1967). *The phenomenology of the social world.* Evanston, IL: Northwestern University Press.

Schutz, A. (1970). *On phenomenology and social relations.* Chicago: University of Chicago Press.

Searle, J. R. (1969). *Speech acts.* London: Cambridge University Press.

Searle, J. R. (1984). *Minds, brains and science.* Cambridge, MA: Harvard University Press.

Searle, J. R. (1989). How performatives work. *Linguistics and Philosophy, 12,* 535–558.

Searle, J. R. (1990). Collective intentions and actions. In P. R. Cohen, J. Morgan, & M. G. Pollack (Eds.), *Intentions in communication* (pp. 401–415). Cambridge, MA: MIT Press.

Searle, J. R. (1995). *The construction of social reality.* New York: The Free Press.

Seidenberg, M. S. (1992). Connectionism without tears. In S. Davis (Ed.), *Connectionism: Advances in theory and practice* (pp. 84–122). Oxford, England: Oxford University Press.

Selznick, P. (1949). *TVA and the grass roots.* Berkeley and Los Angeles: University of California Press.

Seung, T. K. (1982). *Structuralism and hermeneutics.* New York: Columbia University Press.

Shannon, C. E. (1948). A mathematical theory of communication. *Bell System Technical Journal, 27,* 379–428, 623–656.

Shapin, S., & Shaffer, S. (1985). *Leviathan and the air-pump: Hobbes, Boyle and the experimental life.* Princeton, NJ: Princeton University Press.

Shaw, M. E. (1964). Communication networks. In D. Berkowitz (Ed.), *Advances in experimental social psychology* (pp. 111–129). New York: Academic Press.

Sigman, S. J. (Ed.). (1995). *The consequentiality of communication.* Mahwah, NJ: Lawrence Erlbaum Associates.

Silverstone, R. (1994). *Television and everyday life.* London: Routledge.

Simon, H. A. (1957). *Models of man.* New York: Wiley.

Smith, B. (1990). Towards a history of speech act theory. In A. Burkhardt (Ed.), *Speech acts, meanings and intentions: Critical approaches to the philosophy of John R. Searle* (pp. 29–61). Berlin/New York: Walter de Gruyter.

Smith, R. C. (1993, May). *Images of organizational communication: Root-metaphors of the organization-communication relation.* Paper presented at the meeting of the International Communication Association Annual Conference, Washington, DC.

Steuten, A. (1998). *A contribution to the linguistic analysis of business conversations within the language/action perspective.* Unpublished doctoral dissertation, Technical University of Delft, The Netherlands.

Stewart, J. R., & Philipsen, G. (1984). Communication as situated accomplishment: The case of hermeneutics and ethnography. In B. Dervin & M. J. Voigt (Eds.), *Progress in communication sciences V* (pp. 177–218). Norwood, NJ: Ablex.

Stinchcombe, A. L. (1990). *Information and organizations.* Berkeley and Los Angeles: University of California Press.

Strum, S. S., & Latour, B. (1987). Redefining the social link: From baboons to human. *Social Science Information, 26*(4), 783–802.

Stubbs, M. (1996). *Text and corpus analysis: Computer-assisted studies of language and culture.* Cambridge, MA: Blackwell.

Suchman, L. (1987). *Plans and situated action: The problem of human-machine communication.* New York: Cambridge University Press.

Suchman, L. (1994). Do categories have politics?: The language/action perspective reconsidered, *Computer Supported Cooperative Work, 2,* 177–190.

Suchman, L. (1995). Making work visible. *Communications of the ACM, 38*(9), 56–64.

Taylor, G. (1996, February). *Maps, empires and nations in eighteenth-century North America.* Paper presented at the meeting of the SouthEastern American Society for Eighteenth-Century Studies, Tallahassee, FL.

Taylor, J. R. (1978). *A method for the recording of data and analysis of structure in task groups.* Unpublished doctoral dissertation. Philadelphia, University of Pennsylvania.

Taylor, J. R. (1993). *Rethinking the theory of organizational communication: How to read an organization.* Norwood, NJ: Ablex.

Taylor, J. R. (1995). Shifting from a heteronomous to an autonomous worldview of organizational communication: Communication theory on the cusp. *Communication Theory, 15*(3), 1–35.

Taylor, J. R., & Cooren, F. (1997). What makes communication "organizational"? How the many voices of the organization become the *one* voice of *an* organization. *Journal of Pragmatics, 27,* 409–438.

Taylor, J. R., Cooren, F., Giroux, N., & Robichaud, D. (1996). The communicational basis of organization: Between the conversation and text. *Communication Theory, 6*(1), 1–39.

Taylor, J. R., Groleau, C., Heaton, L., & Van Every, E. (in press). *The computerization of work.* Thousand Oaks CA: Sage.

Taylor, J. R., & Gurd, G. (1996). Contrasting perspectives on non-positivist communication research. In L. Thayer (Ed.), *Organization<——>Communication: Emerging perspectives III* (pp. 38–79). Norwood, NJ: Ablex.

Taylor, J. R., & Van Every, E. J. (1993). *The vulnerable fortress: Bureaucratic organization and management in the information age.* Toronto, Canada: The University of Toronto Press.

Thibault, P. J. (1991). *Social semiotics as praxis: Text, social meaning making, and Nabokov's Ada.* Minneapolis: University of Minnesota Press.

Tolman, E. C. (1958). Cognitive maps in rats and men. In E. C. Tolman (Ed.), *Behavior and psychological man: Essays in motivation and learning* (pp. 241–264). Berkeley and Los Angeles: University of California Press.

Tompkins, P. K. (1993). *Organizational communication imperatives: Lessons of the space program.* Los Angeles, CA: Roxbury.

Tompkins, P. K., & Cheney, G. (1985). Communication and unobtrusive control in contemporary organizations. In R. D. McPhee & P. K. Tompkins (Eds.), *Organizational ccommunication: Traditional themes and new directions* (pp. 179–210). Beverly Hills, CA: Sage.

Turing, A. (1936). On computable numbers, with an application to the Entscheidungs problem. *Proceedings of the London Mathematical Society, Series 2(42)*, 230–265.

Underwood, B. J. (1957). *Psychological research.* New York: Appleton-Century-Crofts.

van der Rijst, N. B. J. (1997, July). *Analysis and design of emerging network organizations.* In F. Dignum & J. L. G. Dietz (Eds.), Communication modeling—the Language/Action Perspective: Proceedings of the Second International Workshop on Communication Modeling (pp. 1–12), Veldhoven, The Netherlands.

Van Dijk, T. A. (Ed.). (1997). *Discourse as structure and process.* Thousand Oaks, CA: Sage.

Van Every, E. J., & Taylor, J. R. (1998). Modeling the organization as a system of communication activity: A dialogue about the language/action perspective. *Management Communication Quarterly, 12*(1), 128–147.

Varela, F. (1979). *Principles of biological autonomy.* New York: Elsevier North Holland.

Von Eckardt, B. (1993). *What is cognitive science?* Cambridge, MA: MIT Press.

Walsh, J. P., & Fahey, L. (1986). The role of negotiated belief structures in strategy making. *Journal of Management, 12*, 325–338.

Walsh, J. P., Henderson, C. M., & Deighton, J. (1988). Negotiated belief structures and decision performance: An empirical investigation. *Organizational Behavior and Human Decision Processes, 42*, 194–216.

Walton, D. N. (1996). *Argumentation schemes for presumptive reasoning.* Mahwah, NJ: Lawrence Erlbaum Associations.

Watzlawick, P., Beavin, J. H., & Jackson, D. (1967). *Pragmatics of human communication: A study of interactional patterns, pathologies, and paradoxes.* New York: Norton.

Weber, M. (1922). *Economy and society: An outline of interpretive sociology* (3 Vols, G. Roth & C. Wittich, Trans.). New York: Bedminster Press.

Webster's New World Dictionary of the American Language. (1964). Cleveland and New York: The World Publishing Company.

Weick, K. E. (1969). *The social psychology of organizing.* Reading, MA: Addison-Wesley.

Weick, K. E. (1976). Educational organizations as loosely coupled systems. *Administrative Science Quarterly, 21*, 1–19.

Weick, K. E. (1977). Enactment processes in organizations. In B. M. Staw & G. Salancik (Eds.), *New directions in organizational behavior* (pp. 267–300). Chicago: St. Clair.

Weick, K. E. (1979a). *The social psychology of organizing (revised).* New York: Random House.

Weick, K. E. (1979b). Cognitive processes in organizations. In B. Staw (Ed.), *Research in organizational behavior, 1*, 41–74. Greenwich, CT: JAI Press.

Weick, K. E. (1983). Organizational communication: Toward a research agenda. In L. L. Putnam & M. Pacanowsky (Eds.), *Communication and organizations: An interpretive approach* (pp. 13–29). Beverly Hills, CA: Sage.

Weick, K. E. (1985). Sources of order in underorganized systems: Themes in recent organizational theory. In Y. S. Lincoln (Ed.), *Organizational theory and inquiry* (pp. 106–136). Beverly Hills, CA: Sage.

Weick, K. E. (1988). Enacted sensemaking in crisis situations. *Journal of Management Studies,* *25,* 305–317.

Weick, K. E. (1989a). Organized improvisation: 20 years of organizing. *Communication Studies,* *40*(4), 241–248.

Weick, K. E. (1989b). Theory construction as disciplined imagination. *Academy of Management Review,* *14*(4), 516–531.

Weick, K. E. (1990). Introduction: Cartographic myths in organizations. In A. S. Huff (Ed.), *Mapping strategic thought* (pp. 1–10). Chichester, England: Wiley.

Weick, K. E. (1995a). *Sensemaking in organizations.* Thousand Oaks, CA: Sage.

Weick, K. E. (1995b). What theory is *not,* theorizing *is. Administrative Science Quarterly, 40,* 385–390.

Weick, K. E., & Bougon, M. G. (1986). Organizations as cognitive maps: Charting ways to success and failure. In J. H. P. Sims, D. A. Gioia, & Associates (Eds.), *The thinking organization* (pp. 102–135). San Francisco: Jossey-Bass.

Weick, K. E., & Browning, L. D. (1986). Argument and narration in organizational communication. *Yearly Review of Management of the Journal of Management, 12*(2), 243–259.

Weick, K. E., & Daft, R. L. (1983). The effectiveness of interpretation systems. In K. S. Cameron & D. A. Whetton (Eds.), *Organizational effectiveness, a comparison of multiple models* (pp. 71–93). New York: Academic Press.

Weick, K. E., & Orton, J. D. (1989). One-way transfers and organization cohesion. In J. A. Anderson (Ed.), *Communication Yearbook, 12* (pp. 675–687). Newbury Park, CA: Sage.

Weick, K. E., & Roberts, K. H. (1993). Collective mind in organizations: Heedful interrelating on flight decks. *Administrative Science Quarterly, 38,* 357–381.

Werth, P. (1993). Accommodation and the myth of presupposition: The view from discourse. *Lingua, 89,* 39–95.

Wess, R. (1996). *Kenneth Burke: Rhetoric, subjectivity, postmodernism.* Cambridge, England: Cambridge University Press.

Whyte, W. F. (1948). *Human relations in the restaurant industry.* New York: McGraw-Hill.

Wierzbicka, A. (1988). *The semantics of grammar.* Amsterdam and Philadelphia: John Benjamins.

Winch, P. (1958). *The idea of a social science and its relation to philosophy.* London: Routledge & Kegan Paul.

Winograd, T. (1994). Categories, disciplines and social coordination. *Computer Supported Cooperative Work, 2,* 191–197.

Winograd, T., & Flores, F. (1986). *Understanding computers and cognition: A new foundation for design.* Norwood, NJ: Ablex.

Wittgenstein, L. (1958). *Philosophical investigations: The English text of the third edition.* (G. E. M. Anscombe, Trans.). London: Macmillan.

Wood, D. (1992). *The power of maps.* New York: Guilford.

Yates, J., & Orlikowski, W. J. (1992). Genres of organizational communication: A structurational approach to studying communication and media. *Academy of Management Review, 17,* 299–326.

Zipser, D. (1990). Modeling cortical computation with backpropagation. In M. A. Gluck & D. E. Rumelhart (Eds.), *Neuroscience and connectionist theory* (pp. 355–383). Hillsdale NJ: Lawrence Erlbaum Associates.

Author Index

Subject Index